W9-ASJ-003

British Enterprise in Brazil

Marshall C. Eakin

British Enterprise in Brazil

The St. John d'el Rey Mining Company

and the Morro Velho Gold Mine, 1830–1960

Duke University Press

Durham and London 1989

For Billie Wray Strauss and Bobby Ray Eakin, Sr.,

who made the historian,

and for all those who made the history of Morro Velho.

Contents

———

List of Illustrations

Figures

Maps

Photographs (following page 164)

List of Tables

Preface

The role of foreign enterprise in national development has long been one of the most hotly debated topics in Latin American history. The debate dates back to colonial times when monarchs and administrators pondered the role non-Iberian entrepreneurs should play in the New World empires. Political independence in the nineteenth century opened Latin American nations to a massive influx of British, and later, North American capital, raising new questions about the role of the foreigner in national affairs. With the emergence of strong cultural and economic nationalism in the twentieth century, scholars and theorists have focused increasingly on the role of foreign enterprise and entrepreneurs in the development process.

Despite the attention given to this topic, most of the literature has concentrated on the national and international arenas. While the debate has ranged over macroeconomic issues such as the effects of foreign business on national industry, politics, and the structure of the national economy, little has been written about the effects at the local and regional levels. Beyond the traditional tales of exploitation and repression on the one hand, and the self-serving publications of businesses on the other, we know very little about the operations and development of individual firms and their impact on Latin American communities. Case studies of foreign or national firms in Latin America are a rare commodity, as are longitudinal studies of communities. The scarcity of such studies for Latin America's largest, most populous, and economically powerful country is striking. This book is the most complete and detailed analysis of any foreign firm in

Latin American history, and one of the few microhistorical studies of a Brazilian community.[1]

This study attempts to move beyond the superficiality of the old debate to present a detailed historical analysis of the operations of one foreign enterprise and its impact on a Brazilian community in the nineteenth and twentieth centuries. It is a case study of the expansion of industrial capitalism into the interior of a rural, Latin American country and how the coming of industrial order transforms the lives of people in an agricultural society. Two complementary perspectives guide this examination of the growth of industrial capitalism in the Brazilian interior. First, I show how the expansion of capitalism fundamentally transforms a small, rural community into a large, industrial city. Second, I show how the local conditions and the response of Brazilians to capitalist expansion, in conjunction with international forces beyond the control of this capitalist enterprise, converge to shape the development of industrial capitalism in the Brazilian interior. In short, although the focus of this book is one company and one community, I place both within the larger context of the international economy and Brazilian society.

By any standard, the St. John d'el Rey Mining Company, Limited, stands out as one of the most successful foreign enterprises in Latin American history. Founded in 1830, for over a century and a quarter this British firm developed the largest gold mine in South America —the Morro Velho in Nova Lima, Minas Gerais. The British constructed a powerful business conglomerate of gold mines, iron ore deposits, farms, power plants, and a railway around Morro Velho, eventually controlling over one hundred square miles of real estate in central Minas Gerais. From the mid-nineteenth century until the mid-twentieth the company was the single largest employer and taxpayer in Minas Gerais and the producer of the vast majority of Brazil's gold bullion. A thriving company town took shape around a British community of several hundred at the mine. A rural community of some 1,000 miners, merchants, slaves, and peasants in the 1820s, Nova Lima emerged by the 1930s as a bustling industrial city of some 25,000 with a large working class. The history of the British company and the Brazilian community were inseparably linked, and both form the focus of this book.

The rich company archives provide us with the opportunity to analyze the functioning of a foreign business and its impact on politics, the economy, and society. The experience of the St. John d'el

Rey demonstrates the impressive adaptability of capitalist enterprise to a wide variety of political, social, and economic conditions. The management of the St. John dealt successfully with political regimes ranging across monarchy, republic, corporatist dictatorship, to populist mass politics. The company adapted its operations to a slave economy in the nineteenth century and made the transition to a free labor economy with abolition. Rather than acting as an agent for transforming the *mineiro*, or Brazilian economy, the British accommodated their needs to local conditions and, beyond the community level, had a minor impact on the state or nation. This mining company created a classic enclave economy in the Brazilian interior.[2]

The converging histories of company and community provide new perspectives on a number of important themes in Brazilian history. First, this study adds to the growing list of recent works on Minas Gerais that have begun to broaden our vision of an economic and social history too long dominated by the Rio de Janeiro-São Paulo axis. Despite the critical role of Minas Gerais in Brazilian history since the discovery of gold at the end of the seventeenth century, Brazilians and Brazilianists have traditionally focused their attention on the coastal states of the northeast and the southeast. The economic and social history of Minas has just begun to receive the attention it deserves. A number of dissertations and books on *mineiro* topics by North Americans and Brazilians in the past decade have begun to reshape our vision of Brazilian history and add to the pioneering work of Francisco Iglésias in Brazil, and John Wirth in the United States.[3] Several recent works have analyzed Minas Gerais as it moved from the gold economy of the eighteenth century to the coffee economy of the nineteenth century.[4] Although gold mining had become a very small segment of the *mineiro* economy by the mid-nineteenth century, the St. John d'el Rey stood out as one of the most prominent enterprises (foreign or national) in the region. Two recent books by researchers in Belo Horizonte have examined the history of the Morro Velho mine, one emphasizing the slave labor system in the nineteenth century, and the other the rise of the miners' union from 1934–64.[5] This book is the first comprehensive and systematic analysis of the St. John d'el Rey.[6]

The structure of this book requires some explanation. While chapters 1 and 2 provide an overview of the historical process, chapters 3 to 7 dissect the history of company and community from various angles. The combination of both diachronic and synchronic approaches permits a much more detailed and revealing look into the key features of economic and social change than would have been possible had I adopted a strictly chronological framework. The two approaches are complementary and mutually reinforcing.

Chapter 1 begins the historical overview briefly tracing the rise and decline of the gold-mining economy in the eighteenth century, and focusing on the reemergence of gold mining with British capital and technology in the nineteenth century. This section reconstructs a poorly studied period in *mineiro* economic history ignored by historians who have focused on the gold rush of the eighteenth century, overlooking the smaller gold "rush" under the Empire. In the process this work offers new information on the role of British capital in imperial Brazil. The rise of "British preeminence in Brazil" in the nineteenth century has captured the attention of scholars for decades. Alan K. Manchester and Richard Graham, among others, have described the impact of Great Britain on Brazilian politics, culture, and society.[7] Works on the British role in the Brazilian economy have largely centered on national issues, and very rarely on local, regional, or microeconomic issues. This chapter adds to recent revisionist historiography emphasizing the relatively weak impact of British capital in the early decades of independence.[8]

The history of the St. John d'el Rey in chapter 2 presents the most complete account of the operations and organization of a foreign business in nineteenth- and twentieth-century Brazil. Drawing on the rich archives and annual reports of the company, this chapter builds on the pioneering work of Stanley Stein and Richard Graham on the entrepreneurial and economic history of the British in Brazil.[9] Chapter 3 places the company's history in the context of the changing political culture of Minas Gerais and Brazil, examining the St. John's relations with local, state, and national governments. As this section demonstrates, a low political profile, geographic isolation, operating in a secondary industry within the larger economy, and the construction of an extensive network of political allies were the keys to the success and longevity of the St. John d'el Rey. Careful political work helped insure stability of the firm allowing managers and engineers to concentrate on the crucial technical demands of deep-shaft mining.

The transition from company history to community study begins in chapter 4 with a close analysis of the technological system at Morro Velho. This chapter illustrates in detail the process of industrialization, and the organization of the primary workplace in the company and community. Technological innovation was the key to the company's success, for it enabled management to surmount the challenges of geology, engineering, and labor. Without technological innovation, nothing else would have been possible. Furthermore, it is in the process of the creation and transformation of this workplace that company power and influence most clearly touch the lives of the local people. The construction and evolution of the technological system at Morro Velho is the key to the history of this British business and of the Brazilian community. The evolution of the technological system reveals the inner workings of the managerial and entrepreneurial skills and decisions of the British at Morro Velho. At the same time the system and its transformation provide the key to the changing nature of local society.

The second half of this book examines the composition and structure of the changing community. The St. John's long, continuous control of the Morro Velho mine offers a rare opportunity to study the creation, evolution, and impact of a foreign business on a Latin American community, and to see the converging regional, national, and international forces that shape the history of company and community. Chapter 5 begins by briefly tracing the administrative and political history of Nova Lima and then turns to an analysis of key social and demographic characteristics as Nova Lima moves from an agrarian, slaveholding society to an industrial, working-class city. Chapter 6 then analyzes the major social groups in Nova Lima and the changing composition of local society: from slaves, peasants, and elites in the nineteenth century to industrial workers and elites in this century.

The emergence of a militant, unionized working class, often guided by anti-capitalist, anti-imperialist leadership from the ranks of the Communist party dominates the process of social and economic change during the St. John's final decades in Nova Lima. This militant movement eventually pits Brazilian against Briton, and highlights the cultural, social, and economic differences between the two communities. The vigorous British enclave of several hundred that took shape around the mine had established deep roots with some families that spanned nearly the entire history of the company. A careful look at British society at Morro Velho in chapter 7 reveals a community of miners, managers, and dependents concerned with creating a small version of Britain in the Brazilian interior. Club, church, and school stood at the center of this community, while intermarriage and job security gave it continuity, cohesion, and stability. While the rise of a large working class makes Nova Lima exceptional in the Brazilian interior, the persistence of this British community over generations makes it extraordinary. Finally, chapter 8 draws together the intertwined threads of business, politics, technology, and society and examines the meaning of the experience of this foreign enterprise in Brazilian history.

This history of Nova Lima and the St. John d'el Rey has a long history of its own that deserves a few words so that the reader may fully appreciate the final product. My own personal road to Nova Lima and the St. John d'el Rey began in graduate school in 1978 as I wrestled with a way to convert a broad concern with technology and social change into a manageable dissertation topic. As I surveyed the historiographical landscape I became increasingly convinced that Minas Gerais had been unduly, and unwisely, neglected, given its critical role in Brazilian history since the beginning of the eighteenth century. Turning from the comparatively well studied regions of São Paulo, Rio de Janeiro, and Bahia, I decided to search for a community in Minas Gerais that might serve as a case study of the relationship between technological development and social change. An initial survey of possible sites led me to the Morro Velho mine and to the London archives of the St. John d'el Rey now housed at the University of Texas. A Fulbright fellowship in 1979–80 then led to the "discovery" of the historian's dream—a large and almost untouched company archive in Nova Lima. The existence of these two archives and the extraordinary history of the St. John d'el Rey have subsequently reoriented the dissertation, and shaped the contours of this book, as well as the education of this historian.

A decade ago I began this study as a graduate student firmly within the camp of dependency theory, convinced of the destructive influence of British imperialism in Latin America, and, in particular, the effects of industrialization on the Latin American rural masses. Ten years of interviews and visits to Brazil, immersion in documents, and reflection have gradually, but significantly, reshaped my views. The extraordinary richness and detail of the documentation on the British at Morro Velho, combined with wide-ranging comparative readings on British imperial history, have given me an understanding of the actions and attitudes of British miners and managers that I could not even conceive of ten years ago. Understanding, however, is not toleration, as the old saying goes. I have acquired an enormous admiration for the technological triumphs and achievements of the British in Brazil, while reinforcing my strong distaste for their worldview, their treatment of Brazilians, and many of their actions.

The extraordinary documentation on the British makes the scarcity of materials on the Brazilians, especially the Brazilian masses, even more frustrating. While the lives and deeds of this small group of British expatriates come out in this book in detail, the vast majority of the Brazilians remain anonymous. It is one of the great ironies and frustrations of history that the vast majority of individuals who made the events historians recount leave only traces of their existence. Consequently, the analysis of local society is not as rich and detailed as the analysis of the business. Although I was unable to reconstruct the lives of the Brazilians with the same richness as those of the British, I hope that I have still been able to convey the unrelenting struggle most of them faced as they made the transition from a rural to an industrial order. While seeking to understand this struggle I have also sought to avoid the naive romanticism that pervades so much writing on the Latin American masses. In the final analysis, and for all its flaws, I believe that the industrialization of Nova Lima benefited not only the British, but also the Brazilians. The industrialization of Nova Lima was an impressive, yet flawed, achievement marred by missed opportunities and social injustice. I believe that this study accurately depicts this achievement and all its flaws. I am sure that both those who see capitalism as the cause of, and those who see it as the cure for, all of Brazil's problems will be unhappy with my analysis.

The rich sources on Morro Velho and Nova Lima have also shaped this study in one other important way. From the beginning of my work in company and local archives in 1979 I have continually avoided the urge to write a company history separated from the history of the community of Nova Lima. Likewise, I have avoided the temptation to focus on just one or two major themes in the social history of the community. Instead, I have taken on the rather daunting task of writing about both a major company and a sizable community, across nearly the entire history of modern Brazil. A narrow business history of the St. John d'el Rey would miss the power and impact of the company in human terms, while a history of Nova Lima becomes meaningful only when one recognizes the company's central role in daily life. As a consequence, I have ventured into the domains of the historian of business, politics, mining, technology, slavery, workers, and the British empire. Although this multidisciplinary approach presents many potential pitfalls, I believe that the comprehensive portrait of company and community has made the final product infinitely more valuable than a narrow study of one aspect of the larger story. The result is a book that is neither traditional business history nor a community study in a strict sense. In focusing on the converging paths of company and community this book presents a complex and rich social history of a British enterprise in Brazil.

Acknowledgments

A considerable number of people and institutions have contributed to the completion of this work over the past decade. First and foremost, without the generosity and friendship extended to me in Nova Lima by countless individuals this work would not have been possible. Dr. Iguatemy Mendonça, former president of Mineração Morro Velho, S.A., opened up the archives of the St. John d'el Rey and provided tremendous support and enthusiasm for the project. His successor, Dr. Juvenil T. Félix, and Paulo Cesar de Moraes Sarmento, the company commercial director, both provided outstanding support during my research in Nova Lima and Rio de Janeiro. Roberto Lima and Mary Gill went out of their way to open doors for me, and their help and friendship are deeply appreciated. Padre Cônego João Deniz de Valle kindly allowed me access to the parish registers of Nova Lima, and the late Reverend Ariel Walter Alvin graciously permitted me to copy the Anglican parish registers at Morro Velho. I am grateful to José Lúcio Fonseca for giving me full access to the Cartório de Paz e Registro Civil. The *prefeitura* and *câmara municipal* both provided access to their records. I would especially like to thank the Brazilians and Anglo-Brazilians who kindly permitted me to interview them about their families and communities. I hope this study does justice to the history they collectively helped create and live.

In Belo Horizonte the staffs of the Arquivo Público Mineiro, the Biblioteca Pública de Minas Gerais, the Departamento Nacional de Produção Mineral, and the Instituto Histórico e Geográfico de Minas Gerais facilitated my research. Douglas Libby, Yonne de Souza Grossi, Eliana Dutra, Amilcar and Roberto Martins, Francisco Iglésias, Maria Efigênia Lage de Rezende, and Hélio Gravatá provided useful suggestions and stimulating conversation. The staff of the United States Consulate in Belo Horizonte provided support and advice on countless occasions. In Ouro Preto I spent pleasant and productive days in the library of the Escola de Minas, Universidade Federal de Ouro Preto, and in the archives of the Centro de Estudos do Ciclo de Ouro, Casa dos Contos. I also received help from the Museu de Ouro in Sabará. In Campinas the late Peter Eisenberg and Michael Hall provided me with good conversation and access to the Arquivo Edgard Leuenroth. In Rio de Janeiro my work was aided by the staffs of the Arquivo Nacional, the Biblioteca Nacional, and the Fundação Casa Rui Barbosa. J. Ivins and Frank Davies allowed me to examine the records of the Morro Velho vice-consulate now in the British Consulate General. At Christ Church in Rio de Janeiro the Reverend Roger Blankley allowed me to copy the parish registers from Gongo Soco and Morro Velho. Vera and José Gomes and their family opened their home to my wife and I on several occasions with warm hospitality.

In Austin, William Callaghan and J. W. F. Dulles both gave me access to their own research and files. The good-natured and conscientious labors of Jane Garner, Wanda Turnley, and Carmen P. Cobas were critical to an intense and productive month in the manuscript section of the Latin American Collection of the University of Texas Library. Bobby Eakin contributed to the project in his own way in Austin. John Wirth, John D. French, and Peter Reich each made helpful suggestions along the way. Tommy Hunt did some of the maps, and Paula Covington provided invaluable bibliographic and research assistance.

Last, but certainly not least, John Burke played a crucial role in the selection of the topic when it began as a doctoral dissertation. E. Bradford Burns guided the dissertation and has done more than anyone else in nurturing my work and my career. Fieldwork in Brazil in 1979–80 was funded by a Fulbright Fellowship, and the Vanderbilt University Research Council financed an additional three months in Brazil in 1985. Steven Topik, Warren Dean, and Thomas F. O'Brien read earlier versions of the manuscript and offered constructive criticism that helped me sharpen and polish my arguments. Finally, I would like to thank my friend and partner, Michelle Beatty-Eakin, for the enormous and incalculable amount of time, effort, and love that she has invested in the author and the project. In her own way, she has brought to life the history of Morro Velho.

Preliminary Notes

When the original directors formed a company in 1830 to work gold mines near the city of São João d'El Rei, they anglicized the spelling of the city to give their enterprise a name: the St. John d'el Rey Mining Company. In the 1850s, with the passage of the Companies Act in England, the directors duly registered the company as a limited liability, joint-stock operation and added "Limited" to the company name. Sometime near the turn of the century, company officials accidentally dropped the apostrophe in the "d'el," only to return it to its proper place a few years later. This accounts for the varied spellings of the company name in English. In Brazil the company was often called the "Companhia do Morro Velho" in popular speech and the press.

For most of the period of this study the common unit of currency in Brazil was the milreis (written 1$000). One thousand milreis was known as a *conto de reis*. In December 1942 the milreis became the cruzeiro (written Cr$1).

As is customary, the titles of works in Portuguese are spelled as they appeared on the original title page. The spelling of names has been modernized in the text.

Introduction

I

Gold Mining in Minas Gerais

"in this the legendary land of gold"[1]

The first rays of a brilliant orange sunrise have just begun to appear over the rugged mountain peaks to the east as the bus reaches the crest of the Serra do Curral, leaving the last view of Belo Horizonte behind it in the gray dawn light. For the next ten kilometers the highway twists along the ridges of low-lying mountains, gradually descending into the foothills to the southeast of the Serra. Very quickly the first blinding light of morning gives way as the bus passes into the thick fog and mist that blanket the valleys and hills, a fog that will slowly dissolve as the temperature rises at midmorning. Through the cool mist the passengers—some dozing, some chatting, others wrapped in their own thoughts—descend into the basin that surrounds Nova Lima and the Morro Velho mine. Straddling the steep hillsides, the community overlooks the converging Cristais and Cardoso streams as they flow westward emptying into the Rio das Velhas a few kilometers away. Except for the dense concentration of buildings, the area looks much as it did three centuries ago when the first Portuguese explorers entered these valleys. Houses now cover the once-green slopes above the streams, and today the ridge which separates the two valleys no longer divides the community physically or culturally as it once did.

Following traditional Iberian patterns, the community originally developed in the early eighteenth century around the central plaza on the southern flanks of the ridge facing the Cristais. The plaza with its cathedral, town hall, jail, and shops formed the political and social center of Nova Lima. On the northern side of the ridge facing the Cardoso sit the English-style cottages, where the British staff of the St. John d'el Rey Mining Company, Limited once resided. With its own school, Anglican church, and social life, the British community on these slopes stood apart from the rest of Nova Lima, a cultural enclave of England in the heart of the Brazilian interior. The growth of the town and the departure of the British in 1960 have blurred the old geographical and cultural distinctions between the two basins split by this ridge. Nevertheless, the southern basin remains the social and political center of the community, while the northern basin continues to provide Nova Lima with its economic sustenance; for in this northern basin an enormous industrial plant straddles the Cardoso and surrounds the entrance to South America's largest, and oldest, deep-shaft gold-mining operation.

Brazilian miners today continue to work the rich Morro Velho ("Old Hill") lode as their ancestors have done since the beginning of the eighteenth century. The amount of gold extracted in the eighteenth century remains undocumented, but after the British acquired the mine in the 1830s production rose steadily until the early twentieth century. Since the turn of the century the mine annually has produced over 3 million grams (100,000 ounces) of gold bullion. A mine with a long and productive past, the Morro Velho faces a promising future in light of high gold prices and large ore reserves. While still the dominant economic force in the life of the *novalimenses*, the mine today does not wield the influence of yesteryear. The once quintessential company town has become more diverse and less dependent on the mine in the past three decades. At the height of the British era the St. John employed more than 8,000 people in a community of 25,000. Since 1960 the Brazilian and (today) South African owners of the mine have modernized and reorganized the company, reducing the number of employees to around 4,000 in a town with some 35,000 inhabitants.

The lessening dependency of the town on the mine has been paralleled by the expanding influence of external forces on the community. A two-lane asphalt highway built in the 1950s winds through the peaks and valleys of the Serra connecting Nova Lima with the state capital, Belo Horizonte. Built in the 1890s as Brazil's first modern planned city, Belo Horizonte now boasts a population of two million and an industrial plant surpassed only by those of Rio de Janeiro and São Paulo. Buses now leave Nova Lima three times an hour carrying *novalimenses* to jobs, stores, and schools in Belo Horizonte.

As the booming capital of Minas Gerais radiates outward, housing tracts and light industry have begun to spring up through the Serra along the highway. Today Nova Lima forms a part of Greater Belo Horizonte, and the forested hillsides of the Serra are giving way to new suburbs and industry along this twisting roadway.

Geology and Geography

Although the influence of the mining company wanes as the years pass, the Morro Velho gold mine has always been the fundamental force in shaping the history of Nova Lima. Gold gave birth to the community, nurtured it, and molded it into the town one sees today. Without the mine Nova Lima would no doubt look just like any of the dozens of other small and historically insignificant towns which dot the landscape of Minas Gerais. The extraordinary nature of the Morro Velho lode has singled it out from other gold deposits in Brazil and has made possible the success and growth of the mine and the community. Unlike most gold deposits in Brazil, the Morro Velho lode thrusts deep into the earth's crust and the gold ore has shown little impoverishment with increased depth. On the surface the exposed lode crops out on the flanks of the Morro Velho across the Cardoso stream north of town. The lode plunges at a forty-five-degree angle to the east in a bed of quartz-ankerite-dolomite. Invisible to the naked eye, gold particles are distributed evenly throughout the dark gray ore. These particles occur in both free form and in association with arsenopyrites.[2]

A fortuity of nature made Nova Lima possible, but the ingenuity and sweat of human beings made the community a reality. The same could be said for all of the mining region of Minas Gerais. Millions of years of geological history have laid down great mineral riches beneath the surface of the Brazilian highlands. The labor and technical resourcefulness of countless men and women, however, have made that geological potential into the history of Minas Gerais. To appreciate that history one must continually refer back to the geology and geography which limit and direct the story that begins to unfold in Minas Gerais in the seventeenth century. Human society in central Minas Gerais has taken shape on top of some of the oldest known geological formations. The bedrock which underlies most of the re-

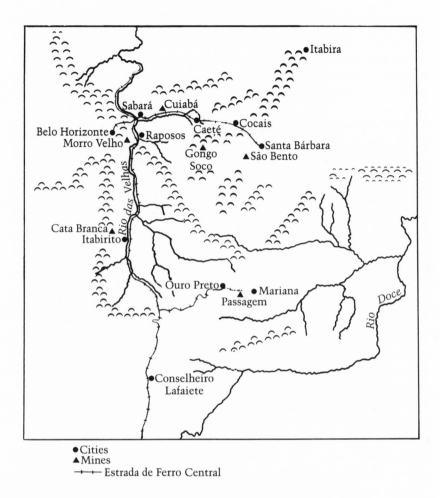

●Cities
▲Mines
—+—+— Estrada de Ferro Central

Map 1 Mining Zone of Minas Gerais

gion dates back some 2.8 billion years. During the last billion years the geological structure has been alternately uplifted, heavily eroded, buried beneath the sea, covered with layers of sediment, crumpled and crushed by movements of the earth's crust. About 500 million years ago the intrusion of superheated magma from deep within the earth recrystallized minerals in the ancient bedrock, forming major deposits of iron, manganese, gold, and other valuable minerals.

During the hundreds of millions of years up to the present the forces of nature have heavily eroded the uplifted portions of Minas Gerais producing a rugged, mountainous terrain, and gradually exposing the deposits of gold. Heavy winds and rains have cut deep valleys, making access, except by river, exceedingly difficult. The highlands produced by uplifting and erosion rise up quickly from the Atlantic coast averaging between three hundred and one thousand meters in altitude, and reaching over three thousand meters at their highest point. The Serra do Espinhaço ("Backbone Range") forms the principal mountain range which runs roughly north to south on a line through Diamantina, Itabira, and Ouro Preto (see map 1). This range separates the two major river systems of the area. To the east the Rio Doce drains south and east into the Atlantic, and to the west the São Francisco and its tributaries (principally the Rio das Velhas) drain to the north and east. A number of small ranges branch off from the Serra do Espinhaço, crisscrossing the gold-bearing region of central Minas Gerais.

The inland location of this area has made it the battleground for contending air masses which shape its weather patterns. From September to March, warm, moist air from the equatorial Atlantic blankets the region, bringing with it heavy (sometimes torrential) rains and temperatures ranging from fifteen to thirty degrees Celsius. From April to August the dry, cool air of the South Atlantic pushes up into the area, dropping temperatures to as low as five degrees Celsius, and temporarily ending the heavy rains. In the low-lying valleys of the gold-mining region hot, sunny days are often sandwiched between cool, foggy mornings and evenings. The heavy summer rains and the cold of winter do not present the most hospitable environment for human settlement.[3]

The Brazilian Gold Rush

Through these foreboding mountain ranges passed the first Europeans late in the seventeenth century. Before 1650 few Europeans had ventured inland from the Atlantic coast more than a few dozen kilometers. Colonists had concentrated primarily along the northeastern coast around the sugar-producing enclaves of Bahia and Pernambuco. Smaller population clusters took shape in the areas of the inland São Paulo plateau and the port of Rio de Janeiro (see map 2). Although the population of the São Paulo plateau numbered only a few thousand inhabitants, their impact was far-reaching. These

Map 2 Brazil and Neighboring Countries

hardy individuals, who could be compared to the mountain men of the North American West, opened up vast areas of the Brazilian interior north and west of São Paulo in search of Indian slaves and precious metals. Known as *bandeirantes*, these men and women explored the mountains and plateaux of the interior as far northwest as present-day Paraguay in pursuit of Indian slaves for the sugar plantations of the coast.[4]

By the early seventeenth century the growing preference for African slave labor on the northeastern sugar plantations began to undercut the slave-hunting economy of the southeast and the *bandeirantes* turned increasingly to the hunt for mineral riches. At the same time the Portuguese Crown began to encourage the search for precious metals in the interior, hoping to duplicate the success of the Spanish in Peru and Mexico. Some gold had been found in the rivers of the São Paulo plateau in the sixteenth century, but in small quantities. By midcentury the *bandeirantes* had begun to focus their attention on the river basins of the interior to the north of Rio de Janeiro and São Paulo.[5]

Controversy surrounds claims to the first discovery of gold in the interior, but the pioneers from São Paulo (*paulistas*) had probably located gold first in the streams of the Rio das Velhas basin in the late 1680s. By the 1690s word of the gold strikes had filtered back to the coast and in the succeeding decades the mining region experienced an enormous influx of prospectors in search of instant wealth and success. The Brazilian gold rush of the eighteenth century stands out as the first truly significant gold rush in Western history in terms of the movement of people and the consequent social and economic consolidation. Never in the history of Western Europe had there been such a massive gold rush as that caused by the news of strikes in Brazil in the 1690s. Nothing comparable would be seen again until the gold rush in California a century and a half later.[6]

As in the Spanish American empire, the Crown demanded its royal fifth (*quinto*). Unlike the Spanish, the Portuguese were hard-pressed to collect it from fiercely independent and widely dispersed miners. As the Spanish had two centuries earlier, the Portuguese immediately acted to construct a political and fiscal apparatus to control the mining region. Unlike the silver mines of central Mexico and upper Peru, the gold mines of central Brazil were widely scattered and separated by rugged terrain, which made policing of the area practically impossible. Consequently, attempts by the Crown to establish central mints and to regulate production and circulation met with much less success than in Spanish America. The shifting and transitory nature of placer mining demanded solutions radically different from those of the centralized, deep-shaft mines of the Spanish empire in the New World.[7]

In the early decades of the eighteenth century the lack of an effective political and military presence in the region led to battles between the *paulistas*, who viewed the area as rightfully theirs, and the Europeans who descended upon the area. The Crown at this point made a concerted effort to impose its authority and soon quelled the conflict. In the aftermath of the dispute, basic political structures took shape under Crown guidance. The political authority accorded to the principal towns merely recognized the social and economic consolidation which had taken place by the second decade of the century. These towns had become important commercial foci with diverse and stratified social groups.[8] In 1711 royal decrees elevated several of the mining settlements to the status of towns. Vila Rica, Sabará, and Mariana received royal sanction, and in the 1720s the area of the mines was officially separated from the captaincy of São Paulo. By the 1730s royal correspondence regularly referred to the new captaincy as *Minas Gerais* (General Mines).[9]

The towns of Sabará and Mariana sit roughly on the northwest and southeast corners of an imaginary rectangle which encompasses the principal gold-bearing deposits of Minas Gerais (see map 1). The early prospectors followed the rivers of the region upstream tracing the alluvial gold back to its origins in search of the mother lodes. Mining in this manner consisted of little more than placer washing techniques. The prospector would gather up the gravelly sands (*cascalho*) of the rivers in a wooden bowl (*batéia*), and then, by gently rotating the bowl, the lighter material would be tipped out, leaving the heavier gold particles on the sides of the *batéia*.[10]

As the alluvial gold gave out and the colonists reached the hillsides from which the gold had been weathered and washed down, they adapted their techniques. Employing groups of slaves, mining *empresários* cut trenches and terraces in hillsides and then diverted streams and rivers to wash down and through the cuts. The slaves kept the loose gravel and water moving across the cuts until the *cascalho* reached either crude wooden stamps and sluices or workers using *batéias*. Waterwheels powered the stamps (sometimes with iron heads), which crushed the *cascalho* into finer particles for the sluices or the washers with *batéias*. Animal hides (or fleece) caught the heavy gold particles and the washing of these hides removed the accumulated gold. Essentially, this type of hydraulic mining comprised a more highly evolved form of alluvial panning. Unlike the labor-intensive, low-technology panning process, hydraulic mining required more capital investment, more machinery (stamps, tools for excavating hillsides and terraces, and aqueducts), and the management of collective labor. From this standpoint, hydraulic mining represented a large step forward in mining technology. A century later the same techniques and organization would play a prominent role in the California gold rush.[11]

The third major type of mining to develop in Minas Gerais was the least common: shaft mining. Deep-shaft mining had been under way in Mexico and Peru for over two centuries. The Portuguese had little mining experience and apparently knew little about deep-shaft technology. The Spanish Hapsburgs controlled the silver-rich mining regions of central Europe and, with the discovery of silver in the New World, the Spanish Crown merely transferred its German experts and their expertise to the overseas colonies. Two factors hindered the development of shaft mining in eighteenth-century Brazil. First, few well-developed lodes exist in Minas Gerais, making the possibilities for shaft mining in the region limited, especially for eighteenth-century miners with scant knowledge of shaft-mining techniques. Second, the lodes that did exist could be developed on an economically viable scale only when the mining techniques of Europeans (especially the Cornish) became readily available to Brazilians. Until these techniques became widely available in the nineteenth century, the typical lode in Minas Gerais consisted of a shallow cut or open pit worked by slaves using crude tools. For as yet unexplained reasons, Brazilian mining entrepreneurs showed little interest in shaft-mining technology and received little encouragement to employ new technology. Consequently, mining went into a long-term decline as soon as the miners had exhausted the sources of alluvial and surface gold. After midcentury, gold production began to fall off dramatically, and the "Golden Age" of Brazil fell victim to technological backwardness.

The erratic fiscalization of gold and the probability of widespread contraband in eighteenth-century Brazil make estimates of gold production a guessing game. The most widely cited figures come from João Pandiá Calogeras's early-twentieth-century study, *As minas do Brasil*, in which he carefully reviews all previous sources and calculations.[12] Calogeras estimated that Brazil produced nearly one million kilograms of gold from 1700 to 1820. About three-quarters of this bullion was produced prior to 1780, with production peaking in the 1750s. Over a period of seven decades Brazil channeled gold bullion into Western Europe in unprecedented quantities stimulating a period of long-term economic expansion. Despite the immensity of gold production in eighteenth-century Brazil, the colony and mother country were not the major beneficiaries of the "Golden Age." By the early eighteenth century Portugal had come under the economic and political domination of the increasingly powerful English nation. Portugal covered its constant trade deficit with England with Brazilian gold, and Lisbon, in the end, became simply a way station for American bullion on its way north. Brazilian gold financed the commercial expansion of England in the early eighteenth century, and, in the last half of the century, its industrial expansion.[13]

The eighteenth-century gold rush fundamentally altered the course of Brazilian history as well. The decline of the sugar plantation economy in the mid-seventeenth century, combined with the loss of Portuguese commercial hegemony to the Dutch and English in Asia and Africa, initiated a process of economic and political decline that has plagued Portugal for centuries. The declining sugar plantations and the population centers they supported extended along the long Atlantic coastline, with the heart of the agrarian economy in the northeast. The discovery and exploitation of the mines briefly pulled Portugal out of economic decline, made Brazil the economic engine of the Portuguese empire, and effectively reduced the mother country to an economic appendage of its wealthy colony. The gold rush also shifted the axis of economic and political power southeast to the São Paulo–Rio de Janeiro region which served as the principal entry and exit point for the majority of the commerce with the mines. Political recognition of this economic shift followed in the 1760s with the transfer of the capital from Bahia to Rio de Janeiro. In the long run, one of the most far-reaching effects of the gold rush was the creation of a strong, national commercial class which, by the later decades of the century, increasingly pressured the metropolis for greater political and economic power. *Mineiro* gold, in essence, fostered the beginnings of Brazilian nationalism.[14]

Finally, the gold rush opened up the Brazilian interior to effective European colonization attracting thousands of immigrants to the mines and creating serious labor shortages in the northeast. These immigrants, slave and free, formed the nuclei of the settlements which developed around the gold deposits of Minas Gerais. The shifting and transitory nature of gold mining, however, inhibited the development of large political and economic centers such as the Zacatecas-Mexico City and Potosí-Lima axes in Mexico and Peru. Far more dispersed, settlements competed for economic and political power. No large city dominated the mining region. Although Vila

Rica served as the capital, Sabará, Mariana, Diamantina, São João del Rei, and several other towns vied for economic and political power in the region.

Mining Communities in Decline

The earliest settlements in central Minas Gerais sprang up on the steep slopes of the river basins and served as commercial supply centers for miners. The oldest and most important of these settlements coalesced around Sabará in the northwest and Vila Rica in the southeast of the mining zone. Sabará quickly became the political and economic center for the numerous small settlements in the Rio das Velhas basin which took shape around the gold-bearing streams and hillside deposits of the offshoots of the Serra do Curral. To the south of Sabará prospectors combed the Macacos, Cristais, and Cardoso streams and the hills above them. Gold deposits with names like Bela Fama, Gabiroba, Faria, Raposos, and Fernão Pães attracted prospectors to the area and a small settlement eventually developed at the confluence of the Cristais and Cardoso. The abundance of a variety of wild tea on the surrounding hills gave the settlement its name: Congonhas.[15]

By 1748 the community had grown large enough to be designated a parish with its own priest, and, falling under the jurisdiction of Sabará, the new parish accordingly received the imposing name Nossa Senhora do Pilar de Congonhas de Sabará (Our Lady of the Pillar of Congonhas of Sabará). Nearly 150 years elapsed before Congonhas achieved the administrative status of town (1891), taking the name of one of its most illustrious families. Villa Nova de Lima, as it was now called, became the administrative seat of the new municipality (município) of the same name. In 1923 the town's name was shortened to simply Nova Lima.[16] Notarial records from the eighteenth century provide us with the meager knowledge we have pertaining to the first century of Nova Lima/Congonhas's existence. Mining claims (datas minerais) indicate that prospectors worked dozens of claims up and down the valleys of the area. The principal families of the community all held important datas and often traded and sold them back and forth. The most important of these deposits by the late eighteenth century were normally open-pit operations that employed slave labor and crude stamping machinery. The richest and largest of these operations belonged to Anna Corrêa da Silva and her children and was located on the southern slopes of the site known locally as the Morro Velho.[17]

Along with the rest of the gold-mining region, the parish of Congonhas de Sabará fell on hard times in the last quarter of the eighteenth century as gold production plummeted and Minas Gerais slid into an economic slump. A Prussian mining engineer, Wilhelm Ludwig von Eschwege, made a survey of the mining region for the Crown in the second decade of the nineteenth century and found little to commend in the mining industry. A shortage of capital investment, antiquated technology, ignorance of mining techniques in general, and resistance to innovation frustrated Eschwege's efforts to revive the stagnant gold-mining industry and to stimulate iron ore production.[18] As an example of the state of the gold-mining industry, he singled out the operation of Anna Corrêa da Silva's son.

A certain Padre Freitas, of Congonhas de Sabará, owner of a rich mine from which he could extract an annual income of fifty thousand *cruzados*. He owned seven wretched two-stroke mills arranged in series and powered by numerous slaves. He could not augment the yield of his mine because he did not possess more space to install others.

A single hydraulic stamping mill would produce as much as the seven he has mounted. Furthermore, there were waterfalls which could be utilized for other equipment. I promised to lend him all possible help for this, even with some sacrifice on my part, but he was not disposed to spend a hundred to make a thousand. Almost all the other miners also proceed in the same fashion.[19]

The French naturalist St. Hilaire summed up the situation of the mining region in his description of Congonhas de Sabará, which he passed through in 1817: "Congonhas owes its founding to miners attracted by the gold which is found in the surrounding area, and its history is that of so many other large villages. The precious metal is exhausted, the workings become more difficult, and Congonhas presently heralds only decadence and abandonment."[20]

In his extensive survey of the mining region Eschwege found the gold-mining industry in Minas Gerais contained many small and medium-size works operating on a shoestring. He cataloged 555 mining claims (*lavras*), the vast majority employing ten slaves or less. A mere 70 employed more than twenty slaves, with but 2 employing over one hundred slaves. Less than two hundred free laborers worked on these *lavras*. He found the use of water power extremely limited, and mining operations wasteful of labor power. No steam engines were in use. Gold production, which had averaged well over 7 million grams annually in the mid-eighteenth century, in 1814 barely reached 400,000 grams from mines, with an equal amount coming from placering.[21] The glories of the Brazilian gold rush had vanished leaving behind a decaying industry in Minas Gerais by the 1820s.

The Anglo-Brazilian Gold "Rush"

The transfer of the Portuguese royal family and court to Rio de Janeiro in 1808 began the transformation of the gold-mining industry which would result in a small-scale gold rush in the 1820s and 1830s. The Prince Regent (later to become King João VI) opened the country to foreign commerce and merchants in early 1808, and by the following decade more than one hundred British merchants resided in the major towns of the coast and the mining zone. One of the most famous of these merchants, John Mawe, traversed the mining region and produced a perspicacious travel account publicizing its potential to British investors.[22] Restrictions remained, however, on foreign investment in mining. Following the declaration of Brazilian independence in 1822, Emperor Pedro I struck down the last of the old colonial obstacles to foreign investment in Brazilian gold mining.

In the colonial period all subsoil rights legally belonged to the Crown which granted the use and benefits of the subsoil to miners. In return for this concession on mineral rights miners paid the royal quinto which, despite the name, varied widely from the theoretical one-fifth of production. This policy of granting mining concessions continued under the empire with the major difference being that foreigners received access to concessions as well as nationals. The Constitution of 1824 made the entry of foreign capital into Brazilian mining a legal possibility for the first time in Brazilian history. Foreigners receiving mining concessions did have to meet special requirements. First, they paid 5 percent higher taxes on production than Brazilians. Second, they had to offer up to one-third of mining company stocks to Brazilian investors. Finally, the mining companies were required to pay a deposit of 150,000 milreis (about £32,000 in 1825 or £14,000 in 1830) to the Treasury as a guarantee against payment of taxes and duties. The constitution of the new Empire of Brazil opened the way to impressive British investment in the nation.[23]

By the third decade of the nineteenth century Great Britain had begun to ride a wave of economic expansion and prosperity growing out of a half-century of industrial revolution and the peace of post-Napoleonic Europe. The former had produced an impressive accumulation of capital and industrial production, and the British crisscrossed the globe in search of markets for their goods and capital. The latter made access to those markets less problematic. The wars for independence in Latin America in the 1820s provided limitless opportunities for the British, and in the century following independence Great Britain inundated the Latin American republics with investments and manufactured goods. British investors pumped some £25 to £30 million into Latin America in the early 1820s, with Brazilian projects taking the single largest share of this capital. The financial and speculative "bubble" burst in 1825, and investment slowed considerably for the next twenty-five years. Investment accelerated after midcentury, and by the 1890s British investments in Latin America probably totaled more than £550 million, with Brazil receiving approximately one-sixth of the total.[24]

From the 1820s to the 1860s the lion's share of British investment went into government loans with very little in other areas. This began to change after midcentury when the major portion of British capital investment funded the construction of railroads, ports, communications systems, and public utilities, and the purchase of government bonds. By the 1890s, for example, nearly 50 percent of British investment in Latin America went into government bonds, another 35 percent to railways, about 7 percent to banking and finance, and 3 percent each to public utilities and mining ventures. Total British investment in Latin American mining hovered around £3.5 million for most of the nineteenth century, rising to more than £20 million in the 1890s and reaching £38 million by World War I.[25] The major focal points of British mining investment were Brazil, Colombia, Mexico, and Chile, with Peru joining the group in the latter part of the century. Gold-mining companies were concentrated in Brazil, Mexico, and Colombia. Almost without exception, the mining companies funded by British investors in nineteenth-century Brazil were gold-mining enterprises. Brazil accounted for some 6 percent of British capital invested in Latin American mining ventures in the 1820s, and probably 3 percent of that invested in the 1890s.[26]

British investment in Brazilian gold mining during the nineteenth century flowed in three major waves. The first appeared in the 1820s and lasted into the 1830s. Great Britain had adopted the gold standard in 1816, and other nations followed her lead in the succeeding decades. The British eagerly sought to stimulate the production of Latin America's precious metals, which had declined in the late colonial period and practically ceased during the revolutionary upheavals. This rush for gold (and silver) began with the floating of joint-stock ventures, the first great venture being the Real del Monte gold mine in Mexico. Before the bubble burst in 1825, speculation ran rampant in London financial markets as seemingly everyone from clerks to the highest politicians scrambled to get into the American mining ventures.[27]

A second, somewhat more intense wave swept into Minas Gerais in the 1860s as a new influx of British overseas investment moved into Latin America. The third, and least intense wave of investment stretched across the last quarter of the century. The mining ventures that arose out of these waves, by and large, did not last long (see table 1). Of those companies established in the first wave, only two survived midcentury. None of the companies founded in the 1860s survived the century, although two lasted into the 1890s. Those founded in the third wave (with one exception) disappeared by 1905. Brazil was not exceptional in the failure of mining ventures. Mining has always been a high-risk enterprise, and Latin America has been the graveyard of many a British mining venture. J. Fred Rippy estimated that the English invested in approximately four hundred mining companies in Latin America after 1820: less than a score became profitable. Of the eighteen British companies to which the nineteenth-century Brazilian gold-mining boom gave birth, however, several did become profitable, including the most successful of all the British gold-mining ventures in Latin America.[28]

Although the gold-mining boom of the early nineteenth century revived a dormant industry, even within Minas Gerais gold mining remained a secondary industry employing around 20 percent of the labor force.[29] Minas Gerais experienced relative economic decline in the nineteenth century, as São Paulo and Rio de Janeiro took off with

Table 1 British Gold-Mining Companies in Nineteenth-Century
Minas Gerais

Dates of Operation	Company Name (Principal Mine)	Nominal Capital (in £s)	Production (in grams)
1824–56	Imperial Brazilian Mining Association (Gongo Soco)	350,000	12,887,000
1828–?	General Mining Association (São José d'el Rei)	?	?
1830–1960	St. John d'el Rey Mining Company, Limited (Morro Velho)	252,000	72,840,000
1833–44	Brazilian Company, Limited (Cata Branca)	60,000	1,181,291
1833–46	National Brazilian Mining Association (Cocais)	200,000	207,900
1834–?	Serra da Candonga Gold Mining Company, Limited (Serra da Candonga)	?	?
1861–76	East Del Rey Mining Company, Limited (Morro das Almas)	90,000	?
1862–96	Don Pedro North Del Rey Gold Mining Company (Morro de Santa Ana & Maquiné)	150,000	2,427,000
1862–98	Santa Barbara Gold Mining Company, Limited (Pari)	60,000	2,682,453
1863–83	Anglo-Brazilian Gold Mining Company, Limited (Passagem)	100,000	753,500
1864–?	Roça Grande Brazilian Gold Mining Company (Roça Grande)	100,000	?
1868–74	Anglo-Brazilian Gold Syndicate, Limited (Itabira)	100,000	?
1873–75	Brazilian Consols Gold Mining Company (Taquara Queimada)	100,000	?
1876–87	Pitangui Gold Mines Limited, (Pitangui)	8,000	285,000
1880–87	Brazilian Gold Mines Company, Limited (Descoberta)	80,000	?
1880–1927	Ouro Preto Gold Mines Company, Limited (Passagem)	140,000	8,210,119
1886–?	São José D'El Rey Gold Mining Company, Limited (Caçula)	?	?
1898–1905	São Bento Gold Estates, Limited (São Bento)	250,000	922,739
Totals		£2,040,000	£102,397,002

Sources: Ferrand, *L'Or à Minas Geraes*; Leonardos, *Geociências no Brasil*; Rodolphe Jacob, *Minas Geraes no XX século* (Rio de Janeiro: Gomes e Simões, 1911).

the coffee boom after 1840. Within Minas Gerais, the southern and southwestern portions of the province (Zona da Mata and the Zona Sul) benefited from the coffee boom, leaving the old Zona Meta-lúrgica to experience economic stagnation. Although the capital of Minas Gerais would remain in the old mining region, the politicians of the Sul and Mata zones would emerge as major figures in *mineiro* politics and would be more interested in cattle and coffee than min-ing.[30] By the mid-nineteenth century coffee accounted for half the value of *mineiro* exports, with cattle, bacon, pigs, cheese, and to-bacco making up an additional 40 percent. Gold never accounted for more than a small percentage of all exports after independence.[31]

British companies moved into Minas Gerais with capital, advanced technology, and Cornish miners, reviving dozens of the abandoned and decaying eighteenth-century mines. The first British mining venture in Brazil also proved to be one of the most profitable. Edward Oxenford, an English merchant, had installed himself in Ouro Preto in the first wave of British merchants arriving in Brazil. Oxenford served as the agent for a number of British mining companies during the next two decades. In the 1820s he explored an old claim known as the Gongo Soco located between Caeté and Santa Barbara. In 1824 he obtained the first mining concession granted to a foreigner and purchased the Gongo Soco from the Baron of Catas Altas for the newly formed Imperial Brazilian Mining Association. This British company had been established in London with an initial nominal capital stock of £350,000. In 1826 it took control of the Gongo Soco property as well as a number of smaller and less important mines in the surrounding area. The association agreed to pay government taxes of 25 percent on production, an amount reduced to 20 percent in 1837, 10 percent in 1850, and 5 percent in 1853.[32]

The Imperial Brazilian set the general pattern which most of the subsequent British mining companies would follow for the next cen-tury. After issuing a call for investors, the company sent a group of Cornish miners to Gongo Soco with a commissioner to direct opera-tions. This core of British miners and managers and their families established a small but vigorous settlement complete with Anglican chapel and parson. By the 1840s the company employed some two hundred Europeans who led a work force of more than five hundred slaves and two hundred free Brazilians. The company introduced the deep-shaft mining techniques of Cornwall and the latest milling pro-cesses. The cost of fuel and difficulties of transport prevented the use of steam engines, but the abundance of water more than made up for the excessive costs of steam power. Water powered the stamping mills, grinding stones (arrastres), and all the amalgamation equipment. The rational and large-scale application of deep-shaft mining and milling techniques made Gongo Soco the most modern mining operation in Brazil.[33]

British capital and technology—combined with a rich lode—produced quick success for the Imperial Brazilian. The Gongo Soco had been one of the legendary mines of Brazil until it fell on hard times in the late eighteenth century. Under the British it yielded consistently large amounts of ore rich in gold. Nevertheless, the mine works flooded and collapsed in complete ruin in 1856, ending three decades of extremely successful operations. According to company account books, the mine produced nearly thirteen million grams of gold worth £1,697,295. Approximately one-fifth of this amount went to the Brazilian government in the form of taxes and duties. Another one-fifth went to investors in the form of dividends, and expenses gobbled up the remaining three-fifths.[34]

The wave of mining speculation and the initial success of the Imperial Brazilian spurred the formation of a score of similar companies in London over the next few decades (see map 1 and table 1). In the 1830s and 1840s the Brazilian Company at Cata Branca and the National Brazilian Mining Association at Cocais met with limited success. The Don Pedro North Del Rey near Ouro Preto, the Santa Barbara Gold Mining Company at Pari, and the Anglo-Brazilian Gold Mining Company at Passagem all began operations in the early 1860s, lasted into the 1880s and 1890s, and were even more successful than the companies had been at Cocais and Cata Branca. With the major exception of the Ouro Preto Gold Mines Company that took over operations at Passagem from the early 1880s to 1927, the rest of the British mining companies in Brazil were dismal failures. With few exceptions, Brazilian mines took much more from British investors than they gave back, and British capital invested in mining had minimal impact on the Brazilian economy in the nineteenth century.

Most of the British mining companies followed the pattern set by the Imperial Brazilian, raising initial capital in the range of £200,000, sending out experienced Cornish miners to open up the old mines on a modern basis, and attempting to construct permanent and productive mining enterprises. The most successful of all the British gold-mining ventures in Latin America took shape in this first wave of Brazilian mining speculation. Formed in London in 1830 to work a group of mines in the area around São João del Rei, the company would take its anglicized name from this city in southern Minas Gerais. Despite its official title, the St. John d'el Rey Mining Company would prosper far removed from the city which brought it into existence and gave it a name.

PART I

The Company

By 1830 Brazil had begun a process of modernization spurred by political independence and the beginnings of coffee cultivation in the southeast. Foreign capital played a critical role in this process, notably in the form of direct investment in British companies. Part one of this study contains the most detailed analysis of any foreign business in modern Brazil, a business that is arguably the most successful foreign company in Brazilian history. The three chapters in this section address three simple questions. First, what was the structure and organization of this British company, and how did it evolve? Second, what was the extent of its political influence? Third, what was the nature of its operations?

Chapter 2 examines the history of the company in detail, relying primarily on company archives. This chapter emphasizes the international, national, and regional forces that shaped the company and its history. The analysis stresses the tremendous adaptability of this capitalist enterprise to local conditions, rather than its ability to transform the regional and national economy beyond Nova Lima. Chapter 3 also stresses the limitations of the St. John, and the surprising weakness of its political influence beyond Nova Lima. Finally, chapter 4 turns to the technological system the British constructed at Morro Velho. Ultimately, the key to the company's success was the ability of the British to control and continually refine this system. An understanding of the evolution of this technological system is the key to understanding the history of both company and community.

2

The St. John d'el Rey Mining Company, Limited

And the English company will come and in turn will buy everything
and in turn will lose everything.[1]

A handful of British investors met in the City of London Tavern on 5 April 1830 to organize the St. John d'el Rey Mining Company. These investors had signed a contract leasing the St. John and San José mines in southern Minas Gerais (near the city of São João del Rei) for a period of up to twenty-five years. Three British merchants and a German physician educated at Oxford owned the mines. The German, George Süch, had obtained an imperial decree in November 1828 to work these mines, and he and his partners quickly leased their rights to the newly formed St. John d'el Rey. Süch had probably been operating as an agent for the founding directors of the company. As early as April 1829 he had contracted with the company's future directors to lease the mines to them.[2]

Apparently, Süch and his partners had all been active in Brazil in the mining boom of the 1820s, and the investors to whom they sold their rights were hardly newcomers to the American mining industry. John Diston Powles, the chairman of the new company, was one of the most prominent London merchants pushing investment in the new republics of Latin America. One of his partnerships—Herring, Graham and Powles—floated the 1822 Colombian government loan. Powles became notorious for his promotion of investment in Latin American mining ventures. He hired the young Benjamin Disraeli to write pamphlets "puffing" the new American mining companies, and included him as a partner in a number of business schemes. Powles served on the board of the Anglo-Mexican Mining Association formed in 1824 to work silver mines in Guanajuato, and he was a partner with Simón Bolívar in an ill-fated Colombian mining scheme. When the speculative bubble burst in London in 1825–26, Powles apparently went bankrupt. The collapse spelled financial crisis for thousands of investors including Bolívar and Disraeli. (The former was plagued by British creditors until his death in 1830, and Disraeli did not settle his debts until the 1850s.) A prominent Conservative, Powles would be a strong ally and supporter of Disraeli in the 1850s and 1860s. Powles quickly recovered from financial collapse, and, in addition to his Brazilian mining company, he continued to invest in Colombian mines. His strong leadership guided the St. John d'el Rey for nearly four decades.[3] Charles Herring, Jr., the superintendent soon to head for Brazil, served on the board of mining companies in Mexico and Chile, and was Powles's partner in the Colombian loan. James Vetch, another company director, was the first commissioner (superintendent) at the Real del Monte silver mine in Mexico.[4]

Like other joint-stock companies formed in the early nineteenth century, the St. John d'el Rey operated in ambiguous legal territory. British law had made joint-stock companies "indictable as a common nuisance" after the South Seas Bubble debacle in the early eighteenth century. Possible fraud, and speculative disasters notwithstanding, joint-stock companies continued to grow in popularity for the next century. By the 1820s investors in joint-stock companies faced two major problems. British law did not recognize the companies as legal entities, and shareholders' liability was unlimited. Lack of legal recognition made it difficult for companies to enter into binding contracts, hold property, and sue. In 1834 Parliament issued "letters patent" to the companies that, in effect, granted them corporate charters and legal status. In 1856 the Joint Stock Companies Act extended limited liability to all registered companies. The St. John d'el Rey Mining Company duly registered, adding a "Limited" to the company name.[5]

When the directors of the St. John organized the company in 1830 they immediately announced an offering of £50,000 in stock to finance mining operations in Minas Gerais. Within a month they had assembled a group of Cornish miners under the direction of Herring and dispatched them to Rio de Janeiro. Herring hired a Cornish mining "captain" who had worked at the Real del Monte and a crew of eighteen. The party arrived in Rio de Janeiro in June and after a tough journey on mules through the mountains with their heavy machinery they arrived at the mines in July. By mid-August work at the mines had begun. Under strict instructions from the London office Herring sent back detailed reports every fortnight describing the progress of the new works.[6] The optimism that filled the early correspondence gave way within a year's time to disillusionment with the prospects of the mines. Legal problems over ownership rights, the creeping realization that Süch and his partners had probably misrepresented the mines' possibilities, and low-grade ore hampered the St. John in the first two years of operations. By mid-1832, the directors, on advice from Herring, had decided to shut down operations and search for new mines. Some of the mining crew remained with Herring as he inspected the various gold deposits in the region. Others returned to England, and a few of the Cornish hired on with other English mining companies in Minas Gerais.[7]

Herring and his agents made a thorough search of the gold mining properties in central Minas Gerais, many of them owned by British investors. By 1833 he had purchased the small Feixos mine near the village of Congonhas de Sabará. At least a score of Englishmen worked the gold deposits around Congonhas, and several had bought up portions of the Morro Velho mining estate. Anna Corrêa da Silva had died in 1829 leaving the estate to her children, including the Padre Freitas so ridiculed by Eschwege.[8] The former manager of the Imperial Brazilian Company at Gongo Soco and several other Englishmen had bought up the heirs' portions.[9] It seems that Herring knew these Englishmen well and had visited Morro Velho on a number of occasions. Recognizing the wealth of the lode, he arranged to work the mine on a trial basis and began proceedings to purchase the entire estate. After issuing a call for more capital, the directors of the St. John d'el Rey authorized Herring to purchase the mine and estate for £56,434, and by the end of 1834 the Morro Velho mine had legally passed into the hands of the St. John d'el Rey Mining Company.[10]

Building the Enterprise

The mine occupied only a small portion of one corner of the Morro Velho estate. The greater part of the estate lay to the northwest of the mine. In fact, the northwestern boundary ran along the crest of the Serra do Curral several kilometers away, and included the forests and

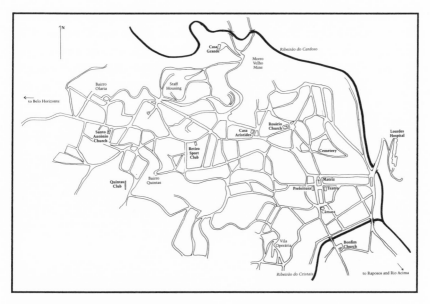

Map 3 Nova Lima, Town Plan

watersheds on the entire southern slopes of the Serra. Little more than an open-pit operation, the mine works spilled down the southern slopes of the Morro Velho overlooking the Cardoso stream (see maps 3 and 4). Across the stream and a short distance to the south a ridge separated the estate from the village of Congonhas de Sabará. On the hillside directly opposite the mine the eighteenth-century Casa Grande surveyed the mine and the Cardoso.[11] Stamps, workshops, and mining machinery lay scattered over the hillside around the open pit. To the west of the pit on a shoulder of the Morro Velho sat the houses and compound of the estate's slaves. Along with the small English crew Herring had brought some fifty slaves with him from the mines at São João del Rei. To this he added the 136 slaves belonging to the newly acquired estate.[12]

Although the ore from the Morro Velho lode proved to be as good as or better than anticipated, the initial costs of renovating the mine and putting its operations on a sound, modern basis alarmed stockholders in England. Stockholders even named a special committee to study company finances.[13] More and more capital had to be funneled into the construction of sturdy aqueducts, stamping machinery, hauling equipment, milling works, and housing for Europeans as well as slaves. As the improvements took shape and the mine's pro-

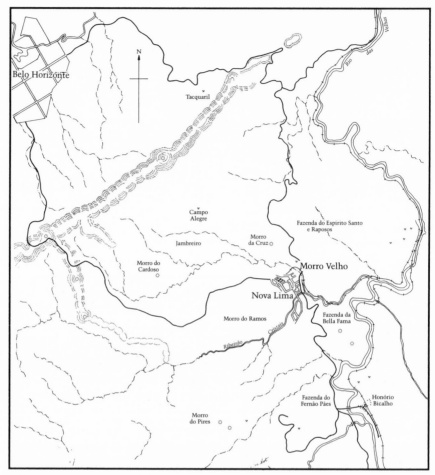

Map 4 Nova Lima and Surrounding Area

duction rose, the investment began to pay off. The company paid its first dividend to stockholders in 1842, and dividends would continue on a regular basis for the next quarter-century. By the mid-1840s Herring had the mine running smoothly, the labor force expanded as production increased, and the company's stock rose in value on the London Exchange.[14]

The prosperity of the mine also stimulated the growth of the British community around Morro Velho and Congonhas as the St. John d'el Rey sent out ever larger numbers of miners and their families. By the mid-1850s the size of the British community at Morro

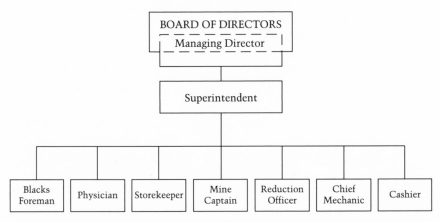

Figure 1 Organizational Structure of the St. John d'el Rey Mining Company, Limited, Mid-Nineteenth Century

Velho hovered around 150, approximately half of those employees of the company. Imbued with the Victorian morality of the era, company directors carefully monitored the spiritual and moral behavior of employees and dependents. The board encouraged employees to take their families out to Brazil. The stability of family life, the directors reasoned, would encourage the men to lead sober and temperate lives, thereby providing the company with better workers.[15] The board hired an Anglican clergyman and his wife to provide religious services and to educate the more than sixty children of the British community. The company had a chapel and schoolhouse erected near the Casa Grande and successfully petitioned Emperor Pedro II for permission to set aside ground for a cemetery for the Protestant English. In 1867, after lobbying by the company's directors, the British Parliament passed a special act legalizing marriages consecrated by Anglican clergy at Morro Velho. By the late 1860s, then, the English at Morro Velho could be born, baptized, married, and buried as easily as if they were in a parish in the English countryside.[16]

Another consequence of the growth of company operations was the development of a well-defined and differentiated organizational structure that would remain basically intact into the twentieth century (see figure 1). In London the company maintained an office in the financial district with a small clerical staff. The board of (five to six) directors, elected by the stockholders who met biannually, usually met bimonthly to discuss company business, set policy, and go over the latest reports from the mines. A managing director watched over the day-to-day operations of the office and acted as the contact between directors, office, and mine. As with many British companies overseas, the St. John employed commercial agents to represent the enterprise in Rio de Janeiro. The agents handled all important commercial and financial transactions, mail, purchasing of supplies, and represented company interests in the Brazilian capital.[17]

The company's chief officer in Brazil was the superintendent who headed mining operations at Morro Velho. The fate of the company depended on the skills and decisions of this man more than any other company official. London could monitor and lay down policy, but the thousands of kilometers between Brazil and England, and the slow pace of communications, forced the board to place the brunt of responsibility on the shoulders of the superintendent at the mines. The St. John d'el Rey was extremely fortunate during its long history to have strong and energetic superintendents during critical years. Charles Herring, Jr.'s able guidance and purchase of the Morro Velho estate in the early years saved the company from failure. George Chalmers, in his forty years at the helm at the turn of the century, would personify the power and importance of a strong and capable superintendent. (Appendix 4 contains a list of superintendents and their tenure at Morro Velho.)

Department heads at the mine made up the next level of management, and they answered directly to the superintendent. Mine, reduction, mechanics, medical, store, cashier, and blacks department heads met with the superintendent on a daily basis to discuss problems and policy. The superintendent coordinated the various duties and personalities. By far the largest branch of operations, the mine department encompassed all work underground with the exceptions of maintenance and repair work. The mine captain headed this department. Supervision of milling and treatment of ore as it came out of the mine came under the control of the reduction officer. The mechanics department handled all types of woodworking and metalworking in the shops and did repairs and maintenance. A surgeon guided the medical department which included care for the English and slave populations, as well as the management of the company hospital.[18] The storekeeper supervised the purchasing and dispensing of the enormous quantity of materials used by the company, from foodstuffs to heavy machinery. Accounting, payroll, and the

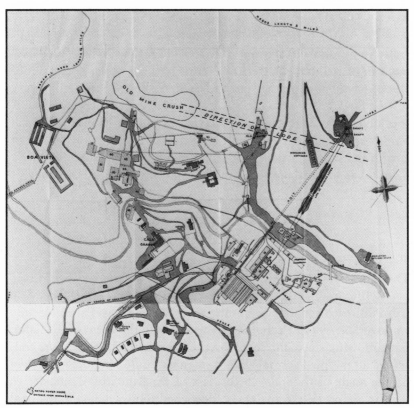

Map 5 Morro Velho Surface Works

disbursement of funds fell under the control of the cashier. Finally, the foreman of the blacks oversaw the control and treatment of hired and purchased slaves who lived in compounds in areas known as Boa Vista and Timbuctoo located on the southwestern shoulder of the Morro Velho (see map 5).

As a rule, Europeans filled the positions of department heads as well as the supervisory positions. The British generally handled supervisory tasks both in and out of the mine, leaving the lower-level jobs and manual labor to slaves and free Brazilians whom they referred to as "blacks" and "natives." The company paybooks mirrored this functional division with separate paysheets for "Europeans," "Natives," and "Blacks." (Slaves did not receive wages but did get rewards for good behavior and occasionally overtime for working on holidays.) Occasionally non-British Europeans worked for the company, especially Germans in the nineteenth century. After World

War I a few select Brazilians (principally lawyers) made their way onto the contract system and the "European" payroll. Europeans generally signed four- to six-year contracts in England and received payment in British pounds sterling. Terms of the contract normally included payment of passage out and back, enabling British employees to visit England for a short time at the end of each contract period. A special feature of the contracts was the payment of "home pay." Each month an employee could have a portion of his wages deposited in a bank in England, usually for relatives left behind. Natives usually hired on as wage laborers and received payment in local currency.[19]

The Mine

The Morro Velho mine actually consisted of a series of three mines paralleling each other as they descended into the same lode. The Bahú followed the lode beginning at its westernmost extremity and was overlain by the Cachoeira to the east.[20] To the north of the Bahú, but following the same lode, lay the Gambá. Each excavation contained an inclined central shaft or mainway following the forty-five-degree angle of the lode, in the case of the Bahú and Cachoeira to depths of 300 to 350 meters. Ladders and footways and occasional platforms for hauling machinery ran the entire length of the central mainways. Known as "stopes," these areas were worked downward in a stairstep fashion known as underhand stoping.[21] Timber supports and rock pillars held up the rock overhead. Water-powered hauling wheels on the surface raised and lowered huge buckets or "kibbles" carrying water and ore out of the mine. Kibbles often served as transport for men and large equipment. In the 1840s crude trams on rails in the mainways greatly facilitated the movement of ore, but the principal method of access and egress for workers was via ladders and footways until the 1870s. Not until the 1880s did the company install "cages" to lower and raise workers into and out of the mine, saving them from the tiring and dangerous trips to and from the stopes.[22]

Until the 1850s miners normally entered the underground works in two shifts of twelve hours each, one shift entering in the early morning and the other replacing it in the evening. The company switched to three eight-hour shifts in 1851.[23] The stopes were the center of activity and consisted of huge caverns continually expanding outward and downward. As in Cornwall, the basic mining techniques entailed the driving of iron or steel rods ("borers") into the rock face. One man held the borer while a second drove it with a sledge hammer ("double-jacking"). At regular intervals, normally at the end of shifts, the boring crew left the stopes and a special crew filled the drilled holes with blasting powder and ignited the charges. Still another crew then cleared and broke up the debris, and others loaded it into trams to be taken to the surface. In the early years female slaves handled the transport of ore in baskets from the stopes to the reduction works. With the advent of the trams the women generally took over at the surface continuing the journey to the reduction works. The great majority of the mining force was employed as borers, with smaller groups handling the tasks of charging, loading, tramming, running machinery, and maintenance.

Slave Labor

With the expansion of operations, the company also acquired large numbers of slaves. Herring and his successors relied on slave labor guided by English miners to provide the company with a stable and secure work force. The management of the St. John turned to slavery with great reluctance. Like good Victorian capitalists they firmly believed in the superiority of free wage labor over African slaves. Yet from the beginning of operations in Brazil, they also failed to attract sufficient free workers to run the mine. For nearly a century free laborers in Minas would shun the mine for the fields of the surrounding region and São Paulo. Free labor was scarce, and the small force the company managed to hire refused to adjust to the industrial rhythms demanded by the British. Absenteeism by the free borers continually plagued management efforts to run the mine at full capacity. Unable to attract productive free labor, the company reluctantly accepted the realities of local conditions.[24]

There is no way to know if the company would have been more productive with a free labor force in the nineteenth century. Company statistics do not permit a valid comparison of the productivity of slave versus free miner. Certainly slave labor appears to have been cheaper than wage labor. In the 1830s and early 1840s when the

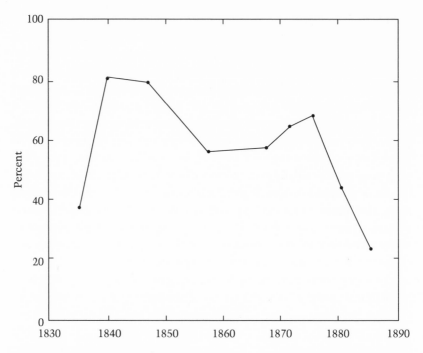

Sources: AR and Burton, *Explorations*, I.

Figure 2 Percentage of Slave Labor in Total Labor Force, Morro Velho, 1835–1885 (selected years)

company purchased its first slaves the price of a healthy, young black male slave ranged from 450 to 600 milreis (or approximately £44 to £59). In Congonhas de Sabará in the 1870s the price had nearly tripled to 1,500 to 2,000 (£112–150).[25]

A truer test of costs, however, was the price of renting slaves, for the majority of the labor force after 1850 was made up of rented slaves. The company rented slaves from two sources: large groups from failed mining companies and small groups from individuals. In the 1860s the St. John rented nearly one thousand slaves from three defunct mining companies. Several hundred more slaves came from a constant turnover of rentals from individuals in the surrounding region. In 1861, for example, the company either rented or returned two hundred slaves from more than fifty different slave owners, an average of three to four slaves per owner.[26] By the 1860s the St. John employed fourteen hundred slaves in almost every aspect of its operations, and captive labor formed the vast majority of the work force (see figure 2). The company was probably the single largest employer of slaves in Minas Gerais, the province with the largest slave population in Brazil.[27]

Management developed an elaborate rating system to evaluate rented blacks. With separate scales for males and females, managers rated "blacks" either first, second, or third class depending on their age, health, and demeanor. Slave owners received contracts for either five years guaranteed, or for one year, with the annual rate for the latter being slightly higher. (Although the shorter contract gave the company greater flexibility in controlling the size of the labor force, the longer contract offered more stability.) In 1858, for example, a first-class black male cost 240 milreis on a five-year contract, and 250 on a one-year contract. (First-class females cost 120 milreis on either type of contract.) Prices seem to have risen slightly in the 1870s.[28]

Libby has calculated the cost of a rented slave versus the cost of a free laborer in the 1860s and 1870s. The combined cost of rent, provisions, and overtime pay for rented slaves on an annual basis shows clearly the financial advantage of the first-class slave over the free miner in 1867 (350 milreis v. 465), and in 1879 (377 v. 682).[29] Company officials were making the same type of calculations on a regular basis, yet continued to believe that the free miner would be more productive in output than the slave. Although Libby's calculations do not take into account certain "hidden" costs (medical care, dependents, housing, supervision), they do demonstrate—along with the company's profitability—that industrial slavery was not only viable, but profitable, in nineteenth-century Brazil. The St. John d'el Rey constructed an efficient industrial enclave using slave labor. In the process, the company adapted to local conditions, as it would eventually adapt to the demise of slavery.

In 1845 the British Parliament passed the Aberdeen Act which, among other things, prohibited British citizens, regardless of residence, from purchasing slaves. Throughout the nineteenth century the British Foreign Office worked diligently to end slavery and the slave trade, and this act represented a major step in the struggle for abolition. The realities of the Brazilian labor market forced the St. John into confrontation with British foreign policy. The board of directors lobbied successfully to include a provision allowing British citizens to keep slaves purchased before the passage of the law, and to strike a clause prohibiting the renting of slaves.[30] Company slaveholding (largely through renting slaves) would continue to expand and, ultimately, create enormous friction between this British firm and British diplomacy (see chapter 3).

The St. John d'el Rey profited from the demise of British mining companies at Cata Branca, Cocais, and Gongo Soco, hiring nearly 1,000 slaves from companies failing in the 1840s and 1850s. The St. John d'el Rey "rented" 385 slaves from the Brazilian Company of Cata Branca in 1845; 182 slaves from the National Brazilian Mining Association of Cocais in 1861; and approximately 400 slaves from the creditors of the Imperial Brazilian of Gongo Soco in the 1860s.[31] With its renting policy, the St. John was able to hire slaves in the peak of their productive years, and to discard them at no cost as they became less productive. In the superintendent's words, "By judicious removals, dispensing with the services of those who are inefficient and the introduction of effective Blacks the general force of the Company is becoming much improved."[32] From the company's perspective this procedure contained the most attractive features of the slave- *and* free-labor systems; it provided a captive labor force with minimal social obligations.

The company protected its investment in a captive labor force with careful paternalism. The mine superintendent reported back to the board on the health and welfare of the captive labor force, and careful records traced the birth and death rates of the blacks. The company built a hospital run by their own physician, and they hired a Roman Catholic priest to minister to the spiritual needs of the slaves in the company-built church.[33] Marriage and procreation received every encouragement and special gifts were given out regularly to the parents of newborn children and to newlyweds. Parents of newborn children received a bottle of wine and one milreis (1$000—about 24 pence or 50 cents in 1866) and newlyweds the same. The company allowed slaves and free blacks to marry. As the great majority of company slaves were males, this allowed them to settle down and reproduce without the company having to hire extra female slaves (see chapter 6).[34]

From the earliest days in São João del Rei the company had set up an elaborate system of rewarding "deserving" slaves with emancipation. Company blacks received a special issue of clothing which they wore at fortnightly Sunday reviews (*revistas*) on the front lawn of the Casa Grande. Good behavior was rewarded with special stripes on the *revista* clothing and with medals. After five- to ten-year periods of probation the slave could be freed by the superintendent.[35] Beginning in the 1850s, the directors set manumission "goals": to free ten slaves at Midsummer (St. John's Day), and another ten at Christmas. They rarely met their goals in times of labor shortages.[36]

Several factors motivated the emancipation process. In the eyes of the board, gradual emancipation for "good behavior" resulted in more responsible freedmen. The desire to relieve the company of unproductive, elderly, and infirm slaves also guided manumission decisions.[37] As the abolition movement gained strength in the 1870s and 1880s, and as the price of hired slaves increased with the end of the Atlantic slave trade, two additional factors influenced the company's emancipation process. First, the board hoped that healthy and productive freedmen would stay on in their old jobs as free wage laborers, recognizing the "beneficence" of the company. By freeing trusted workers in their productive years, the company hoped to supply itself with skilled, cheap, wage labor and to reduce overhead costs by no longer having to provide for slaves and their families. Second, in the two decades preceding abolition the company pushed the emancipation process with one eye on potential social upheaval from slave rebellions, and the other eye on the perceived inevitability of abolition. The emancipation program served the St. John d'el Rey well, reducing potential social conflict, cutting costs, supplying new free laborers, and providing a convenient ideological salve for the consciences of the slave-owning Victorian English. The company freed 191 of its own slaves between 1830 and 1882, and 87 of the "rented" Cata Branca company slaves between 1845 and 1879. Some 50 of these 278 freed slaves partially or entirely paid for their freedom (see chapter 6).[38]

The overwhelming predominance of slave labor began to decline in the 1870s and 1880s in both absolute and relative terms (see figure 2). This shift reflected forces at work on the international scene and within Brazil. Abolitionist forces in Great Britain had been pressuring the Brazilian government for decades to end slavery and the slave trade. British diplomacy, backed by warships, effectively halted the Atlantic slave trade in the early 1850s. With the African slave supply suddenly choked off, the future of Brazilian slavery now rested on the ability of the slave population to reproduce itself and thrive. The passage of the Law of the Free Womb, or Rio Branco Law, in 1871, effectively spelled the death knell of Brazilian slavery by providing for the eventual emancipation of all children born to slaves. Although not totally effective, the law did make reproduction of the slave population an improbability, if not an impossibility. As supply fell below demand slave prices rose, making slavery less economically attractive for large employers like the St. John d'el Rey.[39]

The rising cost of hired slaves coincided with a decline in the number of company-owned slaves. Death had reduced the company's slave force, but emancipation had been an even more effective factor in the decline. The company, in effect, consciously chipped away at its own slave labor force. The process of emancipation received a forceful push forward in 1879 by judicial action. Abolitionists publicized the case of the Cata Branca slaves, revealing that the company had failed to free the slaves in 1859 as the original rental contract (1845) had stipulated. Joaquim Nabuco denounced the St. John in the Brazilian parliament, and the English-language press in Rio took up the cause. The British Foreign Office had pressured the St. John to free the slaves for years, and now sided with Brazilian critics of the company.[40] In 1882 Brazilian courts forced the company to free the remaining Cata Branca slaves and pay them back wages. Of the original 385 slaves rented from the Cata Branca mine, the company had freed 87, another 223 were freed by the courts, and the remainder had died. The St. John freed its last 28 slaves the same year.[41]

For the six years remaining before abolition, a few dozen hired slaves formed an insignificant portion of the labor force. The number of slaves working in the mine dropped to 91 by June 1886, and to 21 by the end of 1887.[42] By 1888, the transition to a free-labor system had effectively been completed, and the Lei Aurea merely liberated a small number of hired slaves in the company's employ. Rather than acting as a modernizing force promoting abolition and the growth of capitalist free labor, the company simply responded as best it could to the shifting slave- and free-labor markets, and British diplomatic displeasure.

On the issue of abolition, as well as other major social and political issues, company management preferred to remain out of the public eye and the public political arena. Acutely aware of the Foreign Office's position, and the growing force of abolitionism in Brazil, the St. John d'el Rey saw abolition as inevitable and did what it could to accommodate to the perceived decline of the slave system. The Cata Branca fiasco represented one of the few times that the company failed to handle its affairs quietly through its political allies. To avoid such open political battles the company carefully cultivated the friendships of state political leaders and lobbied behind the scenes throughout the nineteenth century (see chapter 3).

The tremendous expansion of the labor force in the 1850s and 1860s reflected the financial success of the company. By the mid-1860s the success and stability of the St. John d'el Rey had spawned another generation of mining ventures in Minas Gerais. Companies with names like "East del Rey" and "North del Rey" attempted to capitalize on the reputation and success of the Morro Velho mine. (See table 1 for a list of these companies.) These companies, like most of their predecessors, met with limited success and soon passed from the scene. The noted British adventurer, Richard Burton, visited Minas Gerais and Morro Velho in late 1867 and poked fun at these imitators while professing his admiration for the sound management of the St. John d'el Rey. In the years prior to Burton's visit the mine reached record production and profit levels under the superintendence of the strong-willed Irishman James Newell Gordon. The latter hosted Burton for over a month during which time the famed world traveler scrutinized every aspect of life and labor at Morro Velho. A descent into the depths of the mine left Burton deeply impressed with the vast underground workings and the complex timberwork system which supported the works.[43]

Disasters and Hard Times

Within a few short months of Burton's visit the Morro Velho mine nearly joined the long list of failed mining ventures in Minas Gerais. On the night of 21 November 1867 a fire broke out in the lower levels of the mine and in a short time spread throughout the works. The sea of timberwork that had awed Burton fueled the inferno and carried the flames into every area of the mine. After fighting the blaze for days and eventually diverting water from nearby aqueducts into the mine, Gordon ordered the shafts sealed to cut off all oxygen. As the fire consumed the timberwork, however, the walls of the galleries came tumbling down, rendering the excavations completely unworkable. In a matter of days three decades of financial success lay in ashes.[44]

After the collapse of the mine, and to reduce costs, the company began to rent out its own slaves, to release hired slaves to their owners, and to send home a number of the British miners. Some remained in Brazil and hired on with other British mining companies, particularly the Passagem mine near Mariana.[45] Unwilling to let this once-profitable investment die, the directors and Gordon resolved to reopen the mine via two parallel shafts to be located to the east of the old works. These two vertical shafts would drop directly into the lode below the original workings and thus avoid the crush in the old mine. The use of new hauling equipment over the shafts would also greatly speed up the movement of men and ore. After sending out a special team of rock drillers, work on the new "A" and "B" shafts began in November 1868.[46]

Seven lean years followed for stockholders as the St. John suspended dividends and raised capital to pay for the new shafts. For nearly an entire year, midway through the project, flooding in the shafts held up work and drove up costs. Hard rock and cave-ins delayed the work, and the drilling team did not reach the lode until November 1873, at almost forty meters below the surface. The total cost of the new shafts eventually passed £50,000, almost equal to the original purchase price for the Morro Velho estate.[47] While cutting the new shafts the company limped along, working the upper levels of the old mine, re-treating previously rejected ore, and by working a small mine nearby which the St. John had purchased in the early 1860s.[48] Stockholders and management held on with the hope that the newly opened mine would continue to produce ore of comparable quality and quantity to the old mine. As the miners opened out the lode at the bottom of the "A" and "B" shafts, the ore fulfilled their expectations and the future seemed promising once again.

The reopening of the mine in the early 1870s revived dividend payments and production levels, but serious administrative and managerial problems developed by 1875. After the initial resurgence in production with the opening of the new shafts, production began a precipitous decline, and the board decided to send out a review team to Morro Velho consisting of the company secretary, Pearson Morrison, and one director, Frederick J. Tendron, to survey the situation.[49] Much to their surprise and dismay the fact-finding team found rampant corruption and mismanagement. In his twenty years at the helm Superintendent Gordon had accumulated a number of personal business ventures on the side and had even entered into other mining activities, fraudulently diverting labor, materials, and capital from the Morro Velho works. The superintendent's contract always carried clauses prohibiting him from engaging in any business other than that of the company while in Brazil. Among other things, Gordon had bought part interest in a nearby mine. He had silently taken one-third interest in the major commercial outlet in Congonhas and was compelling all company employees to buy there. He had also charged the company for labor and materials employed for his own personal uses.[50] Even more seriously, it appeared that Gordon had been "milking" the mine of its best ore instead of developing the mine on a sound and orderly basis. His strategy for working the lode had come under fire in the 1860s and resulted in the firing of an experienced Cornish mining captain, Thomas Treloar.[51] John Jackson, the Cornish mine captain who replaced Treloar, now told the board in London that Gordon had been unfairly working the mine after its reopening to achieve high production figures.[52]

After some bitter exchanges the review team fired Gordon and attempted to pick up the administrative mess he left behind.[53] Over the next five years the mine suffered as a series of superintendents from within the company ranks attempted to put the mine back in order. Gordon's replacement, Pearson Morrison, took ill and soon died in Brazil. The company physician and then the chief engineer served brief stints and both proved ineffectual administrators. As production continued to drop, the board once again sent out one of its directors to survey the situation at Morro Velho. S. E. Illingworth found the establishment in disarray, under weak administrators, and quickly let London know they should be shopping for a new superintendent.[54] In their anxious search the directors interviewed a young civil engineer and liked what they saw. On 30 October 1884 the board of the St. John d'el Rey hired the young engineer and immediately sent him out to Brazil. The selection of George Chalmers proved to be the wisest decision the company ever made. Chalmers would not only revitalize operations, he would completely rebuild the Morro Velho into one of the most famous gold mines in the world during forty years at the helm.[55]

A Cornishman of Scottish descent, George Chalmers was working in the mining industry in Cornwall when the St. John d'el Rey management hired him. A newlywed, and just shy of his twenty-eighth birthday, Chalmers arrived at Morro Velho in December 1884,[56] facing tremendous administrative and logistical problems there. For the previous five years the parade of superintendents had failed to take charge of operations, and morale had declined as well as production

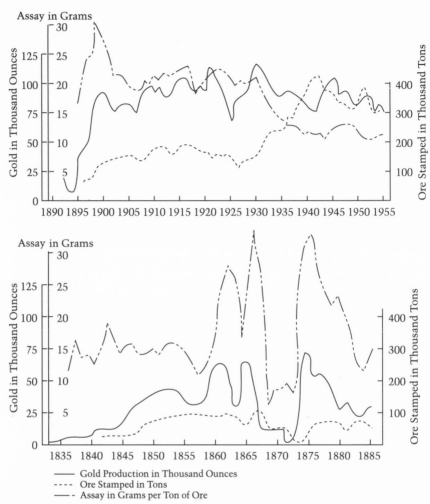

Figure 3 Gold Production, Tonnage Stamped, and Assay, 1834–1955

(see figure 3). He immediately restructured the supervisory staff and completely overhauled all aspects of labor and industrial processes. An even greater problem, however, stemmed from the layout and system of working the Morro Velho lode. Although the "A" and "B" shafts had reached the lode below the old mine, the shafts had been sunk directly into the lode, placing all mine traffic and operations directly in the very rock which the company excavated. Furthermore, the old methods of opening up large subterranean caverns supported by vast amounts of timberwork had been continued in the new mine. As the mine deepened, rock pressure increased, placing greater and greater stress on timberwork raising the chances of another major crush.

Chalmers had little time to deal with this situation before disaster struck. On the night of 10 November 1886 the mine captain, James Rogers, was called down into the mine. Timbermen had measured and cut a log to be fitted into the vast support system only to find that rock movement had lowered the section for which the timber had been cut. Rogers weighed the situation and resolved to have the dangerous rock section removed by the morning shift. They never had the opportunity. At 5:30 A.M. the entire section of rock broke away and brought down timber supports, a hauling engine, and the main platforms in that section of the mine. Luckily, this occurred as shifts were changing and few people were in the mine at the time. Rescue parties quickly descended and freed some twenty or thirty trapped miners. The falling rock had buried another ten men. The disaster, however, had just begun. The fall set off a chain reaction and for the next few weeks the mine slowly collapsed, section by section, as miners and administrators helplessly felt the ground below them tremble with each new fall.[57]

The initial fall heavily damaged the mine, but Chalmers felt that production would be halted for less than six months.[58] He sent Rogers off to England to explain the situation to the board, and then he proceeded to cut operating overhead as much as possible. He laid off the free labor force, a number of the British staff returned to England, and purchasing fell to a bare minimum. By early December it had become clear that the mine would be a total loss, and Chalmers sadly reported to the board that the excavation would have to be abandoned. In London directors and stockholders began to debate the future of the company. Two options appeared to be open. The company could be dissolved and accounts settled with creditors, or management and stockholders could hold on as they had in the 1830s while finding another promising mine to work. After carefully assessing the situation, Chalmers resolved to avoid both these options and to reopen the mine for a second time in less than twenty years. As Chalmers drew up plans and began to present his case to the board, the company went into liquidation. After a half-century of exceptional financial success, the St. John d'el Rey seemed to have reached the end of the road.[59]

An ordinary man would have closed down the company's operations and quietly accepted defeat. George Chalmers was not an ordinary man. Refusing to bow to the pessimism of the board and stockholders, Chalmers began to argue in his letters to London that the old lode had years of life ahead of it. Despite fifty years working the same lode, declining production in the previous decade, and two crushes in twenty years, he believed a new mine in the same lode could once again be a profitable enterprise. He proposed a plan to sink two new parallel shafts to reach the lode below the old workings. This time the shafts would be sunk to the north of the old lode and all of the main trafficways would sit in solid rock away from the workings. These shafts, labeled "C" and "D," would reach the lode at a depth of seven hundred meters below the surface, an unheard-of depth for mining in the nineteenth century. No mine had ever been worked to that depth without a consequent impoverishment in the quality of the gold ore. Chalmers's idea met with scorn and derision in England from both mining experts and stockholders.[60]

Undaunted, Chalmers hastily put together plans for the "third" mine and hurried off to London to present his case before the board. He argued that despite the depth of the new shafts, the lode and works would actually be closer to the surface than in the old mine. Modern hauling machinery would reduce the amount of travel time between the stopes and the mine entrance to two and one-half minutes as opposed to the twenty minutes it took in the old mine. To those who argued that ore quality inevitably declined with depth, he carefully pointed out that the ore in the lode had been consistent for over fifty years and that the samples taken from the lowest levels of the old mine before the fall were as high in gold content as at any time during the previous decades. A modern milling operation and more efficient shafts and tunnels, he maintained, would result in higher production and greater gold recovery. Chalmers's logic soon convinced the chairman of the board, and together they persuaded directors and stockholders to follow them in this bold plan. In July 1887 the St. John d'el Rey Mining Company, Limited, went through formal reorganization, and Chalmers returned to Brazil to work his miracle.[61]

Rebuilding

Chalmers's plans called for the construction of a completely new mine and mill. The old workings on the slopes of the Morro Velho would be abandoned and operations moved farther to the east into the center of the Cardoso basin. Chalmers planned to sink the "C" and "D" shafts to the east of the old shafts, placing them on the summit of the Mingu Hill east of the Morro Velho. These twin shafts would descend 700 meters with the "C" shaft handling pumping and the "D" shaft hauling. An adit (the entrance tunnel to the shafts) 364 meters long would intersect the shafts at the depth of a little over 100 meters to serve as the entry and exit for men, materials, and ore. The adit entrance would lay at the base of the Mingu Hill on the northeastern edge of the basin, and the Cardoso would run between the hill and the future surface works. He planned a steel bridge to span the stream connecting the mine and mill. The Cardoso basin would serve as the center of the new industrial park. The plan called for the dismantling of the old mine works at the far western rim of the basin. This plan placed the mine and mill to the east of the Casa Grande and the majority of the English cottages. The ridge on the south side of the Cardoso basin separated the mining complex from the center of Congonhas de Sabará (see map 5).[62]

As 1889 began, the London office dispatched boring machinery and a specialized crew of "sinkers." Work on the main adit began in April and on the shafts in May. After a short time it became clear that the boring machinery did not produce results in the hard Morro Velho rock, and hand boring combined with electric blasting became the key elements of shaft sinking. Workers on the main adit and shafts intersected exactly as planned and the new shafts reached the seven-hundred-meter mark in April 1892, three years to the month from commencement of driving. The next step involved tunneling "cross-cuts" south into the lode in order to open it out. Aiming to avoid the errors of the last two mines, Chalmers designed a new method of working the lode. He planned to work the lode with overhand instead of underhand stoping on a series of levels or horizons simultaneously. This system would avoid the tremendous rock pressures and expensive timberwork system by using a "cut-and-fill" technique along with the overhand stoping. On each horizon miners would cut up into the lode instead of down into it. The ore would then slide into the horizon below to be loaded and trammed away. Earth from the surface would be used eventually to fill in worked-out areas. Working the small areas and then filling them to reduce the chance of falls avoided the buildup of excessive rock pressure as the mine deepened. As miners opened out the lode with this system the size and quality of the mineral proved even higher than Chalmers had anticipated. After years of waiting, here lay proof that the Morro Velho lode still held untapped wealth despite its great depth.[63]

Chalmers also personally designed the new surface works, principally a new mill. Scattered haphazard across the southern slopes of the Morro Velho, the old mill had for more than half a century relied on wooden stamps with iron heads driven by huge waterwheels. Over sixty kilometers of aqueducts stretching across the countryside provided power for the stamps as well as the rest of the mine's machinery. The high costs of steam power (in view of the scarcity of coal, the cost of importing it, and the cost of wood) compelled the St. John d'el Rey to turn to water for power. Water powered over 130 stamp heads which crushed the ore and then forced it through wire screens onto long tables called strakes. Mixed with water, the finely ground silt moved across the strakes and onto woolly skins which caught the free gold particles. This method captured about half the gold content of the ore. The silt was then transported to the far eastern end of the Cardoso basin to the "Praia Works," which consisted of a series of amalgamating processes. Approximately another 25 percent of the gold content was removed at the Praia Works, and the still rich, but refractory, refuse was then stored in huge piles to await the day when more efficient processes would be able to get at the remaining 25 percent of the gold content.[64]

The new mill, built in front of the adit entrance, would eventually contain 130 Californian stamps mounted in a long row on the high ground above the surface works. The ore would come out of the adit entrance pulled by mules and then a moving chain pulled the cars of ore up to the mill where it would be dumped into the stamps. The silt produced then moved through wire screens and onto the strakes, pulled by gravity. Automatic shaker tables separated the gold particles from the silt and channeled the free gold into special recovery vats. The rejected silt was then piped into a retreatment plant which achieved over 90 percent recovery with the cyanide process that had been developed in South Africa in the 1890s.[65]

Chalmers designed the entire mine and mill with one goal in mind: to construct a high-output mine. The Morro Velho mine, he argued, was not a high-assay mine with ore of exceptional quality. It produced ore of consistent, but medium-range quality. Consequently, to produce an adequate profit the company would have to achieve high output. Stockholders could not expect high dividends from rich ore finds but could expect consistent exploitation of an unfluctuating medium-quality ore. High production became the primary goal. Steady assay value and high output provided the keys to success, and Chalmers designed the new mine and mill to handle record amounts of ore on a normal basis.[66]

Work on the new mill began in 1893, and delays plagued Chalmers at every step. A naval revolt in Rio nearly toppled the government and greatly hindered shipping of vital materials. Company management fumed over the refusal of the British Foreign Office to take direct action, break the naval blockade in Rio de Janeiro harbor, and facilitate British shipping.[67] Locally, scarce labor and materials combined with heavy rains slowed work and raised construction costs. Again and again the board called on stockholders to purchase new bond and mortgage issues to finance the new works. Meantime, the old mill continued to process ore from both the upper levels of the old mine and the newly opened lode. Until the new mill went into operation the increased output and income promised by Chalmers would not be forthcoming. As debts mounted and Chalmers expanded his plans to produce a model mine, the board became increasingly impatient, ordering him time after time to cut back costs and to focus on opening the mill. Chalmers did not want to put the mill into operation until everything had been put into place. Under great pressure from London, he started up seventy of the first hundred stamps in mid-1896 and production began to rise. Despite a decade of waiting, reconstruction, and mounting debt, the St. John d'el Rey now began the road back to financial stability and success.[68]

Water power had been central to the success of the old mine and Chalmers saw it as the key to the new mine's future. He envisioned a mine steadily deepening, and a mill steadily increasing its operations with expanded ore production. The increasing demands for power to operate machinery as output expanded clearly could not be provided by the old wooden waterwheels. A modern mine would have to have new and efficient power sources. Chalmers decided to transform the power of local streams and rivers into electricity via a series of generating plants. As the mine descended and output rose, the company could develop a number of power plants on the waterways of the surrounding countryside.[69] In the mid-1890s Chalmers built four small plants within a few kilometers of the mine and mill, providing the company with about 500 HP. By 1910 Chalmers had built another series of larger generating plants on the Peixe River to the south of the mine bringing total power generation up to 2,100 HP., more than three times the total power generated in the 1880s. Small, portable gas- and oil-fired engines provided emergency power in times of drought. The water power available in the earlier mine had produced about 450 HP. The total power generated by water, electricity, and occasional use of gas and steam plants came to almost 3,400 HP.[70]

By the turn of the century George Chalmers's mine had become a successful reality. Stockholders began to receive regular half-yearly dividends in the late 1890s as production took off. Production in the old mine had peaked at over 200,000 metric tons of raw ore during a handful of years in the mid-nineteenth century. Under Chalmers's modern operation the new mine reached that record level within three years of the opening of the new mill, and by 1910 passed the 400,000-ton mark. Within five years of the opening of the mill, gold bullion production had surpassed the record levels of the 1860s and continued to climb (see figure 3). By the second decade of the twentieth century George Chalmers's vision had been vindicated. Amid the ruins of the old mine in 1886 he alone had the foresight to envision the untapped potential of the lode. He alone saw that a new, modern, efficient plant could be built and be a success. Fighting the pessimism and skepticism of mining experts, directors, and investors, Chalmers had singlehandedly persuaded the doubtful to back his plan.

In 1901 the chairman of the board, Frederick J. Tendron, went out to Morro Velho for the formal dedication of the new mine. At the request of the board and stockholders he placed a plaque with the following inscription above the entrance to the mine. The plaque still hangs over the main adit entrance.

> The Directors of the St. John d'el Rey Mining Company Limited have placed this tablet to record their appreciation of the immense services rendered by GEORGE CHALMERS, A.M.I.C.E., in the reopening of the Morro Velho Lode and in designing and construction of the Surface Works.[71]

George Chalmers had saved the Morro Velho and the St. John d'el Rey Mining Company, Limited. He could now sit back and observe the fruits of more than a decade of labor. He was forty-four.

Labor Troubles

Although George Chalmers revolutionized the technological system at Morro Velho, one aspect of operations refused to conform to his careful plans: labor. Throughout the history of the company the recruitment and maintenance of an adequate, trained labor force continually eluded the company. The reliance on slavery provided a secure labor supply, but an inadequately skilled one in the eyes of management. The gradual abolition of slavery pushed the St. John toward free labor, yet, despite repeated efforts, the company could never attract sufficient free labor to satisfy its needs. Especially during periods when the company wanted to increase production levels, management was constrained by a shortage of free labor.[72]

With the gradual demise of slavery in the 1870s and 1880s free workers became the major source of labor. After the collapse of the mine in 1886 the majority of this labor force found itself out of work and many migrated out of the area. Some hired on with other, smaller mines in the province, some headed for the coffee fields of São Paulo, and many probably returned to agricultural labor. Furthermore, the construction of the new state capital, Belo Horizonte, twenty kilometers to the northwest, siphoned off additional workers at higher wages than the company was willing to offer. Consequently, as the mine came back into operation in the 1890s the labor crisis intensified. The mine now required even more workers than before and the supply had been seriously depleted. Moreover, the bulk of local labor did not take to full-time mining. Company management for decades complained of the seasonal nature of free laborers, and the majority of the company's local labor supply apparently came from the ranks of small landowners and agricultural workers. During the peak of planting and harvesting seasons, these people left the mine and headed for the fields, only to return with the end of planting and harvesting. It seems that few wanted to go down into the mine, and even fewer wanted to make mining a full-time occupation. The local peasantry supplied the company with a seasonal labor supply when peasants chose to supplement their agricultural income. In the 1890s the labor supply had become so depleted that Chalmers told stockholders that "the scarcity of labour has rendered it necessary to place almost every man, woman, and child capable of work on the new surface plant."[73]

As a result of a half-century of problems recruiting free labor and the impending abolition of slavery, the company concluded in the last third of the nineteenth century that the solution to the labor shortage lay outside Brazil. As early as the 1850s the St. John had experimented with the importation of cheap labor from the Azores. From time to time small groups of Germans had been hired, but, like the Portuguese islanders, they had left after a short time. English miners, particularly the Cornish, formed the bulk of the supervisory mining staff, but English labor would emigrate only for wages higher than the company wanted to offer. "Cornish lads" could be had cheaply, especially after 1870 and the collapse of the Cornish mining industry. These lads served in apprentice-type positions and received low wages. Company labor agents in Cornwall hired numerous groups of these youths in their teens, but more often than not they were too small and weak, or they ran away shortly after their arrival at Morro Velho.[74]

As the labor shortage became more pronounced in the 1870s the company began the first of several larger labor experiments. (Several state governments—notably São Paulo—and enterprises attempted to promote European immigration to Brazil in the late nineteenth century to supply their need for workers. While hundreds of thousands of workers headed for the cities and plantations of São Paulo, few immigrants chose to locate in Minas Gerais.)[75] The company contracted labor agents from China and Japan, and in 1882 over one hundred Chinese arrived at Morro Velho as the St. John attempted to copy the methods of the Californians. To the dismay of management, at least half the Chinese adamantly refused to enter the mine, others ran away, and many took ill. By the time the mine collapsed in 1886 few remained on the company payroll.[76] An experiment with Japanese laborers met with similar results shortly before the First World War. After negotiating with a Japanese emigration company, 107 workers arrived at the mine in August 1913. All had left the area by October.[77] The St. John also turned to Spain and Italy for workers. Large numbers of Spaniards and Italians had begun to immigrate to Brazil and southern South America in the late nineteenth century and the company hired labor agents to channel these immigrants to Morro Velho. The agents induced many to come to the mine by paying their passage across the Atlantic. Once in Brazil, the majority either slipped away to São Paulo or quickly left Morro Velho after hearing of higher wages on the expanding coffee plantations to the southwest.[78]

The Spaniards and Italians who stayed on with the mine proved to be a headache for management. Coming from the more economically developed Mediterranean, with its well-developed labor movements, these workers soon became the leaders of the first serious strikes in company history. On at least five occasions between 1897 and 1925, Spanish and Italian workers led strikes and organized Brazilian workers. Not one to rely on finesse to achieve smooth labor relations, Chalmers made sure that working-class organizations never developed by harassing organizers, infiltrating nascent movements, and effectively crushing most strikes with help from the local militia from Sabará. (Company "police" were little more than night watchmen.)[79] In general, company efforts to import cheap labor failed miserably. Few workers stayed on, and those who did proved more trouble than they were worth. Until the onset of the world economic crisis of the 1930s, the company would continue to work the mine below capacity for lack of sufficient labor. By the 1920s competition from the plantations of São Paulo and the growing Belo Horizonte combined to produce the most severe labor shortage in the company's history.[80]

Expansion

During the first three decades of this century the operations and assets of the St. John d'el Rey increased phenomenally under Chalmers's careful guidance. He followed a policy of continually developing the Morro Velho lode, opening up new exploratory horizons at greater depths while continuing to work proven ore reserves on upper horizons. As the lower exploratory horizons confirmed the value of the lode, work on lower levels followed and the process was repeated. New shafts driven at the easternmost extreme of the lode in the lower horizons deepened the mine. New horizons tunneled eastward from the shafts opened up the ever-deeper exploratory sections of the lode in a stairstepping fashion. By World War I the Morro Velho had become the deepest mine in the world, reaching down some 1,958 meters below the surface.[81] Temperatures rose as the mine descended, and at 2,000 meters rock temperatures had reached fifty degrees Celsius. Working conditions became intolerable, and Chalmers once again faced a formidable challenge: how to cool and ventilate a mine at such unprecedented depths? In conjunction with a young company engineer, Eric Davies, Chalmers designed a plant to cool air and blow it from the adit level down the shafts. The first of its kind in the mining world, the cooling plant gradually lowered temperatures in the bottom levels of the mine to acceptable limits. Once again, full activity resumed, guaranteeing (for the time being) the continued descent into record depths.[82]

The growth of company operations under Chalmers increased the size and variety of departments. New shops for the electricians, smiths, and mechanics went up around the mill. The size of the mill increased to 130 stamps, a new amalgamating plant took shape, and the company built its own brickmaking and lumber yards, as well as its own farm. The number of houses built for Europeans and Brazilian laborers rose along with the growth of the labor force. By 1910 the St. John d'el Rey employed over 2,500 people in a community of approximately 10,000. The European payroll listed about 150 employees, and the British community hovered around 400.[83] To meet the new demands of this growth Chalmers expanded old departments and set up new ones in an organizational restructuring. To the old medical, mine, cashiers, store, reduction, and mechanics departments Chalmers added several new departments. An estate department took control of the company's now vast real estate holdings, a new electrical department took charge of the new power plants, and a drawing and survey department handled the growing mountain of drafting and survey work. At the end of the First World War Chalmers built a two-story office annex alongside the Casa Grande to house the previously scattered departments under one roof.[84]

Unable to remain satisfied supervising the development of mining operations, Chalmers began to develop systematically the company's real estate holdings and a number of pet projects. Throughout the nineteenth century the company had purchased woodlands to keep the mine supplied with timber and charcoal.[85] Chalmers and his predecessors also carefully bought up the principal watersheds in the region to protect both the local water supply and the water power that was so central to the survival of the mine. Strategic acquisitions of small, bordering properties to avoid claims conflicts, purchasing of promising gold deposits in the vicinity, and the development of the company's farm properties to supply foodstuffs, all bolstered the St. John's real estate portfolio. By the 1950s the company owned well over one hundred square miles of property in central Minas Gerais, making it the single largest property owner in the region.[86]

Envisioning a day when the mine would eventually reach exhaustion, Chalmers made efforts to locate and develop manganese, diamond, and iron ore deposits. The first two efforts proved elusive, the third farsighted. Chalmers had long studied the iron ore situation in Brazil and hoped to utilize the enormous Brazilian reserves both for export and for the manufacture of iron and steel. The Serra do Curral between Belo Horizonte and Villa Nova de Lima (the name was shortened in 1923) formed the northwestern boundary of the original Morro Velho estate and contained millions of tons of high-grade hematite with over 60 percent iron content. Chalmers explored these deposits (known as Aguas Claras) and acquired additional iron ore lands to the south near Itabirito. He constantly pushed the board to develop these lands but met with little success. Although the directors of the company granted Chalmers permission to begin purchasing iron lands in 1902, they watched his purchasing and plans with little enthusiasm. They could see little value in pursuing iron ore mining while gold mining at Morro Velho flourished.[87] Furthermore, the problems of transporting the iron ore to the coast and foreign markets hindered the exploitation of these enormous reserves until the 1950s. Chalmers's iron ore dreams never developed in his lifetime, but he stands as a farsighted pioneer in his efforts.[88]

Chalmers also had the company plant hundreds of thousands of eucalyptus trees hoping to use this fast-growing species as fuel for producing charcoal.[89] The charcoal could be used to smelt iron ore to produce steel which the company could use or sell in Brazil. Several preliminary studies on the economic feasibility of producing steel, both by electric and charcoal smelting, were carried out by the St. John d'el Rey in the first decade of the century.[90] To Chalmers's dismay, the company chose not to pursue iron and steel production (although the European/Brazilian Companhia Belgo-Mineira would successfully run a charcoal-based iron and steel complex in Sabará beginning in the 1920s). Chalmers's inability to persuade the board to pursue iron and steel production is an indication of the conservativism of company directors and demonstrates a lack of entrepreneurship. One interesting side project rose out of the technology used to produce the company's charcoal. One of the main by-products of the process was ethanol which the company used during the First World War to power all its vehicles. In 1917 the company operated what was, no doubt, Brazil's first alcohol-powered fleet of automobiles. Nevertheless, the process proved unfeasible when the company could not recoup the cost of producing the ethanol by marketing the principal by-products of the distillation process, and in the early 1920s the machinery was dismantled.[91]

Perhaps the most successful of Chalmers's fertile ideas was the construction of an electric railroad. As soon as the mine had come back into full operation in the late 1890s Chalmers began to push the board to finance the construction of a private electric railway between the mine and the Central do Brasil some eight kilometers to the east. Throughout the long history of the company the principal source of transport had been bullock carts on the narrow, dusty, and mountainous roads of Minas Gerais. In the late nineteenth century the Central had pushed up from the south, connecting the interior of Minas Gerais with the coast, but the line passed through Honório Bicalho and Raposos east of the mine. The company had to ship goods to the station at Honório Bicalho, and then transport them on bullock-drawn carts the last eight kilometers. This frequently resulted in damage to goods and sometimes these few kilometers took longer to traverse than the entire trip by rail, especially in the rainy season when the dirt roads turned to mud.[92] Running on the company's hydroelectric system and carrying workers as well as supplies, Chalmers believed that the railway could pay for itself in service and convenience within a few years. The company handled all construction for the tramway through the hills between Raposos and Villa Nova de Lima. In 1913 the electric railway went into operation. The cost of the 7.9-kilometer ride was 1$000 (about 16 pence or 32 cents in 1913) and cargo costs for the company ran about half of that for the bullock carts. About four thousand passengers rode the thirty minutes between the two communities each year. The movement of goods, the quicker access to outlying labor, and better communications made the railway one of the St. John's foremost assets.[93]

Chalmers's remarkable reign at Morro Velho coincided with the years of the First Republic (1889–1930). The company continued to profit from Brazil's internal political stability, but found itself ever less isolated geographically and more involved in state and national politics. The rebuilding of the mine coincided with the construction of the new state capital, Belo Horizonte, just over the Serra do Curral (twenty kilometers) from Morro Velho, and these two developments made the company increasingly visible in state and national political circles. A long line of prominent state and national political figures visited the mine, including seven presidents.[94] Despite the inconvenience, the "Companhia do Morro Velho" (as the company was known in Brazil) rarely turned down requests for visits, fully understanding the importance of good public relations. This careful cultivation of the political elite over decades served the company well when a strong nationalist campaign to protect mineral resources began just before the First World War. While North American entrepreneur Percival Farquhar and his Itabira Iron Syndicate were repeatedly vilified by politicians and the press over the next two decades, the St. John quietly continued to mine the vast majority of Brazil's gold.[95]

The so-called "politics of the governors" dominated by the "coffee and cream" alliance of Minas Gerais and São Paulo heightened the influence of *mineiro* politicians and drew the company into more active lobbying. Concomitantly, the rise of an increasingly interventionist state raised even more concerns over taxation and tariffs.[96] However, Chalmers's reputation as a builder, company lobbying, and the modernizing mentality of a European-oriented elite eased the St. John's potential conflicts with the Brazilian state. By the end of World War I the company had assigned several employees to fulltime public relations work (behind the scenes, of course). These key officials spent most of their time in Rio de Janeiro and Belo Horizonte wining and dining bureaucrats and politicians, and frequenting the corridors of power in key offices and ministries.[97] By the 1920s the company had a circle of powerful friends in high places in local, state, and national politics (see chapter 3).

Despite the expansion of the company's political and economic power in Brazil it fell victim to international forces with the outbreak of war in Europe in 1914. Supplies from England that were critical to mining operations became harder to obtain as submarine warfare swept across the North Atlantic and rationing became essential in England. For the first time the St. John began to turn to the United States for parts and machinery. Brazil also felt the economic shocks set off by the war, and to stabilize the monetary system the government placed an embargo on gold shipments. Reluctantly, the company began to sell its gold in Rio de Janeiro. When the Brazilian government lifted the embargo the St. John decided to ship the gold to New York to avoid the risks of shipping in the submarine-infested waters of the European North Atlantic.[98]

The war also deeply touched the British community in Morro Velho on a personal level. At the outbreak of hostilities in Europe the British community numbered well over three hundred with about half that number employed by the company.[99] Many of the prominent company officials and families at the mine had been with the company since the mid-nineteenth century, weathering the hard times after both major crushes. The intermarriage of these families with prominent local families helped to cement company ties with the community and created a bilingual-bicultural sector which straddled Anglo and Brazilian societies (see chapter 7). The entry of England into the Great War touched newcomers and old-timers alike and fanned the flames of patriotism. A large number of young Englishmen left Morro Velho and volunteered for military duty, draining the St. John of valuable and highly trained personnel. The board managed to persuade the British government to exempt Morro Velho employees from war duty on the grounds that the mine and its gold were vital resources for the allied effort in Europe. Nevertheless, the young male employees could not be restrained, and more than a score left for Britain. Late in the war the labor shortage became so acute at the staff level that the board came close to shutting down the mine until the end of the conflict. Despite supply and personnel shortages the St. John d'el Rey limped through the war years.[100]

The 1920s marked a transition period for the St. John as it moved out of the Chalmers era and into the tumultuous 1930s. In 1917 George Chalmers turned sixty and completed thirty-three years as superintendent of the Morro Velho mine. Always looking to the future, he had been carefully grooming the oldest of his two sons to replace him. A. G. N. Chalmers and his younger brother, J. W. P. (George and Billy to their father), attended boarding schools in England and then, following in their father's footsteps, trained as engineers. J. W. P. (with his father's help) eventually became a partner in Rooper and Chalmers, the St. John's consulting engineering firm in England.[101] A. G. N. returned to Morro Velho after the war under his father's wing and became his assistant with the blessing of the board. Gradually he took over the day-to-day operations of the mine as his father spent more and more time on his *fazenda* fishing, hunting, farming, and working on plans to drive a more direct route to the bottom of the ever-deepening mine.[102]

In 1924, the fortieth anniversary of his joining the company, George Chalmers became general manager at the mines, and his son, superintendent. Two years later A. G. N. took over full control and his father became consulting engineer in Brazil.[103] The older Chalmers continued to work on his direct-route plans and to develop his farm as his health declined. A heart condition weakened him in 1927, and on the advice of his family he left for England in early 1928 for medical treatment. Shortly after arriving in England in February he collapsed and died of heart failure. Dozens of newspaper obituaries in leading Brazilian newspapers and hundreds of letters and telegrams from the powerful testify to the influence and reputation of the man who built the Morro Velho mine.[104]

A. G. N. Chalmers assumed his father's mantle but could not live up to his remarkable achievements. A severe labor shortage continued to hold back production, his managerial style apparently produced conflict among the staff, and the company directors grasped for ways to pull the mine out of its operational doldrums. Embittered by company infighting, mounting criticism over his handling of matters, and faced with an increasingly unsympathetic board, A. G. N. stepped down in 1930. As he returned to his father's estate and the life of the gentleman farmer, the Chalmers era passed away. New management took control of the mine, and, along with the nation, the St. John d'el Rey entered into a new and tumultuous era.[105]

Politics, Nationalism, Growth, and Decline

The board of directors chose A. H. Millett, the company's business manager at Morro Velho, to replace Chalmers at the helm. (Millett had come to Morro Velho in 1912 and rose to the position of business manager in the late 1920s.)[106] For the next decade company operations expanded in an unprecedented fashion under Millett's astute guidance. This expansion first required a fundamental reorganization of company management in Brazil. Millett became manager and superintendent, and for the first time since the 1880s the superintendent at the mines did not have a technical background in min-

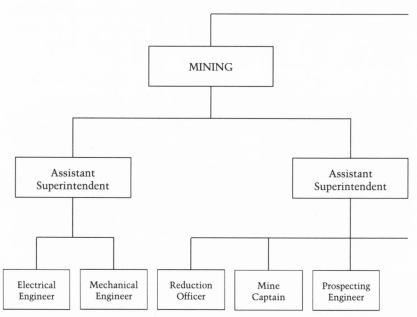

Figure 4 Organizational Structure of the St. John d'el Rey Mining Company, Limited, circa 1930

ing. Two assistant superintendents handled mining operations. One took charge of underground duties while the other handled the shop departments and operations aboveground (see figure 4). Millett continued to manage the business affairs of the company and relied on his assistants for counsel on the technical side of company operations. For the first time in the company's history a mining engineer took control of the mine, resulting in a good deal of criticism of the approach of Chalmers in the previous decade.[107]

Nineteen-thirty also marked the one-hundredth anniversary of

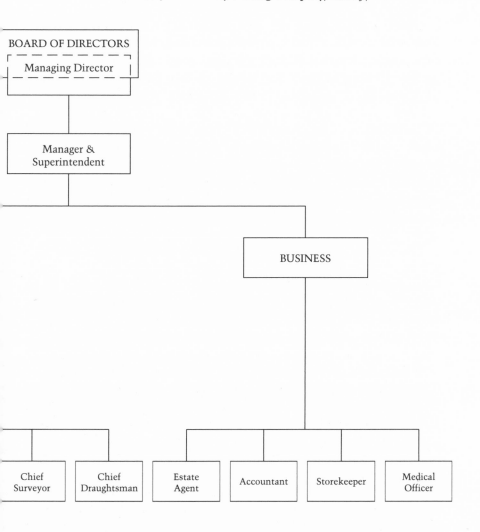

the St. John d'el Rey's arrival in Brazil. As the company entered its second century of operations in Brazil, fundamental changes were taking place that would profoundly alter the future of the company.[108] In October 1930, just months after Millett took control, a revolt led by Getúlio Vargas toppled the First Republic, ending four decades of political supremacy by the big coffee states. Since the 1890s São Paulo and Minas Gerais had dominated the national political system via the so-called "politics of the big states." *Mineiro* and *paulista* politicians manipulated an electoral system which alternated the presidency among those who represented the interests of the "coffee and cream" alliance. Internal political divisions and the onslaught of new political forces weakened the system and produced its collapse in the elections of 1930. The revolution of 1930 ushered in an era of mass politics personified by the charismatic Vargas. He ruled Brazil under various guises for the next fifteen years. As in a number of European and Latin American nations in the 1930s, the working class rose as a new political force. Vargas understood the growing power of the working class, and like Perón in Argentina and Cárdenas in Mexico, he skillfully organized labor as a potent source of mass support. He won over labor providing it with basic social benefits: a minimum wage, maximum working hours, pension plans, and health regulations.[109]

This revolution reverberated throughout Brazil and transformed life in Nova Lima. To the anger and dismay of the St. John d'el Rey, the government's new Ministry of Labor officially recognized the union which the miners of the Nova Lima area formed in 1934. In a matter of months the company watched decades of anti-union efforts go down the drain. Last-ditch efforts to form a counter-union which could be manipulated by the company failed miserably.[110] The formation of this miners' union and the new social legislation brought about fundamental changes in the community. First, the union finally provided Brazilian workers with a unified and powerful voice with which to confront the company management. Second, the social legislation completed a transformation which had been gradually taking shape for the previous half-century. The legislation provided miners with strong incentives to become full-time, year-round company employees and to abandon seasonal work patterns. By making mining a full-time career, workers gained access to the new social benefits and the accrued advantages of seniority. As a result, seasonal labor rapidly diminished and the mine force became more stable. By the mid-1940s the majority of the company's employees had been on the payroll for at least a decade.[111] Ironically, the new social legislation had finally produced the exact situation which the company had for so many decades sought in vain to achieve: the formation of a steady, skilled, and adequate mining force.

Vargas also pursued a policy of strong economic nationalism. The Great Depression had shattered the coffee-export economy of the First Republic. Vargas turned to protectionism and fiscal restrictions and moved away from the more liberal economic policies of the republican era. This shift reflected desperate defensive measures. In the face of drastically declining coffee exports, declining revenues, and the exhaustion of gold reserves in the treasury, Brazilian leaders formulated policies aimed at cutting imports, promoting industries that produced local substitutes, and sought ways to reverse the flow of hard currency out of the country. Designed to protect the Brazilian economy, these policies severely punished foreign companies that imported large quantities of essential materials, as did the St. John. Higher tariffs on vital supplies (chemicals, machinery, spare parts) drove up operating costs and forced the company to seek national suppliers.[112]

The currency restrictions of the new regime struck an even more punishing blow. In order to stem the flow of profits to foreign investors, and to halt the outflow of hard currency, the Brazilian government began to limit exchange transactions and profit remittances. The government had begun to purchase the company's bullion during World War I and had continued the practice into the 1930s. With the government controlling gold sales, the new restrictions created currency exchange problems for the company.[113] The income from gold sales accounted for virtually all of the company's revenue. The Brazilian government effectively limited profit remittances by paying for the gold with a mix of local currency and sterling. New regulations limited sterling remittances to one-third of the value of the gold sales, and the government paid the company in local currency for the remaining two-thirds of the gold's value. Company officials lobbied intensely to fight the new regulations, going all the way to Vargas himself on the matter, with no success. They achieved no more than a promise that they would be allowed the full one-third with no additional restrictions.[114] The astute Vargas placed national needs above his favorable view of the company's work.

Fortunately for the St. John, this bold new intervention by the state coincided with an abrupt jump in the world price of gold from $20.67 to $35.00 an ounce in 1934.[115] Higher revenues from rising gold prices and an accumulating surplus of Brazilian currency that could not be converted to sterling created a peculiar situation at Morro Velho. The company was able to maintain previous profit and dividend levels, but it could not raise production to even higher levels without creating even larger surpluses, and at the same time risking further remittance difficulties with government fiscal authorities.[116] Profits continued to flow to England at a steady pace. The surplus currency, however, had to be put to use, and the company embarked on a massive reinvestment program. (This reinvestment and the use of national suppliers, of course, were exactly what the protectionist economic policies had been designed to produce.) During the 1930s the company began a number of construction projects which consumed the currency surplus and, at the same time, provided company and community with valuable capital improvements. The company began to reopen old mines in the surrounding area and began a second major mining operation in Raposos some eight kilometers from Morro Velho. During these years the St. John completed the final phase of George Chalmers's hydroelectric plan, building three huge dams on the Peixe River to the south of Nova Lima. Another major project was the construction of two thousand housing units for Brazilian workers. Management hoped that cheap, subsidized housing would attract workers to Nova Lima.[117]

The phenomenal expansion of the St. John d'el Rey during the Great Depression masked the domestic and international tensions that finally erupted in the 1940s, shaking the foundations of the company. The first of these forces was the rise of a vocal and militant labor movement. The government-sanctioned union gained strength in the 1930s, and in the 1940s began a series of long and costly strikes that would contribute to the demise of the British company (see chapter 6). Rampant inflation in the postwar years drove up company costs and moved the workers to demand ever higher wages. While inflation raced ahead the official exchange rate remained fixed against the dollar from 1940–45, and again from 1947–52. The devaluation of the pound sterling by 30 percent against the dollar—and thereby against the cruzeiro—in 1949 further damaged the St. John and raised costs.[118]

The union gradually came under the influence of anti-imperialist, anti-capitalist leaders, many drawn from the ranks of the Communist party of Brazil, which had been building a base in Nova Lima since the early 1930s. With the growing strength of Brazilian nationalism and the disparity between foreign management and a Brazilian working class, the union leadership had little problem finding a means to galvanize the rank and file. In addition, nationalistic, pro-labor government officials pressured the company to adopt stronger safety standards, better working conditions, and more comprehensive social services.[119]

In retrospect, it appears that the St. John made two costly mistakes. First, management failed to Brazilianize the staff in any significant way. Chalmers had argued for the need to integrate prominent Brazilians into positions of visibility and to bring more Brazilians into positions of responsibility in company operations. Yet, as late as the 1950s, the upper levels of the company management in Brazil (with the notable and logical exception of lawyers) were almost entirely British. The St. John did form an "advisory council" of prominent Brazilians, but not until the mid-1950s and then only to attempt to combat rising nationalism through lobbying.[120] The failure to hire Brazilians also hindered the nation's development. Had the St. John hired Brazilian engineers (and the School of Mines in Ouro Preto produced many) and technicians, the practical training and transfer of technological know-how would have been invaluable in the growth of the *mineiro* economy. Second, the company decided to fight the union and government regulations every step of the way, and confrontation soon became a way of life. Workers and nationalistic government officials continually criticized the St. John on issues of safety, health conditions, and social benefits, even as wages and operating costs rose dramatically. The average daily wage (including bonuses and overtime) rose over 400 percent between 1935 and 1950, while the cost of living in Nova Lima rose at approximately the same pace.[121]

Company confrontation tactics resulted in long strikes and unfavorable publicity exacerbated by growing nationalism in Brazil. The strikes punished the company severely, shutting down production for weeks. Overall productivity per worker had begun a slow rise in the 1940s with the elimination of some auxiliary personnel, but productivity of the underground mine force had been declining (see figure 5). Management could cut back on personnel aboveground, and thereby raise overall productivity, but the company's fate hinged on the ability of the underground force to get the ore out of the ground and to the surface. Productivity underground was the heart of operations and profitability. From 1915 to the beginning of the Second World War the value per ton milled at Morro Velho varied very little, fluctuating between forty-seven and fifty-six shillings. Between 1940 and 1954 the value rose from fifty-one shillings per ton to ninety-two, an increase of just over 80 percent. More impressive was the rise in working cost per ton, from thirty-two shillings per

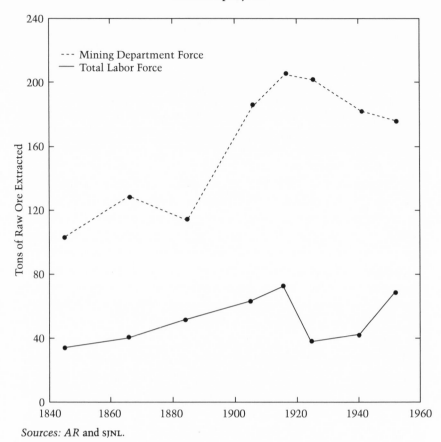

Sources: *AR* and sjnl.

Figure 5 Productivity per Worker per Year, Morro Velho

ton in 1940 to seventy-nine in 1954, an increase of nearly 150 percent! In short, working costs per ton outpaced value per ton by close to two to one from 1940 to 1954.[122]

Clearly, the time and income lost to strikes shook the financial stability of the St. John d'el Rey, producing the first yearly deficits in this century (see figure 6). By the mid-1950s the once stable investment had become a risky venture. International forces further affected company operations. World War II had created supply problems and materials shortages as had World War I, but these hindrances had been temporary.[123] More far-reaching and fundamental for the world gold-mining industry was the international monetary system constructed at Bretton Woods after the war. International agreements froze the price of gold at $35 an ounce, where it would

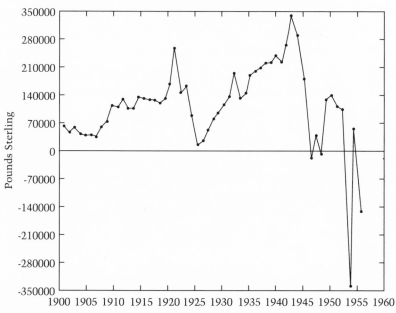

Source: AR

Figure 6 Profits and Losses, St. John d'el Rey Mining Company, Limited, 1901–1956

remain until the late 1960s. Income per unit of production now had a fixed ceiling, and few gold mines anywhere could operate keeping costs below that level.[124] A cost-price squeeze shut down gold mines around the world.[125] Combined with inflation, and the wave of long strikes, the freezing of gold prices spelled the end of British prosperity at Morro Velho. By the mid-1950s, only drastic measures could have kept the company operating with a profit.

Furthermore, the plant laid out by Chalmers at the turn of the century had become increasingly obsolete and in need of major renovation. The company desperately needed a new deep shaft to the lower levels of the mine to speed up the handling of ore and reduce wasted traveling time along the numerous shafts and horizons. (Workers spent a full hour traveling from the mine entrance to the lower levels of the mine!) Ironically, just at the time when the company most needed to renovate and to invest in new capital improvements, the St. John was also facing a severe financial crisis. Mounting problems compelled the board of directors to seek drastic management changes at the mine. After hiring several outside consultants to study the situation, the board hired a Canadian mining engineer,

G. P. Wigle, who had revitalized several gold mines in Canada before coming to Morro Velho in 1946 as an assistant superintendent. Wigle became superintendent in 1953, began work on a new deep shaft to the bottom of the mine (nicknamed "*maracanã*," after Brazil's enormous soccer stadium built in 1950), and promptly sacked a large number of the top-heavy British staff. He instituted a new labor policy which emphasized worker productivity and provided incentives for steady and efficient labor. The so-called "Canadian Plan" failed, however, as workers continued to battle management for benefits and higher wages and as financial troubles forced the suspension of the new shaft. Wigle left Morro Velho frustrated and beaten after one year as superintendent. With him went the St. John's last chance for survival.[126] Without continued investment in new technology to raise productivity in the face of rising costs, the company was doomed.

The end of the British era at Morro Velho came suddenly and swiftly in the late 1950s. The decade-long financial crisis and labor troubles gradually eroded the value of company stock on the London Stock Exchange, and a group of astute North American investors bought controlling interest in the company in 1957.[127] The investors, led by New York stockbroker Leo Model, did not have the least interest in buying a failing gold mine. They had their eyes on the enormous and still-undeveloped iron ore reserves that Chalmers had so intently pursued fifty years earlier. The world iron and steel industry had surged in the postwar years, and Model hoped to find a buyer for these immense reserves.[128] Consequently, Model and his associates sold the iron lands to the Hanna Mining Company of Cleveland, Ohio, in 1960, and the latter began a long battle with the Brazilian government to mine and export the ore. Eventually, Hanna and a Brazilian mining magnate, Augusto Azevedo Antunes, formed a multinational firm controlled through their ownership of the St. John d'el Rey's mining rights. In essence, the St. John d'el Rey became a paper company through which this Brazilian subsidiary of Hanna (Minerações Brasileiras Reunidas) now works the huge ore reserves at Aguas Claras, Mutuca, and Itabirito, all to the south of Belo Horizonte.[129] Hanna closed the London office of the St. John and moved all the English operations to Cleveland, thus ending 130 years of British enterprise in Brazil.

In the late fifties and early sixties the Brazilian government provided subsidies (via their gold purchasing price) to help keep the

Morro Velho enterprise afloat.[130] Government officials did not want to see the demise of one of the most important economic forces in Minas Gerais, and they dreaded the social and economic disruption the mine closing would cause in a company town of thirty thousand inhabitants.[131] Unwilling to take on the gigantic social and economic problems of a failing gold mine, Model and Hanna virtually gave it to a Brazilian mining engineer, Fernando Mello Viana.[132] The son of George Chalmers's close political ally in the 1920s, Mello Viana entered into a partnership with newspaper publisher Horácio de Carvalho and banking magnate Walter Moreira Salles in the mid-sixties. In the mid-1970s, the three sold 49 percent interest in the mine to Anglo American Corporation of South Africa, the world's largest gold-mining company (De Beers of diamond-mining fame is an affiliate). In 1980 Siderúrgica Hime S. A., jointly owned by Anglo American and Bozano, Simonsen of São Paulo, bought out the remaining stock from Carvalho and Moreira Salles.[133] The high price of gold in the past decade has once again revitalized the Morro Velho, as the South African and Brazilian owners have reinvested several hundred million dollars out of profits during the past decade renovating the old mine and reopening other mining properties in the surrounding region.[134]

The Financial Balance Sheet

The end of the British era at Morro Velho brought to a close one of the most successful foreign enterprises in modern Latin American history. During a century and a quarter, the St. John d'el Rey racked up profits totaling £8,024,495 (see table 2). Approximately one-fifth of this total was accrued before the collapse of the mine and reorganization of the company in the 1880s. The company accumulated the remaining four-fifths between 1892 and 1956. On an annual average this makes Chalmers's mine almost three times as profitable as the earlier mine(s). Taking into account good years and bad, and beginning with the formation of the company in 1830, the St. John d'el Rey annually averaged better than £60,000 in profit.

The small venture of 1830 had blossomed from an initial capital stock of £50,000 to £800,000 by the early twentieth century (see table 3). This capital stock growth had taken place in a series of steps.

Table 2 Profits of the St. John d'el Rey Mining Company, Limited,
1831–1956 (in pounds sterling)

Date	Profit	Annual Average
1831–87	1,675,758	29,924
1887–1956	6,348,737	90,696
1831–1956	8,024,495	63,686

Source: AR 1831–1957.

Table 3 Capital Stock History of the St. John d'el Rey Mining Company,
Limited, 1830–1957 (in pounds sterling)

Date	Issue	Total Nominal Capital Stock	Total Actual Subscribed Capital Stock
1830–31	5,000 shares at £10 each	50,000	37,387
1834	6,000 shares at £5 each	80,000	57,500
1834–42	£5 installment on the above 11,000	135,000	98,398
1856–71	Additional offerings coming to £70,812	205,812	176,978
1872	Additional offerings raise total to	220,000	190,000
1874	Additional offerings raise total to	253,000	223,000
1888	Company reorganized with new capital stock of	252,000	120,603
1891	Stock raised by £180,000 to	432,000	217,186
1893	Additional £30,000 raised	462,000	272,068
1895	Additional £138,000 raised	600,000	370,152
1904	Creation of 100,000 preference shares at £1 each	700,000	624,255
1910	Creation of additional 100,000 preference shares at £1 each	800,000	646,265
1957	Authorized stock raised to	1,300,000	721,414

Source: AR 1831–1957.

From the initial capital of £50,000 the amount rose to £135,000 by
the 1840s, and to £175,000 by the time of the first major mine crush
in 1867. The reconstruction of the mine raised the capital stock to
£253,000, where it stood at the time of the crush in 1886. The reconstructed St. John d'el Rey carried a capital stock of £252,000 which
rose in the 1890s to £600,000. In the first decade of this century
the company issued 200,000 shares of preferential stock at £1 each.
(Preferential shares were nontaxable in England.) Total capital stock
remained at £800,000 until the takeover in the late 1950s.[135] The St.
John's assets and production levels placed it in the category of the

large mines of the gold-mining industry, but considerably below the larger companies of the Transvaal.[136]

The unusual nature of the world gold-mining industry played a key role in the cycles of company prosperity and penury. Gold was a commodity with insatiable consumer demand and a stable price on the world market. Consequently, a gold-mining company did not face the same hard times as other producers of primary goods during the world financial crises of the past two centuries. In the 1870s, 1890s, and 1930s, for example, when general crises struck the Western economy, the gold-mining industry flourished. These were precisely the decades when the St. John rebuilt after major disasters (1870s and 1890s) or dramatically expanded operations (1930s). The special nature of gold as a commodity set the gold-mining industry, and the St. John, apart from other producers of primary products such as coffee, sugar, and minerals. Until the Second World War the management of gold-mining companies confronted financial and economic cycles fundamentally different from those faced in other sectors of the Western economy.

Company management always took a conservative approach to finances. With a few prominent exceptions, virtually all financing for the development of the enterprise came from capital raised in stock issues and from reinvesting earnings in the mine. From the beginning management set aside a "reserve fund" for emergencies, an action whose wisdom was demonstrated in 1867 and in 1886 when the mine collapsed in ruin. The money in this fund was usually invested in British stocks, normally in railways with a yield of 4 to 5 percent.[137] In the first rebuilding, management turned to the issue of new stock to finance the new shafts. In the 1880s and 1890s management again turned to new stock offerings, but also took out major loans to finance the extraordinary costs of building a completely new mine and mill. All of these loans had been retired by the end of the First World War. In the 1950s the company often turned to bank loans to meet cash-flow problems created by rapidly rising payrolls.

The St. John d'el Rey had had its hard times with the two major crushes in the nineteenth century, but, in the long run, it proved a very wise investment with a good return. The company began to pay regular dividends in 1842 and continued to do so until the disaster of 1867 stopped dividends for seven years. Dividend payments resumed between 1874 and 1882, lapsing again until the Chalmers mine came into operation in the late 1890s. Rates of return fluctuated wildly

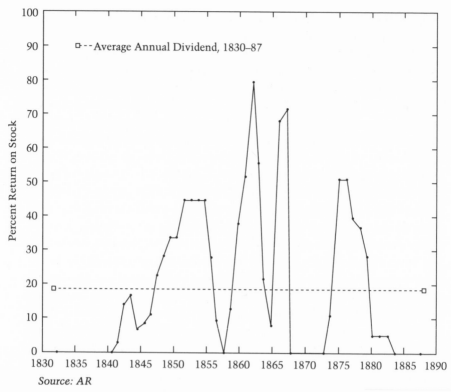

Figure 7 Dividends Paid by the St. John d'el Rey Mining Company, Limited, 1830–1887

throughout the nineteenth century, ranging from no payment to as high as 80 percent at their peak (see figure 7). During the fifty-eight-year period from 1830 to 1887 the company made dividend payments in thirty-five years, or 60 percent of the time. Total dividends for the period (before taxes) came to £1,453,100, for an average of £25,053 per year. Average actual capital stock for the period comes to £134,018, giving an average yearly return on investment of 18.7 percent. The company did achieve "windfall" profits during certain years, but when these are averaged out with the lean years, even the return of 18.7 percent is impressive, particularly in an industry where only three companies in a score survived more than a decade. Indeed, such a rate of return made the stock of the St. John d'el Rey one of the highest-yielding investments of any British enterprise in Latin America or the overseas empire in the nineteenth century.[138] Despite the regularity of dividend payments and high earnings, the rate of return on stock in the twentieth century never achieved such heights. In this century both ordinary and preferential stock gave a 10 percent return.

When compared with other companies in Latin America for which data are available, the St. John's returns for the nineteenth century are again impressive, and the returns are comparable to the other firms for the twentieth century. The British-owned Rio Flour Mills, for example, produced returns between 10 and 15 percent in the first two decades of this century, while the Brazilian-owned Companhia Paulista de Estradas de Ferro averaged a 10 percent return during the last three decades of the nineteenth century. The most successful of the British-owned railways in Argentina normally returned 7 to 8 percent (1868–1914), while the British railways (as a whole) in the same period averaged between 2.7 and 8 percent. The overall average return for the British companies in Latin America analyzed in a recent volume edited by D. C. M. Platt was 6 to 7 percent. Platt estimates that British investors received an average of 5 to 6 percent on comparable domestic investments. South African gold-mining companies had just begun to emerge in the late nineteenth century, and a recent study puts their return at just over 5 percent between 1887 and 1913.[139]

Rates of return on capital parallel the figures for stock dividends.[140] Between 1842 (when the company first began to turn a profit and pay dividends) and 1886, the St. John had an average rate of return of 14 percent. As with dividends the range was enormous, varying from slightly negative returns during the rebuilding of the mine in the early 1870s to the extraordinary figure of 50 percent in 1876. (The latter figure probably confirms the assertion that Superintendent Gordon was "milking" the mine in his last years.) In the 1840s the rates averaged around 10 percent, rising into the 20s in the early 1850s and falling drastically in the late 1850s after an important disaster in the mine. From 1860 to 1867 the rate again averaged over 20 percent, dropping quickly during the rebuilding years. In the late 1870s the rate once again reached the high 20s with the reopening of the mine, and in the 1880s the rate dropped again, registering a negative 2.4 percent in 1884, the year George Chalmers arrived on the scene.

Rates in the twentieth century offer a more sensitive measure of profitability than dividends with their annual 10 percent return in good years and bad. The range is not as wide as in the pre-Chalmers years, with a low of −4.7 percent in 1956 and a high of 14.1 percent in 1922. Rates fluctuated greatly during the rebuilding years in the 1890s (.7 to 12.9 percent), and then stabilized at around 9 percent from 1898 to 1924. In 1926 and 1927 the rate dropped under 2 percent and averaged just over 5 percent from 1925 to 1935. For the next decade the rate remained strong and stable with very little fluctuation (7.2 to 9 percent). In the postwar years (1946–56) the company registered negative rates in three years, and rates under 4.4 percent in seven years. The average rate for the years 1888–1956 was a healthy 6.8 percent.

Of course, the key to the financial success of the enterprise ultimately lay in the production of gold bullion. From initial figures of 100,000 to 300,000 grams in the 1840s, production rose steadily, reaching 1 million grams annually by 1850 and 2 million by the 1860s. These figures placed the Morro Velho in the first rank of deep-shaft gold mines, although they pale in comparison with the enormous placer production in the last half of the century in California, Alaska, Canada, and Australia.[141] The second mine in the 1870s achieved the 2 million-gram mark only briefly before production fell off drastically in the 1880s. The Chalmers mine surpassed the 2 million-gram mark soon after going into full production, and passed 3 million grams per year by 1900. By World War I annual gold production had passed 3 million grams, and it hovered between 3 and 4 million grams per year until the 1940s, when the mine reached an all-time high of over 4,700,000 grams at the end of World War II. Production remained relatively steady in the 3–4 million-gram range for the next decade, as company costs skyrocketed, dooming the St. John d'el Rey (see figure 6).[142]

The St. John d'el Rey's success made it the most powerful private operation in Minas Gerais in the nineteenth and twentieth centuries, its revenues and expenditures rivaling those of the provincial government in the nineteenth century. The company's assets at Morro Velho reached £100,000 in the 1860s, rising to £340,000 by the 1880s. The rebuilding and expansion of the mine at the turn of the century raised assets to more than £1,000,000 by 1906, and £2,500,000 by the late 1930s. By 1950, the company's assets in Brazil were valued at nearly £3,500,000.[143] In the relatively backward *mineiro* economy in the nineteenth century the revenues of the company (£138,649 in 1860) nearly equalled the revenues of the provincial government (£143,594 in the same year). Even with the enormous growth of the *mineiro* economy after World War I, the company's revenue continued to run at about one-fifth (£645,179 in 1935) of that of the state.[144]

The company pumped considerable amounts of money into the regional economy in central Minas Gerais in taxes, wages, slave hire, and purchases of foodstuffs and wood. Taxation (local, state, and national) seems to have run at about 5 to 7 percent of the value of annual gold production from the 1850s to the 1920s.[145] As already noted, the St. John found itself in a constant tax struggle with the government, winning some battles and losing others. The overall effect was a gradual rise in total tax payments. Although the combined rate of federal, state, and municipal taxes declined from around 9 percent (£46,000) in 1930 to less than 5 percent (£41,000) in 1937, the costs of the new government pension program alone effectively taxed the company another 7 percent (£60,000) by the latter year.[146] Ironically, in 1940 the St. John was paying far higher income taxes in England (£120,000) than it paid in taxes in Brazil (£50,000)—although combined taxes and social welfare payments in Brazil came to around £100,000. About 75 percent of the company's taxes went to the state of Minas Gerais.[147] Wages and slave hire, which also went essentially to Minas Gerais, regularly accounted for half of the company's expenses throughout its history. In addition, the St. John purchased enormous amounts of beans, rice, *mamona* (castor) oil, corn, and wood, accounting for another 25 to 35 percent of its annual expenditures.[148] Clearly, this British business was the most important economic force in Minas Gerais apart from the state government.

Conclusion

As these figures indicate, the St. John d'el Rey Mining Company, Limited, stands out as a preeminently successful foreign enterprise in Brazil. Spanning 130 years of Brazilian history, from its inception in the City of London in 1830 until the Hanna Mining Company transferred corporate headquarters to the United States in 1960, the company owed its success—and ultimate failure—to a complex interaction of local, national, and international factors. The company benefited from the sheer luck of having located one of the richest and deepest gold deposits in the world. Luck, however, does not account for longevity and financial success. The exceptional management of the St. John, particularly under Chalmers, enabled the company to overcome crises. As Richard Graham has pointed out, the principal cause of the difficulties facing British companies in Brazil "was the gross mismanagement of their affairs by the directors and local managers."[149] The St. John management's willingness and ability to introduce technological innovation allowed them to surmount geological, technical, and social challenges. Finally, management at Morro Velho and in London developed a powerful and extensive political network in Brazil to protect and promote its interests. The history of the company demonstrates clearly the tremendous adaptability of capitalists and capitalism to local conditions.

Conversely, the company failed when it could no longer innovate and meet new challenges produced by geology, business, and politics. Ultimately, international market forces in the form of fixed gold prices, and national forces in the form of an inflation and wage spiral, brought the firm to financial collapse. Unable to invest in new labor-saving technology to raise productivity, British management lost control of this once profitable enterprise. Economic nationalism in Brazil and labor militancy in Nova Lima aggravated the company's problems, and its extensive but battered political network could not salvage it. The St. John entered Brazil in the 1830s with key elements the mining industry desperately needed: capital, know-how, and technology. By the mid-twentieth century, however, the company had overstayed its initial welcome and had little that Brazilians could not manage by themselves. By the 1950s the complex and constantly changing forces of the international economy, national development, and local society finally turned against the St. John d'el Rey, bringing to an end 130 years of British enterprise in Brazil.

Today the city of Nova Lima retains few traces of the British era at Morro Velho. On the hillsides at the western edge of the city the distinct cottages built for British employees now house the Brazilian staff. The British club and lovely Quintas area now serve the Brazilian management. In the impressive aqueducts, plant, and houses one is struck by the traces of the once mighty British enterprise in Minas Gerais. Most of the British left Morro Velho and Nova Lima in the late fifties and early sixties when control of the company moved to the United States. Many of the British, however, had deep roots in the community, having raised families there, and a number were third- and fourth-generation *morrovelhenses*. On the company payroll one still finds the names of Heslops, Gills, and Hodges, among others. The local phone directory contains the descendants of Kemps, and Clemences, and Joneses. Some have Brazilianized over the generations, losing the English language and contact with the old homeland. Others have bridged both cultures, raising truly Anglo-Brazilian families. The triumph and tragedy of the British era have passed, but the lives of the *novalimenses* continue to revolve around the fortunes of the mining company in their midst. George Chalmers and his countrymen have departed, but their descendants and the thousands of people they touched remain dependent on the mine which provided, and continues to provide, the community with its very life and labor.

3

The Politics of a Foreign Enterprise

We are all very conscious of the fact that in these modern days no
foreign company can operate successfully either in Brazil or elsewhere
without cultivating to the greatest possible extent the co-operation of
leading people in the country where it carries on its work.[1]

The political influence that accompanies economic power has long
been one of the most controversial aspects of the presence of foreign
business in Latin America. Visions of coups d'etat and powerful fruit
companies in Central America and gunboat diplomacy in bankrupt
Caribbean nations have long colored our perceptions of the political
power of foreign business in the region. The role of foreign capital in shaping national politics and the national economy has been
one of the central issues in the debate over theories of development
and underdevelopment. Until the 1960s evolutionary and diffusionist theories formulated in the United States and Western Europe
dominated studies of Third World development. These liberal analyses viewed the diffusion of capitalism as beneficial and crucial to
the future of Third World nations. Trade served as the engine of
growth for all economies, and the fewer barriers to trade the better.
As capital and technology from the developed nations flowed into
underdeveloped nations the latter would recapitulate the "stages of
growth" already experienced by the former. The expansion of capitalism would spur economic and political modernization.[2]

In the decades following the Second World War powerful critiques
of liberal development theories began to emerge with some of the
most influential challenges coming from Latin American social sci-
entists. In the 1940s and 1950s the United Nations Economic Commission for Latin America (ECLA), led by the Argentine economist
Raúl Prebisch, formulated an influential non-Marxist critique of
neoclassical analyses of Latin American development. In the ECLA

critique the inequality in terms of trade between the industrial nations and the developing nations prevented the latter from developing fully. The latter formed the "periphery" of the international economy, selling raw materials and agricultural products to (and buying manufactured goods from) the industrial nations at the "center." ECLA economists argued that, in the long term, the terms of trade between the center and periphery increasingly favored the former. They argued that the state, in conjunction with a rising national bourgeoisie, had to intervene to promote industrialization through import substitution, agrarian reform and regional integration. The analysis proposed political solutions for the problems of economic underdevelopment. The ECLA analysis rejected the rosy optimism of evolutionary and diffusionist theories, but accepted the need to promote the expansion of capitalism, although with the careful intervention of the state.[3]

Marxist theories, on the other hand, blamed capitalism for Latin America's underdevelopment. The development of the West, in effect, underdeveloped the Third World. The Marxist critiques of liberal theories built on classical theories of imperialism, primarily those of Hobson and Lenin. V. I. Lenin's reinterpretation of the pioneering work of the English journalist John Hobson has dominated studies of imperialism in Latin America for most of this century. For Lenin, imperialism represented the highest stage of capitalism. The industrial nations, according to Lenin, had built up an enormous surplus of capital which they needed to export overseas in search of higher profits. In his classic analysis, powerful financial groups combined with industrial capital to form monopolies that would dominate the capitalist world and, through imperialism, the nonindustrial world. The economic might of Europe and the United States was the foundation for its political hegemony over the Third World. In addition, this political and economic power (so goes the argument) allowed foreign businesses to extract profits at levels higher than possible in domestic markets in the industrial nations.[4] Partly through its powerful analysis, and partly through the dominant role of Marxist-Leninists in leftist political movements, Lenin's work on imperialism has dominated critiques of capitalism in twentieth-century Latin America.

Perhaps the most influential non-Leninist interpretation in Latin America has been the so-called "imperialism of free trade" approach pioneered by Ronald Robinson and John Gallagher.[5] In a critique of the periodization of previous theories of imperialism (Marxist and non-Marxist), Robinson and Gallagher argued that Great Britain pursued a policy of "trade with informal control if possible; trade with rule when necessary."[6] British power was, following the logic of the argument, effected in two (often) converging ways—via the Foreign Office and via British business. When the latter wanted to achieve its goals it could rely on the former to back it up. Simply stated, diplomatic and business interests converged, creating an "informal empire" in contrast to the formal empire in Asia and Africa. Great Britain was making the world safe for capitalism, and British companies were the agents of the new capitalist order in the rise of economic (or business) imperialism.

For these theorists, British business distorted the politics and economics of Latin American nations primarily through domination and control of the export sector and the manipulation of that sector. Foreign business, according to this logic, monopolized the export sector and loans, and used this economic leverage to extract favorable treatment from the already receptive political elites who acted as their "collaborators" in the national system. This leverage and the assistance of the collaborating elites provided British (and later North American) business extraordinary influence in national politics as the foreigner developed the export sector to the detriment of diversification in the internal market. The power of external forces, in essence, dominated and distorted the Latin American economies and polities, severely restricting national autonomy.

Dramatic changes in the world economic and political system since the First World War forced theorists of imperialism to revise and extend the dominant explanations developed at the beginning of the century. The Great Depression and the rise of welfare states, the rise of multinational corporations, and decolonization are the most striking of the changes that had to be incorporated into the new versions of the dominant theories. Although the theories acknowledge the emergence of political independence in the Third World, they stress the enormous and growing power of multinational corporations to influence profoundly political and economic events in the former colonial areas. Once again foreign business is central to imperialism, but with even greater power and less dependence on the assistance of the "home" state to achieve its goals. In the latest stage of capitalism, some areas of the Third World have achieved previously unanticipated levels of industrialization as multinationals invest in manufacturing in conjunction with the latest version of collaborating elites and the host state.[7] For one powerful new current of theorists the principal means of domination is through an unequal exchange between rich nations and poor nations. Through the exploitation of very cheap labor the multinationals transfer the wealth of the Third World back to the First World.[8]

The most important and influential critique of the evolutionary and diffusionist theories has come from a diverse group of analyses often mislabeled dependency theory. With a vast array of proponents and approaches, dependency is more of a paradigm than a theory. *Dependentistas* come in all shapes and sizes, Marxist and non-Marxist.[9] While theories of imperialism have looked at the world system from the center outward, dependency views the system from the perspective of the periphery. Strongly influenced by theories of imperialism and the ECLA analysis, *dependentistas* share a common analytical approach. They argue that Latin America emerged and grew out of the expansion of capitalism, and that external forces have shaped Latin American history since its origins. Latin America's position on the periphery of the international economy has made it dependent on the center nations for its growth and development.[10] *Dependentistas* diverge on the extent and precise nature of this dependency.

Fernando Henrique Cardoso and Enzo Faletto's *Dependencia y subdesarrollo* (first edition, 1967) has been the most important and influential work on development theory to come out of Latin America in the past quarter-century.[11] Like many *dependentistas*, Cardoso and Faletto also argued that the place of Latin America in the international system was crucial to any analysis of its development. External relations, they argued, are central, but the key to understanding development and underdevelopment lies in the social class relations in each nation. The interaction of these changing class relations with external forces produces various outcomes in each nation. Cardoso and Faletto depicted two basic types of situations in Latin America: enclave economies where national wealth was controlled by foreigners, and economies where the key resources were controlled by nationals. The banana enclaves of Central America (controlled by foreign multinationals), for example, were very different from the coffee economy of Brazil (controlled by Brazilians).

From each of these two basic economies rose various paths conditioned by the changing nature of class relations in each nation. Cardoso and Faletto charted major periods in the evolution of dependency in Latin America and sketched the various historical paths in a broad range of cases. Among the first of the dependency theorists of the 1960s and 1970s, Cardoso and Faletto were also the most sophisticated and their work the most enduring. The appeal of their paradigm was that it offered a set of relatively simple analytical tools, theoretical rigor, and a sensitivity to differing historical experiences. The multiple paths of development and underdevelopment could be explained with a single paradigm. Furthermore, they did not fall into the simplistic economic determinism that characterized so many analyses.[12]

Despite the vast differences between the various theories of development and underdevelopment, all give foreign business a central place in the analysis. For the proponents of capitalism, foreign capital promotes development. For the critics of capitalism, foreign capital creates underdevelopment. The power and influence of foreign business is key to the construction and maintenance of imperialism and dependency. For most theorists of imperialism and dependency, capitalism is the source of Latin America's ills, and foreign businesses its principal agents. Their view of foreign capital represents the virtual antithesis of liberal theorists.

While liberal theories have been attacked and critiqued for nearly two decades, theories of dependency and imperialism have not gone unchallenged. D. C. M. Platt, in particular, has argued in numerous books and articles that the proponents of economic imperialism, Marxist and non-Marxist, overstate the volume, importance, and power of British business in Latin America.[13] A growing group of historians (especially in Britain) has called for microlevel studies of businesses and business practices to test the assertions of theories of dependency and imperialism that stress the political and economic power of foreign business in Latin America. For these scholars, the empirical test of the theories lies in case studies, cases which seem to confirm the relative political and economic weakness of foreign business, particularly in nineteenth-century Latin America.[14] Business imperialism, they argue, is a myth. Theorists of dependency and imperialism counter by arguing that the nature of the source material understates political influence and coercion. In other words, foreign businessmen and their local "collaborators" did not normally leave documentary evidence of their political dealings. Therefore, the argument goes, microlevel studies, by their nature, will not find confirmation of the political influence of foreign business.

This chapter examines the political economy of the St. John d'el Rey and weighs the company's political power at the state and national levels. The central question this chapter attempts to answer is deceptively simple: to what extent does the economic success of the St. John d'el Rey (analyzed in chapter 2) translate into political influence, and what is the extent of that influence? While one case study cannot resolve the long-standing theoretical debates over the role of foreign business in Latin America, the experience of this enormously successful firm can contribute important empirical evidence to the debate. The longevity of the St. John d'el Rey bears eloquent testimony to the company's ability to operate within a foreign context, and to the enterprise's sensitivity to the changing political culture of Brazil since 1830. The long-term success of the St. John demonstrates, more than anything else, the striking adaptability of capitalist enterprise. Clearly, the company's ability to surmount the varied technical, social, and economic challenges encountered hinged on management's skill in navigating the shifting tides of Brazilian politics over a century and a quarter. This chapter will show that the company's success was built on quiet negotiations and compromise with an increasingly activist state.

The power of this British enterprise to influence politics at the local level in Nova Lima was enormous, and company and community relations will be discussed in detail in chapters 5 and 6. At the state level the St. John acted as a significant interest group in the Minas political system, but did not in any way achieve a position of domination or exceptional leverage. On the national scale the company had the ear of powerful officials and often that of the head of state himself, but was never able to dictate the terms of treatment. The company had to work diligently, though often unsuccessfully, to convince national leaders just how Brazil would benefit from the extension of favorable treatment to a British firm.

While it is true that documentation for political deals and influence may be lost to the historian, the archives of the St. John d'el Rey do contain a good deal of confidential material documenting company efforts to influence Brazilian politics. No doubt, much more was never documented for obvious reasons of secrecy and confidentiality. The true test of political influence, however, does not rest entirely on "secret" documents. The important question is this: to what extent did foreign business see its political goals achieved? In short, we may not always be able to see the backroom maneuvering, but we should be able to see political results and compare them to the "wish list" of foreign business. This analysis demonstrates the ability of the St. John d'el Rey to achieve some of its political goals. More importantly, it stresses the limits of political influence, despite the company's economic power and prestige.

The political analysis in this chapter will show that, at least in this one case, the power of British business in Latin America was more limited and restricted than theories of imperialism and dependency have posited. As one of the most enduring and profitable of all British businesses in Latin American history, the experience of the St. John d'el Rey demonstrates the power of market forces and the state in shaping and constraining business practices and limiting economic and political leverage. Furthermore, although the company did succeed to a large degree due to its dexterity in political affairs, this British business exerted much less political influence than would be expected of a powerful foreign firm. The following pages will carefully examine the company's operations to show the principal forces that shaped and limited company operations and to what extent the St. John was a prisoner of national and international forces beyond its control. Although the St. John demonstrates the resilience and prosperity of a British enterprise in a foreign culture, its history also shows the need to recognize the limits of British business power and the key role of market forces and the state in determining success and failure. Certainly the St. John's state and national political clout was strikingly weak when compared with the notorious power of a United Fruit in Central America, or an International Harvester in the Yucatán.[15]

It is important to place the St. John d'el Rey's influence in proper perspective by issuing several caveats. First, although certainly the most powerful and successful of all the gold-mining companies in Brazil, one must remember that gold was a small and secondary segment of the national economy. After 1840 coffee would rise as the principal export and motor of the Brazilian economy. A truer test of British political and economic power must come from more dynamic sectors of the economy, and gold rarely made up more than 1 percent of export earnings in this export-oriented economy. Second, and unlike coffee or other agro-exports, gold has not historically been subject to the market fluctuations of the international economy. The price of gold did vary, and in the 1930s increased dramatically, but the St. John d'el Rey did not function within the classic export pattern of drastically fluctuating demand and prices. In fact, during the major economic crises of the Western economy (1848, 1873, 1893, and 1929) the St. John was in periods of tremendous expansion or major renovation.

Third, although the gold-mining boom of the early nineteenth century revived a dormant industry, even within Minas Gerais gold mining remained a secondary industry. Minas Gerais experienced relative economic decline in the nineteenth century as São Paulo and Rio de Janeiro took off with the coffee boom after 1840. Within Minas Gerais the southern and southwestern portions of the province (Zona da Mata and Zona Sul) participated in the coffee boom, leaving the old Zona Metalúrgica to experience economic stagnation. Although the capital of Minas Gerais was to remain in the old mining region, the politicians of the Sul and Mata emerged as major figures in *mineiro* politics and were more interested in cattle and coffee than in mining.[16] The St. John d'el Rey, therefore, operated an exceptionally successful foreign enterprise, but one that was an economic enclave, outside the economic mainstream, isolated from the economic heartland of both the nation and Minas Gerais. As a British enterprise, the company benefited from the European *mentalité* of the imperial elites. As a gold-mining enterprise the St. John suffered from the benign neglect of provincial and federal governments more interested in agriculture and cattle raising than in an isolated and secondary industry.

Given the changing nature of Brazilian politics, the company could not, and did not, employ the same tactics throughout its long history. Four major political periods, each with its own features and political style, presented the company with differing and evolving challenges. This chapter will deal in detail with each of these periods and outline the shifting nature of the political context within which the company operated. Under the Empire (1822–89) the company received a warm reception from a regime highly favorable to foreign capital in general but with little active interest in gold mining. Under the First Republic (1889–1930) an activist state began to emerge, and although the modernizing, European mentality of the elite remained paramount, political leadership became increasingly nationalistic. The Vargas regime (1930–45) that followed the Republic ushered in an era in which the activist state came of age accompanied by a pronounced economic and cultural nationalism. Nevertheless, as I will argue below, the political elites still found it fairly easy to reconcile their nationalism with foreign investment in the national economy. Finally, the postwar years (1945–60) are marked by the rise of mass politics and an activist, nationalistic state that made the operations of foreign business extremely problematic due to the incorporation of new sectors of society into the political system. The elites still found ways to accommodate foreign capital, but the demands of mass politics made this accommodation increasingly difficult.

The St. John d'el Rey operated successfully over decades by developing a powerful network of political allies. From its very inception company management understood the importance of establishing strong ties with Brazilians who would work within the local, provincial, and national political systems to protect company interests. Under the Empire the company began to assemble a network of influential friends, and George Chalmers consolidated this network during the heyday of the First Republic. As a result, the company weathered the rising nationalism of the 1930s and 1940s, relying heavily on its friends to help check the activism of an interventionist state. In the postwar years of mass politics the network continued to protect the St. John d'el Rey from the harshest of its nationalistic critics, and the company even strengthened its network. Ultimately, not even its strong political allies could save the company from the dislocations of the postwar international economy in the form of fixed gold prices and rampant inflation. Had the international gold market been more favorable, the St. John could conceivably have survived as a British firm into the present.

Empire and Isolation, 1830–1889

For most of the nineteenth century the St. John d'el Rey operated with little government interference and only an occasional need to become actively involved in political matters. The mentality that characterized the political and economic elite of imperial Brazil favored foreign investment and respected the technical and economic competence of the British. The Brazilian elites welcomed the British with open arms beginning in the early nineteenth century and sought to emulate the British in economics, politics, and social affairs with the hope of duplicating their successes.[17] This Anglophilia, however, did not blind the Brazilians to certain practical necessities, nor did it mean unquestioning aping of the British. The Brazilians would gradually learn to press the British and restrict their initial "open arms" policy. By the late imperial years the Brazilian state and provincial governments had begun to assert themselves and place some demands on British capital. These efforts were small but telling evidence of a growing nationalism that would not fully manifest itself until the following century.

Throughout the imperial period the major political issues that preoccupied the company were taxation and tariffs at the provincial and national levels. Although the English mining companies succeeded in lowering tax duties and tariffs under the Empire, the battle over tax and tariff rates was never-ending. Independence opened the doors to foreign investment in mining but maintained the old (fluctuating) Portuguese *quinto* as the rate of taxation. The new English mining companies initially paid an additional 5 percent tax on production.[18] The British mining companies banded together in the 1830s and 1840s and through numerous petitions to the Emperor they reduced the production tax on gold to 5 percent by the early 1850s, and eliminated that by the end of 1859. By then the gold-mining industry had fallen on hard times with the bankruptcy of major mines at Cata Branca, Cocais, Caeté, and Gongo Soco. The surviving mining companies persuaded the imperial government to reduce taxes to attract new investment.[19] The imperial regime also often allowed the companies to import their equipment and supplies free of tariffs in order to stimulate the growth of the mining industry. Occasionally, *mineiro* politicians attacked the special privileges of the British mining companies. Bernardo Pereira de Vasconcelos, a *mineiro* and the leader of the conservatives in the Brazilian parliament in the 1820s and 1830s, adamantly opposed mining concessions to British companies.[20] The companies usually responded by publishing their replies to the charges emphasizing the low profits and exceptional costs of this small industry.[21]

The St. John d'el Rey cultivated a network of prominent Brazilians to present its views in political circles and in the provincial assembly. The company could count on the Baron of Cocais, the Baron of Catas Altas, and the Count of Linhares, among others, to come to their aid as fellow mining entrepreneurs.[22] The company followed a policy of retaining prominent lawyers for their legal advice and political connections. In the 1860s the company retained a member of the powerful Viana family of Sabará. In the 1870s they employed

Ignácio Ferreira da Fonseca of Ouro Preto to represent company interests.[23] Perhaps the most powerful ally of the company was Commendador Francisco de Paula Santos, grandfather of Henrique Santos Dumont of aviation fame. Paula Santos had numerous landholdings and was the major creditor of the defunct Imperial Brazilian Company. He rented several hundred slaves to the St. John, supplied the mine with timber, and led the successful lobbying effort at the Court to repeal the gold production tax in the 1850s.[24]

One important test of political influence rose not over taxes, but over conscription of laborers. In the late 1860s the demands of Brazil's war with Paraguay placed pressure on provincial authorities to conscript soldiers for the war effort. Friends had helped the company receive an exemption for free laborers at the mine. With labor already difficult to come by, the St. John could ill afford losing workers to a draft. Ultimately, the jealousy of other British mining companies that were not exempted and the pressure of provincial authorities forced the company to compromise with the government, allowing the conscription of a token few to give the impression the company was not receiving favored treatment. The superintendent personally arranged the compromise with the provincial president while they traveled together from Rio de Janeiro to Juiz de Fora.[25]

The tax issue, however, was once again the central dilemma facing the St. John in the last years of the empire, and early years of the republic, and it was one that demonstrated the limits of the company's power and influence. In 1867 the imperial government restored a tax of 2 percent on gold production. (In the 1870s the state government also imposed a two-milreis tax on each slave employed in mining.)[26] In 1875 the provincial assembly, after intense debate, imposed a 4 percent tax on gold exports (later raised to 5 percent), clearly aimed at the St. John d'el Rey, which by this time produced the bulk of the nation's gold.[27] Unable to round up the votes to have the tax repealed, the St. John took the issue to the courts to have it declared unconstitutional, arguing that only imperial authorities had the right to levy export taxes. Despite employing powerful local figures in its legal effort, the company ultimately failed in its efforts, and the precedent was set. While pursuing the legal battle in the courts, the St. John and other English mining companies also approached the Brazilian minister in London, the Baron of Penedo, to ask his support for the repeal of the law. The baron served as Brazil's minister in London for four decades and had very close relations with British investors and bankers.[28] The St. John also approached the baron's son-in-law with a generous offer of remuneration for help in repealing the law. The mining companies argued that such legislation would frighten away potential British investment in Brazil.[29]

The British Foreign Office refused to come to the aid of the St. John d'el Rey because of the company's refusal to release the Cata Branca slaves. Lord Salisbury summed up views of the Foreign Office for the Consul General in Rio de Janeiro in no uncertain terms. "The protection of H[er]. M[ajesty's]. Legation cannot properly be extended to a British Co. whose proceedings have been examined by the Law Office of the Crown, & have been declared by them to be in violation of the Slave Trade Acts."[30] Although the tax was declared unconstitutional on several occasions by national authorities, the state government went ahead with its collection beginning in the 1880s.[31]

Despite its failure on this critical issue, the company had, by the 1880s, established friendships with key political figures and was a long-standing and productive enterprise well known to imperial authorities. Pedro I had visited the company's initial operations in São João del Rei, and his son had several interviews with company officials during his long reign.[32] While touring Minas Gerais in 1881, Pedro II spent a day at Morro Velho descending with the empress to the bottom of the mine. Superintendent Pearson Morrison fascinated the emperor with the marvels of deep-shaft mining while stressing the needs of the gold-mining industry for lower taxes and tariffs.[33] The company periodically entertained provincial presidents at the Casa Grande, attempting to demonstrate the benefits of foreign investment and making a case for lower taxes and tariffs.[34] The political network in the late imperial years, however, was small and normally called upon only in times of political dangers such as the imposition of new taxes. The construction of a broad, carefully cultivated, political network would not come until the rebuilding of the mine during the heyday of the First Republic.

Modernization, George Chalmers, and the Activist State, 1889–1930

The fall of the Empire in 1889 came as no surprise to the management of the St. John d'el Rey and had few immediate repercussions on the company. The process of modernization under the republic had been well under way long before the political transition of 1889, and the new regime opened the way to the rise of a more activist state, although the new government loudly proclaimed its economic liberalism.[35] Rising taxes, new duties and tariffs, and greater regulation demonstrated the encroachment of the state into the economy and into the affairs of the St. John d'el Rey. This process of increasing state activism had also been evident prior to 1889, would increase noticeably under the republic, and would flourish after the Revolution of 1930.

The most important short-term change implemented by the new regime was the promulgation of a new constitution. Under the old imperial system the Crown had followed the colonial practice of maintaining ownership of all subsoil rights, while issuing concessions to those who wished to mine. The major shift from colonial to imperial regime was the opening of mining to foreign entrepreneurs —a move that triggered the mining boom after 1824. The St. John operated under a concession granted to George Süch in 1828 to mine in Minas Gerais.[36] The concession did not tie the company to a specific site, a factor that would benefit it enormously in the twentieth century. The new mining code implemented after the Constitution of 1891 fundamentally altered the imperial code by merging surface and subsoil rights.[37] Suddenly property owners controlled not only the surface but all rights to the subsoil. The logic behind this legislation was simple: the state should step out of mining and return all rights to property owners thereby unifying surface and subsoil. The new code created countless headaches for mining companies and especially for the St. John.

The company undertook a careful policy of land purchases surrounding Morro Velho in order to guarantee control of the surface over the mine.[38] This presented a major challenge with a mine that had reached down two kilometers below the surface by 1914, and ran west to east at a forty-five-degree slope for nearly two kilometers. The company now had to have extremely accurate underground surveys to make sure of the location of the mine as it moved progressively eastward toward Raposos. The company never felt comfortable with the mining laws in the Constitution of 1891, and spent the next four decades working for the creation of a new mining code. Several presidential administrations in the first twenty years of the republic made efforts to protect and stimulate the mineral resource industries in Brazil. Despite continual lobbying by the St. John and by Brazilian mining interests, and despite the support of Presidents Campos Salles, Rodrigues Alves, and Afonso Pena, the efforts to develop mineral resource industries produced few results.[39]

In 1899 the president of Minas Gerais appointed a commission to study ways to revive the once promising mining industry. Composed of mining investors and the company's close friends, Teófilo Ribeiro and Afonso Pena, the commission made a series of recommendations that could have easily come out of the St. John's boardroom. The commission called for the reduction of the state export tax on gold, elimination of tariffs on mining equipment, lower freight insurance rates on gold, and more foreign investment in mining. Nothing came of the commission's report.[40] In 1903, at the state industrial, agricultural, and commercial congress in Belo Horizonte, another commission made similar recommendations after a strong report from Chalmers on the needs of the mining industry. Again, nothing came of the recommendations. The federal government did create a Superior Mining Council in 1915 with George Chalmers as a member. As if to demonstrate the political impotence of the mining lobby, the new mining legislation that went into effect after the First World War ignored Chalmers's and the industry's recommendations during the previous two decades.[41]

Increasing taxes, new duties and tariffs, and new government regulations presented the St. John with important financial burdens that had not existed under the empire. The first major financial and political challenge of the 1890s was to maintain the company's traditional customs exemptions on imports of supplies and machinery. A complex tariff structure complicated the work of the St. John, and the management now spent more and more time lobbying to protect exemptions on specific items.[42] After the visit of President Campos Salles and the president of Minas Gerais in the late 1890s the state reduced the gold tax rate to 3.5 percent from 5 percent. Rui Barbosa presented public and private arguments that helped the company achieve the reduction. The Campos Salles administration also lowered customs duties for imports of equipment from 45 percent to 5 percent.[43] Despite the sudden upsurge in support for the mining industry a long struggle had begun that would increasingly go against the British as they fought to maintain exemptions and keep tariff costs down. Most mining equipment entered the country with a 5 to 7 percent duty after Campos Salles's visit and help.[44] Nevertheless, all tax exemptions were abolished in 1927. The pattern after 1900 was for the company to avoid tariff problems by turning increasingly to national suppliers (creating the very response that the government had hoped for with its protectionist measures).[45]

Transportation became another major headache for the St. John by the turn of the century. Supplies and equipment from England traveled 8,000 kilometers by sea, 550 kilometers by rail, and an additional 8 kilometers over mountainous dirt roads.[46] The rail line from central Minas to Rio de Janeiro had been completed in the 1890s, yet different rail gauges forced users to transship goods at Conselheiro Lafayette. More important the Estrada de Ferro Central passed through Honório Bicalho and Raposos to the east of Nova Lima (see map 4). The St. John spent large sums moving goods from the rail line by oxcart, and the rains often made the 8-kilometer journey a trip of days and even weeks![47] Transport costs for bullock-drawn carts between the rail line and the mine ran close to £4,000 per annum at the turn of the century (or equal to about 8 percent of total profits).[48] When George Chalmers decided to build an electric railway from the mine to Raposos, he turned to his network of political allies to persuade the state government to allow the company to build it. An official decree opened the way, and in 1913 Chalmers inaugurated rail service on the electric "tramway," saving the company transport costs and establishing closer ties with the population of nearby Raposos. The rail line cut transport costs in half almost immediately.[49]

Government control of the Estrada de Ferro Central and efforts by national authorities to regulate and tax the national rail network demonstrated the rising activism of the republican regime. The company unsuccessfully fought efforts to apply railway regulation to the *bonde*, arguing that the line clearly did not qualify as a railroad and therefore did not fall under government regulatory laws.[50] More important than regulation of the company's line was the imposition of mandatory insurance fees on all goods, an effort to raise revenues without raising freight rates. As the insurance fee depended on the value of the goods, the company faced enormous new costs, in effect, another production tax on gold bullion. The company lobbied long and hard to avoid the new fees, with A. G. N. Chalmers meeting personally with state president Fernando Mello Viana and state secretary of agriculture Daniel de Carvalho, both close friends of the company.[51] Stressing the financial crisis created by a severe labor shortage, company management persuaded the government to exempt the St. John from the railway fees. Nevertheless, additional new taxes negated the revenue gain, and the exemptions were soon lifted.[52]

The export tax on gold remained the company's major fiscal burden. Unable to have the tax declared unconstitutional under the empire, the St. John initially attempted to have the tax removed by the new republican government. Despite intense effort the tax remained and the St. John never achieved more than periodic reductions in the size of the tax, which fluctuated between 3 and 5 percent after 1900. The tax cost the company around £12,000 annually during the First World War, or about 3 percent of company revenues. In 1926 the St. John convinced the state government to lower the export tax from 3.5 to 1.5 percent due to the company's enormous labor difficulties and the financial hardships resulting from lower production. The company estimated that the reduction would mean a saving of £8,000 per year. Management showered praise and gifts on Teófilo Ribeiro, the lawyer who had done the lobbying that produced the reduction. A. G. N. Chalmers told the board that Ribeiro was the company's greatest friend in Brazil.[53] The export tax represented, in reality, a production tax on gold bullion and, in the 1930s, would be replaced by a direct production tax. The 1920s were the heyday of government support for the gold-mining industry. Chalmers had constructed a powerful mining complex and a network of political allies. His close friend, Fernando Mello Viana, after serving as state president was then vice-president of the nation, and the severe labor crisis and cutbacks in operations at Morro Velho made politicians receptive to company appeals for fiscal restraint.

Despite the receptive attitudes of politicians, the rising activism of the Brazilian state had become a clear pattern by the 1920s. The economic impact and dislocations created by war in Europe after 1914 would fuel state activism and turn the St. John increasingly to Brazilian markets for the sale of its product and the purchase of supplies. The economic impact of the war on Latin America was immense. The war in the North Atlantic hindered traditional trading relations with Europe and the United States, and the economic chaos in Europe hit Latin America hard. More specifically, Brazil and other countries turned to regulation of internal financial and commercial markets to soften the blows of wartime economic shocks.[54] The fluctuating exchange rates and the near impossibility of shipping gold to

England presented the St. John with severe challenges, but these represented forces beyond their control. Initially, the company shipped gold to New York and turned to the United States for key supplies now unobtainable in England.[55] In 1917 the Brazilian government suddenly placed an embargo on all gold shipments to stem the flow of specie and to bolster the national currency. Although the company initially did not welcome government control of gold exports, the St. John worked out an arrangement whereby the national mint purchased all gold bullion at the New York price.

The contract arrangement caused no loss of revenue and the company directors recognized what they termed the "good propaganda" from the sale of all gold to the government. This arrangement continued (in various forms) until the 1960s.[56] One unexpected side effect was the reduction of transport costs; as the government took possession of the gold at the mill, the company no longer had to handle transport and the consequent insurance fees.[57] Government control of company gold sales also represented an important shift for Brazil. For nearly a century the majority of the country's legal gold production had been leaving the country. Henceforth, the government would have additional means to accumulate hard currency and support Brazilian currency.

The rising activism of the state forced the St. John d'el Rey to become increasingly active in the backrooms of political lobbying. Under George Chalmers's astute management the company built a broad and effective political network at the local, state, and national levels. The positivist modernizing mentality of the elite under the republic converged conveniently with the St. John's expansion. Although nationalism, most visibly in the form of an activist state, began to emerge as a key force by the turn of the century, the elite continued to view foreign investment and technical expertise as essential elements in the development process.[58] The company had six decades of experience in Brazil when the Empire fell and had developed a fine sense of the nuances of the Brazilian political culture. Chalmers built on this experience and fine-tuned the St. John's integration into state and national political cultures. Chalmers gained widespread respect and admiration for the technical and business marvels he produced with the rebuilding of the mine and mill in the 1890s. Although he enormously disliked the socializing and niceties of public relations, Chalmers understood the need to cultivate close ties with Brazilian business and political figures. Although never comfortable in Portuguese, he developed close friendships with powerful state and national leaders, often inviting them to his personal *fazenda* (Jaguara) for hunting and fishing trips.[59] Chalmers's personal charisma, his towering figure, and his technical achievements made him an almost legendary figure even among the business and political elite. For most Brazilians, George Chalmers *was* the St. John d'el Rey Mining Company, Limited.[60]

One striking episode demonstrates the St. John's economic prowess and the limits of its political power in Minas Gerais under the Republic. In the first decade of the century the state government, unwilling to become any more dependent on the Union, turned to the company for a loan to carry state finances through a difficult period. Although appalled by the request, company management reluctantly acceded to maintain good relations with the state government and to avoid possible tax increases. The state borrowed £50,000 at 6 percent interest to be credited to the company's tax account with the state. The state government also promised not to raise taxes on gold production while the loan was being repaid (1901–8). In effect, the state leaned on the company and the St. John had little choice but to make the loan. Success in rebuilding the mine had brought the company more visibility than it wanted.[61]

By the First World War it had become clear that Chalmers and his department heads could no longer handle the growing demands of public relations work. The company slowly moved toward the creation of a full-time public relations department without fully envisioning it. One employee began to emerge as a pivotal figure in public relations work—Jacques Santiago Paris. An extraordinary figure with a cloudy personal background, Paris had been born in Uruguay, apparently of Franco-Hispanic parents. He spent a number of years wandering in Argentina and Bolivia trying his hand at a wide variety of commercial enterprises with little success. He married in Bolivia at the turn of the century, fathered a son who later fought in the Chaco war, and left his wife and child around 1914, never to return to Bolivia (although he wrote and sent money occasionally). Somehow Paris found his way to Morro Velho and began working for the company in the estate department in 1914 or 1915 as a purchasing agent.[62] Very quickly his ability with people and his fluency in Spanish, Portuguese, English, and French insured his rise within the company. By the end of the war he was used frequently as a troubleshooter in lobbying on tax and duties problems that arose.[63]

By the 1920s Paris had become, in effect, a full-time lobbyist operating in Belo Horizonte and Rio de Janeiro. Paris wined and dined bureaucrats and politicians, developing a wide network of friends throughout the political system and bureaucracy in Minas and Rio. His personal charm and handling of personalities became legendary among company management who marveled time and again at his ability to find the *jeito* that saved the St. John from new taxes, duties, and regulations. The "public relations" work of Paris represented the shady side of company operations as he traded favors and made deals in the backrooms and clubs of the bureaucratic and political networks in Minas Gerais and Rio de Janeiro.[64]

In the 1920s, for example, the company business manager accidentally discovered that the St. John had not officially registered the changes in capital stock and company regulations since 1888 as required by Brazilian law.[65] The company operated under the imperial decrees of 1828 to George Süch and the transfer of Süch's mining concession to the St. John in 1830. When the St. John d'el Rey Mining Company added Limited to its name and registered under England's Companies Act of 1862, the company was also registered in Brazil. The same procedure was followed when the company was reorganized in 1888 after the mine disaster.[66] Failure to register the numerous new issues raising capital stock from £252,000 to £800,000 was supposed to carry a fine levied on each share, which would have been astronomical had the government discovered the unregistered changes. After an initial panic, and at Jacques Paris's suggestion, company officials passed a general resolution that mentioned the combined capital changes and made no reference to the numerous gradual changes. Jacques Paris then quietly walked the changes through the Brazilian bureaucracy, paid normal registration fees— as if all the capital changes had just taken place—and management breathed a collective sigh of relief. With Paris's quiet work and the sleight-of-hand resolution, the St. John avoided a massive fine and skirted Brazilian law.[67] In the early 1930s his efforts led to the exemption of company goods from a customs duty that saved the St. John about £10,000 per annum. Paris was invaluable to the company and virtually irreplaceable.[68]

Paris became the company's public relations man and in the 1920s was assisted by two young Franco-Brazilians: Carlos Galery and Braulio Carsalade. Both were the sons of Frenchmen who had come to Nova Lima to work for a short-lived French mining company at Faria to the south of the town. Their fathers married into the Ribeiro Wanderley family, one of the old, established local families. The two cousins—Carsalade and Galery—spoke Portuguese, English, and French. Each would begin to work with Paris in the 1920s, technically as employees of the estate department.[69] Carsalade replaced Paris after the latter's death in 1934.[70] Less flamboyant than his predecessor, Carsalade was an exceptionally effective replacement for the next two decades. Galery worked for the company in various capacities—as a clerk, translator, and public relations man. He was an invaluable ally during the 1930s and 1940s when he was *prefeito* of Nova Lima and a major local political figure (see chapter 6).

By the 1920s the company had a circle of powerful friends in high places in local, state, and national politics. These Brazilians were convinced of the contribution of the company to regional and national economic development, and they deeply admired British culture and technical competence. A brief sampling of the company's "friends" demonstrates its success in developing a political lobby. The St. John's chief legal officer, Flávio Fernandes dos Santos, was the *prefeito* of Belo Horizonte in the 1920s.[71] One of the company's closest allies was the brilliant young lawyer, Daniel de Carvalho, who served as state secretary of agriculture in the 1920s and as minister of agriculture in the 1940s (among other positions). (The mining industry fell under the jurisdiction of the state secretariat and the federal ministry of agriculture.)[72] Augusto de Lima, one of the most visible political and intellectual figures of the era (and a native of Nova Lima), diligently defended the company's interests as a state and federal deputy, newspaper editor, and in a wide variety of powerful posts.[73] Fernando Mello Viana, state president and then vice-president of Brazil in the 1920s, was a close personal friend of Chalmers and had family ties to the St. John dating back to the mid-nineteenth century.[74] In short, the company built a network of friends and constantly cultivated them with favors, gifts, and remuneration. Although the company by no means faced smooth political sailing, its economic power and its political allies guaranteed Chalmers and his successors a careful hearing of company views—often in the governor's office, or in the presidential palace.[75]

The St. John d'el Rey had responded to the rise of the modernizing, activist state under the First Republic by broadening its political network and developing its public relations work to confront the increasing challenges of government intervention in the business world. The greatest challenge to the St. John was the rising nationalist sentiment that viewed foreign business as too powerful and too privileged. The company's careful cultivation of political figures and its decades of integration into the regional economy blunted the more severe criticisms of nationalistic politicians. The collapse of the elite consensus of the coffee and cream alliance in 1930, however, would usher in a new, and difficult, era fundamentally altering the St. John's delicate position as a foreign enterprise in Brazil.

Nationalism, Expansion, and Getúlio Vargas, 1930–1945

In 1930 the St. John d'el Rey prepared to celebrate one hundred years of continuous operations in Brazil. The wife of the chairman of the board designed a special medallion, and the Brazilian mint cast several hundred of them in gold, silver, and bronze as the company prepared an official ceremony to present the medallions to high-level federal and state officials.[76] Before the ceremonies could take place, however, civil war broke out and a coup toppled the government of President Washington Luís, effectively destroying the alliance and ushering in a decade and a half of rule by Getúlio Vargas. The so-called Revolution of 1930 represented the collapse of the oligarchical rule of the large coffee states and the emergence of a new politics based increasingly on centralization of power, economic nationalism, and an appeal to the masses for support via the rhetoric of social justice.[77] As in all major political controversies, the St. John maintained a low profile and carefully monitored events to ensure that company affairs would not be endangered by the turn of events. Company officials had been reporting back to London on the rising dissatisfaction of opponents of the regime, and expected violence to break out after the hotly disputed elections in 1930. When fighting broke out in early October, Minas Gerais played a critical role in the coup, and for weeks the fighting around Belo Horizonte between rebels and loyalists cut off the company from the outside world.[78]

The change of regime did not produce a radical shift in relations between the Brazilian government and the company. Rather the new regime accelerated the changes that had been emerging at least since the First World War: increasing state intervention in the economy and growing cultural and economic nationalism. The company maintained its ties with key officials in the new government, in particular, Getúlio Vargas, who eventually emerged as the strongman who would rule Brazil through the Second World War. Vargas had first visited the mine shortly after his appointment as treasury minister in 1927 and left company officials with a favorable impression and the belief that he would be sensitive to their problems. He left the ministry before acting on any concrete concerns but did not lose contact with the company. Vargas or members of his immediate family visited the Casa Grande on at least four occasions between 1927 and 1938, and he apparently was enchanted by the hospitality and the setting.[79] After Vargas led a coup in November 1937 to halt preparations for elections, he imprisoned many of his chief political foes and asked the St. John to allow ex-presidential candidate and former São Paulo state president, Armando de Salles Oliveira, to remain at the Casa Grande under house arrest. Salles Oliveira spent five months under police observation and house arrest at Morro Velho. Although the company management resented the imposition, they acquiesced to avoid any bad feelings on the part of the Vargas regime toward the St. John d'el Rey.[80]

The company's political network remained intact, although some old friends now faced exile or prison. Others, however, now rose to positions of prominence in the new government. Unable to hold the public ceremony to celebrate the company's centennial, management settled for private presentations of the medallions to key officials. To maintain a nonpartisan profile and to reward old friends, the St. John made sure to present medallions to old political allies, even though they might be in the opposition—or even under house arrest. When Managing Director C. F. W. Kup visited Brazil in late 1930 he met with the finance minister, the president of the Bank of Brazil, the governor of Minas Gerais, as well as officials of previous governments. Kup and Superintendent Millett met with Vargas for a half-hour interview to present him with a centennial medallion and to discuss the state of the gold-mining industry.[81] The troubled political waters after 1930 were becoming more difficult to navigate and the company would spend the next three decades resisting rising nationalism and the encroachment of the state in company affairs.

The St. John felt the force of the rising activism of the Vargas regime in four main areas: exchange policy, taxes and tariffs, labor organizing, and nationalization of natural and human resources. In each area the company achieved compromise with the government but found itself increasingly restricted in its actions. All of these areas represented various facets of the rising nationalism of the Brazilian government and the desire by Brazilians to assert greater control over their economy and society. As a foreign enterprise the St. John d'el Rey felt the rising nationalist pressures on all sides. With more than a century of experience operating in Brazil, the company was able to meet the growing challenges of nationalism for two decades until an unfavorable international economy converged with these challenges to bring an end to the British era at Morro Velho.

The first concrete challenge of the new regime to business operations came in the efforts of Vargas to place restrictions on foreign-exchange transactions (see chapter 2). The government's decision not to allow more than one-third of the currency paid for the company's gold to be converted into sterling created a capital-flow crisis for the St. John. Jacques Paris and company officials lobbied intensely to fight the new measure, with no success. They achieved no more than a promise that they would be allowed the full one-third.[82] For the next two decades management continually dreaded the possible restriction of all profit remittances. One unfavorable ministerial or bureaucratic change could bring an end to all remittances, effectively nationalizing all company assets by cutting off the flow of revenue to British investors. Technically, the Brazilian government permitted the one-third remittance to allow the company to pay for machinery and supplies in England. In fact, only one-third of the sterling remitted went to such purchases, the rest going to stockholders in the form of dividends. This was in direct violation of the remittance law, and, had the Brazilian government discovered the payment of dividends and pressed the company, it could have shut off all future profit remittances. Occasionally, the company chose not to challenge new fees and duties to avoid any inquiry into the destination of remittances. The company, in effect, could not bring too much attention to the financial "burden" of new imposts without endangering the remittance allowance.[83] (It is possible that the government knew of the company's deception and allowed the situation to continue to maintain extra leverage over the St. John, but there is no evidence of this.)

The enormously favorable jump in the price of gold in 1934 countered the potentially devastating impact of the currency restriction.

The sudden jump in the value of production reached levels that ensured that the one-third remitted sterling would cover the dividends and other expenses at previously established levels in London. In 1929 one-third of the value of gold production came to around £150,000. In 1937 the figure approached £300,000. Dividend payments remained virtually unchanged.[84] At the same time the company's labor situation radically improved with the collapse of the coffee economy after 1929 and with the consequent rise in unemployment in agriculture. Although the labor market did not improve dramatically for employers as it did in Western Europe and the United States, the St. John's extreme labor shortages of the previous decade disappeared. For the first time in the history of the company, labor abounded and the St. John could turn to expansion plans to take advantage of the abundant labor supply and the large surpluses of currency.[85] Favorable forces in the international gold market and the regional labor market mediated the impact of the new government restrictions. Once again, powerful market forces beyond company control shaped the St. John's destiny.

Ironically, the decade of the 1930s was a period of economic expansion and financial stability for the St. John d'el Rey despite the rising activism of the Brazilian state and a worldwide economic crisis. As company revenues climbed, the government also began to take a larger share of the company's income. New burdens imposed by the government included the elimination of old customs exemptions, the imposition of new customs duties, and a wide range of secondary fees and taxes. Jacques Paris and Braulio Carsalade spent most of their time working to eliminate or soften these new costs.[86]

The St. John achieved some success in the mid-thirties as Vargas decided to try to revive a gold-mining industry now reduced to small-time operations and the St. John d'el Rey. Facing default on the foreign debt, the regime recognized the benefits of producing more gold.[87] Decrees abolished state and municipal taxes on gold mining and exempted the industry from customs fees in 1934. These tax gains were erased when the Vargas government returned the old export tax to 3.5 percent, raising company costs another £5,000 per year. In addition, a 6 percent Brazilian income tax on company profits went into effect for the St. John in 1932.[88] The export tax was abolished in 1938 in a carefully negotiated compromise with government officials. In exchange the company agreed to raise the valuation of its lands, thereby replacing the government's lost tax revenue.

An unwritten understanding between government and company officials kept total taxation around 8 percent of total revenue. The new constitution of 1937, for example, prohibited state export taxes and phased out the old export tax over a three-year period (3.6 percent in 1938, 2.9 percent in 1939, and complete removal in 1940), but the government then instituted a new 3 percent tax on production, a new tax on power production, on capital employed, and a sales tax.[89] The general government pattern was to give with one hand and take away with the other. The overall effect was a gradual rise in total tax payments. Although the combined rate of national, state, and municipal taxes declined from around 9 percent in 1930 to 5.6 percent in 1939, the costs of the new government pension program alone effectively taxed the company another 6 to 7 percent.[90]

Potentially more damaging than any tax or duty was the rewriting of the Brazilian constitution and the formulation of a new mining code. The new regime implemented legislation that reflected the nationalist sentiments of the era. The St. John worked hard and long to influence the new legislation, particularly the mining code and the sections of the constitution that dealt with ownership of natural resources. Under the new regime the government abandoned the mining code of the republic and returned to the concessionary approach of the empire, and the nation once again became the owner of all mineral rights. Mining claims established prior to the implementation of the new mining code remained in private hands. The new code distinguished between different types of mining claims, creating new headaches for the mining industry. Most important, the company had to make sure it established legal title over all its wide-ranging deposits: iron, manganese, watersheds, and a long list of gold claims. Under the new laws, claims not only had to be established before implementation of the new legislation, claims also had to be worked, or they reverted to the control of the state which considered them abandoned.[91]

The new regime also established guidelines to insure Brazilian control of national resources. Legally, all mining companies had to be Brazilian corporations with a Brazilian board of directors.[92] The St. John d'el Rey saw the nationalistic handwriting on the wall and created a new dummy company, the Companhia de Mineração Nova-limense (CMN), that actually held the mining rights to all the St. John's properties. The new "paper" company was theoretically a Brazilian corporation, created and organized in the country, with stock issued in Brazil. The St. John, however, controlled the stock, and the board consisted of the company's Brazilian lawyers and some company officials. The St. John continued (and continues) to operate its mining claims through the mining rights of the CMN. The mining done today at Morro Velho and at the iron deposits is done under claims controlled by this paper company.[93]

Nationalism also resulted in the passage of laws that restricted the ability of foreigners to work in Brazil. The so-called "Two-Thirds Law" required that two-thirds of all company employees at all levels be Brazilian.[94] Although the British made up less than 1 percent of the payroll, certain areas of the staff were entirely British. The company worked hard to get around the new regulations, even helping Anglo-Brazilian *morrovelhenses* clearly to establish their Brazilian citizenship to insure the "Brazilian" quotas were met.[95] Finally, the rising nationalism had repercussions even among the children of the English as the government began to require all schools in the country to offer basic levels of Portuguese instruction and Brazilian social studies.[96] The company had to hire Brazilian instructors to teach morning sessions that met the educational guidelines of the government; in the afternoons the children attended classes in English. These steps helped create a generation of English children who were truly bilingual and bicultural, though the children no doubt resented the double load.

The final area where the St. John felt the impact of rising government activism was, in the long run, the most far-reaching in its effects. A crucial new political innovation of Vargas was his efforts to organize labor as a key base of political support. Vargas, much like Cárdenas in Mexico and Perón in Argentina, recognized the emerging power of the laboring classes and worked to integrate them into a corporatist regime.[97] Vargas created a new Ministry of Labor and implemented social legislation that established basic social benefits and workers' rights for the first time in Brazil. These measures frightened the management of the St. John who had worked for decades to crush any efforts at organization by the workers, and they saw the new programs as socialistic.

In 1934 the workers began to take advantage of the new regime's orientation and a group of miners asked the Ministry of Labor to help them establish an official union.[98] Superintendent Millett and the company made last-minute efforts to organize a union controlled by "trustworthy" employees and failed. The União dos Mineiros da

Morro Velho became official in May 1934 and set into motion forces that would produce conflict in strikes in the following decades. In the 1930s the union pressured the company to implement the new social legislation, and the St. John grudgingly established a pension plan, health insurance, disability insurance, and health and safety guidelines in the mine. The company fought these changes inch by inch, creating enormous ill will in the government bureaucracy and among the community in Nova Lima. Nevertheless, the battles of the late thirties took place in offices and union halls, and not in the streets in the form of strikes. Differences were mediated by the government with the company generally losing each issue after long negotiations and delay tactics. Not until the 1940s would the full fury of the union be unleashed in bitter strikes that crippled the St. John, bringing it to the brink of financial collapse.[99]

The union and the Ministry of Labor pressed the company on a series of issues that compounded the problem of rising labor costs. Health, safety, and retirement issues dominated the conflicts between workers and management. The most bitter and prolonged of the health disputes rose over the crippling disease of silicosis, or "white lung." Beginning in the 1930s the union and government officials began to pressure the company to recognize the disease as a major problem for the miners, particularly the borers underground. Initially, management refused to concede the existence of the disease, arguing that miners were suffering from pneumonia, bronchitis, and related lung problems, but not silicosis. The company initially challenged government test results, but after a decade of government reports and outside consultants, management had to concede the widespread incidence of silicosis in the underground force.[100] This led to a series of government regulations that restricted the number of years a miner could work underground. Furthermore, the company (after a long and bitter struggle) had to pay an "insalubrity" bonus to those working underground. The related costs of health care for the silicotics and the size of the insalubrity bonus placed important new burdens on the company payroll.

Under the new social legislation the company had begun to provide workers with health care and disability pensions in the 1930s. The scope and costs of setting up clinics and paying pensions also added new burdens to the payroll. The company had to set up a Caixa de Aposentadoria e Pensões that handled the pension fund and soon found that the Caixa leadership (drawn from union ranks) were strong antagonists of management.[101] In short, by the 1940s the union struggled not only for wage increases, but for additional funds for pensions, insurance, and health and safety programs. The growing costs of social legislation quadrupled between 1944 and 1950 from £41,759 to £173,422. In 1950 the cost of social legislation added another 10 to 11 percent to payroll costs.[102]

The emergence of a strong local Communist party played a critical role in the rise of the union movement in Nova Lima. The Brazilian Communist party (PCB) had begun to develop local cells in the 1920s and early 1930s, and slowly developed a strong local network of leaders. When the union was organized in 1934 Communist workers very quickly established themselves as leaders in the mine and union.[103] The Communist movement in Nova Lima had to maintain a low profile in the late thirties and early forties as a result of an aborted coup by the party in 1935 and government repression. The leader of the national party organization, Luís Carlos Prestes, was jailed, and the party went underground or into exile.[104]

The major leadership roles in the union movement came under the control of Communists, some with secret training in Eastern Europe and the Soviet Union. Apparently, the strength of the party's membership came from the skilled workers in the mine, and particularly from the recently opened Raposos mine.[105] The party resurfaced with the fall of Vargas in 1945 and emerged as the most powerful Communist party in Latin America, and the fourth largest political party in Brazil. The Dutra administration outlawed and suppressed the PCB after 1947, forcing the faithful underground once again.[106] Company management, facing several long and bitter strikes, turned to the government to help stamp out Communists in the miners' union movement. Taking advantage of the government's anti-Communist offensive, the St. John in 1949 dismissed all workers suspected of having Communist ties, accusing them of sabotaging mining operations. The fifty-one fired workers, many with more than ten years of seniority, took the company to court in a legal battle that lasted three years. Ultimately, the company won the case and the dismissals held up, although lower courts ruled against the St. John several times during the appeals process.[107]

The issue of nationalism dominated worker-management relations. To a large degree the strength and unity of the union movement rose from the split between a Brazilian work force and a British staff. Workers were very much aware of the substantial dividends remitted to England to stockholders. Government regulations compelled the St. John to publish annual accounting figures in the official state newspaper and Brazilians could easily see the size of profits and dividend remittances.[108] Workers looked to the profits and wanted the company to direct more of its funds to wages and less to English stockholders. Union leadership used this issue effectively in an era of rising nationalism to strengthen working-class unity and hold the workers together during long strikes. In short, the workers believed that the company could afford to pay them higher wages and provide better benefits. Even after the suppression of the Communist leadership in the union, their non-Communist successors followed the old policies, though with less of the language of anti-imperialism and anti-capitalism.

Militant Labor, Nationalism, and the End of the British Era, 1945–1960

The events of the years between 1930 and 1945 demonstrate the growing political weakness of the St. John d'el Rey as it attempted to confront challenges from militant labor and from a more activist and nationalist state. National and local forces crippled the company, revealing the inherent weaknesses of this representative of foreign capital. With the end of the Second World War the St. John d'el Rey entered into its final years of operations under British control. In these final years the international economic system, Brazilian economic problems, and the rise of a militant labor movement combined to bring the St. John to the verge of bankruptcy. The company still had the means to combat militant labor and continued to work for political accommodation with government officials. The forces that would ultimately bring down the British firm were inflation in Brazil and a weak international gold market. Last-gasp efforts to work with the Brazilian government via the old political network failed to produce an arrangement that could save the company from takeover. In the end, 130 years of British enterprise collapsed in the face of these combined pressures, and North American investors took control of the company.

Although the company increasingly faced hostile bureaucrats and vocal politicians, its network and contacts within the political system remained intact, and the St. John continued to cultivate new allies. The political struggle became more difficult as nationalism became an increasingly public issue taken up by politicians and the middle and working classes. Newspapers and political campaigners found the company an easy target. Here was a city of poor workers, many disabled and crippled, built around a prosperous and relatively affluent foreign community. The contrast was stark and visible. Furthermore, here was a company that extracted enormous wealth for over a century from a community that was clearly impoverished.[109]

In response to rising public and political pressure the company stepped up its public relations work. Braulio Carsalade retired in the early 1950s, and the St. John brought in a new man, Anthony Vereker, who mounted a campaign in the press to improve the company's image and to counter unfavorable stories. Vereker paid journalists to write stories in a wide variety of publications (a common practice in Brazil) that placed the company in a positive light. He also played a leading role in organizing an "Advisory Council" of prominent Brazilians to defuse the issue of foreign management and control of the mine.[110] This council provided the St. John with additional ties into the national and state political networks. Furthermore, the company decided to hire a former military man to head the personnel department, believing that this would also defuse the foreign/national issue and allow management to employ a tougher stance toward strikes. General Nelson de Melo had been chief of staff of the Brazilian Expeditionary Force in Italy during the Second World War and was serving as staff chief to the minister of war when the company hired him in 1954. He left the St. John's employ in 1956 after being appointed chief military adviser (*chefe da casa militar*) to President Juscelino Kubitschek.[111]

As the financial crisis mounted in the mid-fifties, the company found itself in an inescapable bind. The international economic system of the postwar had frozen the price of gold and limited the income per unit produced. Rising inflation and nationalism in Brazil produced strikes, large losses, and constantly rising costs. Trapped between a frozen income ceiling and rising expenses, the company saw no way out of insolvency without the aid of the Brazilian government. In the end the struggle compelled the St. John to go to the government and lobby for its survival. The only means to avoid a complete shutdown would be to meet rising costs with higher gold prices, and the only way to higher prices was through government subsidies on gold purchases. In the last years of the British era the struggle for government subsidies became the paramount concern of management. After long consultations with company officials, and after examining company financial records, the government decided to subsidize the price of gold to allow the company to stay afloat. The Superintendency of Monetary Affairs (SUMOC) worked out a formula that would guarantee the St. John a price high enough to keep the mine operating. This subsidy would continue under the new Brazilian owners in the early 1960s. The Brazilian government chose to work with foreign capital and help the mining company through the crisis rather than face the end of operations at Morro Velho.[112]

The financial troubles of the St. John eventually led to a takeover by a group of New York investors led by stockbroker Leo Model.[113] Low stock prices and the immense iron ore reserves of the company attracted Model and his partners. They did not have the slightest interest in a failing gold mine, and they looked for ways to get rid of the mine while exploring the ways to begin mining and export of the iron ore at Aguas Claras, Mutuca, and Itabirito. Initially, the new owners considered closing the mine, but Brazilian law required them to pay severance to the thousands of company employees that would have run into astronomical figures.[114] In the meantime, Model searched for a suitable buyer for the iron lands. In 1960 Hanna Mining Company of Cleveland, Ohio, bought the St. John d'el Rey, transferred ownership to the United States, and sold the Morro Velho to Brazilian investors. The Brazilian government played a key role in the transfer of ownership. First and foremost, the government of Juscelino Kubitschek, a *mineiro*, did not want to see the closing of a mine that supported a community of thirty thousand. The social and economic costs would be unacceptable. The government had two alternatives: nationalize the company or help the owners through the crisis. Nationalization would have presented enormous problems for a regime that had committed itself to welcoming foreign capital to Brazil. The pressures for nationalization would reach fever pitch, however, under the Goulart administration in the early 1960s, focusing on Hanna's ownership of the iron lands.

Politics and Business

The longevity of the St. John d'el Rey testifies to the company's ability to maneuver adeptly through the constantly evolving political culture of Brazil. This political aptitude allowed the company to continue operating across two centuries and to surmount the challenges presented by rising state activism throughout its history. The key to the St. John's efforts was the construction of an extensive network of political allies at the local, state, and national levels. This network tied the company into the bureaucratic and political machinery of Brazil, allowing the St. John to handle effectively the rising challenges presented by increasing nationalism and state activism.

In the nineteenth century the company could count on the receptive attitude of the imperial regime to foreign capital, and could respond to restrictions on operations in a very favorable political context. Even before the fall of the Empire the state became increasingly more active in the form of fiscal and tariff restrictions, and the company (guided by Chalmers) continued to build a broad network of powerful friends. Although the company succeeded in many of its efforts to fight off new taxes and fees, it is important to note that the St. John never dominated the political exchange between the business and the government. The company was in a fairly weak negotiating position, having to persuade politicians that support for gold mining helped not only British investors, but also the Brazilian economy. In an industry almost exclusively controlled by foreigners this was not an easy task. They did succeed in keeping taxes and fees at relatively low levels for decades, their strongest argument always being the need to keep an ailing industry from dying out.

The political turning point for the St. John and for Brazil came in the 1930s with the Great Depression and the rise of Getúlio Vargas. Building on the milder activism of the republican state, Vargas initiated an era of developmental nationalism that slowly began to place greater and greater restrictions on foreign capital. The response of the St. John was to employ full-time lobbyists in Rio de Janeiro and Belo Horizonte to confront the constant stream of new taxes, fees, and restrictions. An old, well-entrenched political network allowed the company to meet many of these challenges and to soften the blows. In addition, the St. John was aided by a highly favorable international gold market until the end of the Second World War. Even under the nationalism of the Vargas years the company maintained its ability to operate profitably. Vargas welcomed foreign capital and knew the St. John firsthand, but he wanted the company to operate on terms more favorable to Brazil than had been the case in the past.

The most difficult political times for the St. John d'el Rey came in the 1940s and 1950s as mass politics and rising nationalism made foreign control of a vital national resource more problematic. Ultimately, however, the company was able to handle the political turmoil and continue to rely on its political network. Despite intense nationalism and a series of presidents who promoted government intervention in the economy, the company continued to work closely with the Brazilian government. The demise of the British firm was due not to political problems but to the rampant inflation in Brazil and the freezing of gold prices on the international market. The government even attempted to help the St. John overcome these twin problems by subsidizing gold prices.

As the preceding discussion has shown, the history of the St. John d'el Rey indicates that (at least in this case) the power of foreign capital to exert control over political and economic conditions in the host country is much weaker than the literature on dependency and imperialism seems to indicate. Rather than operating from a position of strength, the St. John operated from a position of weakness when negotiating with the Brazilian government. This became more evident as the decades passed. The relative weakness of the company in the political arena is clear in nearly every major issue affecting operations. The St. John did achieve some success in the debates over taxation and tariffs, but management faced constant challenges and a continual erosion of its position. On the most important of all issues, the mining code and mining law, the company was never able to make an impact on legislation. In effect, it had no choice but to react to fundamental and far-reaching changes in legislation that came out of the executive and legislative branches of the Brazilian government. The company did not operate a firm central to the national economy, nor even to the mining economy. Had the St. John produced iron, steel, or petroleum, its relationship with the Brazilian government would have been very different. With the rise of an activist state, particularly after the First World War, the company essentially fought a long and expensive struggle attempting to hold down the rising costs from new social legislation, fiscal restrictions, and tariff problems. The political influence of the St. John must be seen as relatively weak throughout its long history, despite its network of political allies and its ability to adjust to changes in Brazilian politics.

In the first century of operations the weakness stemmed from the St. John's role in a peripheral industry, its strength from its demonstrated success and investment in the local economy. After 1930 the threat of nationalization hung over all relations between the business and the government. The position of weakness when dealing with the Brazilian government no doubt also derived from the nature of the enterprise: a mining operation with an enormous amount of fixed capital investment. Unlike a merchant house, or plantations that could be removed to similar environments elsewhere, a gold mine and its fixed capital trapped the company and provided it with less leverage than corporations with more movable assets. The St. John initially offered the Brazilian government something it lacked: capital investment, technology, and know-how. By the twentieth century this investment was dwarfed by the growth of the state and national economies, and the small size of the gold-mining industry in those economies. The Brazilians no longer needed the British as much as they had in the early nineteenth century. The St. John, by failing to Brazilianize its staff and operations, became a visible target for nationalists. The British overstayed their welcome, and the St. John paid for its failure to see this.

The St. John d'el Rey was able to translate economic power into political influence, and the company does demonstrate the success of British capital in a foreign political culture. The company did have political resources, and its objectives periodically converged with those of local, state, and national elites (in keeping down workers and the PCB, for example). But the political methods and maneuverings of the company show its weakness in state and national politics. The example of the St. John seems to suggest that scholars must look more closely at generalizations about the power of foreign capital in Latin America. General theories must take into account the complexities and subtleties of business operations and discard stereotypes that tend to see all foreign business as essentially the same. Foreign business, as the case of the St. John d'el Rey demonstrates, is often successful and powerful, but that power may not necessarily translate into the ability to control or significantly shape the host political system.

In addition, this case demonstrates the need to recognize the limits on the power of foreign business. The role of the state must be reexamined to counter notions of its weakness and inability to restrain foreign capital. The executive and legislative branches of government in the host country both need to be examined to see their role in restraining foreign capital, and not just in acquiescing to it. We must pay more attention to the role of market forces that shape business practices. Not all foreign business could monopolize markets, control supplies, and dominate sectors of the international economy as did multinational fruit or mining corporations. In short, we must develop typologies of businesses emphasizing such factors as movable versus immovable assets, partnerships versus joint-stock operations or multinational corporations. We need to develop more sophisticated analyses of the relationship of foreign diplomacy and foreign business. The simplistic vision of British business and British diplomacy marching forward in unity is no longer viable, but that does not mean that the two never converged. More sophisticated explanations must take into account both the unity and divergence of interests.

Finally, the example of the St. John highlights the need for a more sophisticated analysis of the interaction of external *and* internal forces in the shaping of the Brazilian economy and Brazilian society. While the older liberal theories failed to appreciate the power of the external connections to the international economy, theories of dependency and imperialism have overstated that power. The approach of Cardoso and Faletto seems to offer a promising paradigm that recognizes the complexity of the interaction of endogenous and exogenous factors, and the advantages as well as the disadvantages of foreign capital in the process of development. Nevertheless, their work remains highly theoretical and needs to be tested and refined against a broad range of microlevel studies.

Dependency theorists are correct in arguing that external forces have shaped Brazil's development, but the failure to examine how those forces have interacted and were mediated by internal forces has produced a distorted and inaccurate view of Brazilian history. Foreign companies have exerted formidable power in Latin America during the past two centuries, but all foreign capital was not equal and we must recognize the variations and limits of that power. A United Fruit may have dominated politics in Central American nations, but in a nation like Brazil a company as successful as the St. John d'el Rey could not hope for anything like United Fruit's political influence in the "American Mediterranean." The St. John did exercise enormous power, a power that was largely concentrated in its home community —a power that diminished with the distance between Nova Lima and the outside world.

4

Technology and Labor in
the Workplace

It is always the direct relationship of the owners of the conditions of
production to the direct producers . . . which reveals the innermost
secret, the hidden basis of the entire social structure. . . .[1]

The success of the St. John d'el Rey for more than a century hinged
on its ability to surmount a series of obstacles on the international,
national, and local levels. On the international level the company
faced challenges over which it could exert relatively little influence. The price of gold on the world market, a series of financial
crises in the Western nations, two world wars, and the Great Depression presented obstacles that severely tested the entrepreneurial
skills of company management. At the national level the St. John
sought to influence the course of events, but had little impact. The
rise of economic nationalism, government intervention in the workplace, restrictions on profit remittances, and rising tariffs and taxes
all hindered management's ability to generate profits. Finally, the
trajectory of the Brazilian economy ultimately raised obstacles the
St. John could not overcome. Chronic inflation and rising wages
in the postwar period, the rise of a militant working class, and
import-substitution industrialization squeezed the company and created major problems for British management when combined with
the worldwide decline in the gold-mining industry.

These international and national problems intermeshed with an
equally important set of local obstacles. The St. John constructed
at Morro Velho a technological system that evolved as management
grappled with problems of geology, mining techniques, and labor.
This technological system *was* the very essence of the St. John d'el
Rey. The company was, in a sense, a system designed and operated
with a single goal: the production of gold bullion at acceptable levels

of profit. This chapter analyzes the technological system the British constructed at Morro Velho, and how it formed not only the core of business operations, but also the foundations of life and labor in Nova Lima. The emphasis is on the company and the workers at the local level. The St. John operated largely as an enclave, with little transfer of technology; the system therefore had its greatest impact in the community.

As employed here, the concept of technological system consists of the coordination and control of three primary elements: raw materials, techniques, and labor.[2] The St. John d'el Rey sought to control and shape the components of its technological system to the greatest degree possible, i.e., to rationalize its operations in the pursuit of profit. The gold ore that formed the raw material processed by the system provided fewer opportunities for control than the other two components. The company had the good fortune to locate one of the world's finest gold deposits, yet it depended on the persistence of quality ore—on a fortuity of nature—for its very life. What distinguishes the St. John from other companies (particularly those mining gold in Brazil) was its management of the two remaining components of the system. Given the nature of the gold ore, the company pursued two inseparable goals: continual technical innovation and a steady rise in the productivity of labor. Technical innovation lies at the heart of the success of the St. John d'el Rey and the history of Nova Lima. Technical innovation provided the firm with the way to profit and some semblance of control over gold ore and labor. Continual innovations permitted the company to extract the ore, to refine it at acceptable profit levels, and to raise the productivity of labor in a century of operations when labor was perpetually scarce, and then recalcitrant. Ultimately, the inability to continue technical innovation and to raise labor productivity was crucial in the demise of the British management.

The time has come to recognize the fundamental role of technology in Latin American history and the need for detailed empirical studies of the interaction of technology and society. Although scholars of widely divergent ideologies acknowledge the importance of technology in economic growth, development, and underdevelopment, the history of technology in Latin America has languished in its own state of underdevelopment. Since the arrival of Europeans to the Americas in the late fifteenth century, the introduction of foreign technology has played a crucial role in the history of Latin

America. The technological gap between Iberians and Native Americans facilitated the conquest and colonization of the Americas, while the British used their own technological superiority to construct their colonial empire.[3]

In Latin America technology has been the most concrete and direct point of encounter between foreign capital and local society. Steam engines, railroads, telegraph lines, and the repeating rifle are but a few examples of the tools that the Europeans used to construct their empires and to establish their powerful presence in Latin America in the nineteenth century. Today the technological backwardness of Latin America continues to play a key role in its dependence on the industrial nations of the North. Foreign technology has always been the most concrete, physical manifestation of foreign investment in Latin America, and the industrial workplace has been the most direct point of encounter between local society and so-called "external forces." At Morro Velho the British constructed a technological complex that brought Africa, America, and Europe face to face deep in the Brazilian interior. Historians of Latin America need to pay greater attention to these points of encounter and to the relationships between technology and society.

Although I argue in the following pages that technical innovation holds the key to understanding the rise and fall of the St. John d'el Rey, and the transformations in local society, I am not arguing for technological determinism. Technology does not mechanically determine social change. Society and technology interact in a dialectical process, the power and influence of each varying with time and place. As we shall see in the following pages, technology can often provide the stimulus to social change, yet social processes can also act as a stimulus, or a brake, on technical innovation. This chapter illustrates the dynamic interaction between society and technology at their most pronounced point of intersection—the workplace—and it analyzes the resulting technological and sociological change this interaction produces.[4]

In Nova Lima the St. John d'el Rey Mining Company *was* the dominant technological system, and society in Nova Lima grew up around it. As a company town built around an extractive industry, Nova Lima clearly and dramatically illustrates the close relationship between technology and society. At the height of its expansion in the 1930s the company was the dominant force in the community. The St. John employed nearly 40 percent of the adult population, including virtually all adult males. Of the remaining adult population (nearly all females), half were wives of company employees. In short, workers, wives, and dependents accounted for more than 90 percent of the local populace. The technological system at Morro Velho more completely than most systems enveloped the lives of the entire community.

This chapter focuses on the three components of the technological system with the emphasis on techniques and labor. The analysis in this chapter provides a comprehensive picture of the technological system from the extraction of ore at the rock face through its treatment to the production of the finished gold bullion. In the process I concentrate my analysis on the process of technical innovation— from the goals and motivations of management to implementation and changing labor structures in the workplace. Clearly, the major goal of management is to abolish labor, while the principal goal of labor is to preserve jobs in the face of technical innovation. As we shall see, the two goals are rarely in conflict and generally do not divide management and labor.

Although the discussion sweeps across a century and a quarter, several distinct periods emerge as the focus of the analysis: the implantation of the system in the mid-nineteenth century, the construction of the modern industrial operation under Chalmers's guidance beginning in the 1890s, and the era of technical stagnation after 1940. The industrial revolution forged by George Chalmers in this small Brazilian community in the early twentieth century stands out as the key conjuncture in social and technical change as the system reaches full maturity, having eclipsed the system of the nineteenth century but standing on the verge of a new stage of much-needed modernization. As a consequence, the period 1890–1940 serves as the baseline for the analysis in the following pages.

The World Gold-Mining Industry

The evolution of the world mining industry shapes the major structural features of the technological system at Morro Velho. The German, Mexican, and Cornish mining traditions dominate world mining until the late nineteenth century when the rise of powerful mining industries in North America and South Africa eclipse the older industries. The changing nature of mining in Morro Velho re-flects this larger shift in the world mining industry. The Germans had risen to the forefront of European mining in the Renaissance with the discovery of silver in Saxony. German miners, and particu-larly metallurgists, played a key role in the rise of mining indus-tries in England and Spanish America. The Tudor monarchs brought German miners to England in the sixteenth century to develop cop-per and tin deposits in Cornwall, and the Spanish Hapsburgs called upon German experts in the initial stages of the monumental silver strikes in Mexico and Peru. The Cornish had become the pioneers in deep-shaft mining by the nineteenth century, and the Mexicans turned the ancient amalgamating techniques of Europe into an in-dustrial process. By the early nineteenth century the Mexican amal-gamation process, German metallurgical chemistry, and Cornish shaft-mining techniques formed the foundations of modern precious metals mining.[5]

Although the eighteenth-century gold rush had made Brazil the world's leading producer of gold bullion, technical stagnation and de-clining alluvial reserves led to a drastic drop in production as Russia emerged in the late eighteenth century as the world's leading pro-ducer (see table 4). Brazil returned to the ranks of the major producers after the gold-mining boomlet of the 1820s and 1830s, particularly as the Morro Velho began to consolidate and expand its operations. Russian gold production declined at the beginning of the nineteenth century, only to rise again by 1850 when gold production in Califor-nia quickly dwarfed that of other areas of the world. After 1849 the great gold rushes in California, Australia, Alaska, Canada, and South Africa would transform the gold-mining industry and emphasize the fragility of the Brazilian industry. The emergence of the fragile Bra-zilian gold-mining industry as one of the two major producers in the first half of the nineteenth century reflects the poverty of the indus-try prior to the great rushes. Brazil reemerged as a major producer with advanced methods and the deepest mines in the world for two simple reasons: British capital and Cornish expertise.

The Cornish dominated British mining, and the British domi-nated mining in nineteenth-century Brazil. British mining compa-nies brought to Brazil the capital needed to industrialize mining, a profound knowledge of deep-shaft mining, milling operations, and managerial methods. Two centuries of experience in the lodes of Cornwall, a deep appreciation of German technical expertise in ore

Table 4 World Gold Production, Percent by Regions, 1800–1980 (selected years)

	1800	1850	1865	1904	1980
South Africa	—	—	—	22.5	55.2
Canada	—	—	2.5	4.7	4.1
United States	—	61.1	37.5	24.3	2.5
Russia/USSR	2.7	19.0	12.4	6.5	21.1
Brazil	18.5				2.9
Colombia	23.4	9.9	6.1	6.6	1.4
Mexico	8.0				.5
Rest of Latin America	21.2				2.5
Australia	—	—	35.3	25.1	1.4
Europe	6.5	1.6	1.0	1.4	.7
Others	19.7	8.4	5.2	8.9	7.7
Totals	100.0	100.0	100.0	100.0	100.0

Sources: J. Arthur Phillips, *The Mining and Metallurgy of Gold and Silver* (London: E. and F. N. Spon, 1867), p. 127; J. H. Curle, *The Gold Mines of the World*, 3rd. ed. (London: George Routledge, 1905), pp. 1–3; Marcos A. C. Maron and Alberto Rogério B. da Silva, *Perfil analítico do ouro* (Brasília: Ministério das Minas e Energia, Departamento Nacional da Produção Mineral, 1984), p. 71.
Note: Dashes (—) indicate negligible production.

processing, and a willingness to adapt the amalgamation process to local circumstances form the essence of the British contribution to Brazilian mining in the nineteenth century. The British possessed the capital and the know-how. The gold deposits of Minas Gerais provided them with a focus for their entrepreneurial talents.

Gold-mining technology at Morro Velho experienced revolutionary changes in the last quarter of the nineteenth century with the emergence of science-based technology and the enormous expansion of gold mining around the world. The Second Industrial Revolution witnessed the merger of science and technology, while the gold rushes in California, Australia, Alaska, Canada, and South Africa transformed the dimensions of the industry. Prior to the great gold rushes mining had been dominated by a long empirical tradition. As the geological and chemical sciences matured at the end of the nineteenth century mining absorbed the new scientific ideas, and a new science-based technology began to take shape. The rise to dominance of the mining engineer epitomizes the emergence of this new technological wave.[6] By the end of the nineteenth century the major European powers and the United States had begun to produce a sizable body of scientifically trained mining engineers who were taking control of the industry. The era of the prospector, Cornish captain, and amalgamating master had passed. The economical exploitation of the deep lodes required capital and know-how beyond the reach of the individual prospector or the practical miner. Henceforth, the great bulk of gold mining would be controlled by corporations, and grounded on scientific principles. The growing number of geologists and mining engineers in the late nineteenth century began to transform mining with the application of their knowledge to the practical problems of the industry.

Historically, the discovery of gold in South Africa has proven the most significant of the late nineteenth-century finds. Since the discovery of gold in the Transvaal (Witwatersrand) in the 1880s, South Africa has completely dominated world gold production, accounting for well over half the production of the noncommunist world in the past two decades, and more than 40 percent of the gold ever produced.[7] With the unprecedented size and concentration of its gold mines, South Africa became a hothouse for research and development, and modern gold mining entered into a new scientific and technological era.

As any mining engineer knows, however, scientific principles and technology must be adapted to the vagaries of local conditions. The development of deep mines will vary from the Transvaal to South Dakota depending on the specific problems faced by miners in those areas. This holds true for the development of mining at Morro Velho. A number of crucial local factors guided the development of the Morro Velho mine. First, with few and sporadic exceptions the Morro Velho has been the only deep-shaft mine in Brazil and has rarely been able to count on the expertise and experiences of a local community of miners and mining entrepreneurs. Unlike the Transvaal, for example, where a large and experienced community of miners and mining professionals interact, the staff of the St. John d'el Rey sits isolated and out of close, personal contact with other mining professionals. Second, this isolation also means that the Morro Velho does not have a large and experienced mining force in the region on which it might draw. The St. John throughout its history found that it had constantly to train new deep-shaft miners, unlike the South Africans who could and do draw on a large population that has experience in the dozens of mines in the Transvaal and Orange Free State.[8]

The gold rushes of the late nineteenth century and the boom of the mining industry spurred technical innovation producing a revolution within the industry. Between 1870 and 1930 the gold-mining industry experienced its own "industrial revolution" moving into an age dominated by corporate mining. The experience of Morro Velho and the people of Nova Lima offers a microcosm of the changes that transformed mining during these six decades. This technological revolution had three dimensions: mechanical, chemical-metallurgical, and managerial. From a mechanical standpoint mining progressed in six fundamental areas. First, in the 1860s and 1870s dynamite replaced black powder in blasting. Second, hand boring gave way to machine drilling. Third, the use of cages in hoisting men and ore came into widespread use. Fourth, at the end of the nineteenth century electricity began to supplant steam engines and waterwheels as the major source of power in mining operations. Fifth, California stamping machinery became generally standard worldwide in the last half of the century, and in the first decades of this century stamp mills gave way to ball milling. Finally, mechanical ventilation became widespread as mines reached ever deeper levels, and in the early twentieth century air cooling (pioneered at Morro Velho) came into use.

The greatest single innovation came in metallurgical chemistry where the cyanide process revolutionized ore processing and transformed the entire industry. The patenting of the cyanide process in 1887 and its development in South Africa produced a boom in older, worked-out mining areas where previously uneconomical ore could now be processed profitably. It made possible the exploitation of the immense reserves of South Africa.[9] To a lesser degree the development of two other processes (flotation and chlorination) also replaced the amalgamation process that had dominated gold mining since the sixteenth century. Recovery rates rose from 50 to 60 percent with the amalgamation process to 90 percent and higher with cyanidation.[10]

From a managerial perspective the technological revolution in gold mining marks the end of the era of the individual prospector. The legendary prospector with his burro on the American desert gave way to the faceless, impersonal corporation. Mining became an enterprise requiring large amounts of capital and expertise, something in the reach of the very rich or the corporate shareholders. The enormous industrial plants of the Comstock, the Homestake, and the Transvaal relegated the placer mining of the "forty-niners" and the lone prospector to a secondary role in the industry.[11] At Morro Velho this process had already begun in the 1830s, with Brazil having experienced its own gold rush a century earlier. The process reached its peak under George Chalmers as the company's operations mushroomed and the capital stock multiplied.

One sweeping, secular trend vividly emerges from this analysis of the evolution of the technological system at Morro Velho: the gradual abolition of labor by machines. The mechanization of the system replaced and reorganized labor while transforming the nature and structure of the workplace. This does not mean, however, that the demand for labor diminished. On the contrary, it rose. For as these innovations took hold and raised productivity they also allowed the St. John to expand the scope of its operations, thereby increasing the demand for labor. Paradoxically, the technological revolution at Morro Velho created a labor shortage rather than a labor surplus.

In a sense, technical innovations were the engine of local growth. They allowed the company to continue to grow and expand and to surmount the obstacles presented by nature and society. Without technical innovation the mine would have closed down long ago in the face of low-grade ore, hard rock, increasing temperatures, increased rock pressure, or low productivity. Technical innovation kept the mine productive, the company profitable, and the community growing. Through its control of the means of production the St. John not only shaped the development of the technological system, but the growth of the community as well. Throughout most of its history the company managed to control technical matters and the geology of the lode remained favorable while the labor factor continually eluded company control. Technical innovation and favorable geology allowed the St. John to meet the challenges of operations until the 1930s when the century-long labor shortage ended and workers became militant. The most difficult of the three components to control, labor ultimately became the breaking point within the technological system called the St. John d'el Rey Mining Company, Limited.

The Morro Velho Underground

Geology and Technology

The geological structure of the Morro Velho lode shaped the development of the mine. The lode is essentially a thin ribbon that lies between folds of clay-like schist ("country rock" or "killas" as the Cornish called it). Millions of years ago a mineralizing solution under great pressure flowed into the rock that forms the ribbon-like channelway between the layers of schist. The mineralizing solution replaced the rock with quartz carbonates and sulphides, the distinguishing features of the Morro Velho lode. This schist has been squeezed and folded over millenia giving it the unique shape and structure that characterize it today. This metamorphism left the channelway at a pitch of forty-five degrees in the upper levels flattening to seventeen degrees about two thousand meters below the present surface. As the pitch flattened, powerful pressures crumpled and folded the lower levels of the lode leaving it contorted and less uniform than the upper levels.[12]

The channelway that we now call the Morro Velho lode stands out with its incredible depth and consistently uniform gold content. Few lodes in the history of mining rival the Morro Velho's length along the pitch, and even fewer can match the consistency of its ore to such depths. The depth of the lode allowed the St. John to pursue mining to record depths for the mining world in the first four decades of this century. The uniformity of the gold assay both blessed and cursed the mine. On the one hand, it has allowed the mine to continue operating for well over two hundred years. On the other, the uniform scattering of gold particles throughout the ore forces the company to extract enormous quantities of mineral, thereby increasing tonnages milled and operating costs. A mine with more highly concentrated gold content would allow the extraction of less ore while maintaining high assay. This uniformity and persistence of gold is the basis of both the mine's longevity and Chalmers's scheme to make the Morro Velho a high-output operation.[13]

The uniform structure and pitch of the lode enabled the company to develop the mine to unprecedented depths. Chalmers, however, opened up the mine at a time when little was known about deep mining, and the cautious scheme he followed shaped the fortunes of

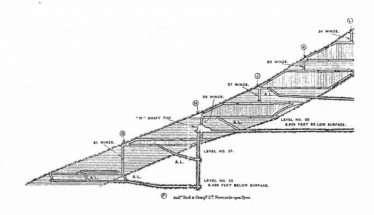

Figure 8   Morro Velho Mine, circa 1940

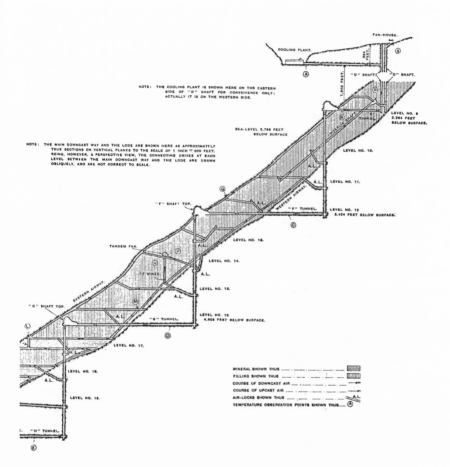

the St. John d'el Rey. Lack of knowledge about deep lodes and financial prudence compelled Chalmers to open up the lode with a series of shafts and tunnels in a stairstep fashion (see figure 8). After the original "C" and "D" shafts cut the lode at what were then incredible depths, Chalmers opened up the lode simultaneously on several horizons. As the lower horizons proved fruitful, Chalmers drove deeper shafts and tested lower, exploratory horizons while working the upper horizons. In retrospect, one deep shaft to the bottom of the mine would have been more efficient and would have been the method of attack today, but Chalmers in the 1890s had no way of knowing if the lode could be expected to continue to such depths.[14]

The availability of power further influenced the development of the mine and surface works. Local geographical conditions determined the St. John's source of power. Lack of coal and the expense of burning wood for steam power ruled out the use of steam engines. The abundance of water made possible the hydraulic and hydroelectric power that enabled the mine to exist and expand. The high volume of water also provided the reduction department with a vital and cheap source of industrial solvent. By the 1930s the St. John used about two million gallons of water per day. As a consequence, the company carefully monitored rainfall from year to year. Low rainfall slowed the reduction process and reduced power production. Water became the lifeblood of company operations.

Finally, the particular period in which a mine is developed also plays a key role in its evolution. Chalmers's mine had to pioneer work in deep-shaft drilling and development precisely because it was opened up in the early 1890s prior to the large-scale exploitation of the later deep-shaft mines of South Africa. On the other hand, over half a century of experience working the lode at its upper levels also provided the St. John with important advantages that a company just arriving on the scene would not normally enjoy. Chalmers could build his mill and mine knowing full well the properties of the ore and, to some extent, the structure of the lode.

Extracting the Ore

The heart of company operations and the single largest segment of the work force labored in the mine underground. The actions in-

Table 5 Total Labor Force by Departments, 1871–1980 (selected years)

Year	Mine	Reduction	Shops	Estate	Others	Total
1871	463	397	269	—	575	1,704
1880	526	251	212	—	339	1,327
1892	148	55	252	—	90	545
1904	813	470	264	284	162	1,993
1908	834	420	255	n/a	n/a	2,597
1917	848	504	355	385	1,130	3,222
1924	829	559	557	373	904	3,173
1939	2,044	888	692	847	3,692	8,163
1943	3,074	893	622	772	2,323	7,684
1950	2,107	n/a	n/a	n/a	n/a	5,134
1960	2,397	388	579	502	736	4,602
1980	2,138	141	511	86	635	3,511

Sources: AR and miscellaneous reports, SJNL.
Note: n/a means figures not available.
—estate department not yet in existence.

volved in removing ore from the earth determined the success or failure of the company more than any other single factor. Without the ore nothing else was possible. About one-third of the company labor force worked underground (see table 5). Workers normally entered the mine in eight-hour shifts at six in the morning, two in the afternoon, and ten at night.[15] They entered the mine via the main adit and walked the three hundred meters to the "D" shaft to be lowered into the works. Timekeepers at the shaft area carefully noted arrivals and departures for pay purposes. The constant need to man machinery and the depth of the mine raised certain problems in changing shifts. Enginemen, cagemen, and trafficmen who handled the hauling machinery received extra pay to go down early to replace their counterparts. Those working in the stopes also went down early to replace the previous shift and were paid extra for their travel time.[16] The depth of the mine by the 1920s had made the traveling time between surface and stopes in the lower levels of the mine nearly one hour.

Dating back to the earliest days at Morro Velho the company had decreed Sunday a day of rest (as it was in British mines).[17] For maintenance purposes a skeleton crew manned pumping machinery and kept an eye on power machinery. In addition, the company found itself compelled to observe Brazilian holidays. In the nineteenth century the free labor force underground invariably refused to show up for work on religious holidays (which were frequent). On holidays it was not uncommon for the company to be left without a single free Brazilian laborer.[18] The captive labor force on these days proved invaluable in keeping up production. In the twentieth century the government standardized the number of official civil and religious holidays diminishing the number somewhat. Nevertheless, the total number of full working days normally ran to around 25 to 26 per month through the 1950s. This meant that the company could only count on some 300 to 310 full working days per calendar year.[19]

The key figure underground was the borer. He began the long extractive process that was to end with the final casting of the gold bullion. Borers in teams of twos and threes handled the punishing job of drilling and blasting holes into the face of the lode. In the nineteenth century miners employed the technique known as "double jacking." That is, one man would hold an iron borer while the other drove it into the rock with an eight-pound sledgehammer. Between blows (up to thirty per minute) the holder adeptly rotated the iron borer for greater effectiveness. From time to time the two would trade places.[20] In the 1870s the St. John began experimenting with power drills driven by compressed air. The drills, however, drained off valuable compressed air from hauling operations. Only four or five could be used during the peak power months of the rainy seasons, and none during the dry season. After 1900 the increased power in the mine brought about the gradual elimination of hand drilling. The company wanted desperately to mechanize the drilling process since two men working a power drill could do the work of ten men hand drilling.[21]

Borers typically made up close to one-third of the underground force. Guided by constant sampling and their nose for paydirt, they held the key to the correct pursuit of the lode, and it was they who determined ultimately whether production rose or fell. In the 1920s the mine generally employed one hundred, three-man teams spread over stoping locations on several horizons. In each team two men handled drilling and a third backed them up providing replacement drill bits. As hand drilling disappeared, the team system continued virtually intact. Two miners operated the compressed air drills while a third provided them with the replacement bits and helped them set up machinery. The teams spent their shift drilling thirty-six-inch holes in the rock face. A normal shift drilled some thirty holes. The drills were heavy and cumbersome, the rock and air hot, and the stopes full of fine dust. The oppressive heat in the mine prevented the company from employing wet drilling which would have cooled the drill bits and cut down on the dust. Combined with the heat, the humidity from wet drilling would have severely hampered miners. Dry drilling produced a fine silica dust that filled the stopes and crippled the lungs of miners with silicosis (white lung).[22] Despite efforts by Chalmers to develop protective masks, the workers refused to wear them due to the heat and discomfort. The borers instead tied kerchiefs over their noses as they still do today. In the heat, miners often stripped down to their shorts and hats. Many went barefoot and the incidence of foot bruises and cuts was high until the company forced everyone to wear a uniform brand of heavy boots in the 1940s.

In the nineteenth century the company issued candles to workers for illumination underground. A miner normally placed the lighted candle in clay and placed the clay base on his hard leather hat or in the rock alongside his work area. After the reopening of the mine in the 1890s Chalmers replaced the old system of oil-fired torches underground with electric lighting in the mainways. Candles, however, continued in use in the more inaccessible areas.[23] Prior to World War I carbide lamps came into use, and by the 1930s the use of battery-powered lamps had become widespread. In the 1950s helmet lamps powered by a battery pack on the belt came into use and, at the same time, hard hats became common. Previously, hard hats had been rare except on supervisory personnel. Miners often wore soft hats, but rarely put up with the uncomfortable hard ones.[24]

At the end of their shift the borers filled two or three holes with dynamite and then blasted the rock. They repeated this process two more times. The drilling and triple blasting would open up the rock to a depth of some two meters.[25] Blasting at the end of shifts insured the least number of men would be on the stopes in positions of danger. Normally the miners would set the dynamite and light the fuses, and then scurry for cover around corners. In the early decades of the nineteenth century the company used blasting powder. Nobel's dynamite came into use in the 1870s, quickly raising productivity.[26] Both the blasting powder and dynamite made the work of men on the stopes exceptionally dangerous. Smoke and nitric acid produced by blasting often caused the miners in the area to suffer from nausea, loss of equilibrium, and fainting. (Miners at Morro Velho describe someone overcome and shaky from inhalation of bad air as *sambado*,

Table 6 Fatalities at Morro Velho Mines, 1904–1950 (selected years)

Year	Fatalities	Per 1,000 Workers	Per 1,000 Workers Underground	Per Million Lbs. of Ore Raised
1904	9	4.52	11.07	.020
1908	11	4.24	13.19	.032
1917	4	1.24	4.72	.009
1924	6	1.89	7.24	.017
1939	12	1.47	5.87	.015
1943	5	0.65	1.63	.006
1950	2	0.39	0.95	.002

Sources: AR and Black Books, sjnl.

in reference to their staggering movements which faintly resemble dancing a samba.) Along with the usual dangers of unexpected rock bursts, the use of explosives complicated the miner's life. A large number of fatalities resulted from blasting accidents—either from blasting at the stopes or from handling explosives (see table 6). At times, charges failed to ignite and the following shift would unknowingly drill into these unexploded charges igniting them. The life of the borer, in short, was the most endangered of all the miners. He worked at the forefront of operations exposed to the dangers of dust, heat, rock bursts, and explosives. All made his life difficult and, often, made it short.[27]

The revolution in mining technology was a mixed blessing and did not produce a clear-cut advance in safety for miners at Morro Velho. New technology eliminated some of the unsafe conditions that produced fatalities in the nineteenth century. Better hauling equipment replaced the dangerous ladders and weak wire ropes that killed many miners in the old mines. The new technology also brought with it new dangers: silicosis from power drilling, the exposed high voltage overhead wires for the trolleys, and chemical pneumonia from blasting materials. Although the fatality rate dropped at Morro Velho in the twentieth century, it failed to show the number of lives shortened by nonfatal accidents, silicosis, and other industrial diseases. Throughout the history of the mine the major cause of accidental deaths was unpredictable "rock bursts." The Chalmers approach to mining the lode eliminated the disastrous rock falls that plagued the mine in the nineteenth century. Smaller, isolated rock bursts could not be eliminated in a mine with the depth of the Morro Velho.

In the twentieth century three-quarters of all fatalities in the mine were from rock bursts. Even Superintendent Wigle, the company's managing director, and a board member were nearly killed by one rock burst while inspecting the mine in 1947.[28]

Comparing fatality rates, particularly for different kinds of mining in various areas of the world, is difficult but instructive. Without a doubt, mining was a dangerous occupation at Morro Velho. By all measures the fatality rate at Morro Velho declined appreciably after the First World War. When compared with other mining regions, the Morro Velho appears to have a good record. The rate of fatalities (per million lbs. raised) in the copper mines of the Upper Michigan peninsula in the second decade of this century (.206) was astronomical when compared with the rate at Morro Velho in the same period (.009). However, the fatality rate per 1,000 workers employed at Morro Velho (4.52 in 1904) was significantly higher than similar rates for the United Kingdom (1.14) and Colorado (2.80). The diamond mines of South Africa did have a higher rate (6 to 7) at roughly the same time (1890s). The Morro Velho rate, however, dropped quickly soon after. Finally, the fatality rate per 1,000 employed in South Africa in the 1960s (1.20) was far higher than Morro Velho's rate in the 1940s and 1950s. Although safety could have been improved (and lives saved) at Morro Velho, its record appears to compare favorably within the industry and improves over the decades.[29] Regardless of the impersonal statistics, Brazilian and foreign workers alike understandably shied away from the dangers of work underground, making labor recruitment difficult for the St. John d'el Rey.

In the mid-nineteenth century the borers usually worked along the same systems as their Cornish counterparts in England. Work was let out by one of three methods: contract, tribute, or wages. Under the contract system a group of miners would agree to work a particular section of a mine and to drive a fixed amount in an allotted period. Tribute miners would agree to drive for a fixed amount per foot depending on the estimated value of the ore. Both systems encouraged the miner to increase productivity, which accounts for the company's efforts to push these two systems over the fixed daily wage. Under tribute work the more feet driven, the higher the amount earned. Under contract, a certain productivity was assured, and the miners could either pace their work or work hard early on to be able to ease off later. This system also normally required the miners to purchase their own blasting implements (fuses, dynamite, caps) and candles from the company. The materials were then debited from the miner's account, and the setting of contracts required the miner to keep these costs in mind. From the point of view of the company this also forced conservation of materials.[30]

By the turn of the century the contract system and such incentive labor had become optional or relegated to borers on development workings. Borers on normal stopes received regular daily wages. The company provided blasting materials and candles at no cost. Candle consumption became a key concern of the management and Chalmers ordered a cutback in distribution in 1903 which prompted a bitter strike by miners, spearheaded by Spaniards. The company was forced to quit charging for "extra" candles, but consumption did fall.[31] For the hardworking and ambitious miner, the contract system could often provide significant extra income. In the 1950s when productivity became a central issue of management, efforts were made to reinstitute contract labor practices and productivity bonuses, but the miners did not respond to the dangled carrot.[32]

After blasting, the borers left for the surface and a crew of carmen and trammers took over. These workers broke down the newly blasted ore and loaded it into one-and-one-quarter-ton (20 cubic feet) capacity cars. This backbreaking labor required the carmen to break down the ore into manageable size with sledgehammers, and then shovel it into the cars whose top edge was nearly four feet off the ground. Trammers then pushed the cars along rails from the stopes to the winzes, or winches, which raised the ore to the mainways. The rails in the ever-changing stopes were necessarily temporary, and therefore rough and difficult. At the mainways the rails were more permanent and the tramming by hand more easily accomplished. The work of loading and tramming took up nearly one-third of the underground labor force and was the least mechanized aspect of operations in the mine. The company attempted to utilize mechanical scrapers and loaders at various times but the devices have always proved too unwieldy to be efficient on the stopes. The ever-changing nature of the rails running between the stopes and winzes prevented any mechanization of the tramming process. One car loaded with ore required two men to push it, and often two teams traded off in the trip from stopes to mainways.[33]

The Chalmers system of working the horizons involved cutting a drift (horizon or level) from the shafts into the lode and extending across its entire length. Workers then sunk winzes into the new horizon from the horizon some three hundred feet above. The two vertical winzes carried ore up to the horizons above, to be carried to the surface, and lowered filling down to the stopes. This procedure fully used the mine cars which arrived at the worked-out stope area with filling to be dumped. Miners loaded mineral into the emptied mine cars and pushed them to the winzes. When this "cut-and-fill" technique was employed, stoping always proceeded in an overhead manner as the filling formed the floor for subsequent operations. The trammers pushed their loads of ore to the winches exchanging loaded cars of ore for cars with filling as the winzes pulled the ore up to the permanent levels. Compressed air powered the winches until the 1930s when the St. John began a long and gradual process of converting the hauling machinery to electric power to divert more compressed air power to the drills on the stopes.[34]

In the permanent levels hauling was handled by a variety of methods. Mules hauled the cars above Horizon 21 with the exception of 19 where electric hauling machinery pulled the cars. Trolley wire locomotives operating off an overhead cable did the hauling on 20 and 22, and below that trammers pushed cars in the mainways. The mules numbered over a hundred in the 1920s and lived in the mine year-round. They often died from the effects of living underground, from tetanus, and from fatigue. The high temperatures kept them out of levels below 21. Storage battery locomotives gradually replaced the mules in the mine, but the last mule did not retire until 1950. By that time electric trolleys, electric cable hauling, or storage battery locomotives handled all hauling in the permanent levels.[35] (The overhead cable carried 550 volts and occasionally killed the unfortunate miner who accidentally touched the overhead line with hands or equipment.) The main hauling equipment in the mine labored in the shafts. Beginning in the twenties the major shafts were converted from hydraulic to electric-powered winding engines.[36] These engines raised and lowered "cages" loaded with miners and, below the cages, cars of ore or filling.

Labor

Although the long trip from stopes to surface required ten transfers of the ore cars from the deepest levels, it was still much more efficient and smoother than in pre-Chalmers days. In the first decade at Morro Velho the company employed female slaves to carry the ore up ladders from the stopes. Kibbles on carriages moving up inclined planes replaced the women in the 1840s.[37] These planes often proved less than smooth and the chain link (and later wire rope) broke constantly causing expensive repairs, and often the deaths of the miners below.[38] In the late 1870s the company installed modern hydraulic hauling machinery in the "A" and "B" shafts and finally replaced the ladders underground in the 1880s.[39]

The men who manned the hauling equipment were vital to the operations of the mine. These positions required men with at least a minimal knowledge of mechanics and with the skill to operate equipment with pinpoint accuracy. The slightest miscalculation in hauling or in the performance of the machines would mean death for those men being moved or, at a minimum, significant damage from the impact of the falling load. Machinists had to take special care not to overwind the machinery. Lowering or raising correctly was a matter of carefully developed touch. In the shafts the number of levels served by the hauling equipment required a system of bells to warn those at each level when the cages were about to be moved up or down. The machinist had to pay close attention to the bells, which served as his "eyes" for equipment and men he never saw. A sudden and unexpected movement could toss a miner entering or leaving the cage plunging to his death down the deep shafts. Lack of care or skill in winding by the machinist could send the whole cage plunging to the bottom of the shaft.[40]

In addition to those directly involved in the process of removing and transporting the ore underground, a number of miners served in auxiliary positions. A few dozen men did masonry and timbering work and handled mechanical and electrical maintenance. The special conditions of the different areas of the stopes or mainways sometimes required timber or steel supports, and masonry was sometimes used to provide extra support for walls subject to heavy passing traffic. A small maintenance crew from the mechanics and electrical departments monitored the operations of underground machinery and when heavy repairs were necessary they would send equipment to the shops on the surface. Young boys traditionally played a key role in this auxiliary labor force. For nearly a century they worked underground in apprentice-type positions carrying tools, drill bits, water, and messages. Some even operated the electric locomotives. As late as the 1920s nearly one hundred youngsters worked underground. In the 1930s social legislation theoretically eliminated the use of workers under the age of eighteen. Apparently, the company continued to employ minors who were willing to lie about their age.[41]

A small group of workers also manned the underground pumping machinery which worked round the clock to keep the mine safe from flooding. Although a "dry mine" by world standards, the continual accumulation of water from underground springs and seepage into the old workings called for constant pumping. Ironically, water brought to the mine especially for this purpose drove the pumping equipment. Water falling down twelve-inch steel mains from the top of "C" shaft drove the enormous pumping machinery located at the adit level. By means of an ingenious system of connecting rods the machinery on the descending levels pulled the water up from the levels below.[42] Without the round-the-clock pumping the mine would be faced with flooding in the lower levels in a matter of days. Whenever strikes broke out the miners always allowed the personnel in the pumping and electrical departments to continue working to keep the city supplied with power and to prevent the mine from flooding.

A hierarchy coordinated the work of the labor force underground. Chargemen (feitores) supervised the work of a number of crews on the stopes, and in turn, shift bosses supervised groups of chargemen. By the 1920s the shift bosses reported directly to the assistant mine captain (normally one per shift). The assistant mine captains then reported to the mine captain in charge of all underground operations and subordinate only to the superintendent himself. From the very beginning the St. John's management encouraged the best Brazilian (slave and free) laborers to take positions of responsibility as chargemen.[43] With very few exceptions Europeans filled the rest of the upper levels of the hierarchy. Not until the late 1940s and 1950s did this begin to change, and then only slightly as a few Brazilians moved into the upper positions. In the mine only one assistant mine captain was not part of the English community—Janis Karklin, an Estonian who had emigrated to Brazil in the 1920s.[44]

The Brazilians were acutely aware of their exclusion from positions of responsibility, and it fueled the antagonism between the two communities and between management and labor. Regrettably, the British had little faith in the capabilities of the Brazilians. Although the School of Mines in Ouro Preto produced hundreds of engineers beginning in the 1870s, the company preferred not to hire them. It appears that in the 1880s, and once again in the 1930s, the company did hire a Brazilian mining engineer, but in both cases the move was calculated to curry political favor, and both engineers were placed in minor positions outside of the mine.[45] Fairly typical of the management's view of Brazilians was Superintendent Millett's assessment of the Brazilian candidates for assistant medical officer in the 1930s. He confided to the managing director that "none of them gave the appearance of outstanding personality, but this is nothing much to be wondered at when racial characteristics and habits are remembered."[46] This racial and cultural prejudice would hurt the company in the long run. More important, management's reluctance to hire locally trained technicians and to train Brazilians limited the transfer of technological expertise, holding back the nation's development.

The supervisory personnel made sure (among other things) that the company rules and regulations were followed. These rules involved more than proper work habits, they also regulated breaks, meals, and health care. Miners normally took breaks about every two hours, and halfway through their shift they would eat a meal. Prior to the 1930s men would bring their meals down with them and eat sitting on the ground or on makeshift chairs built from scrap timberwork.[47] Beginning in the thirties social legislation forced the company to set aside special eating areas. These areas were normally carved out near the less-dusty mainways and contained heavy tables and warmers for holding food. Water carriers traveled throughout the mine bringing welcome refreshment to the parched miners during working periods. In the local mining vocabulary the snack periods were known by the anglicism "snaps."[48]

The overall process underground then was relatively simple in its essentials. Borers arrived for eight-hour shifts, and they drilled a group of holes for blasting on the stopes. At the end of their shift they filled and blasted a number of the holes. Carmen loaded the blasted ore into standard one-and-one-quarter-ton mine cars, and trammers pushed the loaded cars to the winches and winzes returning to the stopes with cars of filling. The ore then traveled up the shafts and across the horizons working its way up to the main adit where it then exited at the mouth of the mine and the reduction process began.

Aboveground: From Gold Ore
to Gold Bars

The complex interaction of man, machine, and mineral underground continued in the processing of ore on the surface. The work underground determined the amount of ore brought to the surface, but the work of the reduction crew aboveground then became the limiting factor in gold bullion production. If the surface works could not keep up with the advance in the company's ability to mine the ore, production increases underground would be for naught. The continual refining of the reduction process, therefore, had to accompany the streamlining of work underground. After the surface works designed by Chalmers came into full operation at the turn of the century, the underground process became the major focus and greatest single limit on production levels. By the 1930s the efforts to raise ore production had been successful enough to turn the company's attention to raising the capacity and efficiency of the surface works.[49]

The treatment of Morro Velho ore as it passed through the surface works involved a complex and interlocking series of mechanical and chemical processes, ultimately terminating in the casting of pure gold bars.[50] A series of factors shaped the structure of these processes. As with any mining plant the particular composition of the local ore determined the design of the treatment process. Morro Velho ore fits into a category of gold ores characterized by high sulphide and arsenopyritic content.[51] This type of ore requires three types of treatments to extract: free gold particles, gold found in conjunction with sulphides, and gold found in conjunction with arsenopyrites. These three considerations determined the overall structure of the treatment process.

The ultimate goal of any treatment process is 100 percent recovery, something never achieved in practice. Approximately 50 to 60 percent of the gold content of the Morro Velho ore could be obtained through purely mechanical processes. Historically, the other 40 to 50 percent (that found in association with sulphides and arsenopyrites) provided the great technological challenge. Prior to the 1890s the company constantly tried various chemical processes to raise the recovery rate, but with little success. The major chemical treatment prior to the 1890s was amalgamation, a process which had been in use in various forms for centuries. To the chagrin of the St. John d'el

Rey, amalgamation did not prove as effective on the Morro Velho ore as it had on ores in other areas of the world. Beginning in the 1890s, however, the recovery rate began to rise dramatically with the introduction of the recently patented cyanide process which proved to be an effective means of recovering gold in sulphide ores. The more refractory arsenopyrites had to be roasted and then treated. By 1930 the surface works combined mechanical, cyanide, and roasting processes to achieve over 90 percent recovery. The remaining 10 percent proved economically unfeasible to treat, and the gold-bearing tailings were stored in special areas to await the day when their treatment would be economically viable.[52] The reduction works, then, consisted of a series of processes which, in combination, produced a high recovery rate at an economically viable level.

In the old mine the ore had been taken from the mouth of the mine to the reduction works in ore cars on crude rails. In the Chalmers mine an endless chain hauled the ore cars from the adit mouth to the reduction works. Chalmers built the reduction works on the hill overlooking the adit and the valley to harness the force of gravity for the reduction process. As the mineral went through the various steps in the process, gravity and water carried it along. First, however, the ore cars had to be lifted up a seventeen-degree incline and across the Cardoso stream directly in front of the adit to reach the reduction works. The endless chain pulled the one-and-one-quarter-ton cars up in a continuous series (seven going up, seven going down simultaneously). At the top of the incline workers detached the loaded cars, weighed and tipped them, and reattached the emptied cars to be sent back down the incline. The reduction crew weighed the cars when full and then empty to ascertain the exact weight of the discharged ore.[53]

The tipped cars discharged the ore onto manganese steel bars set five inches apart. These bars let the smaller pieces pass and then delivered oversized fragments into a rock breaker which crushed the ore to five-inch size.[54] The two rock streams then rejoined and passed through more crushing to reduce the fragments to two-inch size. The reduced pieces of ore passed onto a twenty-five-foot diameter table revolving at 1.25 feet per second where women picked out the waste rock, which amounted to some 4 to 5 percent of the material. By the 1930s these women represented the last vestige of female labor in the industrial labor force. Originally, female slaves had carried ore out of the mine in baskets, but this work had been mechanized with the introduction of the inclined hauling planes in the 1840s and 1850s. The endless hauling chain mechanized hand tramming which in the nineteenth century had been handled by both sexes taking the ore from the mine entrance to the reduction works.

The nineteenth-century reduction works had also begun the crushing process with large "jawbreaker" machines to break down the large rocks. The secondary crushing, however, had been handled by women, and not by mechanical crushers. Spalling (the breaking down of ore) was handled exclusively by women, as was the case in British mines. Armed with four-pound hammers, women passed their shifts endlessly reducing the ore into fragments just as the modern crushing machinery did in minutes. The move from spalling to mechanization raised productivity dramatically. In 1867, for example, the spalling force received and reduced 107,087 tons of ore from the mine. Estimating 310 working days for (an average of) 154 women spallers, they each reduced approximately 2.2 tons of ore per day. In 1930 the machinery at the Morro Velho mill crushed about 530 tons per day as compared to the 340 tons for the 154-woman force in 1867.[55] The dozens of women in the spalling area formed a majority of the reduction work force and a significant number of the total mine labor force. In 1878 the reduction department employed 349 people (24.1 percent of the total labor force), 240 of whom were women. They made up 68.8 percent of the reduction force and 17 percent of the total labor force. By 1924 the department employed 559 people (17.6 percent of the total labor force)—only 132 of whom were women. Females had dropped to 23.6 percent of the reduction force and scarcely 4 percent of the total labor force.[56] The machinery of the Chalmers mine eliminated this female hand labor. Social legislation in the 1940s made it difficult to continue using women for industrial work. The company then mechanized picking-table operations, removing the last women from the industrial process.[57]

The milling process changed more in style than in structure in the first century of British operations at Morro Velho. Basically, the process involved the reduction of the ore fragments into a fine dust which, combined with water, formed a dark, gray, muddy pulp. A vertical bucket elevator lifted the crushed ore fragments from the picking table and deposited the broken ore into a special bin car. This electrically driven car ran on rails along the entire length of the stamps and could deliver its load at any point along the line of stamps. In the nineteenth century wooden stamps powered by overshot waterwheels formed the heart of the milling process. The 135 stamps were grouped in six series and scattered over the uneven hillsides behind the Casa Grande. Part of the beauty and efficiency of the Chalmers mine was the construction of an integrated stamping mill. The Chalmers reduction works eventually contained 140 California stamps set in paired boxes of five stamps each. Operating much like the camshaft and pistons of an automobile a 330-horsepower electric motor powered the stamps via a main-line shaft in front of the batteries. A separate clutch pulley connected to the main line drove each set of ten stamps. The main cam on each battery rotated, alternating the blows of the individual stamps. The din of the California stamps sounded six days a week for more than half a century. On Sundays an eerie silence descended on the town when the mill shut down.[58]

Chalmers built the batteries and stamps of hard Oregon pine (despite the availability of fine hard woods in Minas). The iron stamp heads varied in weight from 850 to 1,000 pounds, and normally dropped ninety-four to ninety-five times per minute. These heads dropped onto cast-iron dies sitting in cast-iron coffers. The electric bin car moved along the platform to the rear and above the stamps discharging mineral into the coffers at regular intervals and the stamps crushed the ore into a fine dust. As water entered the coffers from the company's water system, the fine dust mixed with it forming a pulp which passed through the front of the coffers. This pulp passed through mesh screens containing fifty to sixty holes per square inch to insure a very fine mixture. In the early 1930s the mill averaged about five tons of mineral per stamp head per twenty-four hours.[59] This compares with about two tons per head per day in the nineteenth century. The Chalmers mill allowed for handling larger quantities of mineral more efficiently and consolidated in a single area.

The concentration process was the first of three methods for removing the bulk of the gold in the Morro Velho ore. This purely mechanical procedure removed gold by taking advantage of its high density. In some ways it may be seen as a highly complex version of the panning process of the prospector. As with milling, the process changes more in style than in principle in the nineteenth and twentieth centuries. After the pulp passed through the fine mesh grates, it passed onto a complex series of tables called "strakes." In the nineteenth century these strakes were covered with oilcloth and watery pulp passed over them and eventually onto woolly skins. Chalmers covered the strakes with cotton duck and gave them a more sophisticated design. In both cases the vibration of the tables as pulp passed over them eventually brought about the separation of free gold particles as the lighter silt (tailings) flowed off the tables.

The amount of labor involved in their operation forms the key difference between earlier and later strakes. Prior to the Chalmers period the strakes required the manual labor of large numbers of workers in direct contact with the emerging gold concentrates. This presented management with the problems of occasional theft and the need to place Englishmen in supervision over the washing of the strakes and skins—a costly and often ineffective procedure.[60] The strakes designed by Chalmers sat below the discharging stamps in a series of descending terraces on the hillside under a single roof. The force of water and gravity moved the pulp down the levels of tables to the final concentration point. Faced with the problem of hand washing and security, Chalmers designed an automatic washer system which eliminated the need for all but two small boys with hoses to handle the three levels of strakes. The concentration process removed approximately 60 percent of the gold content of the ore at a very low cost. Except for the large volume of water consumed by the process the logistics of the automatic, mechanically operated, gravity-induced operation were quite simple and free of high labor costs. The total cost of concentration in the 1930s averaged about 2 to 2½ pence per ton milled—about $.50 for a ton which produced one-third ounce of gold at $35.00 an ounce![61]

With mechanical separation complete, the second major process for removing gold from the ore began. This chemical process was designed to extract the gold content of the ore (approximately 40 percent) found in association with arsenopyrites and sulphides. Since the Middle Ages, and on a large industrial scale since the sixteenth century, amalgamation has been used to remove the gold associated with sulphides. Amalgamation is a simple process involving the mixing of mercury with gold ore. When the gold sulphides come into contact with mercury the affinity of gold for mercury causes the two to combine, separating the former from the sulphides. The resulting alloy is then distilled to remove the mercury and isolate the gold.[62] At Morro Velho the St. John d'el Rey began experimenting with the amalgamation process soon after the purchase of the mine. Throughout the nineteenth century the reduction officers (generally

Germans) attempted to adapt the various forms of amalgamation to the local ore. By 1840 the management had brought in a number of German specialists who tested six different versions of the process before settling on one of them.[63] This process, combined with the mechanical removal of gold on the strakes, served as the twin pillars of the reduction process throughout the nineteenth century. Together these two processes captured approximately 60 to 70 percent of the gold content of the ore.[64]

After the sands or pulp had been removed from below the strakes, funnels discharged the sands into grinding circles of stone called *arrastres* to produce a fine silt. The reduction crew then took the sands in large bowls to amalgamating barrels. The crew added water and mercury, and then mechanically rotated the barrels for twenty-four hours to produce a fine, pasty mixture. At this point the gold and mercury had alloyed forming the amalgam.[65] Workers then poured the paste into "saxes," vibrating boxes that carried off residue sand and water. In the saxes free mercury rose (due to its lighter specific gravity) and the amalgam sank. Every ten to twelve days workers filtered the amalgam through a canvas cone which operated much like a coffee strainer. After straining they kneaded and rolled the amalgam into fifteen- to twenty-four-ounce balls which they squeezed, wrung, and beat in chamois leather until no sign remained of free metal. The balls normally contained about 60 percent mercury and the rest was a mixture of gold and silver. (The constant exposure to mercury must have had severe long-term effects on the health of these employees.)

Workers then placed the puttylike amalgam in covered crucibles with a pipe leading off and "retorted" the mixture. Heating the crucible for six or seven hours condensed the mercury. The condensing mercury evaporated into the pipe flowing into a special container, leaving gold and silver alloy in the crucible. At this point the gold and silver still contained impurities, especially iron and arsenic. To remove these impurities the metal was placed in new crucibles with flux, borax, and bicarbonate of soda, and then placed in an air furnace heated by charcoal.[66] The heat drew off impurities and the gold and silver fused. After about forty-five minutes a worker would take up the crucible with tongs and pour the fluid into lightly greased, cast-iron, oblong molds producing gold bars. At this point a black slag of fused salts which contained the dissolved impurities still covered the gold. A few blows with a hammer knocked off this slag. The company normally cast ingots three times a month, producing fourteen bars per casting. Each bar weighed approximately 1,600 *oitavas* (5,738 grams).[67]

The amalgamation process, however, created special problems for the St. John d'el Rey and the community. The arsenopyrites did not respond to the process, and a large portion (perhaps one-third of the gold content) of the ore escaped. The only way to treat these ores was to calcine, i.e., roast them before the amalgamation process. The company attempted this at various times during the nineteenth century, always with poor results. The major roadblock remained the same—the roasting of the arsenopyrites produced poisonous arsenic fumes. The first time the company tried the process in the 1830s two slaves were overcome by the fumes and died.[68] Consequently, a major portion of the ore went untreated. During the Chalmers years the company tried again building two roasters on the railway line six kilometers from the reduction works. Arsenical sands were shipped to the roasters which could handle eight to ten tons of sand per day. The roasting produced six to seven tons of material, about 1 to 2 percent being pure arsenic. The roasted material was then returned to the mill for retreatment with the normal cyanidation process. The original danger from arsenic fumes continued, alleviated to some extent with the construction of flues hundreds of feet long. Nevertheless, fumes from the roasters completely devastated the surrounding countryside. Landowners in the area complained endlessly about runoff in streams which killed crops and livestock.[69] The men employed at the ovens also suffered from inhalation of the fumes. The gases caused ulcerations on the skin and perforation of the septum. The process, ironically enough, was discontinued in the 1950s, not because of environmental or health dangers, but because the poor market for pure arsenic in Brazil made the roasting process uneconomical![70]

Much to the good fortune of the St. John d'el Rey a new industrial process came into use in the late nineteenth century just as George Chalmers began rebuilding the mine. Patented in 1887, and developed in South Africa in the 1890s, cyanidation quickly replaced amalgamation as the major treatment of gold ores. Like amalgamation, it is a relatively simple chemical process involving the combination of gold and a soluble. In this case gold combines with potassium or sodium cyanide. Precipitation or electrolysis then separates cyanide from the gold.[71] Chalmers turned to the cyanide process in the late 1890s and designed experimental equipment to adapt the process to the treatment of Morro Velho ore. By the 1920s this process had been perfected and along with the automatic strakes it formed one of the two major components of the reduction process. Recovery rates rose rapidly from 60 to 70 percent with the amalgamation process to over 90 percent with the new process. Cyanidation required a finely ground sand so Chalmers adjusted the stamps to achieve the finest possible pulp, and he introduced the newly developed tube-milling process. (Basically, tube mills are revolving barrels that grind the already-reduced ore.)[72] The tube mills discharged on to more strakes that again separated out fine particles and then discharged the pulp into steel-plated vats where the sands settled. These settlers filled up in about twenty-eight hours, and then revolving paddles (mullers) stirred the sands to a thick pulp before discharging it into more steel vats holding approximately forty tons of sand and twelve to fourteen tons of water. Revolving paddles again stirred the mixture and sodium cyanide was then added to the solution and agitated for twelve hours, at which point the solution reached equilibrium and was run through filters to prepare for precipitation.[73]

The cyanide solution flowed into a series of boxes where the gold separated from the cyanide and combined with zinc plates. These boxes handled up to five hundred tons of solution per day and were cleaned in rotating intervals of four to twenty weeks. When removed, the zinc was treated with acid to isolate the gold. The use of electrolysis gave way in the 1920s to the chlorination process. By passing chlorine gas through melted bullion twice, the process produced 996 to 997 fine gold. Together with the gold concentrates from the mill, the zinc box "slimes" then went to the melting house for the final step in the reduction process. Workers melted down the free gold from the mill and the zinc box slimes with a highly oxidized flux in crucibles.[74]

Every two months the reduction officer, in the presence of the superintendent, removed the gold bars from the company's safe, weighed them, and then bolted the bars in small, wooden boxes each containing three bars and stamped with the company seal.[75] Throughout the nineteenth century the company sent its gold bars to Rio de Janeiro for sale or, more often, for shipment to London. Prior to the construction of the Central do Brasil a mule troop carried the gold every two months to Rio de Janeiro. With the arrival of the railroad to Minas Gerais in the late nineteenth century the troop escorted the bars as far as the railway station at Honório Bicalho. After 1913 the bullion moved to the Central on the company railway and from there to Rio de Janeiro. Amazingly, there is no record of any attempt to rob the troop or train in the entire history of the company. Beginning in the First World War the company sold its bullion to the Brazilian government. This move forced the St. John to begin refining its own gold instead of having it refined in London.[76] In the late 1940s the company began to air freight the gold to the mint in Rio de Janeiro. Today the gold sells mainly on the open market in Rio and São Paulo.[77]

Mechanization and Labor

Labor formed the most expensive component of operations within the technological system at Morro Velho. Throughout the entire history of the company, labor costs accounted for more than half of company expenses and sometimes approached two-thirds of the budget.[78] The cost of labor, and more importantly, the inability to attract sufficient labor, drove the company to mechanize. In the 1860s the chairman of the board wrote the superintendent stating management's concern over the labor issue. "In the present state of your labour market, economy of manual labor and the substitution of machinery, in every practicable form, is of the most vital importance."[79] The labor situation did not improve in the last half of the century and worsened during the First World War, prompting Chalmers to remark that "the only effective way of meeting the inevitable shortage [of labor] will be by the replacement of hand labour as much as possible by machine work."[80] Mechanization, however, never reduced the need for labor so much as it freed the replaced labor for use elsewhere in operations. It did not reduce levels of skills nor subdivide workers' tasks.[81] Company management saw this very clearly. A. G. N. Chalmers remarked in the 1920s that "the introduction of labour saving devices must be looked on more as a means of preventing the mine force increasing as we proceed into depth, rather than as a means of reducing the force necessary to operate it."[82] Machines replaced labor but the lack of a surplus labor force until the 1930s kept the machines from solving the labor shortage.

The greatest degree of mechanization took place in the reduction process rather than underground. From the 1870s until the 1970s manual labor gave way to increasing mechanization, and female labor virtually disappeared from the scene. In the late 1870s the reduction department accounted for nearly one-quarter of the entire labor force, with females accounting for a sizable two-thirds of the department's labor force. Women were employed in nearly every phase of the process. They helped tram the ore from the mine entrance to the spalling floor where a group of women and girls broke down the ore into sizes suitable for stamping. They carried the sand from the strakes to the amalgamation house, and kept watch over the stamps keeping the coffers unclogged. Women, in essence, carried the burden of handling and treating the ore up to the process of smelting and refining. Men occupied the positions of responsibility, however, and handled the technical tasks.

Over the next century mechanization eliminated all the tasks handled by women. The critical period of transition took place with the construction of the new mine. The new reduction works vastly reduced the role of women in every aspect of the process. Crushing machinery and jawbreakers replaced women spallers and their mallets. The endless chain hauling eliminated the need for hand tramming from mine to surface works. The new stamps required less maintenance, and men and boys took charge of cleaning them. The integration of the works and the clever use of water, gravity, and piping eliminated the need for the hauling of sands between strakes and amalgamation. By the first decade of the twentieth century the new surface works had come into full operation and the participation of women in the reduction labor force had fallen to 19 percent.[83] The percentage of the labor force in the reduction department had fallen (largely due to mechanization) from one-fourth in the 1870s to one-fifth, and women now made up less than one-fifth of the reduction force as opposed to the two-thirds share in the 1870s. Better design of component parts gave the company greater control over the system. Men and machines within this design pushed women aside and out of the workplace.[84]

Mechanization and innovations in technology saved labor underground as well, but labor in the mine was less susceptible to replacement for a variety of reasons. The first obstacle to mechanization was the importance of the borer and the difficulty of replacing him completely with a machine. Power drilling proved vastly superior to hand drilling, and one machine could do the work of a dozen men, but this meant that the same number of men could now be used to work more areas. The Chalmers mine expanded constantly, and a labor shortage plagued the company. Chalmers never reached the point at which the need for borers was satisfied. Chalmers constantly searched for more men to handle more machines. In a smaller, or contracting, operation the mechanization might have put people out of jobs. At Morro Velho it merely provided slight relief for the company during a long-term labor shortage.

Another hindrance to mechanization underground was the difficulty of adapting machines to the idiosyncracies of the stopes. How could the company use machines for loading and shoveling when the conditions for moving and setting up the machines were so difficult and the stopes so irregular? The company constantly tried out new machinery for handling the labor-intensive tasks of cleaning and shoveling but always ran into the problem of adapting machinery to the shifting conditions of the stopes.[85] The bulk of the underground force consisted of borers, carmen, and trammers, and the expanding need for the first, along with the difficulty of replacing the last two, made mechanization underground unlikely. As a result, the major innovations underground (dynamite, power drilling, electric lighting, power hoisting) all increased production per man but did little to diminish the size of the labor force.

Instead of diminishing with technical innovation, the size and share of the mine department force increased in the last century. Prior to World War II this occurred due to the needs of an ever-expanding mine. After the war the size of the force stabilized as its share increased. This took place as other sectors of the labor force decreased (see table 5). In the 1870s the mine department accounted for about 40 percent of the total labor force. This figure dropped with the collapse of the mine and then rose again as the new mine opened out. By 1910 the share had returned to about 35 percent. The labor shortage of the 1920s halted the rising percentage, but the booming labor market of the 1930s pushed the percentage up again. At the beginning of World War II the company had reached an all-time high in number of employees (8,163), and the mine department reached a full 50 percent of the total labor force. Over the next four decades the size of the mine department gradually dropped to around two thousand men, yet, proportionally, its share rose to more than 68 percent of the total labor force.

The sectors of the company labor force that did diminish had little to do with the actual processes of mining and milling. These sectors included the estate, shops, electrical, survey and drawing, hospital, store, cashier, and transport departments. In the 1870s these auxiliary departments had employed roughly one-third of the company labor force. By 1908 this had risen to one-half. A number of these departments changed little in size and share during the century following 1870. The company hospital never exceeded 1 percent of the total labor force, employing two to three dozen people throughout the last one hundred years. The cashiers' office remained basically a handful of clerks, and the survey and drawing office (created by Chalmers) generally employed a few dozen draftsmen and engineers.

The two major employers outside of the reduction and mine departments were always shops and estate. The shops originally handled mechanical work and skilled trade labor such as carpentry, molding, masonry, metalwork, and various types of construction. The company relied on the shops to build and repair machinery. Although most heavy machinery had to be imported, the company could not rely on overseas suppliers for replacement parts and repair work. A damaged generator or engine could cripple production, and the St. John could not wait months for replacements. As a result, the company (especially under Chalmers) developed a policy of self-reliance that expanded the shops beyond that which would be found in a European or South African mine. Chalmers prided himself on a shops department that built and maintained many important pieces of equipment at the mine. Chalmers even envisioned producing steel at Morro Velho to avoid importing valuable parts.

By World War I the duties of the shops department had greatly expanded beyond normal maintenance tasks. Besides the usual tasks the department had built and run its own brickyard to supply masonry materials for the mine and company buildings. The enormous water system that supplied the mine and mill had to be maintained and fell under the domain of the shops. With the rise in the use of electricity and the construction of generating plants the department took on new engineering duties. As these plants increased and became more important, Chalmers separated the electrical operations into a new department that built and maintained the ever-growing number of plants and guided the shops when repair work was needed.

The estate department handled a wide variety of functions and eventually accounted for one-tenth of the entire labor force. The estate department grew out of the old stores department. Stores handled purchasing, operation of the company farms, and housing. As the size of company real estate holdings increased at the turn of the century, the stores department was relegated to handling supplies and purchasing. The new estate department then took on the interesting mix of activities related to the management of real estate. The company farms produced milk, beef, pork, and cereals to provide employees (mainly the British) with subsidized foodstuffs. The company lands had to be inspected regularly and boundary markers checked. Establishing clear title to land in the Brazilian legal system has always been very difficult, as the St. John learned. Squatters and legal claims consumed hundreds of man-hours in and out of court, and litigation never ceased. A small force of watchmen handled these inspections and also guarded the boundaries of the mining plant. Prior to the creation of the municipal police force in the 1930s, company watchmen, in effect, served as local police.

The real estate holdings of the St. John d'el Rey included more than two thousand houses by the 1940s, and the estate department took charge of building and maintaining these houses. Workers paid rent directly to this department. In a sense the estate department also cleaned up the town. Since almost all the real estate in the community and the major access routes, water supply, power supply, and recreation areas belonged to the company, the estate department maintained and cleaned just about every important building in town. A weak and impoverished city council often turned to the company to handle jobs vital to local affairs such as the construction of roads, bridges, sewers, and schools. In this company town the estate department essentially served as a department of public works.

The St. John also owned and operated a hotel, a bakery, and a store, which the estate department ran. The hotel provided unmarried Englishmen with a home and good food. It served as a club, library, and billiards parlor. The bakery (which operated in the first quarter of the century) provided the English employees with low-cost bread. A number of other projects begun under the department expanded and eventually were separated off under the transport department. Transport ran the electric railway, the company automobile and truck fleet, and the garage. During the heyday of eucalyptus planting, this department took control of these operations. The woodlands and equipment were along the rail line and more easily handled by transport.

The enormous number of auxiliary functions taken on by the St. John d'el Rey reflects its drive toward self-reliance and its efforts to control every aspect of its destiny. This drive for control created a small business conglomerate and enabled the St. John to dominate Nova Lima. Community development and growth had always been inseparably linked to company fortunes. The wide variety of functions that all these operations demanded increased the company payroll far beyond the needs of an ordinary mining enterprise. Functions that had little to do directly with mining and milling weighed heavy on the company ledger. As the St. John expanded in the early part of the century, half the company payroll consisted of employees outside the mine and reduction departments. With the labor shortage underground in the 1920s this percentage rose to 60 percent.

In the 1940s the onset of financial problems and strikes forced the St. John to look closely at the payroll. Company management began a slow process of paring back the fat put on in the expansionist years. With the growth of the world economy and transportation systems the old self-reliance of the isolated mine became less important. Equipment could be purchased quickly and more cheaply than that built on site. Housing became a burden, and a cash shortage compelled the company to begin selling it to tenants. At every turn management closed down and cut back auxiliary enterprises, focusing more of its resources on mining and milling. By the late 1950s auxiliary departments had shrunk to one-quarter of the labor force, and the percentage remained stable to the end of the British era. The old business conglomerate that had seen its heyday in the first four decades of the century had expanded the payroll with secondary functions. The reduction of this sector of the labor force and the elimination of auxiliary operations reflected the passing of the old order constructed by George Chalmers.

End of the Revolution

The 1930s marked the completion of the industrial revolution begun by George Chalmers at Morro Velho in the 1890s as the company moved into a period of technological stagnation after four decades of technological revolution. The transition converged with the larger social and economic patterns affecting Brazil and Nova Lima in the

1930s: the world economic crisis, the rise of an interventionist and nationalist state, and the emergence of an organized working-class movement among the miners. The rise in the price of gold in 1934 also buoyed the world gold-mining industry and provided a favorable context for changes. The St. John attempted to confront these problems with an important shift in managerial regimes and style. The superintendency of A. H. Millett (1930–40) in many ways bridged the Chalmers era and the period of decline after 1940. Under Millett the company moved from the more personalized regime of Chalmers to a more modern business enterprise run by businessmen and mining engineers. The regime of the new experts modernized company organization and began efforts to move the mine from the Chalmers vision to a new system. The hiring of geological consultants and mining engineers to study the mine and make recommendations to management attests to the company's desire to move into a new era.[86] Millett completed the mining complex as envisioned by Chalmers halting development in depth, finishing the power scheme he initiated, and marking the end of the process of major technological innovations begun in the 1890s.[87]

The end of development in depth of the mine clearly signals the end of the Chalmers approach to working the Morro Velho lode and the beginning of efforts to implement a new approach. Increasing rock pressures in the lower levels of the mine increased the chances of deadly rock bursts; the folding of the schist in which the ore lay became more problematic, and the lode more erratic. Heat and ventilation problems also increased as the effectiveness of the cooling plant diminished with depth. Finally, the discovery and development of new ore deposits (one in the lode and one outside it) sealed the decision to halt further development in depth at 2,453 meters (8,051 feet) below the surface. This new find, labeled the "X" orebody, allowed management to turn its efforts once again to the more easily worked upper horizons of the mine. (Although production of raw ore rose dramatically after 1930, this did not necessarily bring about a dramatic rise in gold production; for as tonnage rose, assay value gradually declined. The company could maintain old gold production levels or slightly raise them by processing more of a lower grade ore.)[88]

Equally significant was the development in the 1930s of the Raposos mine some eight kilometers from Morro Velho. The Raposos mine has possibly been worked for as long as the Morro Velho, but with much less success. The St. John purchased the mine in 1899 hoping to develop the lode later, and to protect company mineral rights in the area by keeping out possible competitors. The company did explore the mine on several occasions during the Chalmers era, always suspending operations for lack of labor or financial problems.[89] In the 1930s the company had the capital, labor, and incentives to open up the mine and test it out.[90] The company built an aerial ropeway from the Raposos mine to the Morro Velho mill. The ore was crushed at the mine, loaded onto one-ton buckets, and sent the eight kilometers over the mountains to Morro Velho.[91] Throughout the forties and fifties the Raposos mine contributed a full one-fourth of the company's total gold production.[92] The "X" orebody had extended the life of the Morro Velho, but the Raposos mine had made possible the continued prosperous existence of the company. Development of the new mine bound Raposos ever closer to Nova Lima and created a satellite community of workers.

Patterns of Change

The opening of the Chalmers mine and the construction of the new surface works produced a small-scale industrial revolution in Nova Lima. In the half-century before the arrival of Chalmers the St. John d'el Rey constructed a fairly sophisticated technological system at Morro Velho that experienced a major crisis with the collapse of the mine in 1886. This disaster allowed George Chalmers to start anew and lay out a new mine and mill—a completely new technological system. In the half-century following the mining disaster Chalmers and the management of the St. John revolutionized mining at Morro Velho and transformed Nova Lima. Morro Velho became the site of one of Brazil's largest and most modern industrial plants, and Nova Lima became a full-fledged working-class community. In the quarter-century that followed the revolution the process of technical innovation came to a standstill, ultimately undermining the financial stability of the company.

Within the framework of the technological system the raw materials component experienced the least change. Assay value did diminish at the lowest levels of the mine, but the discovery and exploitation of new orebodies allowed the company to maintain the system.

Clearly, the technical and labor components of the system experienced the greatest transformations and wielded the most impact. The shift from waterwheels to hydroelectric power, from human and animal labor to mechanization, and from slavery to wage labor formed the essence of the technical and labor transformations. In the half-century after 1880 the technological shifts in the Morro Velho system produced a clear set of patterns. First, technical innovations relentlessly abolished human labor and made the remaining labor force increasingly productive (see figure 5). Second, these innovations allowed the St. John repeatedly to meet the challenges of deep-shaft mining (increased rock pressure, heat, ventilation) and gold recovery (cyanidation, chlorination, roasting). Third, the successful confrontation of these challenges enabled the company to expand far beyond the normal functions of a mining enterprise to dominate the community through employment, purchasing, and public works. Ultimately, this domination of local life made the St. John d'el Rey the focus of social and economic problems in the community; for as the company created jobs and extended its power it provided a single, unifying target for the discontent of the working force which it had helped create.

Technology and labor together acted upon and transformed the environment making possible the growth of the mine and the community. Nevertheless, although the environment was less of a transforming agent than technology and labor, the local environment did very much set down certain conditions and limits which in subtle, but fundamental, ways shaped local growth. The very existence of the lode made the mine and community possible, and the geological structure of the lode dictated the lines along which the St. John d'el Rey handled operations underground. The composition of the local ore made mining profitable and also dictated the major components of the reduction process (mechanical separation, cyanidation, roasting). The location of the lode deep in the Brazilian interior also shaped local development. The isolation of the mine from large population centers, transport routes, and other mines made the task of the St. John more difficult, forced the company to become more self-reliant, and provided a spur to innovation and mechanization. The lack of an adequate mining force in the interior compelled the company to search continually for ways to replace labor with machines. Finally, the lack of coal and the cost of burning wood for power made steam engines impossible, just as the abundance of water blessed the company with the means to generate electrical power for industrial operations on a large scale.

While the local environment laid down the possibilities and limits for growth, technology overcame problems presented by the environment and the geology of the lode and made growth a reality. Water provided the necessary source of power, first through direct action then later through the generating plants which converted this force into electricity. Machinery for power hoisting, power drilling, electric hauling, dynamite, electric lighting, and air cooling all provided solutions to the technical problems of deep-shaft mining and each in its own way allowed the company continually to forge ahead and overcome these problems while raising productivity. Likewise, crushing and stamping machinery, cyanidation, chlorination, and mechanization overcame obstacles and drove up productivity. Without these innovations the growth of the mine and the community would not have been possible. Technology became the primary moving force in the growth of the mine and the community it spawned.

Technical innovation at Morro Velho, however, did not rise automatically or inevitably. Several key factors determined the course of innovation. In a broad sense the local environment shaped the selection of technology. In the period prior to World War I the transportation of machinery to the interior affected technological choices, just as the local environment ruled out certain choices (e.g., steam power). A more critical factor was the growth of the world mining industry. Except for the air-cooling plant, all the major technical innovations were pioneered and developed elsewhere, and then adapted at Morro Velho. In other words, the dynamism and innovativeness of the world mining industry time after time contributed to the success of this Anglo-Brazilian mine. Morro Velho profited from the technological revolution in the world mining industry beginning in the 1860s. In this sense the state of the world mining industry also shaped the growth of Nova Lima.

Technical innovation and industrial expansion at Morro Velho also responded to larger processes in the world economy. The mine and the community took shape as a result of the expansion of British capital and its penetration into the Brazilian interior. In many ways the technological triumph at Morro Velho reflected the technological and industrial triumph of British capitalism just as the technological decline in the twentieth century mirrored the decline of British capitalism. The rise and fall of the British at Morro Velho forms one small chapter in the rise and fall of British preeminence in the century and one-half following the Napoleonic wars.

Ultimately, the driving force behind the technological system and innovation at Morro Velho was the profit motive. Like any capitalist enterprise, the St. John d'el Rey sought to maximize profits, in this case through the rationalization of the technological system at Morro Velho. Technical innovation at Morro Velho functioned on two levels. On the one hand, it enabled the company to solve purely technical problems (heat, depth, gold recovery) which rose from time to time. On the other, innovation enabled management to reduce costs by abolishing labor, rationalizing processes, and providing greater control over the elements of the system. Technical innovation replaced costly labor, made it more productive, and raised profits.

Despite the presence of rich gold ore, and the heroic technical innovations of the Chalmers era, labor stands out as the key component in the technological system at Morro Velho. As the constant labor shortages and strikes so vividly demonstrate, ore and tools are meaningless without men and women to handle them. The technological revolution created the conditions for the rise of an industrial working class. It created a large number of skilled workers, but not a working class. These workers were not organized or fully conscious of their common conditions and concerns. The Vargas regime culminates the process of class formation with the implementation of social legislation and the creation of a ministry of labor. The new social legislation stimulated the workers to stay on the payroll, to organize, and to define themselves as a class with common interests. Technology did not produce a working class in some mechanically determined fashion. It facilitated the creation of the working class in Nova Lima. The technological revolution at Morro Velho helped create and nurture the very forces that later halted the revolution.

Forces too powerful for British management to control, focused in the labor movement, ultimately stifled innovation and ended the British era at Morro Velho. Caught between the rigidity of the postwar international monetary system, and the inflation, economic nationalism, and government interventionism which translated into militant unionism and strikes, the St. John could no longer modernize the system to meet challenges. Caught in a cost-price squeeze and unable to renovate and modernize an aging industrial plant and mine, the St. John d'el Rey found itself trapped. The company needed to continue to mechanize and eliminate costly labor, yet financial problems exacerbated by a militant labor force prevented the company from acting. Without renovation the financial problems became increasingly difficult to face, and as they increased, renovation became impossible. The failure of the No. One Main Shaft under G. P. Wigle in the early fifties symbolizes the failure of this effort. Labor troubles spurred by national economic problems blocked plans for technological modernization and doomed the British enterprise.

PART II

The Community

The first half of this book examined the St. John d'el Rey Mining Company, Limited, placing special emphasis on British management, company politics, and technological innovation. While the St. John was a significant economic and political force in the state and nation, I have stressed the inability of the company to control and shape events in Brazil. The image of a profitable foreign enterprise dominating and controlling events certainly does not hold for this preeminently successful firm. While the stereotype of the omnipotent foreign company collapses before the evidence when looking to the larger political arena, the stereotype comes closer to reality when one turns to the impact of the St. John at the local level. If one is to speak of political power, economic domination, and social control, then one must turn to the role of the company in Nova Lima; for it is at the community level that the power of the St. John to dominate and shape the lives of Brazilians is most evident.

This is not to say that the people of Nova Lima are powerless to shape their own history. To the contrary, as I emphasize (especially in chapter 6), the people of Nova Lima are also actors in the historical process shaping the development of the company and the community. Nevertheless, they are responding to historical forces that are largely beyond their control. Others dictate the terms of the struggle. As previous chapters have shown, the technological system that was constructed was not an autonomous force, but rather rose out of an interaction between the technical demands of gold mining, international and national economic forces, major social changes taking place in Brazil, and the efforts of *novalimenses* to shape the system to their own needs and desires. The technological system was the focal point of change in the community, but a focal point that reflected the influence of larger forces on the national and international scenes. Therefore, the process of history that unfolded in Nova Lima consisted of the interaction of the local people with the larger forces of the world economy and national politics as reflected in the changing nature of the technological system. People and machines interacted, but in a process that reached far beyond Nova Lima. The fate of both the people and the machines was shaped by forces on several continents.

The next three chapters examine the mixed blessings of gold mining in Nova Lima. Chapter 5 traces the administrative and political evolution of the community, its evolving economy, its main demographic features, and urban ecology. Chapter 6 analyzes the major social changes in the community: the rise and decline of slavery, the formation of a working class, and the emergence of a vocal, militant union movement. Finally, chapter 7 looks at the most privileged members of the community, the British who ran the Morro Velho mine for a century and a quarter. In short, these three chapters present a cross section of the social groups and social changes that accompany the process of technological change in Nova Lima across two centuries.

5

From Rural Village to
Industrial City

N[oss]a. S[enhor]a. do Pilar de Congonhas de Sabará—here names are
long, apparently in direct inverse ratio of the importance of the place or
person named—though very drowsy, is tolerably neat, and wears
a kind of well-to-do-in-the-world look.[1]

Rising up twelve hundred meters above sea level, the Serra do Curral
forms a natural boundary dividing the *municípios* of Belo Horizonte
and Nova Lima. Looking down from the crest of the Serra, one is
struck by the immense differences between the two communities.
Laid out in geometrical design as Brazil's first modern, planned city
in the 1890s, Belo Horizonte has exploded in the last four decades.
Cement, steel, and glass have pushed aside trees and grass. Three
million inhabitants, and miles of concrete and asphalt, spill across
the broad plateau and up against the rugged gray-green Serra and a
wide, blue horizon. *Mineiro* urban planners and politicians picked
a worthy location for their state capital. To look south of the Serra
toward Nova Lima is to peer into a much longer and vastly different
past. A few kilometers off in the distance the city sprawls haphaz-
ardly over a series of low hills in a depression nearly one hundred
meters lower than Belo Horizonte. Chance and geology, rather than
planners and politicians, dictated the location and urban ecology of
Nova Lima. Over decades prospectors, peddlers, peasants, and slaves
gradually settled in anarchic fashion on the hillsides overlooking
the converging Cristais and Cardoso streams. The latter flowed by
the southern slopes of the Morro Velho, and a low ridge separated
it from the Cristais to the south. While miners consolidated claims
on the slopes of the Morro Velho in the Cardoso basin in the eighteenth century, the hamlet of Congonhas de Sabará took shape on
the southern slope of the ridge overlooking the Cristais (see map 3).
When the St. John purchased the Morro Velho estate in 1834, the

hamlet had been in a period of stagnation for decades. A decaying *matriz* looked across a dusty, dirt plaza at a dilapidated town hall, a few homes, and stores. The French traveler St. Hilaire passed through Congonhas in 1817 observing a village that probably changed little in the half-century before the arrival of the St. John. "Congonhas owes its founding to miners attracted by the gold which is found in the surrounding area," he wrote, "and its history is that of many other large villages. The precious metal is exhausted, the workings become more difficult, and Congonhas presently heralds only decadence and abandonment."[2]

The decadence and abandonment that characterized so many villages in the old mining zone would end for Congonhas with the arrival of the British in the early 1830s, setting the community apart from its neighbors. The technological system the British constructed at Morro Velho formed the core of the company's operations and played a crucial role in the success, and failure, of the enterprise. This technological system also transformed a small, rural community of peasants, slaves, miners, and merchants into a large, urban, working-class city. The evolution of the technological system at Morro Velho helped make Nova Lima one of the largest centers of industrial slavery in nineteenth-century Brazil; the home of a melting pot of races and nationalities by the turn of the century; and, eventually, home of one of the largest concentrations of industrial workers outside of São Paulo and Rio de Janeiro. The St. John d'el Rey dominated the life of this company town. The technological system constructed by the British not only defined, and redefined, the nature of work and the workplace, it also shaped and reshaped the organization and structure of local society.

The evolution of the technological system analyzed in chapter 4 is the key to the process of social change in Nova Lima. Chapters 5 to 7 examine the human side of company operations. These chapters dissect the community concentrating on the evolution of Nova Lima from a small, rural community of some fourteen hundred inhabitants in the 1830s, to a thriving industrial city of twenty thousand by the 1950s. The expansion of capitalist enterprise formed the driving force in the transformation of Nova Lima, and the technological system was the locus of change. This chapter shows the relationship of the expanding technological system to the community's urban development, its economy, and changing demographic profile. Chapters 5 and 6 then analyze social groups and their relationship to the evolving technological system.

From Congonhas de Sabará to Nova Lima

Gold gave Nova Lima life and shaped its history. *Bandeirantes* in search of gold in the streams of the Rio das Velhas basin probably began to settle on the hillsides around the Cardoso and Cristais streams in the last decade of the seventeenth century and in the first years of the eighteenth century. Nossa Senhora do Pilar de Congonhas do Sabará was one of the several hamlets (*arraiais*) in the parish (*freguesia*) of Santo Antônio do Rio Acima, a few kilometers to the south. Rio Acima (as it is known today) fell under the jurisdiction of Sabará, one of the four royal towns (*vilas reais*) and the administrative center of one of the four departments (*comarcas*) of the new captaincy of Minas Gerais. The oldest surviving documents (*livros de guardamoria*) from the parish of Rio Acima date from the 1720s and contain *datas minerais* that refer to earlier mining claims that have not survived.[3] Congonhas became a separate parish in 1748 but did not receive its own parish priest until 1752. Under the administrative reorganization of the empire Congonhas became one of the three districts of the *município* of Sabará. While essentially one and the same unit, the district was an administrative and political division, and the parish, an ecclesiastical one.[4]

Congonhas remained an administrative appendage of Sabará for most of the nineteenth century, growing steadily with the expansion of the Morro Velho mine until it eventually would surpass the stagnating Sabará. When the St. John set up operations at Morro Velho in the early 1830s, Congonhas de Sabará was a small village of just over one thousand inhabitants, three decaying churches, three dry-goods houses, one pharmacy, no hotels, and no public schools.[5] By the 1890s the town had grown to nearly eight thousand (despite the recent mine disaster), and the municipality took in fourteen thousand inhabitants, making it larger than Sabará (see table 7).[6] With a wide variety of commercial establishments, two hospitals, and a public school, the town was no longer just another small hamlet in the interior.[7] In addition to four justices of the peace the *município*

Table 7 Population of Nova Lima, 1830–1960

Year	Population
1830	1,390
1840	2,000
1864	5,000
1872	9,701
1890	14,066
1900	16,037
1910	16,759
1920	17,448
1930	22,611
1940	29,714
1950	21,932
1960	27,825

Sources: Burton, *Explorations*, I, p. 195; *AEMG* (1921), II; *Annuario demographico de Minas Gerais*; and RE 1872–1960.
Note: The figures prior to 1890 are for the parish level. Beginning in 1890 they are for the municipality. The 1940 census includes Raposos which was annexed to Nova Lima in 1938, and the 1950 census reflects the loss of Raposos and the district of Rio Acima which became separate *municípios*.

had a town council with nine members, elected every four years. The local council remained faithful to the state political machine, the *Partido Republicano Mineiro* (PRM), guaranteeing a large and favorable voter turnout from the close to nine hundred eligible voters in state elections.[8]

Political "emancipation" arrived with the new republic, no doubt due to the influence of native sons Augusto and Bernardino de Lima. Their family had lived in the area since the eighteenth century, and their father, José Severiano de Lima, had worked a number of local gold claims. Augusto served briefly as governor of the state (March to June 1891), and his brother was state chief of police.[9] Earlier petitions requesting the state to elevate the community to the status of a *vila* as an independent *município* had failed.[10] Undoubtedly, the political pull of the Limas now made the difference. A state decree created the new municipality in February 1891, naming it Villa Nova de Lima in honor of the Lima family. State officials, hosted by the St. John at the Casa Grande, inaugurated the new administrative regime in March to the great pleasure of the company and the local elite. The company and community were pleased to have taxes and local government out of the hands of officials in Sabará who were seen as unresponsive to local concerns. The status of *vila* gave the local town council greater control over taxes, public works, and electoral affairs.[11] The name of the municipality was shortened to Nova Lima in 1923. Full judicial "emancipation" did not come until 1938 with the creation of the *comarca* of Nova Lima, giving the town its own separate courts and notaries.[12]

By the early twentieth century Villa Nova de Lima had developed into a thriving company town around the Morro Velho mine. Although the community had been on the main road between Sabará and Rio de Janeiro throughout the eighteenth century and the first half of the nineteenth century, the major transport routes that emerged in late nineteenth-century Minas Gerais all bypassed the growing mining town. The most important new transport route was the Estrada de Ferro Dom Pedro II (later the Estrada de Ferro Central do Brasil) built between Rio de Janeiro and central Minas Gerais in the late nineteenth century. The railway followed the Rio das Velhas basin to the east of Congonhas and passed through Raposos and Sabará. The railway reached the newly created station of Honório Bicalho eight kilometers to the south of Congonhas in 1890. Although the gauge of the railway changed at Queluz (present-day Conselheiro Lafaiete) in southern Minas Gerais, requiring the transshipment of passengers and freight, the rail connection shortened the trip to Rio de Janeiro from the two weeks by mule of the 1830s to an overnight ride in the 1890s.[13]

The old Sabará-Rio highway continued to link the community by dirt road with its neighbors to the north and south, while cruder dirt roads, barely passable by bullock cart, linked Nova Lima to Raposos and the railway at Honório Bicalho (see map 4). During the First World War the St. John's *bonde* (streetcar) connected the town with Raposos, and the railway, greatly improving transportation and cutting shipping costs. In the 1920s the company undertook the paving of the road to Sabará, which branched off a few kilometers to the north of town and turned west across the Serra to a growing Belo Horizonte.[14] The railway, the new road to the nearby state capital, and the appearance of the automobile, all signaled the end of Nova Lima's long isolation in the interior, and a trend toward greater ties into a regional system that had begun to develop around the new state capital.

The 1920 national census takers counted six passenger vehicles and four trucks in Villa Nova—plus eighty-three oxcarts. The county had no auto roads, as yet, but boasted 110 kilometers of roads for the oxcarts.[15] The *câmara* approved the construction of the community's first gas station to service the small group of automobiles and trucks, and passed a series of safety regulations and registration requirements for automobiles. Finally, a private contractor initiated regular bus service between Nova Lima and Belo Horizonte.[16] The old highway over the Serra would remain the community's main link to Belo Horizonte until the 1950s when the construction of an asphalt highway westward along the steep mountain ridges cut the travel time between the two cities to thirty minutes. Today bus service provides the main linkage between the capital and Nova Lima, carrying hundreds back and forth three times an hour.

Urban Ecology

Until the late nineteenth century the community developed largely in an unplanned and spontaneous fashion. With the rebuilding of the mine and expansion of company operations at the turn of the century, the community's ecology became largely a result of company decision making. In the last half of the nineteenth century distinct *bairros* began to take shape, generally clustered around the major roads overlooking the central plaza in the Cristais basin (see map 3). The eighteenth-century *matriz* faced the municipal building across a dirt plaza. In the 1850s a group of prominent townspeople funded the construction of a municipal theater, making Congonhas home of one of the three theaters in the province.[17] On the same side of the plaza to the south of the theater was the local jail. Across the plaza on the west side homes and businesses took shape. Distinct neighborhoods developed around the plaza on the steep hillsides to the north and west, and on the terrain sloping into the Cristais basin, to the south and east of the plaza. After the turn of the century town officials fenced off the central area of the plaza, planting trees and shrubs and constructing a small kiosk in the center. Between the two world wars the municipal government planted imperial palms around the central plaza, paving the plaza and adjacent streets.

The oldest and most densely inhabited areas were to the north and south of the plaza. To the north the Rosário Church dominated the hill separating Congonhas from the Morro Velho mine.

Begun in the eighteenth century as a church for slaves, the Rosário was one of the three churches in the community. The main street into the neighborhood rose sharply from the side of the *matriz* to the little plaza in front of the Rosário. The town laid out the municipal cemetery on the hillside next to the church looking eastward. To the south of the plaza was the community's third church, the Bonfim, a tiny chapel in ruins by the nineteenth century. The Cristais ran through the *bairro* and a wooden bridge across the stream connected Congonhas with the road to Rio de Janeiro.

More sparsely dispersed homes dotted the areas to the east and west of the plaza, with the main concentration following the Rua do Piolho (Rua Bias Fortes today) that ran northwest from the plaza over the steep Rosário hill and into the Morro Velho estate. The street continued on past the front of the Casa Grande, crossed the Cardoso near the mine entrance, and then rose sharply into the hills as it became the highway to Sabará. Until the construction of the new asphalt highway west to Belo Horizonte in the 1950s all traffic to Sabará and Belo Horizonte had to take this route through the mine compound. Until well into this century the British and Brazilian communities were more or less separated by the ridge separating the two basins. Standing on the ridge where the Rua do Piolho crossed out of the Cristais basin, one looked south to the central plaza and north into the Morro Velho estate. To the west along the ridge were the homes of the British community. Rising up on the hill above the mine to the west of the Casa Grande in the *bairro* of Retiro and continuing west onto the next hillside in the *bairro* that came to be known as the Quintas.

Few Brazilians lived in this area. With the "imperial" mentality that distinguished so many British colonial settlements around the world, management at Morro Velho made every effort to isolate the British from the "natives" in the Retiro and Quintas *bairros*. British management, and many of the workers, clearly saw themselves as members of a "superior" civilization and their small settlement as an enclave of that civilization in a backward land. The British (with some notable exceptions) looked down on the racially mixed Brazilians. To minimize fraternizing with the "natives," Chalmers even went so far as to require all British employees to seek permission before going into the "village."[18]

With the influx of European workers at the turn of the century, some ethnic neighborhoods developed for a brief time. The Spaniards, Italians, Japanese, and Chinese each staked out a specific area of town. The language barrier, efforts to maintain their cultural traditions, and simple anxiety kept the new ethnic groups together. The Japanese and Chinese, however, did not stay long, and the Italians and Spaniards had assimilated into local life by the 1930s.[19] The St. John staked out well-defined *bairros* with the construction of employee housing in the first decades of this century. On the road to Belo Horizonte west of the Casa Grande and the English neighborhood, the company built dozens of homes in neat whitewashed rows on the site of the old brickyard. The *bairro* of Olaria became the center of what would later become the parish of Santo Antônio. Southwest of the town center, on hills overlooking the Cristais basin, two additional working-class *bairros* took shape in the 1930s—Vila Operária and Bairro Cristais. After 1950 the community began to expand westward along the new road to Belo Horizonte, and south along the highway to Rio Acima, although most of the population continued to reside around the urban core radiating out from the central plaza.

The community grew with the expansion of the mine and became densely inhabited. Population density stood at around twenty-two inhabitants per square kilometer in the 1920s. Nova Lima then ranked near the middle of the range in *mineiro municípios* ranked by density. No *município* (with the exception of Belo Horizonte) registered more than thirty-five inhabitants per square kilometer.[20] The expansion of company operations made Nova Lima one of the most densely populated *municípios* in the state by 1960 (with seventy inhabitants per square kilometer). Of 485 *municípios*, Nova Lima ranked twenty-fourth with sixty-nine inhabitants per square kilometer. Nova Lima had a higher density than 95 percent of the *municípios* in Minas Gerais.[21] The heavy vegetation and numerous trees on the sparsely populated hillsides had given way by the 1960s to paved roads and a densely packed urban core.

As with everything else, the St. John dominated the construction and control of buildings and housing in Nova Lima determining housing patterns and urban development. The company had begun building housing for employees from the beginning of its operations in Brazil. The earliest housing accommodated the British community and company slaves. The latter lived in a compound on the western slope of the Morro Velho in an area known as Boa Vista or Timbuctoo. The single males lived together in rooms capable of holding up to twenty people, while married couples had their own houses. A separate building, known locally as the "Convent," housed the single slave women.[22] As slave labor became more difficult to come by, and as the St. John hired increasingly larger numbers of free laborers, management began to build housing for the free labor force. Throughout the history of the company low-cost housing served as a tool to entice workers to migrate to Nova Lima, to work for the company, and to stay. The St. John first began constructing housing for free Brazilian laborers in the 1840s.[23] The company built wooden frame structures raised off the ground, with adobe walls, and tile roofs. Each structure contained twelve rooms and was designed for two workers per room.[24]

The St. John built two types of worker housing, multiple-room dormitories and houses. In the early twentieth century the typical company house rented to a Brazilian laborer had four rooms, each room measuring eleven feet by eleven feet, with walls of sun-dried adobe brick, a tile roof, and windows with wooden shutters (but no glass). Each house had a wood floor raised fifteen inches off the ground and cost the company about £650 to build, about 65 percent of the cost of an English staff house.[25] Houses usually contained a small kitchen. In the 1920s when the company began a desperate drive to attract sufficient labor, management began a building plan which, over the next two decades, expanded the size of company housing by close to 100 percent and doubled the available housing in Nova Lima. In 1920 Nova Lima had close to 2,200 buildings with about 2,000 serving as housing. All but a handful were single-story structures.[26] By 1950 the urban core contained some 4,000 buildings used for housing purposes, and 2,000 of those were company-built, largely in the previous thirty years.[27] In 1913 about 40 percent of the Brazilian work force was living in company housing (1,046 of 2,428). Just over 1,000 workers and 1,754 dependents were renting a total of 2,146 rooms from the St. John d'el Rey. This averaged out to 1.3 persons per room, hardly overcrowding, especially considering the low proportion of dependents to workers (1.7 per worker). In 1937, at the height of company and community expansion, the occupancy density had dropped slightly to 1.2 per room (2,609 workers, 5,913 dependents, in 7,297 rooms). This is almost exactly the same rate as for the nation as a whole in 1940.[28]

The housing situation in Nova Lima in the 1920s compared favorably with that in Belo Horizonte and Juiz de Fora, the other major industrial centers in Minas Gerais. Nova Lima had a density of 5.07 persons per habitation, while Belo Horizonte averaged 6.7, and Juiz de Fora, 7.79.[29] In the 1920s the company charged between 3$000 and 4$000 (about U.S.$.30–.40) per room per month for its housing. The average daily wage of a borer in the mine in 1923 was 7$000.[30] This meant a single male borer would spend about one-half of one day's wage on monthly rent, and a married male borer with children renting a house with four rooms would spend two to three days' wages on monthly rent. (Most workers were single and rented rooms rather than houses.) If company records are accurate, this was substantially below rates charged by local landlords, and the waiting list to get company housing was a long one. Company housing offered electric lighting, running water, and indoor plumbing. In the 1920s the town council contracted with the St. John to build water and electrical systems for the rest of the community, projects that were costly, despite state aid. Eventually, company loans became grants. The end result of company building, and the council contracts, was a community with nearly three-quarters of all buildings with running water and electricity, something which placed Nova Lima far ahead of comparable communities in Minas Gerais by 1950. Most homes continued to use wood-burning stoves, few had refrigeration, and no one had telephone service (outside of the company offices) until the 1940s.[31]

Without a doubt, Nova Lima would not have had electrical service, the water system, or the road system it had by the 1950s, had it not been for the presence of the St. John d'el Rey. Nevertheless, city services were visibly underdeveloped for a community with an industrial infrastructure the size of the Morro Velho. The English management was willing to extend electricity and other services to the rest of the community as long as it did not interfere with normal company operations. The St. John owned most of the buildings in town and maintained a good many local roads, including the main highways, for obvious reasons. The company had an economic interest in maintaining local infrastructure to insure the smooth flow of goods, commerce, and labor. Grudgingly, the company extended grants and loans to the town council to maintain good relations with local leaders and to keep local services adequate to supply the working population and their families.[32] During the First World War the company began to provide the city with street lighting and maintenance of the system, at no charge. In the 1930s the demand for

View of Congonhas de Sabará in the 1860s. Large building at left is the future Casa Aristides.

View of the old mill in the 1860s with Casa Grande (center) and store building (upper right) in the distance. At upper center is the Rosário Church on the hill separating the mine from Congonhas de Sabará.

1860s view of the old mill from the Casa Grande.

View of the Morro Velho from the Casa Grande in the 1860s. In the center is the open cut into the hillside from the original mine. At right is the Catholic church for the slaves with the British cemetery just above. The old mill is at bottom left.

The fortnightly slave *revista* in front of the Casa Grande in the 1860s. Superintendent James Newell Gordon (center) is in the top hat.

Company officers on the veranda of the Casa Grande, 1901. George
Chalmers is seated at left; the chairman of the board, Frederick J. Tendron,
is seated in the center; and the company secretary, M. A. M'Call, is seated
at right.

In the mine, ca. 1900.

The Chalmers mill, ca. 1910. In the background are rows of California stamps with strakes (shaker tables) below. Note the two young boys operating the automated washing system.

Rock drilling in mine, ca. 1950.

Hand-tramming ore in mine cars from the stopes,
ca. 1950.

Hauling mules underground, ca. 1950.

Female workers picking over ore in mill, 1940s.

Company housing for workers, ca. 1940.

electricity in homes and buildings not owned by the St. John led the *prefeitura* to request more power from the company generating stations. Company officials acceded to the request, but only because the completion of new power stations allowed for the use of an older station for community needs (a small two hundred kilowatt hours per year). In addition, the *prefeitura* paid a fee for the electricity.[33]

More striking than electric lighting is the inadequacy of the water filtration and sewer systems in the community. Surrounded by an abundance of fresh-water streams and rivers, Nova Lima is exceptionally well situated for water supplies and drainage. Once again, the presence of the company proved a blessing and a curse. The St. John constructed an enormous system of aqueducts to supply the mill with the more than two *million* gallons of water it required by the 1930s. All the watersheds in the region were acquired in the nineteenth century, leaving the town dependent on company goodwill for access to water. Furthermore, arsenic and other chemicals from the mine and mill contaminated the waters downstream from the industrial park as well as much of the local water table. As a result, a community of abundant water resources has faced serious environmental health problems up to the present from scarce and often contaminated water. The company did little to keep non-company buildings supplied with water or sewers, and the community had fewer than 25 percent of its buildings linked up to water or sewer systems in the 1920s, a time when more than 100 *mineiro* cities had water filtration systems in place. Most of the *novalimenses* took their water from the more than one dozen public spigots.[34] Although a capitalist enterprise pursuing profit rather than public service, the St. John d'el Rey could have done much more to improve local services in a community it dominated. The small investment in local infrastructure would have produced an important return in healthier and more productive workers.

To provide some perspective on the immense local economic power of the company one should keep in mind that in the 1920s the company's annual expenditures were around £500,000, those of the state of Minas Gerais about £2,000,000, and the budget of the Nova Lima town council around £200.[35] Most of the council's money went to employee salaries, maintaining streets, cemeteries, and local hospitals. The St. John paid the salaries of the half-dozen local police.[36] Whenever any major expense arose the council had to turn to the state or the company for funds. In 1922, for example, the St. John

donated thirty *contos de réis* (£60) for the construction and maintenance of a new tuberculosis hospital.[37] In short, the company maintained most local roads, paid the local police, provided electricity,
the water system, and helped fund the local schools. Although not a
classic company town completely built and controlled by the dominant local industry, Nova Lima developed largely as a result of the
growth and plans of the St. John d'el Rey.

Economic Transformations

In some ways the industrialization of Nova Lima anticipated the
shift from agriculture and cattle raising to industry that the old Zona
Metalúrgica surrounding the community would experience in the
mid-twentieth century. The economy of central Minas Gerais had
turned inward in the nineteenth century after the spectacular rise
and decline of the gold export boom in the eighteenth century. The
gold rush had made Minas into the most populous province in Brazil,
and one of the largest slaveholding societies in the Western Hemisphere by the mid-nineteenth century.[38] The southern and western
fringes of the province developed coffee economies linked into São
Paulo and Rio de Janeiro in the mid-nineteenth century while the
old mining zone and the north turned to the production of agricultural products and stock raising largely for internal consumption.[39]
Gold accounted for a very small portion of the state's total production, and a few mines, mainly the Morro Velho, produced most of
the gold. In the 1850s gold, cereals, and sugar cane were the major
products of the hinterland surrounding Congonhas de Sabará.

With the exception of the industrializing Villa Nova de Lima, the
economy of the region changed little until after the turn of the century. The construction of Belo Horizonte in the 1890s did little to
alter the regional economy. The construction industry generated a
great deal of activity in and around the capital affecting labor markets, but the process of industrialization around Belo Horizonte and
in the old mining zone did not take off until the 1940s, accelerat-
ing in the 1950s.[40] Until the 1930s Nova Lima remained an isolated
industrial center in a largely self-sufficient agricultural economy.

The company dominated the local economy as the principal land-
owner, employer, and consumer. By the early twentieth century the

company owned the majority of buildings and most of the land in and around the town, controlling the real estate market. Despite the huge wage payments, consumption of goods, and the enormous technological complex, the St. John did not stimulate the growth of local industry. The British imported, built, or repaired most of their machinery and did not nurture local workshops for the production or repair of industrial goods. The company operated essentially as an enclave economy in the Brazilian interior. Few linkages developed, and the influence of the firm was seen largely in agriculture, services, and commerce.

Even in agriculture the company's impact was greater in the surrounding *municípios* than in Nova Lima. Most of the surrounding farms were small and supplied products for the local and regional economy. As with the surrounding regional economy, the principal products from Nova Lima were cattle, horses, mules, sheep, pigs, chickens, sugar cane, corn, manioc, rice, potatoes, beans, milk, and cheese. In the 1920s farms covered three-quarters of the *município* (570 of 776 square kilometers), but most of them were small, and none had any type of agricultural machinery more sophisticated than plows and hoes for planting or harvesting.[41] The 1920 census lists 390 agricultural "establishments," 84 percent (328) under 100 hectares. The average size of a farm was 146 hectares. Less than 4 percent of the land was under cultivation, 70 percent was pasture, and the rest *"em matta"* (forested). The pattern in the census data is clear: small landholdings, few large producers, and insignificant production.

Agricultural production in 1920 contributed less than 10 percent to the total production of the *município*, while mining contributed nearly 90 percent. The value of gold production placed the *município* among the top ten in total production in the entire state, and gave Nova Lima the highest per-capita production of any *município* in Minas Gerais. Gold production placed the *município* third in the state (behind Juiz de Fora and Barbacena) in value of exports, third in capital investment, second in personnel employed, and fourth in total production (behind Juiz de Fora, Queluz, and Belo Horizonte). Nova Lima alone accounted for nearly 10 percent of the state's industrial production (by value) and 20 percent of capital investment.[42]

The enormous expansion of the industrial operations at Morro Velho in the 1930s (at the expense of the already-small agricultural economy) can be seen in the census figures for 1940. By then the number of agricultural establishments had dropped to 63 (from 390 in 1920) and a mere 219 people were employed by them. Fifty-nine of the establishments were listed as small-scale, and they accounted for more than 70 percent of all agricultural production. Ninety percent of the workers were employed on the fifty-nine small-scale establishments which were all under two hundred hectares. The other four establishments employed twenty-three people and covered two-thirds of the acreage under cultivation.[43]

The local economy that developed around the company was built on services, primarily in small retail outlets. In the 1860s, with the mine at full production, Congonhas had less than two dozen merchants, and one store dominated local retail sales. The Casa Aristides, founded in the 1870s, would remain the principal retail establishment in the community until the Second World War. Traveling merchants and small shopkeepers kept the town supplied with a limited variety of retail goods. In the 1920s the town still had just two dozen commercial establishments, and no banks would set up operations until the late 1940s.[44] The growth of Belo Horizonte after 1900 also hampered the development of local commerce as the state capital became the major producer and supplier of clothes, foodstuffs, and services.

The shifting nature of the local economy from the 1870s to the 1940s can also be seen in the changing composition of the work force in the census figures. Although the censuses are not uniform in their categories, and the numbers (particularly for 1920) appear to present some problems, a clear general picture emerges: the rise of an industrial work force, the decline of the agricultural sector, and the relegation of women to domestic labor. As shown in table 8, between the 1872 and 1940 censuses most of the local work force was employed in agriculture, industry, or domestic service, with small groups in commerce and the "liberal professions."

Table 9 provides a detailed look at the occupational breakdown for free and slave, male and female for the 1872 census. The weakness of the census becomes apparent when it fails to show any workers in mining. Undoubtedly, those employed in mining must have been listed under agriculture or day labor (criados e jornaleiros). The table shows a clear division of labor by sex and slave/free status. Textile work was exclusively a female slave occupation, employing 17.1 percent of all slave women with a profession. Sewing work was an exclusively female occupation taking in 9.7 percent of the female

Table 8 Occupational Breakdown of Population, Nova Lima, 1872–1940 (in percentages)

Category	1872	1920	1940
Agriculture	35.8	29.9	3.3
Industry	17.0	25.0	41.8
Domestic Service	23.7	5.0	45.7
Commerce	1.6	4.6	2.7
Liberal Professions	0.3	3.0	1.0
Totals	78.4	67.5	94.5

Sources: RE 1872, reel 4, part 9, p. 228; RE 1920, v. IV, part 5, no. 1, pp. lxiii and cxix; RE 1940, v. XIII, part 2, p. 362.
Note: Table does not include all working population nor all occupational categories.

Table 9 Slave (S) and Free (F) Population by Profession, Congonhas de Sabará, 1872

Profession		Male	Female	Combined	Percentage of Total	Percentage of Employed
Agriculture	S	948	135	1,083	32.9	40.9
	F	1,426	247	1,673	26.1	33.2
Domestic Service	S	303	564	867	26.4	32.7
	F	87	869	956	14.9	18.9
Day Labor	S	133	213	346	10.5	13.1
	F	656	8	664	10.3	13.2
Industrial Workers	S	0	213	213	6.5	8.0
	F	939	138	1,077	16.8	21.3
Seamstresses	S	0	121	121	3.7	4.6
	F	0	362	362	5.7	7.2
Capitalists/Landowners	F	156	13	169	2.6	3.3
Merchants	F	119	5	124	1.9	2.5
Liberal Professions	F	17	4	21	0.3	0.4
Other	S	20	0	20	0.7	0.7
No Profession	S	301	333	634	19.3	—
	F	594	777	1,371	21.4	—
Total	S	1,705	1,579	3,284	100.0	100.0
	F	3,994	2,423	6,417	100.0	100.0

Source: RE 1872, reel 4, part 9, p. 228.

slave work force and 22 percent of the free females. Nearly half of all females with an occupation, slave (45.3 percent) and free (52.8 percent), worked in domestic service. Only 10.8 percent of the female slaves were employed in agriculture with another 17.1 percent listed as day laborers, probably in manual labor in a wide variety of areas.

In short, women were largely relegated to domestic service, sewing, and, to a lesser degree, agricultural and manual labor.

Male slaves were overwhelmingly concentrated in three areas: agricultural work (67.5 percent of those with occupations), domestic service (21.6 percent), and manual labor (9.5 percent). A large segment (19.3 percent) of the slave population fell into the category "no profession"—most likely small children and the elderly who made up nearly 20 percent of the 3,284 slaves in the census. Free men had a broader variety of occupations and choices. Most were concentrated in three principal groups: agricultural workers (41.9 percent of those employed), industrial workers (27.6 percent), and manual laborers (19.3 percent). A sizable number of free males (8 percent) fell into the categories of capitalist, property owner, and merchant.[45]

By 1940 the occupational composition of the population confirms the rise of industry and the working class around the Morro Velho mine. Of the more than 18,000 people with known occupations, over 8,000 worked in industry, nearly all for the St. John d'el Rey with its work force of 7,500. The agricultural sector that had long been a part of the local economy was now reduced from a majority of the economically active male population to a tiny segment of the local work force and the local economy. Nearly 9,000, the vast majority of them women, worked in domestic service jobs (7,741 of 8,758, or 88.4 percent). By the Second World War the community had evolved a highly segmented labor force. Over 80 percent of all workingwomen were in domestic service, and the same proportion of workingmen were employed by the St. John d'el Rey. Nova Lima was clearly a working-class community built around a single industry and a single company.

The extraordinary growth and size of the company and the working-class community around it can be seen in the census figures for 1920. The national census of industrial establishments in 1920 lists twenty-nine establishments with more than 1,000 workers (operários). Twenty-four of these are textile factories, concentrated in the state and city of Rio de Janeiro (10), and the state of São Paulo (9). Other than the St. John with its 3,000 employees, Minas Gerais had no industrial establishments with over 1,000 workers. The Morro Velho mine alone employed 15 percent of the operários in the state. The textile industry in Minas employed just over 50 percent of the industrial work force (9,519), and the St. John employed nearly as many workers as the next largest industry (food processing) in the state. In effect, the St. John d'el Rey was the third largest industry in the state![46] Although the St. John's prominent role in the industrial economy of Minas would decline in relative terms after 1930, it would continue to employ a significant proportion of the industrial work force. The 8,000 industrial employees in Nova Lima in 1940 still accounted for 9 percent of the *mineiro* industrial labor force.[47] Until the rise of industrialization in Belo Horizonte after 1940, Nova Lima would remain an expanding working-class community in the midst of a largely agricultural hinterland.

Demographic Patterns

Just as the technological transformations at the mine shaped the urban growth and economic features of Nova Lima, they also altered the demographic characteristics of the community. By the late nineteenth century the growth of the parish of Congonhas de Sabará placed it among the sizable communities of Minas Gerais. The most populous province in the empire, with one-fifth of the national population, Minas Gerais contained nearly four hundred parishes, the largest with just under twenty thousand inhabitants. Approximately fifty parishes fell in the ten thousand-to-twenty thousand range, with Congonhas in the next grouping of parishes with just under ten thousand inhabitants. While not as large as the growing southern towns of Barbacena and Juiz de Fora, Congonhas had surpassed the traditional administrative centers in the mining zone—Sabará and Ouro Preto—in size.[48] In the next few decades Minas Gerais experienced an outflow of population, especially to the coffee plantations of São Paulo. Possibly as high as one-fifth of the state population left as the *mineiro* economy stagnated relative to neighboring states.

Nova Lima, however, continued to grow. In the 1920s less than 5 percent of *mineiros* lived in cities of more than five thousand inhabitants. The city (district) of Nova Lima had a population of over ten thousand.[49] As the cities and counties of Minas Gerais experienced a process of population dispersal in the interwar years, Nova Lima grew. After 1940 Nova Lima continued to grow at a steady pace, and the growth of industry in central Minas reversed the dispersal trend, drawing population into the expanding industrial pole around Belo Horizonte. By the 1940 census Nova Lima was one of only twenty-two cities in Minas with a population above ten thousand. By the 1960s the expansion of the state capital had drawn Nova Lima into the rapidly expanding metropolitan area of Belo Horizonte, despite the rugged mountain range between the two cities.[50]

One of the most striking features of the community was the size of its slave population. Undoubtedly, the economic activity generated by the St. John drew an exceptionally large number of captive blacks into the area. The true nature of slaveholding patterns in the parish is obscured by several factors. First, the 1872 census took place during the period of rebuilding after the mine collapse of 1867. The company had cut back on costs by sending hired slaves back to their owners, and the company emancipation program, as well as the decline of an aging slave population (all purchased prior to 1845), drove down the number of slaves in company employ at the time of the census. Second, the census itself is clearly flawed. The census shows *no one* under the occupational category *mineiro* for the parish of Congonhas de Sabará, clearly an impossible state of affairs! Finally, many of the slaves normally employed by the company were probably temporarily in other occupations while their owners awaited the reopening of the mine and the opportunity once again to rent their chattel to the British.[51]

Slaves made up a full one-third (3,284 of 9,701) of the parish population. While Congonhas did not even rank in the top fifty parishes in population, it ranked ninth in the province in number of slaves. The parishes with the largest slave populations were concentrated in the coffee zones in the southern and southeastern regions of the Minas Gerais (Mata and Campos). With the exception of two parishes on the southern fringe of the mining zone (the Campos zone), Congonhas de Sabará held more slaves than any other parish in central Minas Gerais (see table 10). Furthermore, it had a higher ratio of slaves to free persons than any parish in the province. The only possible explanation for this concentration of slaves has to be the economic activity and labor market generated by the St. John d'el Rey and its auxiliary economic activities. Unable to attract sufficient free labor, slaves supplied the labor force in the local economy. Just before the collapse of the mine in 1867 the St. John had employed nearly 1,600 slaves, and the majority of those were hired. This indicates that although the Morro Velho may have been the principal stimulus behind the growth of the slave population, the St. John owned barely one-fourth of the slaves in the parish. The company

Table 10   Slave to Free Ratios, Selected Parishes, Minas Gerais, 1872

Parish (Zone)	Slave Population	Slaves per Free Person
Juiz de Fora (Mata)	7,171	0.9
Mar de Hespanha (Mata)	5,500	0.4
Barbacena (Campos)	4,990	1.8
São José do Rio Preto (Mata)	4,103	0.2
Ubá (Mata)	3,833	0.9
Brumado (Campos)	3,704	0.4
Capela Nova N. S. das Dores (Campos)	3,604	1.2
Congonhas de Sabará (Metalúrgica)	3,284	2.0

Source: RAPM, 30 (1979), pp. 281–303.

slave register records slave rentals from over one hundred different owners in the 1860s and 1870s. As there is no evidence of any other large operation in mining, agriculture, or industry, the only reasonable conclusion is that most of the slaves were held in relatively small concentrations. This would fit the pattern that others have identified for Brazil in earlier periods.[52]

Although there are no comprehensive figures on the slave population of Congonhas, the tax receipts of the St. John indicate that the majority of the slaves it purchased (prior to 1845) were Africans (see table 11). (The tax receipts seem to account for most of the slaves purchased by the company. Receipts normally list prices, slave names, ethnic origins, and previous owner.) The origins of one-fifth of the population of nearly 300 are unknown, while a small 10.3 percent were Brazilian-born *crioulos*. Nearly 70 percent of the slaves were African, with the largest groups from the "nations" of the Congo, Angola, and East African regions.[53] These figures parallel the larger trends in the Atlantic slave trade to Brazil in the nineteenth century.[54] Company officials bought over 90 percent of their slaves in Rio de Janeiro (48.9), Congonhas de Sabará (31.2), and Sabará (12.8). Many bought locally were from surrounding mines that were closing, like the Tacquaril just over the Serra do Curral.

The slave traffic into Congonhas created a predominantly black and mulatto population with a white minority (see table 12). The population trend in the community in the century after the 1872 census has been toward a steady decrease in the percentage of blacks, a steady increase in the percentage of whites, and a fairly stable proportion of mulattoes in the population. In the 1870s a mere 21.2

Table 11 Ethnic Origins and Place of Birth of Slaves Purchased by the
St. John d'el Rey Mining Company, Limited, 1830–1843

Origins	Number	Percentage of Africans	Percentage of Total
Brazil			
Crioulo	30		10.3
Unknown	62		21.4
Total	92		31.7
Senegambia, Guinea-Bissau			
Monjollo	11	5.6	3.8
Gold Coast			
Mina	10	5.0	3.5
Bight of Biafra			
São Tomé	2	1.0	0.7
Congo-Angola			
Congo	47		
Angola	18		
Benguela	17	65.7	44.8
Cabinda	29		
Casange	14		
Rebelo	5		
East Africa			
Mozambique	34		
Quelimane	7	22.7	15.5
Inhambane	4		
African Totals	198	100.0	68.3
Grand Total	290		100.0

Source: Slave Tax Receipts File, SJNL.

percent of the population was white with 36.2 percent listed as black, and the rest mulatto. By the 1890s the number of whites had risen to 34.3 percent, the number of blacks had dropped to 25.4 percent, and the percentage of mulattoes had dropped slightly (to 35.1 percent). By the 1950s the percentage of whites in Nova Lima approached two-fifths (39 percent) of the community, and the percentage of blacks had dropped to just over one-eighth (13.9 percent) of the *município* population. Nearly one-half (47.1 percent) of the community were mulattoes.

Despite the inherent problems of race statistics in censuses over a century, the trend in Nova Lima seems clear. The community has

Table 12 Racial Composition, Nova Lima (NL) and Minas Gerais (MG), 1872–1950

Year		White	Mulatto	Black	Other	Total
1872	NL	21.2	41.7	36.2	0.9	100%
	MG	40.8	34.5	23.1	1.6	100%
1890	NL	34.3	35.1	25.4	5.2	100%
	MG	40.6	34.9	18.3	6.2	100%
1940	NL	32.0	52.6	15.3	0.1	100%
	MG	61.2	19.4	19.3	—	99%
1950	NL	39.0	47.1	13.9	0.0	100%
	MG	58.4	26.8	14.6	—	99.8%

Sources: RE 1872–1950; *Boletim commemorativo da exposição nacional de 1908* (Rio de Janeiro: Typographia da Estatistica, 1908), p. 81; T. Lynn Smith, *Brazilian Society* (Albuquerque: University of New Mexico Press, n.d.), p. 63.
Note: Some figures have been rounded causing totals to equal less than 100 percent.

assimilated the waves of racial groups, producing a racially mixed community. Blacks moved into the community in significant numbers due to the slave trade prior to the 1870s, and Europeans arrived at the turn of the century as the St. John attempted to fill its labor needs. The end result was a whitening of the community, and a strengthening of the mulatto (or mixed-race) population. Throughout the period 1872–1950 the community remained significantly darker than the larger population of Minas Gerais. In the 1870s the white population of Minas Gerais (40.8 percent) was twice that of Nova Lima (21.2 percent). By 1950 the percentage of whites in Minas (58.4 percent) was still 1.5 times larger than the percentage for Nova Lima (39.0 percent).

Since the gold rush of the eighteenth century Nova Lima has also been the recipient of a wide assortment of foreigners. Without a doubt the vast majority of the foreigners in Nova Lima have been attracted by the gold-mining economy. In the late nineteenth century the parish probably reached the highest percentage of foreigners in its history with around 5 percent of the population claiming foreign birth. While certainly not as cosmopolitan as late nineteenth-century São Paulo or Rio de Janeiro, Nova Lima had a much larger foreign community than the typical town in the Brazilian interior. (Foreigners in Belo Horizonte, for example, accounted for around 2 to 3 percent of the *município*'s population.)[55] Of the nearly 500 foreigners (of a population of 9,701) registered in the 1872 census, more than 80 percent were African slaves. Of the 383 Africans in Con-

Table 13 Age Structure of Congonhas de Sabará and Minas Gerais Slave Populations, 1872

Age	Congonhas de Sabará (in percentage)	Minas Gerais (in percentage)
0–10	9.5	12.6
11–20	21.4	20.1
21–30	32.5	21.6
31–40	26.9	11.5
41–50	4.7	12.2
51–60	2.9	10.9
61–70	1.3	7.5
71+	0.8	3.6
Total	100.0	100.0
Male/Female Ratio	107.8	92.6

Source: RE 1872, reel 4, part 9, pp. 226 and 1084.

gonhas de Sabará, all but 54 were still enslaved in 1872. The next largest foreign group, of course, was the British, with some 72 men and women. A small group of Portuguese, and a handful of various European nationals completed the foreign colony.

The foreign population of Congonhas shifted in the late nineteenth century with the termination of the Atlantic slave trade and the abolition of slavery. By the 1920s more than 580 foreigners resided in Nova Lima, accounting for about 3.5 percent of the total population. The single largest group came from England (187), with equally large groups from Italy (157), and Spain (125). A sizable group of Portuguese (82) formed the only other large foreign segment of the population. The British, of course, had come to Nova Lima to run the mine, and after the end of slavery they had imported large numbers of Italian, Spanish, and Portuguese workers. By the 1940s foreigners accounted for less than 2 percent of the community but still held strong at just under 500. The largest groups, though smaller than in the 1920s, were still the English, Italians, Spaniards, and Portuguese. Just as the construction and expansion of the Morro Velho by the British had stimulated the growth of a large foreign community, the end of the British era in 1960 led to the decline of the foreign-born community. By the 1970 census a mere . 3 percent of the population claimed foreign citizenship, barely 100 persons in a *município* of

Table 14 Age Structure, Nova Lima (NL) and Brazil (B), 1872–1960
(in percentage)

Age		1872	1920	1940	1960
0–9	NL	16.1	27.6	27.4	31.4
	B	23.5	30.0	29.6	30.5
10–19	NL	19.8	25.4	20.1	21.3
	B	22.5	23.8	23.7	22.4
20–29	NL	32.0	17.1	24.1	14.9
	B	21.1	17.9	17.4	16.4
30–39	NL	22.6	12.2	13.9	12.2
	B	11.1	11.6	11.9	12.1
40–49	NL	6.5	8.8	7.6	9.9
	B	7.5	7.9	8.4	8.5
50–59	NL	1.9	4.9	4.0	6.1
	B	6.0	4.8	5.0	5.4
60–69	NL	0.6	2.5	2.0	3.0
	B	4.2	2.6	2.6	3.1
70+	NL	0.5	1.5	0.9	1.2
	B	4.1	1.4	1.4	1.6
Total		100.0	100.0	100.0	100.0
Male/Female Ratio					
	NL	102.4	107.2	111.8	96.7
	B	106.6	101.7	100.0	99.8

Sources: RE 1872–1960, and Ludwig, *Brazil*, pp. 60–63.
Note: Figures are rounded to nearest tenth. For the 1872 national figures the age
groups are 0–10, 11–20, 21–30, 31–40, 41–50, 51–60 and 71+.

more than 40,000. The Brazilianization of the community reflected
the gradual decline in the British managerial ranks and the assimilation of Africans and European laborers after the end of slavery and
the labor experiments.

The shifting age structure of Nova Lima reflected the rise and consolidation of industrial order in Nova Lima and the changing labor
system of the St. John d'el Rey. As table 13 shows, in 1872 more
than 80 percent of the slaves were between eleven and forty years of
age, a figure that reflects the utilitarian role they played in the local
economy. Another 10 percent were children under the age of eleven,
and the remaining 10 percent were over the age of forty. The Congonhas slave population was much younger than the overall slave
population of the province. Just over 50 percent of the provincial

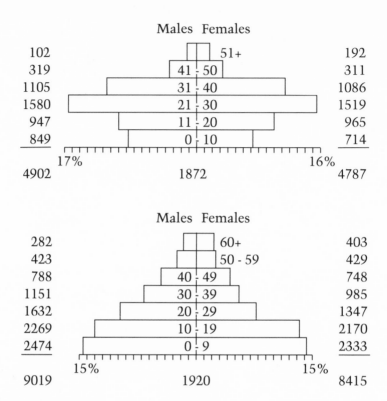

Figure 9 Age Structure, Nova Lima, 1872–1960

slave population was between the ages of eleven and forty, with 35 percent over the age of forty. Even with the aging of company slaves and the decline of slavery by the 1870s, the figures are still heavily weighted toward slaves in their most productive years.

The overall population of Nova Lima in the 1870s (see table 14 and figure 9) was very young with 90 percent of the population under forty years of age. Just over 35 percent of the community was under twenty years of age. The population moves toward an even greater tilt in the direction of youth in succeeding censuses. With 53 percent under age twenty in 1920, 47.5 percent in 1940, and 52.7 percent in 1960. Throughout the decades the age brackets forty and above remain fairly constant with 10 to 20 percent of the population. The prime working population between ages twenty and thirty-nine drops from approximately 55 percent in the 1870s to 27 percent in

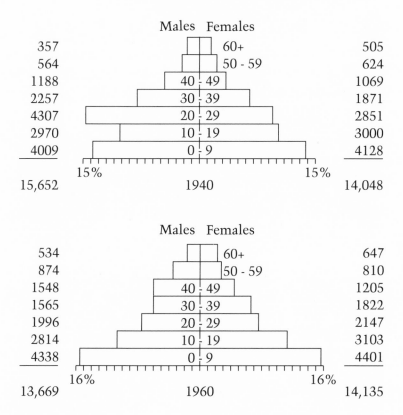

Males Females

357		60+		505
564		50 - 59		624
1188		40 - 49		1069
2257		30 - 39		1871
4307		20 - 29		2851
2970		10 - 19		3000
4009		0 - 9		4128

15%   15%

15,652   1940   14,048

Males Females

534		60+		647
874		50 - 59		810
1548		40 - 49		1205
1565		30 - 39		1822
1996		20 - 29		2147
2814		10 - 19		3103
4338		0 - 9		4401

16%   16%

13,669   1960   14,135

the 1960s. Old age and even middle age were not heavily represented in Nova Lima. National trends parallel those in Nova Lima in that a large proportion of the population (generally around 45 to 50 percent) is under age twenty (see table 14).

Amazingly, and unlike in Nova Lima, the age structure of the nation changes very little between the 1870s and 1960s. Over nearly a century, 45 to 50 percent of the population is under age twenty, another 30 percent is in the twenty-one-to-forty range, and 15 to 20 percent are over forty years of age. Between the 1870s and the 1940s the male/female ratio runs in favor of the male population rising from near parity in 1872 to a distinct tilt toward a significantly larger proportion of males in the population, no doubt reflecting the tremendous expansion of the (overwhelmingly male) labor force at Morro Velho between the world wars. This tilt runs counter to national trends that show a clear pattern of a move toward parity between the sexes by 1940 to a slightly larger female population by 1960. The shifting age structure no doubt reflects the changing nature of the labor system of the St. John d'el Rey. In the nineteenth century the demands of the slave-labor economy, and then the transient nature of free labor before 1930, probably tilted the age structure heavily toward the fifteen-to-forty age groups. As workers settled into full-time careers and remained in Nova Lima, the age structure began to take on a pyramid look.

Given the age and sex structure of the community, it is clear that the St. John employed virtually all adult males in Nova Lima by the 1920s. In the early 1920s the St. John employed 3,173 people, nearly all males. The 1920 census shows 5,418 males between the ages of fifteen and sixty-nine in the *município*. The company, then, would have employed 60 percent of all adult males in the *município*, and the figure must have come close to 90 percent of all adult males in the city of Nova Lima.[56] The 1940 census shows 8,582 males (ages twenty to sixty-nine); the company employed 7,684 people—again, around 90 percent of all males in the community.

Vital Rates

Shifting vital rates provide some of the most graphic evidence of the changes taking place in Nova Lima as the community industrialized. Parish registers for the nineteenth century and notarial registers for the twentieth century contain a wealth of data on the vital statistics of the local population. Each source presents problems. Some parish registers of baptisms, marriages, and burials are available for most of the nineteenth century, but they are not complete and clearly do not include the entire community. The registers include Catholics only, and no doubt many a Catholic did not see fit to register birth and death information. Consensual unions (*amazia*) were common in Brazil, and these couples would not appear in the church records for marriages. Many of the registers have disappeared, and for years in which no priest was present registration no doubt lagged. Finally, registration of baptisms does not always immediately follow birth, thereby throwing off calculations of birthrates.[57] Nova Lima's Cartório de Paz e Registro Civil begins to register births, deaths, and

Table 15 Vital Rates, Nova Lima, 1890–1960 (per thousand)

Year	Birthrate	Death Rate	Natural Increase
1890	6.0	5.2	0.8
1900	19.7	16.4	3.3
1910	17.2	11.3	5.9
1920	23.5	16.7	6.8
1930	19.5	13.5	6.0
1940	45.9	20.0	25.9
1950	54.1	21.3	32.9
1960	44.2	13.9	30.3

Source: CPRC, Births and Deaths.

marriages in the late nineteenth century, although records do not seem to be very comprehensive until after the community becomes a separate *município* in 1891. Although the *cartório* contains the most comprehensive records of vital statistics for the community, it is again unclear if the registers are complete. In a community with a very transient population, many may have failed to register births and deaths properly. However imperfect the records, they provide us with a revealing glimpse of the changing nature of a community as it industrializes.

Crude birth and death rates alike appear to have remained fairly stable in Nova Lima until the 1920s and 1930s. The community's crude birthrate provides the most graphic example of change. Table 15 shows the vital rates for Nova Lima since the 1890s. Although the numbers (particularly for the nineteenth century) are often suspect, the pattern is clear. Despite some fluctuations in the birthrate before 1900, the rate seems to remain fairly stable (around twenty per one thousand) into the 1930s. Then it takes off dramatically, doubling to forty-five to fifty-four per one thousand in the 1940s and 1950s. The dramatic shift emerges graphically in figure 10, which shows the total number of births and deaths registered in Nova Lima from the 1880s to the 1960s. After a brief jump in the early 1930s, the number of births skyrockets in the late 1930s before leveling off at a number much higher than the community had ever experienced.

The pattern in Nova Lima does not coincide at all with national trends. The birthrate in Brazil had reached the mid-40 range in the late nineteenth century and remained stable into the 1960s. The miniature "population explosion" in Nova Lima no doubt reflects the transition to a fully industrial community, and the stabiliza-

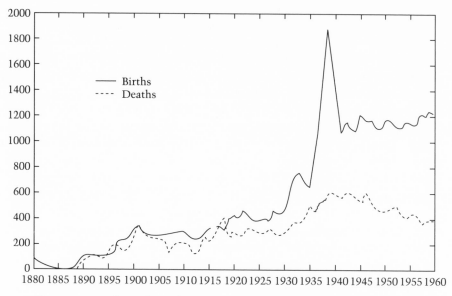

Figure 10   Births and Deaths, Nova Lima, 1880–1960

tion of the work force. As the cycle of transient labor on a seasonal basis faded away, it was accompanied by the influx of a large number of women in their childbearing years and a dramatic rise in the number of married couples. By 1940 nearly half the population was married, and probably many more were living in consensual unions. Furthermore, the percentage of the population in the ten-to-forty age brackets remains fairly steady (at around 55 to 60 percent). Evidence for a large number of consensual unions comes from statistics on legitimate births. In three sample years (1847, 1860, 1900) from the parish registers, illegitimate children accounted for (respectively) 34, 28, and 24 percent of all baptisms. At the turn of the century, then, possibly one in three to one in four children were born out of wedlock.[58]

The natality pattern becomes even clearer through figures for the general fertility rate for Nova Lima. Once again, although figures for the nineteenth century are always suspect, the fertility rate appears to be very low (35.2 per 1,000 in 1872 compared with 138 for the Brazilian slave population). By 1920 the rate has risen to 97.5 per 1,000. The rate nearly doubles by 1940 to 188.0 and continues to be very high into the 1960s. The extraordinary rise in the general fertility rate in Nova Lima puts it into the range of the national rates in the 1930–50 period. The Brazilian rate in these years is in the 177-to-179 range.[59]

Figures on the crude death rate in Nova Lima are somewhat more problematic. While the nation experienced a steady decline in the death rate (from 30 per 1,000 in the late nineteenth century to 12 in the 1950s), the rate in Nova Lima appears to hold steady and at one-third to one-half the national average. In the 1940s the rate in Nova Lima rises to meet the declining national average and remains there before dropping to previous levels and equalling the national rate in 1960. In absolute terms the figures indicate a slightly increasing number of deaths in the 1930s and 1940s (accompanying the rise in population), with a slow and steady decline after 1945. Clearly, the major demographic shift in Nova Lima is nearly the reverse of the national pattern. (The trend in Nova Lima is also contrary to the general Latin American pattern.)[60] This industrializing community witnessed a baby boom, rather than a steady birthrate, and without a dramatic drop in the death rate. Although a baby boom in one community should not be so surprising, the accompanying lack of a decline in the death rate requires closer analysis.

The parish burial registers and the notarial death registers allow an indirect look into morbidity in Nova Lima from the mid-nineteenth century to the 1960s. Although smallpox, influenza, and typhoid struck the community from time to time, the effects appear somewhat minor compared with other causes of death. The company worked with local officials to quarantine the town and isolate the carriers of infectious illnesses, thus reducing the impact of epidemic diseases. Furthermore, the company vaccinated its slaves and free employees and pressed local officials to compel the rest of the community to seek vaccinations. The worst epidemic to strike the community was the worldwide Spanish influenza outbreak in 1918.[61] At the turn of the century the company brought in a new water supply for the town from the heights of the Serra do Curral. The Aguas Claras water and a new city water system built by the company virtually eliminated typhoid from Nova Lima and Morro Velho.[62]

Respiratory and digestive illnesses caused from 50 to 75 percent of all deaths from the 1840s to the 1940s. Gastroenteritis, bronchitis, pneumonia, and tuberculosis were the principal killers. Many of those dying from respiratory illnesses probably died from silicosis (pneumoconiosis), but the diagnosis of the disease was not perfected until the 1940s. Many silicotics were diagnosed as having pneumonia or tuberculosis. About the time of the Second World War heart disease (along with circulation problems) began to emerge as a major killer, as respiratory and digestive illnesses declined in importance. This probably reflects better health care, changes in diet and the water supply, and the onset of the diseases of industrial societies. When compared with figures for twentieth-century Rio de Janeiro, Nova Lima appears to have a different set of problems. Nova Lima has a much higher percentage of heart-related deaths, and the causes of death in Rio are much more diverse.[63]

As with other preindustrial and industrializing societies, Nova Lima experienced extraordinarily high infant mortality rates. The município also experienced the drastic decline in infant mortality experienced by industrial societies. The rate dropped from 221.5 per 1,000 in 1900 to 195.1 in 1920, to 120.9 by 1940, and 61.8 per 1,000 in 1960. By the 1960s the infant mortality rate in the community had fallen to nearly one-quarter of the 1900 figure! This enormous decline is faster and more impressive than the comparable trend in some of Brazil's major urban centers. In 1960 the infant mortality rate in Nova Lima was lower than the rates of Brazil's five largest cities, and the rate of decline in infant mortality between 1900 and 1960 was higher.[64]

As with the rest of the population in the community, infants died largely from respiratory and intestinal illnesses: bronchitis, pneumonia, and gastroenteritis. Perhaps most striking is the very high percentage of stillbirths, an indication of poor prenatal care. Throughout the twentieth century over one-third of all babies in Nova Lima were stillborn. Many of those who were not stillborn died very soon after birth due to complications from delivery and poor prenatal care. Despite the impressive decline in the infant mortality rate by the 1960s, the number of stillbirths (as a percentage of all births) was on the rise. As the baby boom took shape after 1930, it appears that pregnant mothers were not receiving adequate health care. It seems likely that the enormous amounts of toxic industrial effluents (mercury, arsenic, and cyanide, for example) also may have had a role in the high rate of stillbirths.[65]

The rate of natural increase (i.e., crude birthrate minus crude death rate) lags far behind the national average until the baby boom of the 1930s. For the nation the increase hovers around 17 to 19 per 1,000 from the late nineteenth century until 1940. For Nova Lima the

Table 16 Mortality Rate of Company Slaves, St. John d'el Rey Mining Company, Limited, 1842–1883

Year	Slave Population	Deaths	Death Rate (per 1,000)
1842	464	12	25.9
1851	1,201	40	33.3
1855	1,127	32	28.4
1859	1,121	31	27.7
1860	937	32	34.2
1861	1,424	44	30.9
1865	1,225	64	52.3
1870	1,191	41	34.4
1871	1,115	36	32.3
1872	875	28	32.0
1873	778	28	36.0
1874	749	40	53.4
1875	813	37	45.5
1876	814	35	43.0
1877	732	27	36.9
1879	574	24	41.8
1880	398	16	40.2
1883	344	13	37.8
Averages	882	32	36.5

Source: AR 1842–1884.
Note: Figure for 1842 is for adults only.

rate is always less than half that, below 7 per 1,000. After 1940 the national rate rose to 24 to 30 per 1,000, and Nova Lima experienced virtually the same rate, although for very different reasons, as noted above. The increase in population in Nova Lima prior to the 1930s was probably, to a large degree, from in-migration. In nearly every decade after 1890 the absolute difference between births and deaths does not account for the absolute change in the population. Even if one assumes that all the children born in Nova Lima in the 1920s remained in the *município*, the net gain over deaths during the decade would have accounted for merely one-quarter of the population increase between 1920 and 1930. The baby boom of the 1930s could have accounted for a major portion of the increase in that decade and in the next two. The apparent loss of population in the 1940s and 1950s most likely represents the dismemberment of Raposos and Rio Acima from the *município*.

Prior to 1888 slaves represent a special population within the

Table 17 Crude Death Rates for Selected Slave Populations in the
Americas, 1817–1870

Place	Date	Crude Death Rate
S. Amaro Parish, Bahia	1817	47.0
Jamaica	1817–32	26.0
Minas Gerais	1821	62.8
Surinam	1826–48	50.0
Danish West Indies	1840s	50.0
Gongo Soco Mine	1842	28.0
Cata Branca Mine	1842	19.0
Rio de Janeiro	1847	42.7
Rio de Janeiro	1870	38.0

Sources: Schwartz, *Sugar Plantations*, p. 366; Letter Book #4, 7 February 1847, SJUT;
Karasch, *Slave Life*, p. 92; Slenes, "Brazilian Slavery," p. 281.

larger changes taking place in the community. Although, once again,
the figures are often partial and suspect, it is possible to assemble
some figures on the slave population separate from the free population of Congonhas de Sabará. The slave community is too small, and
the figures too incomplete, to venture firm estimates of the crude
birthrate in the slave population. Relatively good figures are available on the crude death rate of the St. John d'el Rey's slave force.
The management carefully monitored the health of their bondsmen,
keeping detailed morbidity and mortality records duly published in
each *Annual Report*. Table 16 shows the mortality rates for selected
years in the nineteenth century.

Mortality ranged from as low as 25.9 per 1,000 in the 1840s to as
high as 53.4 per 1,000 in the 1870s. The average for the years for
which figures are available is 36.5 per 1,000, a figure on the low end
of the range for the few comparative slave populations in the New
World for which statistics are available. Table 17 compares the St.
John's slave mortality with several other nineteenth-century slave
populations. (The age structure of these populations no doubt varied
widely and limits the value of any comparison.) Figures ranged as
high as 62.8 per 1,000 in Minas Gerais in the 1820s to as low as 26
per 1,000 in Jamaica at roughly the same time. Karasch estimates
that the slave population of Rio de Janeiro in 1847 was 42.7 deaths
per 1,000 compared with 31 per 1,000 for freemen. Robert Slenes
estimates a mortality rate of 38 per 1,000 for the slave population of
Rio de Janeiro in 1870. Unfortunately, the parish registers have not

survived for 1872, the year for which we have good enough census figures to calculate a crude death rate for the entire community.[66] As with the larger population of nineteenth-century Congonhas, respiratory and digestive ailments were the major killers.

Marriage Patterns

The changing nature of the technological system, especially its labor requirements, also affects marriage patterns in Nova Lima. In the early decades of company expansion the slave work force exhibited a sex-ratio imbalance even greater than that noted for other Brazilian slave populations in the nineteenth century. Although the slave force was relatively small in the 1840s and 1850s, the imbalance is striking. The company owned 255 adult slaves in 1837, and 77 percent were male. In 1843, 71 percent of the company's 376 slaves were male. This compares with ratios of 65:35 in Vassouras in the 1840s and 60:40 in Rio Claro in the 1870s (both coffee counties).[67] Perhaps even more striking is the shift toward a balance by the 1860s (when the slave force peaks), accompanied by a very high percentage of married couples. Although the company hired the majority of the captive labor force by the 1860s, the sex-ratio balance and the high percentage of married couples seems to hold for both hired and "company" slaves. In 1867 the portion of males in the company slave force had dropped to 53 percent. A survey of the slave force in 1850 reveals that 43 percent of the company's adult male slaves were married, as were an astounding 84 percent of the company's adult females. The numbers are nearly identical for the large group of hired Cata Branca slaves.[68] Between 1845 and 1850 no less than eighty-seven slave couples married. Another twenty-two couples married in the 1850s (as did eight rented couples). In the following years the number of marriages declined rapidly, no doubt reflecting the high percentage of rented slaves and the declining number of company-owned slaves.[69]

These figures are much higher than the general population of slaves in 1872, although the latter figures may not be representative of earlier decades. According to the 1872 census, 10 percent of all males and 5.6 percent of all females were married or widowed. If the slave population under the age of twenty is subtracted from the figures, the percentages rise 16.2 and 7.5 percent, respectively—still far below the Morro Velho figures.[70] In Rio Claro, for example, Dean found that approximately 25 percent of the adult slaves were married. The Rio Claro figure is less than half that for the population of adult men and women, hired and owned, at Morro Velho.[71] In fact, slave marriage rates appear to be much higher than those for the free population. In 1872 only one in four of the community as a whole was married. According to the parish registers, nearly four in ten of all marriages in the parish register sample were slave marriages. (The figures no doubt reflect the flaws of registration.) The balance of males and females, along with the high percentage of married couples, certainly sets the Congonhas/Morro Velho slave population apart from others in Brazil for which we have figures. The figures undoubtedly reflect the success of the St. John's drive to promote marriage and procreation among their slave force.

In addition to a very young population in the late nineteenth century, nearly three-quarters of the community were unmarried. This pattern fits with that found in the province as a whole and in the nation. The percentages are virtually identical.[72] The move toward a more balanced ratio of single to married persons appears in the 1920 and 1940 censuses (44 percent single to 47 percent married in 1920 and 41 percent to 52 percent in 1940), a trend that appears later on the national scene. By 1920 Villa Nova reached close to parity between married and single persons, a parity that does not appear in national figures until the 1940 census. The rising number of married persons probably contributed to the growing percentage of young people in the community as the number of childbearing couples increased. Across the decades the number of widows and widowers runs between 5 and 10 percent, with the former far outnumbering the latter. Widows outnumbered widowers five to one in the 1920 and 1940 censuses. This imbalance probably reflects the hazardous life of the gold miner, and the long-term health problems of men who had worked underground.[73]

Some sketchy information from parish registers allows for the computation of the average age at marriage of males and females in the nineteenth century. In 1847 the average age of males at marriage was 29.3 years and 25.5 for females, a difference of 3.8 years. In 1850 the averages were 31.2 years for males and 25.1 years for females, with a difference of 6.1 years. Finally, in 1860 the figures had dropped to 22.3 for males and 19.6 for females, a difference of 2.7

years. (Unfortunately, the age of marrying couples does not appear with any regularity in the parish registers after 1860.) If these figures are representative, Nova Lima falls within the range for age at marriage found in Europe in the early to mid-nineteenth century: 22.2 to 30 for females and 24.3 to 31.3 for males.[74] After 1900 the average age at marriage for both males and females remains steady and within a narrow range: 24.0 to 27.1 for males, and 21.2 to 23.1 for females. The community did not exhibit the patterns of young age at marriage and high fertility generally associated with contemporary underdeveloped countries.

Local parish registers also provide a sketchy, but revealing, look into marriage patterns and race. Although the registers list slave and free marriages with equal attention to detail, the information must be used with caution. A number of registers are missing for the nineteenth century, and this may lead to undercounting, particularly for the free population, as the registers for slaves appear more comprehensive. Furthermore, the registers list only marriages in the church, and it is impossible to know how many couples may have been living in free consensual unions. Finally, the sample is for a very small population and, therefore, must be seen as a sketchy and incomplete view of local patterns, not as a complete survey of a large population.

Surprisingly, the largest group listed in the registers (for the selected sample years) between 1847 and 1880 are slave marriages. Nearly 40 percent (35 of 91) of the marriages are between slaves. This pattern is more an indication of the role of slavery at Morro Velho than slavery in the community, for the vast majority of the slaves marrying are under the control of the St. John d'el Rey. As noted, the company encouraged the slaves to marry and provided rewards for doing so. Six marriages (7 percent) are between free persons and slaves, the former generally being former slaves. About one-fourth of the marriages are between blacks (*crioulos*). Just over 15 percent are mulatto marriages (*pardos*). Three of the ninety-one marriages are between mulattoes and blacks. A mere 3 are between mulattoes and whites, and none are between blacks and whites.[75] A mere 10 percent of the marriages are among whites (*brancos*), who made up 20 percent of the population. The figure seems to indicate a strong consciousness of the broad color spectrum and a tendency to marry someone of a similar color group. Nevertheless, racial categories in Brazil were very fluid, and the registers do not list consensual unions where racial "crossing" was more likely. The registers also contain a few marriages of mixed nationalities: English and Brazilian (two), Brazilian and Portuguese (one), and one English couple marrying in the Catholic church.

Marriage registers regularly recorded the native *município* of the bride and groom, thereby allowing us an imperfect but revealing glimpse of the origins of the community. Although the sample is small, and takes in only those who married locally, the pattern seems clear and probably holds for the rest of the community. Of the sample of 194 individuals marrying in the parish between 1860 and 1900, an overwhelming majority (173 or 89 percent) listed Congonhas or the surrounding *municípios* of the old Zona Metalúrgica as their place of birth. Another 3 percent (six individuals) came from Minas Gerais. Just one person listed another Brazilian province as his place of birth (Bahia), and a mere fourteen (7 percent) were European-born. This same pattern continues through the first half of this century. An even greater predominance of migrants comes from the surrounding region. Nearly three-quarters of those marrying in the *município* were born in Nova Lima or the surrounding area (32.8 percent from the Zona Metalúrgica and 39.0 percent from Nova Lima). An overwhelming 95.4 percent of those in the table were born in Minas Gerais. The pattern for nearly a century is clear and convincing: the local population, and therefore the labor force in the mine, was drawn from Nova Lima and the surrounding *municípios*. Throughout most of this period the region was characterized by small-scale agriculture and cattle raising geared toward self-sufficiency and local markets. These statistics support the observations of company management. The principal source of labor for the mines came from the peasantry in the surrounding region. The proletarianization of the peasantry parallels similar processes in other areas of Latin America and Europe in the nineteenth and twentieth centuries.[76]

Conclusion

For more than a century the growth and expansion of the St. John d'el Rey slowly transformed what had been a small, rural village into a large, industrial city. The British brought increasingly capital-intensive industry to this small village in the Brazilian interior, yet they encountered a resistance to their plans to implant industry in the community. A free peasantry refused to leave behind their traditional rural order to work in the mines. Unable to attract free wage labor (at the wages they offered), the company purchased and hired large numbers of slaves, Africanizing the racial and cultural patterns in the village. Although the process of capital-intensive industrialization accelerated in the 1890s with the construction of the Chalmers mine and mill, the surrounding Brazilian peasantry continued to resist the efforts to construct an industrial order. In the late nineteenth century the company faced continual frustration as the local peasantry developed a pattern of seasonal labor, moving between their fields and the mine, denying the British an adequate work force in the aftermath of abolition. The importation of European laborers helped the St. John make it through these years of rebuilding but failed to solve their chronic labor shortage.

As the preceding pages demonstrate, the 1930s mark the turning point in the life of the community. The completion of the major technological transformations begun by Chalmers laid the groundwork for the post-1930 company expansion and the demographic shifts in the community. As noted earlier, the enormous expansion of mining operations in the post-Chalmers years was *not* initiated by the company but by major changes in Brazil and the world economy. The collapse of the agricultural (coffee) economy after 1929, the rise of Getúlio Vargas with his social and fiscal legislation, and a dramatic rise in gold prices contributed to the transformations of the 1930s. In the 1920s the mine nearly closed for lack of labor. In the 1930s labor became abundant and flowed into Nova Lima in record numbers. The traditional resistance of the peasantry to work in the mine disappeared, and a stable, industrial working class took shape in the community.

The demographic analysis reflects these changes. Although the town continued to draw on surrounding *municípios* for its labor supply, many remained and settled in Nova Lima, married, and raised families. The result was a major demographic shift, but not the traditional "demographic transition" experienced by Western Europe in the eighteenth century and by some areas of Latin America in the last two centuries.[77] On the contrary, the community experienced an impressive rise in birth and fertility rates and a slow rise in death rates, producing a miniature population explosion. Although the demographic trends in Nova Lima do not coincide with those of the nation, they do parallel other mining and industrial communities in Europe and the United States. Recent research indicates that mining and industrial communities experience high fertility rates and birthrates contrary to the larger national trends toward lower rates in Western Europe and the United States.[78]

The introduction of capital-intensive industry in the interior of Brazil after 1830 did not suddenly transform the traditional rural society. The British were compelled to adapt to local labor markets and a technological system employing slave labor. With the decline and abolition of slavery, the British industrial order faced a crisis, and management attempted to solve it with imported European labor. The experiment allowed the company to continue industrial growth and innovation, but by the 1920s the shortage of labor threatened to bring industrialization to a halt. The long, slow process of industrialization surged forward after 1930 when national and international events converged on the Morro Velho mine and Nova Lima. For a century the slow and erratic growth of the technological system at Morro Velho shaped the growth of the community. At the same time the resistance of the surrounding peasantry shaped the development of the technological system. For all the economic and financial power of this British company, an unorganized, poor, and traditional peasantry held the company's future in its hands. When this peasantry finally made the transition to industrial life, they would remain poor, but they would organize and fight to shape the future of the company—and of their community.

6

From Slave Society
to Working-Class Community

The miners' movement is different from the movements of the
metalworkers, railway workers, bankers, that are strategic sectors of
the economy. Not us miners. We drill into the earth, we die beneath it
in order to extract gold. Our reality is different. Burdensome.
It has the smell of death.[1]

Between 1880 and 1960 Brazil experienced a profound and fundamental social transformation, as the largest slave society of the Western Hemisphere made the transition to free wage labor and, eventually, to the rise of an industrial working class in major urban centers.
Despite its relative isolation and small size, Nova Lima made the
same transition, in many ways a microcosm of the larger change
taking place in cities like São Paulo, Rio de Janeiro, or Porto Alegre.
Slavery was at the heart of nineteenth-century Brazilian society, and
the rise of an industrial working class is an essential feature of urban
Brazil in the twentieth century. This chapter will examine these two
phases in the history of Nova Lima, focusing on the rise of an industrial working-class community in the years after the First World
War. The first part of this chapter analyzes the nature of local society in the nineteenth century by looking briefly at the three major
social groups: slaves, elites, and the free masses. The second part
turns to the transition to free labor in Nova Lima and to the rise of
a working class. This section emphasizes the conditions of workers,
their concerns, their struggles to organize, and their efforts to take
control of the politics of the community. Finally, the chapter links
the plight of the workers to the larger forces that affect the company
and the community: the world gold market, inflation, and the rise
of mass politics in Brazil after 1930.

While the pursuit of profit drove forward company expansion, the
pursuit of a better life guided the struggle of the *novalimenses*. The
former produced an industrial city, the latter a militant, unionized,

and politicized working-class community. Control of the technological system placed the British in a position to shape the growth of the community and to direct the flow of profits to Great Britain. In many ways the story of the people of Nova Lima is the struggle to wrest an ever-larger share of the wealth of the Morro Velho from the British who controlled the mine. It is a struggle that results in few victories for the community. Across three centuries the wealth of the Morro Velho mine has played the central role in the fortunes of the *novalimenses*, and control of that wealth has eluded them for the past 150 years. Indeed, the most striking feature of the history of Nova Lima is the contrast between the poverty of its people and the immense wealth they extract from the Morro Velho mine.

The Slave Community

Slavery was central to nineteenth-century society in Congonhas, just as the rise of the working class is the dominant feature of society in twentieth-century Nova Lima. A slave economy permeated all aspects of local society, adding a third major social group to a free population already split in two. Local society consisted of a small elite of landowners, mineowners, and merchants; a large group of small farmers and laborers; and a considerable population of captive blacks. From the 1840s to the 1870s a large part of the slave population in Congonhas was either owned or hired by the St. John d'el Rey. By the 1870s, as the St. John began a slow transition to free labor, half the slaves in the parish were outside the company's control. Although parish registers and notarial documents provide us with some brief glimpses at the slave population outside the company's control, the archives of the St. John are the richest and most complete record of slave life in the parish. As a consequence of this uneven documentary base, the following analysis emphasizes the company slaves (hired and owned), although not to the exclusion of non-company slaves.

The first census of the slave population of Congonhas is the 1873 registration (*matrícula*) required by the passage of the Rio Branco Law in 1871. At roughly the same time the first national census took place providing us with two counts in 1873.[2] In the 1870s one-third of the parish population was enslaved. The figure was no doubt much higher in previous years. In the 1860s, for example, the St. John alone

Table 18 Slaves Purchased by the St. John d'el Rey Mining Company, Limited, 1830–1843

Year	Purchases
1830	18
1831	84
1834	151
1835	71
1836	29
1837	4
1838	3
1839	65
1840	30
1841	37
1842	1
1843	7
Total	500

Source: Slave Purchase File, SJNL.
Note: Figure for 1834 includes 136 slaves purchased as part of the Morro Velho estate. No slaves were purchased in 1832 and 1833.

employed over fifteen hundred slaves in a community estimated at five thousand. Given the lack of large landholdings in an essentially subsistence agriculture economy, most of the slave population in non-company hands was probably widely distributed. No reference exists in the published literature or archival documents consulted to suggest any of the local elite had large numbers of slaves. The major centers of economic activity in the parish (aside from the Morro Velho) were several small mining properties. All operated on a small scale and sporadically. Few were likely to employ many slaves.

The St. John purchased approximately five hundred slaves between 1830 and the passage of the Aberdeen Act in 1845 (see table 18). Generally, the company made large purchases in the slave market in Rio de Janeiro, although records indicate a significant number of slaves were purchased in Sabará and at Morro Velho. The purchases made at Morro Velho, no doubt, were prearranged sales with slave brokers who brought the slaves to the company for the completion of the transaction. This was true, for example, of the purchase of the slaves from the nearby Tacquaril Mine, just over the Serra do Curral near the road to Sabará. In 1840 and 1841 the company working the Tacquaril mine went into liquidation and sold most of its slaves to the St. John.[3]

The vast majority of the slaves purchased between 1830 and 1845 were from west-central Africa, Angola, and Mozambique.[4] Generally, the company labeled slaves by their "nation," as a *crioulo(a)*, or by their place of purchase. Hence, Africans were listed as João Mozambique, Maria Conga, Miguel São Tomé, and the like. Slaves born in Brazil were listed with *crioulo(a)* as the last name, and those purchased from other mines as Pedro Tacquaril, Joaquim Cata Branca, or Fernando Cocais. Although the company left numerous records of slave purchases, emancipations, punishments, illnesses, and the like, an exact census of the company's slave population is difficult, in part, because of shifting name patterns. At times a slave may be referred to by first name and nation, by first name only, or by first name and an initial. Furthermore, the nation or purchase location may be dropped and replaced by a new designation to distinguish the slave from others with the same first name. João Mozambique, for example, may appear in the company records as João B. (to set him apart from other Joãos), João Mozambique, or later as João Carreiro, because of his particular occupation at the mine.

Slave Life

As noted in chapter 5, slaves worked in virtually all aspects of company operations. The majority of the males worked as borers in the mine, while many worked as craftsmen or apprentices to craftsmen. Most of the women worked in either the reduction process or in textile production. As in England, women "spallers" broke down the ore into tiny fragments once machines and men had broken the rock into small pieces. The company produced clothing (for slaves and miners), blankets, and assorted items using slave women as seamstresses. Aged slaves and children under ten did little work, but teenagers and unproductive older slaves were used in menial labor and domestic service. In contrast to the majority of Brazilian slaves, the captive blacks at Morro Velho were mostly involved in industrial and artisanal pursuits. Very few were employed in the agricultural tasks so familiar to their fellow chattel on Brazilian plantations.[5]

The slave force lived in isolated housing on the western slope of the Morro Velho in an area known as Boa Vista or Timbuctoo (a term with apparent connotations of the African origins of the slaves). In the late 1830s the company constructed ten houses, eighteen by ten feet each, for sixty slaves.[6] By the mid-1840s the compound contained fifty houses and was growing rapidly with the addition of hired slaves from the failed mining enterprises at Gongo Soco, Cocais, and Cata Branca. Eventually, the single women were housed in a compound that was closed and locked each night and known locally as the "Convent." Married couples had separate houses or apartments, and single males were housed in groups of ten to twenty in a single building. The growing number of freedpersons complicated the housing situation in the 1870s, as some families contained freed and enslaved members. The company had to alter the slave quarters at Timbuctoo, building a wall to separate free and slave quarters in 1878.[7]

The company provided what management considered adequate clothing. Male slaves received two suits of clothing annually: rough wool garments for the winter months and cotton garments for the summer. Underground workers also received a heavy woolen shirt and a heavy leather hat. Women received a thin wool shift, a heavier wool petticoat, and a large square kerchief worn around the neck and over the chest. Each slave also received a new cotton blanket annually. All the slaves went barefoot.[8] In addition to work clothes, all slaves received their special *revista* clothing, described in detail by the superintendent.

All the blacks, men, women, and children, are likewise furnished with a dress for Sundays, consisting, for the men, of a white cotton loose frock, with red collar and cuffs, a pair of white cotton trousers, with a red strip down the outer seams, a patent black leather waist belt, having in front a brass plate, with the words "Morro Velho" on it, and a red Glengarry cap. For the cold season they have a blue woollen loose frock, with red collar and cuffs. The women have a white cotten gown, with two or three red stripes across the skirt, a coloured hankerchief wrapped, according to the fancy of the wearer, round the head, and for the hot season a cotton scarf, with various coloured stripes; for the cold a spencer and cape of red cloth.[9]

The slave force received three meals a day consisting of the standard regional foodstuffs: beef, pork, maize, beans, rice, and vegetables. The standard food allowance called for two pounds of fresh beef per week per adult, nine pounds of corn meal and flour, four and one-half pounds of beans, and thirteen ounces of bacon, as well as vegetables and salt. Meals were prepared communally and distributed around the mine compound and underground.[10] Females nursing infants received additional rations. Breakfast usually consisted of a cold maize porridge (angu) and coffee. Lunch was distributed on the job, and dinner was eaten in the slave compound. Slaves were allowed to cultivate their own personal garden plots and keep pigs and poultry to supplement their diet and their income.[11]

If the daily diary of the superintendent is an accurate measuring device, the slave population at Morro Velho did not present major problems of social control. Runaways, stealing, and insubordination were the most common challenges to company authority. In 1859, for example, a dozen slaves fled the premises, most of those hired slaves. Most runaways recorded in the diary were returned within a few weeks, some having fled the mine to their owner's home. The most common punishments for stealing and insubordination were *palmatórias*. These were inflicted at a public ceremony in the slave compound. More persistent runaways and habitual thieves were sometimes placed in irons, or their clothes were marked to draw attention to them in public. Occasionally, a major incident drew a flogging. Slaves received lashes for striking an Englishman, fighting, or major thefts. Suicide as a means of resistance seems to have been very rare, although the diary does record a few vivid examples.

Some slaves created constant problems for the English as the following example indicates. In July 1862 Marcellino Novo, a company slave,

> working in the Iron Smithy—an acknowledged thief who has had for many years an iron on his leg as the only preventative to his prosecuting theft actively—had the iron taken off a few months ago with the view of giving him another trial; but having renewed his plunder and assumed his former functions as a practised thief amongst the Blacks, it became unavoidable to place the iron again on his leg as [the] only means likely to restrain him from extensive theft. This morning he concealed himself behind a forge not in use, and had a short piece of cord around his neck in pretence of about to commit suicide. I understand severe punishment has been tried without producing the least effect. He is a vigorous and healthy man not old and possesses exquisite skill and cunning in

his art. Restraint seems better than active punishment. The plan of encouraging him to do well has had little if any effect.[12]

Marcellino was eventually sold, as were other "problem" slaves.

In the 1840s a former company physician attacked the St. John in the British press, accusing the company of mistreating its slaves and causing a high death rate. Management dispatched a special envoy to Morro Velho to survey the situation. Thomas Walker, M.D., had been a regimental surgeon for many years in a variety of naval assignments in India.[13] Walker's report, read with a critical eye, provides a valuable, detailed look into the company's slave population at midcentury, and the *mentalité* of the slave owners.[14] At Walker's suggestion the company implemented a series of regulations for disciplining slaves. These regulations, in theory, made it impossible for the British miners to punish slaves, leaving all decisions on punishment in the hands of the superintendent. All slaves had the right to complain to the superintendent of any ill treatment by the British miners and officers, a right that was surely meaningless for most slaves, as most were no doubt thoroughly intimidated by their subordinate status. All punishments were ordered and overseen by the superintendent and were duly noted in his diary. Whether for fear of punishment or simply resignation to their fate, the slave population at Morro Velho required a minimal amount of policing. With the exception of the unrest provoked by the Cata Branca court case in the late 1870s, no other records indicate that the company ever faced significant group resistance by its slave force. A handful of overseers were sufficient to handle the more than fifteen hundred slaves on the Morro Velho compound in the 1860s.

In addition to providing what management perceived to be adequate housing, clothing, and diet, the St. John offered rewards to the slave force to encourage marriage, procreation, and good behavior. In keeping with the paternalism of the management, the company encouraged marriage and procreation believing that both would lead to more "responsible" workers and to a strengthening of "moral" behavior among the slaves. The superintendent bestowed bottles of wine and one to two milreis on couples who married or who gave birth to children. Conversely, the superintendent and the board took a harsh view of childbirth among unmarried mothers, though they could do little about the situation other than attempt to segregate single women.[15] As pointed out in chapter 5, the company incentives appear to have worked. In the 1850s half of all male slaves, and three-quarters of the females, were married, many to free persons. It should be pointed out that the company did not encourage marriage and procreation to produce a breeding population. After 1 January 1868 the St. John freed all children born to their slaves and the Cata Branca slaves. The primary objective of the management was to promote stable, responsible, and moral workers and to move them along gradually toward emancipation. Paternalism, not demography, formed the underpinnings of the system.[16] The slaves established ritual kinship ties among themselves through the use of *compadrio* (godparentage). The pattern in the parish registers of Congonhas is clear and convincing—slaves almost always turned to other slaves to serve as godparents for their newborn children. As with the pattern among Bahian slaves studied by Stuart Schwartz, slaves did not turn to their masters to serve as godparents. The pattern holds for both company and non-company slaves.[17]

Despite the tremendous shocks of the "middle passage" and the pressures to shed African customs and languages, slaves at Morro Velho did manage to maintain some of their heritage. Scattered references note that certain slaves were "kings and queens" watching "over the interests and welfare of their respective nations."[18] In February 1859, for example, the superintendent, noting that Jacinto Tacquaril had fallen to his death in the mine, added in passing that he "was chief of the Mozambique nation."[19] Occasionally, the different "nationalities" dressed in their native costumes and performed dances for the benefit of foreign visitors.[20] Despite these meager attempts to preserve African customs and traditions, the forces of assimilation must have been very powerful. Most of the Africans probably arrived in Brazil as youths with a brief experience and socialization into the customs and traditions of their tribal heritage.[21] The diversity of tribal backgrounds, the variety of languages, and the exposure to Brazilian-born slaves must have undermined ancestral traditions, gradually eroding memories of life in Africa. No doubt, the costumes and dances of the nationalities displayed at Morro Velho must have reflected the influence of Brazil and the intermingling of tribal groups as well as African customs. The constant influx of Africans into the slave trade in Brazil, and to the mine at Morro Velho, worked to Africanize Brazilians, but the wide variety of non-African influences that surrounded the slaves were a powerful means of acculturating them to Brazilian society.

One powerful assimilating force was the imposition of Roman Catholicism on the slave population. The British, rather than attempt to convert the slaves to Protestantism, chose to expose them to the dominant religion of the country. The paternalism of the British led to the hiring of a Roman Catholic chaplain to minister to their chattel. When the company hired a Portuguese priest to serve the company as slave chaplain in 1860, the chairman of the board summed up management's view of the role of religion among the slaves at Morro Velho. The board, he advised Superintendent Gordon:

> trust that in addition to the performance of weekly religious services of the church (the chaplain) will occupy himself with the personal instruction of the negroes in the elements of christian truth & by means thereof inculcate upon them the practice of moral habits in their daily life. The mere formal performance of the public service of Religion, will it is to be apprehended, do but little to advance *people of their class* in the knowledge and practice of Christian duty, unless accompanied by such intercourse between them and their Pastor, as is here suggested. *It is well known that in the African mind there is no antagonistic element to the reception of christian truth &* that patient and judicious teaching are not likely to be thrown away upon these persons, who have every claim upon us to give them every possible help for their social advancement.[22]

One can only speculate on the impact of this forced exposure to "christian truth" on the slaves at Morro Velho. The company required them to attend mass on Sunday mornings in a chapel built especially for the slaves on the southern slope of the Morro Velho directly across the Cardoso basin from the Casa Grande.[23] The padres hired by the St. John do not seem to have been terribly concerned about their flock. Complaints about the first chaplain, Padre Saraiva, in company correspondence indicate that he did not even accompany funeral processions from the chapel to the slave cemetery nearby. Furthermore, one of his successors, according to the superintendent, "made a small fortune" on the Sunday collection.[24] At any rate, the slaves' exposure to Catholicism must have been minimal at best.

Most of the company's adult slaves spent the majority of their day working or restricted to the slave quarters after eight at night. During the daytime hours when the slave was not working, and on

Sundays after the morning *revista* and mass, slaves were free to move about the Morro Velho estate, and even to go into Congonhas. Several times each week the slaves were given permission to go into the "village" to make purchases. Although not closely monitored, the slaves were able to move about the village with relative freedom—"while precautions are taken," as one company official put it, "to prevent their abusing this privilege by partaking too freely of ardent spirits, every facility is given them for enjoying themselves moderately."[25]

Manumission

Death and disease gradually diminished the number of able-bodied slaves in the employ of the St. John d'el Rey. Emancipation further reduced the size of the company's slaveholdings. In the early 1850s, the company established an emancipation system to free company and Cata Branca slaves on a regular basis. As early as 1852 the board had set up a system to award medals to slaves for "good conduct."[26] By 1855 the board instructed the superintendent at Morro Velho to set up a system "by which some of the most meritorious of the Blacks at Morro Velho should be granted their freedom periodically throughout the year."[27] In the late 1850s the company began to set emancipation goals, asking the superintendent if it would be feasible to free ten slaves annually, five of the company's and five of the Cata Branca contingent.[28] By 1859 the board instructed Superintendent Gordon to step up the pace of the program, freeing ten slaves at midsummer (St. John's Day), and an additional ten at Christmas.[29] Ten slaves freed biannually remained the goal of the management into the late 1870s, although Gordon did not consistently meet the goal during his tenure.

The company carried out its emancipation program for nearly half a century (1834–82), freeing an average of six slaves per year. Each slave received a letter of freedom (*carta de alforria*) duly registered and witnessed in the local *cartório*. The St. John freed 191 (or 40 percent) of its own slaves, while the rest must have died (or been sold) over those five decades. As a part of the emancipation program the company freed 87 of the original 385 Cata Branca slaves, while the courts freed another 165 in 1879. The remaining 133 had died prior to the court case. Between the slaves purchased by the company prior to 1845 (500), and Cata Branca slaves (385), the St. John "owned" nearly 900 slaves. Subtracting those manumitted by the company (278), and those by the courts (165), leaves nearly 450 slaves who must have died while in company service. In short, the St. John manumitted about one-half of its slaves (with help from the courts), and the other half died in servitude. (These numbers do not take into account the growth of the company and Cata Branca slave populations through new births. Furthermore, after 1867 all newborns were freed and are not in the adult emancipation totals.)[30]

Several factors motivated the creation and maintenance of the emancipation system. First, the company saw the program as a way to mold the behavior of the slaves by rewarding those demonstrating "exemplary" behavior. The board made it clear to the superintendent, and he to the slaves, that emancipation was bestowed as a reward for "good behavior." The company devised an elaborate reward system placing slaves on a probation list, then awarding emancipation to a select group who had been on the list for five to ten years. At weekly Sunday morning *revistas* (reviews), slaves wore special clothing with medals and cloth stripes indicating their progress on the road to possible emancipation. The following excerpt from the superintendent's personal diary is a description of one such Sunday *revista* in the 1860s.

The Blacks instead of being arranged in lines as in the ordinary Review, were arranged in a pretty close semi circular body, occupying the Space in Front of the Casa Grande Portico. The officers of the Company filled the three sides of the Platform of the Portico, the Superintendent being in the centre of the side towards the doorway.

On the steps in the center of the Portico stood Joao Cornaz (and) Eduardo Tacquaril who were about to receive their letters of Freedom. Next stood the following Candidates about to be placed on the Good Conduct List . . .

There were arranged semi circular lines the Candidates both Men & Women, who had their distinguishing dress, & their Medals, & stripes according to their respective periods they have been on the good candidate list.

Uniform shawls of Turkey Red on the women candidates, handkerchiefs on the general women deficient in number—there are no more in stock. The women had the proper number of stripes on the petticoat marking their time of probation at the end of 1866. The men candidates with the uniform jackets had also their stripes on the cuffs up to the same date.

The motionless mass of people watched with fixed interest the proceedings while they were very briefly addressed on behalf of the Board, and informed what had been done by the company since 1848 towards improving the condition of the people under their care.[31]

The company's general manager explained the rationale for the system to one superintendent in the following terms:

If these people [the slaves] are constantly reminded of the boon offered to them as a reward for persistent good conduct by seeing their comrades decorated, freed, or otherwise advanced on the list it is much more likely to influence the whole body more than if these assemblages are held at distant and uncertain periods. The Board would therefore desire that these assemblages of the Blacks to witness their fellows being rewarded for good conduct be held twice a year.[32]

Always with an eye on the balance sheet and profits, the board instructed the superintendents to choose candidates for emancipation with care. The elderly and infirm, those no longer productive, and children predominated. In the late 1870s, with the rise of abolitionism and the increasingly apparent decline of slavery, the company made selections with "an eye to those most likely to remain at M[orro] V[elho] and work as free labourers."[33] Paternalism and the profit motive guided the emancipation system of the St. John d'el Rey.

Management's view of the company slave force is summed up in a passage written at midcentury displaying all the paternalism, condescension, rationalization, racism, and self-congratulation that characterized this British enterprise's handling of its slave force.

What the directors have done, and are doing is this:—*they are seeking to improve the moral condition of the Negroes;* they provide them with good food, good clothing, and other comforts; they encourage a spirit of industry amongst them, by dividing them into classes, and encouraging the most deserving; they endeavour to teach them the difference between right and wrong, by means of religious instruction and religious worship; they cause their children to be brought up to mechanical arts. In this way, and by encouraging matrimony amongst them, they are endeavouring gradually to improve their condition—*to elevate them in the scale of humanity*—and so to prepare them for any change which the course of events may hereafter bring about.[34]

Unfortunately, the slaves left no written record of their view of the system.

The Free Community

While slaves accounted for one-third of the population of Congonhas, at least into the 1870s, the remaining two-thirds of the community was a diverse group. Of the 6,417 free persons in the 1872 census, most were native Brazilians occupied in small-scale agriculture. As table 9 indicates, the free population was divided between a very small elite (landowners, capitalists, merchants, and professionals) and a very large working population (farmers, manual laborers, industrial workers, seamstresses, and domestic servants). Free adult males (with a profession) were concentrated in agriculture (41.9 percent), industry (27.6 percent), and day labor (19.3 percent). In other words, nearly 90 percent of adult males either worked for the St. John or farmed their own land or the land of others. Virtually all free adult women (98.2 percent) were concentrated in four professions: domestic service (52.8 percent), sewing (22.0 percent), agriculture (15.0 percent), or industry (8.4 percent). Of the 5,046 free citizens of Congonhas de Sabará with a known profession (probably close to the entire free adult population), 93.8 percent fell within the categories above composing the free masses.

The remaining 6.2 percent of the free adult population fell into the category of elites and middle groups linked to the elite. The census lists 169 "capitalists/landowners," no doubt including many small and medium-size landowners and petty capitalists. Furthermore, the 124 merchants in the census also, no doubt, include a large number of small businessmen who were not far removed from the masses. Finally, the census counts twenty-one citizens in the liberal professions. For the purposes of our analysis, the elite will be defined as wealthy and prominent landowners, capitalists, and merchants, as well as prominent local officials in government and military service. Using this working definition, the Congonhas elite probably consisted of less than two dozen prominent citizens and their families as well as the middle sectors linked to them. The overall composition of the free community, then, would consist of a small elite (1 percent) and a somewhat larger group of professionals, merchants, capitalists, and farmers (5 percent) serving as the poorly defined boundary with the masses (94 percent).

As the demographic survey in chapter 5 indicated, the community expanded with the growth of mining operations between 1830 and 1890, but the basic composition of Congonhas changed very little. It remained a society with a small elite, a large slave population, and an even larger free peasantry working the land in small-scale agriculture. These free peasants resisted the process of industrialization for decades, continuing to work their fields and showing a reluctance to become miners. The management of the St. John complained for decades of their inability to attract free labor and of the resistance of the surrounding population to mining work. Prior to the 1870s the company could turn to slavery as an alternative to free wage labor. From the 1870s to the 1920s, however, the demise of slavery and the continued resistance of the local peasantry created enormous difficulties for the St. John d'el Rey as the company expanded operations and constructed a modern industrial mining complex.

The company had trouble competing with other employers in the region for the scarce wage labor force. The difficulty in attracting sufficient labor was not just wages. In the 1920s the company often lost workers to the coffee fields of São Paulo or the construction industry in Belo Horizonte. When company labor recruiters attempted to lure construction workers away from road-building work near Belo Horizonte in 1924 with wages double the rate for road building, the workers all refused, pleading a fear of working underground in the mine. The wages of borers and carmen in the mine in the 1920s was equal to or superior to wage rates for workers in Rio de Janeiro and São Paulo. The difference, in the minds of workers, was apparently in the working conditions in the mine versus conditions in factories and fields.[35]

Management clearly diagnosed and lamented the cause of the labor shortage. The surrounding population was mainly composed of an agricultural population with small plots, and the men were unwilling to work in the mine during the planting and harvesting seasons.[36]

In short, they came to work for the company during the slack months of the agricultural cycle when they could leave their own fields to be tended by their families while they supplemented family income with their wages from the St. John. These *roceiros* made very rational calculations judging the price of crops each season, determining whether to plant, how much to plant, when to leave their fields, and when to return. The resistance of free labor was not so much based on peasant conservatism as it was based on capitalist calculations. The collapse of the agricultural economy, along with the benefits of social legislation, finally persuaded the peasantry to abandon farming for full-time mining in the 1930s.[37]

The combination of economic crisis, the expansion of the St. John, and the Vargas social legislation ended the company's labor shortage in the 1930s and drew many of these subsistence farmers into the industrial order at Morro Velho. Very clearly, this agricultural population does not fit the controversial pattern of debt peonage, or forced labor, as appears to be the case in the plantation societies and mining centers of places as diverse as turn-of-the-century Yucatán or the central highlands of Peru.[38] Despite the presence of a very successful and expanding foreign business, the surrounding population resisted efforts to draw them into the industrial labor pool. The St. John, unlike other foreign businesses in Latin America at the turn of the century, did not turn to coercive measures to supply its labor force. While International Harvester and its associates in Yucatán, and the Cerro de Pasco Corporation in Peru, turned to debt peonage and repression to solve their labor shortages, the St. John turned instead to imported wage labor after the abolition of slavery. Local elites and foreign business did not, and could not, control the free peasantry in the region around Morro Velho and Congonhas de Sabará.

Elites

Congonhas was a two-class society—of elites and masses—with a third subclass of slaves until the late 1880s. One-third of local society consisted of captive blacks, and nearly all of the remaining two-thirds of the community were peasants or manual laborers. Wealth from mining, commerce, or agriculture, and social status derived from political positions defined the local elite. The size of mining, commercial, or agricultural operations set the elite apart from the small-scale farmer. A handful of the population owned mining claims that were more than just personal or family operations. Although merchants were numerous in the community, again a handful did business on a large scale employing more than just family members in the business. Although some of the elite had significant landhold-ings, few produced more than wood from forests on their properties. Finally, a key distinguishing feature of the local elite was appoint-ment to political office. The cream of local society invariably also held the most important political positions in nineteenth-century Congonhas: justice of the peace, scribe, and peace officer (*subdele-gado*). By the turn of the century, and with the creation of the *muni-cípio* of Villa Nova de Lima, the town council became the key to local political power. Until the 1940s these key posts were always dominated by a group of prominent local families.

After 1834 strong business ties to the St. John d'el Rey were the lifeblood of the local elite. Eventually, the few local families with significant mining claims all sold them to the company. Many of the elite who were "land rich and cash poor" benefited from the expan-sion of mining operations at Morro Velho as the company purchased their surrounding properties, lands that would have had little mar-ket value had the British not developed the Morro Velho. Further-more, the most consistent source of wealth for the local elite came from sales of provisions to the company, a business that endured over decades. The local elite sold the St. John wood, charcoal, beans, corn, manioc, and *mamona* (castor) oil in large quantities, often acting as the intermediary by purchasing the supplies in regional markets. The growth of the labor force, particularly the free labor force, stimulated commerce in Congonhas, particularly benefiting a few individuals who dominated the most important retail outlets in town. Finally, a close relationship with the company guaranteed the local elite the influence of the St. John in supporting local politi-cal control. Business and politics were mutually supporting as the Congonhas elite controlled both.

Notarial registers, company records, and secondary sources reveal a very small group of families in the Congonhas elite in the nine-teenth century, many with ties to the community dating back to the previous century. The Lima, Ribeiro, Rocha, Cunha, Jardim, and Fonseca families settled in the area by 1800; they intermarried with frequency and established bonds through godparentage, creating a complex web of kinship networks and business alliances.[39] In the second half of the nineteenth century a few outsiders married into these families after establishing strong business ties and achieving commercial success. These established families, and the newcomers, dominated local society into the 1920s.

The Lima family illustrates many of the key features of the local elite in the community. The family probably settled in Congonhas in the early years of the eighteenth century and over several generations intermarried with many other prominent families (see appendix 5). The main line of the family traces back to José Maria da Cunha Jardim and his wife Maria Constança de Lima in the mid-eighteenth century. The couple had five children. Their daughter Ana Jacinta married Captain Silvério Araújo de Lima, a local miner and militia officer. One of their sons married into the Jardim family in the late eighteenth century and among their sons was José Severiano de Lima. Juca, as he was known in the family, owned a small mining claim on the slopes of the Morro do Pires to the south of Congonhas known as the Fazenda do California. He married Maria Firmina Diniz Barbosa, the daughter of Diniz Antônio Barbosa, the local schoolteacher, and they raised seven children born in the 1850s and 1860s. The gold mine produced a small income and Juca employed a few slaves, but his main income came from supplying goods, mainly timber, to the St. John d'el Rey. Eventually, Juca sold the mining claim to the company and the family moved closer to the center of town. His income was sufficient to send two of his sons, Augusto and Bernardino, to the famous *colégio* for the sons of the *mineiro* elite in Caraça. One daughter, Emília, taught for thirty years in the Nova Lima "*grupo escolar*," and the school was eventually named after her. José Severiano de Lima Junior took a law degree in São Paulo and was the scribe of the Minas Gerais Court of Appeals before his death in 1942. Augusto and Bernardino would outshine their brothers and sisters, bringing state and national attention to the Lima family of Congonhas.[40]

The Limas are an excellent example of the mobility of the local elite and of its ties to the company and to one another. Augusto and Bernardino both became key figures in state politics in the late nineteenth century. Augusto de Lima served as interim governor of the newly created state in the early 1890s and as a federal deputy for many years in Rio de Janeiro. Bernardino served in several state political posts in the 1880s and 1890s. Eventually, both brothers settled in Belo Horizonte and would spend the last thirty years of their lives there (and in Rio). Augusto's descendants continue to reside in Belo Horizonte; his eldest son, Augusto de Lima Junior, followed in his father's literary footsteps and directed the Arquivo Público Mineiro while writing on the history of Minas Gerais. Some of Bernardino's family remained in Nova Lima; and one son, Manoel Franzen de Lima, would be *prefeito* of Nova Lima; and another, João, *prefeito* of Belo Horizonte in the late 1940s. Although branches of the Lima family remain in Nova Lima, Belo Horizonte became the home of the main line of the family, a pattern repeated by other elite families. The pattern of the Limas is representative of the local elite. Most had roots in the community dating back to the early mining years of the eighteenth century. Intermarriage among the elite families was a persistent trend over generations, as was the eventual relocation of elite families in nearby Belo Horizonte.

Not quite as prominent or as successful as the Limas, the Jardim family also spanned several generations of elite leadership in Congonhas (see appendix 5). Like the other older families in Congonhas, the Jardim and their family branches arrived in the area as early as the 1730s. The Jardim and Lima families intermarried over generations. In the mid-nineteenth century the most prominent member of the family was Lt. Col. Francisco de Assis da Cunha Jardim, owner of the Faria mine to the south of Congonhas at Macacos. He served on the town council of Sabará and was a justice of the peace in Rio Acima.[41] Much like José Severiano de Lima and Francisco de Assis da Cunha Jardim, Lt. Col. Francisco Daniel Rocha also was a major supplier of goods to the St. John d'el Rey. The colonel and his kin were also intermarried into the other elite family networks. Two Rochas served as justices of the peace in the 1860s. The colonel was the senior partner in Rocha & Cia., one of the most important commercial outlets in Congonhas, and was a major supplier of the St. John d'el Rey. The colonel was one of the major slave traders and slave owners in the area and ran the only other significant industrial operation in the surrounding region—a textile mill nearby at Marzagão.[42]

The Ribeiro family also intermarried into the same kinship networks, engaged in local commerce supplying the company with goods, and family members served in prominent political posts. In the mid-nineteenth century Francisco Felizardo Ribeiro, the family patriarch, served as a major in the local militia, a justice of the peace, and supplied the St. John with much of its charcoal and timber. Two of his daughters married into the Rocha family, and another into the Diniz Barbosa family (linking him to the Limas). One son, Belisário, married the daughter of an English family and worked in important clerical positions for the company for fifty-six years. Two of his children married into the English community.[43]

The key features of the elite were clear in the last half of the nineteenth century. All derived their wealth from commerce with the St. John d'el Rey. They monopolized positions of prominence in local politics (judges, militia, notaries), and the families intermarried extensively beginning in the mid-eighteenth century. Some newcomers from outside the community married into the elite network in the late nineteenth century. Aristides de Paula Ferreira, for example, arrived in Villa Nova de Lima as a young man in the 1890s, soon emerged as an ambitious businessman in the main store in the villa, and married the boss's daughter. His father-in-law, Col. Ignácio Furtado de Magalhães, had come to Congonhas from Cocais in the 1870s and become a business partner of the Antônio Pereira Borges and the Barros Taveira brothers, three Portuguese merchants who ran the major retail store in Congonhas. With the secret aid of Superintendent James Newell Gordon, their store became the dominant commercial emporium in the village. Magalhães bought out his partners in the late 1870s. Paula Ferreira married Olga de Magalhães Mascarenhas in 1894, and he became a major figure in local politics. The commercial outlet remained the dominant retail store in Nova Lima into the 1940s and was known locally as the Casa Aristides.[44]

In the eighteenth century the Lima, Jardim, Ribeiro, and Rocha families and their kin established their leadership roles in the community through control of the important agricultural and mining enterprises in the surrounding area, and by monopolizing the few political and military posts in Congonhas. With the arrival of the British in the 1830s, and the expansion of mining operations at Morro Velho, the elite continued to monopolize local political power, but their economic roles underwent a transformation. Those with mining claims sold them to the British by the 1860s. The wealth of this small elite multiplied as they became wholesale suppliers to the St. John and retail merchants for the community. In the 1880s their fortunes took a turn for the worse with the collapse of the mine. In the early years of the twentieth century some began to establish ties in the recently created Belo Horizonte. The elite network remained the dominant force in local politics until the 1930s when the attractions of the state capital and the rise of new populist politics altered the nature of local governance.

Working-Class Society Emerges

Two major transformations converged in Congonhas in the last years of the nineteenth century: the transition from slavery to free wage labor and the construction of a new mining complex on the ruins of the old mine. By the 1870s the company had begun to turn to imported labor as a means of decreasing its dependence on slavery and as a way to make up for the shortage of free Brazilian labor. The St. John made many unsuccessful efforts to import foreign workers, finally giving up in the 1920s. Even with the few hundred imported workers the company continued to suffer major labor shortages as the surrounding peasantry continued to balk at working in the mine. The continued resistance of the local and regional labor force, the end of slavery, and the importation of foreign workers characterized a community in transition from the slave economy of the nineteenth century to the working-class society that would emerge in Nova Lima after 1930. The rebuilding of the mine laid the groundwork for the rise of an industrial working-class community. The Great Depression and the Vargas regime would complete the process.

As with much of the history of the masses in Latin America, a dearth of sources hampers our ability to reconstruct life in the community during these years of transition. Other than short-lived efforts, Nova Lima has never had a newspaper.[45] Workers and their families left few written records, and most records of community life are from the perspective of the company and the local elite. Photographs, statistical sources, notarial registers, and interviews provide additional insights into the life of the community, yet our view of this emerging working-class society is sketchy and incomplete. Given the paucity of information, the following description of the masses is even more anonymous, impersonal, and sketchy than the preceding analysis of local elites. The description focuses on four aspects of local life: religion, sports, education, and politics.

Despite the large influx of Africans in the nineteenth century and the arrival of hundreds of foreign workers at the turn of the century, the community remained overwhelmingly homogeneous in at least one respect—religion. At the turn of the century close to 95 percent of the population were Brazilians, virtually all nominally Catholic. The African population had been assimilated, although spiritist centers did coexist alongside Catholicism as they did in the rest of Brazil. Catholicism, more than any other factor, bound the people of Nova Lima in a common cultural tradition. Even the hundreds of imported workers came from largely Catholic countries (Spain, Italy, and Portugal). The Catholic church, even in its minimal social role, bound the community together with common rituals, festivals, and values. The architectural dominance of the *matriz* on the town plaza symbolized the cultural influence of the church in the community. In Nova Lima one entered the world a Catholic receiving the sacraments of baptism, marriage, and burial in the church. Furthermore, Catholicism served to separate the Protestant British community from the Brazilian populace.

Even the major holidays celebrated in the community originated as Catholic religious festivals. The most important of these, and the major community event each year, was *carnaval*. In the four days preceding Ash Wednesday, the samba schools of Nova Lima performed locally and in Belo Horizonte, as they continue to do today. The company's major annual celebration, St. John's Day, formed the centerpiece of the "June Days" celebrations at midsummer. Just as religious holidays provided the means for communal celebration, a religious figure provided the focal point for miners and their families seeking solace and aid. Saint Barbara became the patron saint of the miners and of the community. Miners carried her image into the mine each year on her saint's day to bless their work.[46]

Aside from religion the most important form of communal experience was sports. Nova Lima contained a number of sports clubs, mainly those backing football teams competing in the surrounding area. The British formed the Morro Velho Athletic Club in 1896, the beginnings of what would become the English Club in the Quintas. Two important Brazilian sports clubs were founded at the turn of the century. Founded in 1916, the Retiro Football Club had some fifty paying members by the 1920s. Prominent local leaders (with some company help) formed the Villa Nova Athletic Club in 1908. With some three hundred paying members by the 1920s, the club fielded a football team that rose to the first division of Brazilian competition.[47]

Table 19 Percentage Literate in Nova Lima, Minas Gerais, and Brazil, 1872–1970

	1872	1920	1940	1950	1960	1970
Nova Lima	9.6	51.7	64.7	69.0	70.2	77.7
Male	12.7	59.5	69.7	73.4		
Female	6.3	43.5	59.0	64.8		
Minas Gerais		20.7	33.0	38.2		58.9
Brazil	15.8	24.5	38.2	42.7	53.6	60.3

Sources: RE 1872–1970; AEB-1965, p. 35.
Note: Figures for 1872 are for population age seven and older. All others are for age five and older.

Schools provided another important means of community experience. Unlike the British (who had their own school), slaves and workers in Nova Lima did not have access to any type of schooling until the twentieth century. The small local elite either hired private tutors for their children or sent them to boarding schools. The first public primary school in Nova Lima opened in 1909. As with most of the public works projects in Nova Lima, the St. John d'el Rey donated the land for the school and financed its construction. In the 1930s the town council raised funds to build a secondary school and the St. John put up one-fourth of the capital. In the 1940s the financial burden became too much for the council, and the company reluctantly agreed to fund the school.[48]

Despite the lack of schools, the community made great strides in the twentieth century raising the local literacy rate far above state and national levels (see table 19). At the time of the 1872 census not one of the community's 3,284 slaves was literate. Of the remaining two-thirds of the parish (6,247) less than 15 percent were literate. (The rate dropped to under 10 percent when including slaves with the rest of the population.) About twice as many men as women were literate. The census notes that only 59 (less than 7 percent) of the parish's 909 children (between the ages of six and fifteen) attended school. The majority of these, no doubt, were children in the English school and the children of the local elite.

By the 1920s literacy (for those age seven and older) had risen dramatically to 51.7 percent. About 60 percent of males were literate while only 40 percent of females. When compared with the rest of the state, the literacy rate in Villa Nova seems nothing short of phenomenal. The literacy rate for the state barely surpassed 20 percent, and not a single major city could claim a rate above 30 percent.[49] By 1940 the literacy rate in Nova Lima (for those five and older) had risen to almost 65 percent, with nearly 70 percent of the males being literate, and 59 percent of all females. By 1950 these figures had risen further to 69 percent literate, 73.4 percent for males and 64.8 percent for females. Community literacy rose to just over 70 percent in the 1960 census, and to close to 80 percent by the 1970 census. This extraordinary rise in literacy far outpaced the rising rates in the state and nation. Rising literacy seems to have accompanied industrialization and urbanization in Nova Lima, just as it did in the nations of the North Atlantic in the nineteenth century.

Early Working-Class Organizations

Four important transformations in the international community, Brazil, and Nova Lima converged in the 1930s, culminating in the emergence of a fully developed working class in the community. The construction of a modern, industrial mining plant begun by George Chalmers had been completed by 1934. Despite the strenuous efforts of company management, decades of labor recruitment had failed to staff this modern industrial plant with the working class necessary to run the mine and mill. The social legislation of the Vargas regime after 1930 provided the peasantry with strong incentives to take up mining as a full-time, year-round profession. At the same time, the unemployment and low agricultural prices produced by the collapse of the coffee economy during the Great Depression pushed the peasantry out of traditional agricultural work. Finally, the jump in gold prices on the world market in 1934 provided the St. John d'el Rey with the means to expand operations and employment at the very moment that an abundant labor force became a reality. In short, the convergence of local, national, and international events helped produce the consolidation of the working class in Nova Lima.

The emergence of a militant and politically potent working class is the dominant feature of Nova Lima after 1930. Unionization was the vehicle and voice of this militant working class in its struggle for control of local politics, higher wages, social and health benefits, and a higher standard of living. The emergence of the Communist party in both Nova Lima and Raposos shaped union policies and sharpened the division in local politics. The militancy of the working class, its battles with the St. John d'el Rey management, and its internal struggles dominate community life between 1930 and 1960. This militancy, and these struggles, remain a vivid part of the historical consciousness of the community.

Although the consolidation of the working class took shape in Nova Lima in the 1930s, the process extended over decades with the transition from slavery to imported labor to the creation of a stable work force drawn from the surrounding peasantry. Efforts by workers to organize and confront company management date back at least as far as the 1850s when free Brazilian borers made an unsuccessful effort to organize a strike.[50] In the 1870s a group of English miners made their only known effort to strike and forced the company to make wage concessions.[51] In 1880 women sand carriers went on strike for a brief period to protest a reduction in wages.[52] Nevertheless, prior to the rebuilding of the mine in the 1890s working-class efforts at organization were very weak. Although slavery disappeared in the 1880s, the collapse of the mine in the 1880s hindered the growth of a working class and working-class organizations.

The arrival of imported Spanish and Italian workers in the 1890s marked a new era in labor relations in Nova Lima. These men came from countries with an already well developed tradition of unionization and political organization. The Spanish in particular created tremendous headaches for company management. The Brazilian work force, led by Spanish miners, introduced the strike as a political weapon for the working class, initiating major work stoppages in 1897, 1898, 1900, 1903, and 1904. Italians and Germans also played a prominent role in these strike actions. On each occasion Chalmers received the help of police and troops from Sabará to handle strikers. The strikes were usually violent, and four died in a shoot-out between Spaniards and Brazilians in the 1903 strike.[53] Although no evidence of the political tendencies of the strikers has survived, the local police believed the leaders were anarchists. This would certainly fit the general pattern of labor movements in Brazil at the turn of the century.[54]

The first working-class organizations also began to appear in the 1890s and the first decade of this century. In 1891 workers formed the *Club dos Broqueiros* (Borers' Club) as a mutual-aid society to provide support for the families of injured workers and those killed in the mine. The company kept a ledger with voluntary worker contributions to the mutual-aid fund. While strongly opposed to unions and government-mandated social programs, the St. John management supported the club as a "proper" approach to social welfare for the workers. For a time the workers ran the organization on their own, but they eventually returned control of the club and fund to the company.[55] Both Spanish and Italian workers formed their own mutual-aid societies (Sociedad Española de Socorro Mútuo and Societá Italiana di Mutuo Socorro), which company management supported.[56]

While management approved of the paternalism of the mutual-aid society, it took all possible measures to crush working-class organizations not under company control. All working-class organizations before the 1930s were short lived. The Junta Auxiliar dos Operários (formed in 1902) did manage to elect officers and publish a pamphlet with its goals and objectives. The company infiltrated the organization and kept a close eye on its activities, harassing the leadership. Loss of employment, or the simple threat of it, helped dismantle efforts such as this one.[57] The company promoted the formation of an "International Club," hoping to compete with working-class clubs and to exert greater influence over the behavior of company employees. The purpose of this type of club created by management was to "smash" the "junta" that "caused the Company such serious trouble and loss," according to George Chalmers. The paternalism of the nineteenth century took new forms in the twentieth century.[58] In 1919 a group of workers organized a branch of the "Sociedade Epitácio Pessôa" based in Belo Horizonte. Once again the company infiltrated the organization to keep tabs on its activities and leaders.[59]

The rise in working-class organization brought with it an increasing concern by management for the safety of the English staff and company property. Although no direct attacks took place, anonymous threats worried management. In 1912, after several activists were dismissed from the payroll, George Chalmers received an anonymous letter, purportedly from the "Black Hand" (*Mão Negra*). The letter contained the threat of violence with "dynamite and poisons" if the company continued to harass organizers. Although Chalmers typically shrugged off all threats, the company built a barbed-wire fence around the mining complex, increased the number of watchmen, and rerouted some roads away from the main buildings in the surface works. By the First World War constant tension between workers and management had replaced the labor peace of the pre-Chalmers era.[60]

Ironically, the last major working-class action prior to the Depression was a strike by Brazilian workers protesting the pay of Spanish miners. In response to the acute labor crisis that nearly closed the mine, the company brought in more Spanish miners in the 1920s. The St. John had to pay the Spaniards higher wages than the Brazilians to induce the former to immigrate to Morro Velho. The Brazilians soon discovered the pay differential, and after a bitter strike (broken up by the regional militia) a new wage settlement produced a compromise.[61] Like all the other important working-class actions prior to the 1930s, the 1925 strike focused on wage issues.

The Emergence of a Miners' Union

The rise to power of Getúlio Vargas and the social legislation of the early 1930s provided the miners of Nova Lima with the means to organize and collectively challenge the St. John d'el Rey. In May 1934 a group of miners culminated months of discussions with the creation of a "Union of the Miners of Morro Velho." (The name was changed to the "Union of the Workers in the Industry for the Extraction of Gold and Precious Metals of Nova Lima" in 1940.)[62] Groups of miners had been meeting in the home of a shoemaker for some time and founded the union on their own, afterward informing the Ministry of Labor of their actions. Representatives from the ministry subsequently arrived in Nova Lima to extend formal government recognition to the union. Superintendent A. H. Millett made a last-ditch effort to form a counter union controlled by "friendly" employees, but the ploy failed when the ministry declared the organization to be illegal. By June nearly two thousand workers had joined the new union. For decades company management had made every effort to prevent the rise of a collective working-class movement outside its control, knowing full well that a unified working class would provide workers with a powerful means to fight for higher wages, better working conditions, and increased benefits. As Millett commented to the managing director in London, "unless I am very much mistaken, [the union] is going to give us a lot of trouble."[63] He was not mistaken.

Over the next quarter-century the union became the vehicle for a bitter struggle between Brazilian workers and British management. This struggle focused on efforts to raise wages, increase benefits, and improve health and safety in the mine. Incidents of labor violence were rare in the late 1930s as company and workers negotiated and debated issues through the mediation of the labor ministry. By 1942 labor violence had emerged as a major feature of life in the community, and in 1943 workers went out on the first of a long series of strikes that would cripple the company by the midfifties. Strikes and violence increasingly polarized the British and Brazilian communities and, by the late forties, divided the Brazilian community. Nationalism divided Brazilian and Briton.

Nationalism had long been a divisive force, emerging as a major factor in the early years of the century with the rise of labor conflict. The economic and cultural nationalism of the 1930s further exacerbated the tension between the poverty of the Brazilian workers and the comfortable life-style of the British managers. In the 1940s and 1950s British control of this national resource, as well as the poverty of the working-class community, became an issue that galvanized workers and drew national attention. Communists and Fascists attacked the company demanding nationalization, graphically portraying the exploitation of poor Brazilian workers by a very profitable British firm. In 1940 a prominent Fascist, A. Tenório d'Albuquerque, published *Escándolo no Morro Velho*, a scathing denunciation of the St. John d'el Rey. Roberto C. Costa, a prominent Communist, denounced the company in *A cortina de ouro (Morro Velho)* (1955). Costa wrote the polemic while serving time in jail for "inciting the people (*o povo*) 'to plunder the American Consulate' " in Belo Horizonte. Like d'Albuquerque, Costa marshaled published data to highlight the exploitation of the workers by a foreign firm exporting considerable profits back to England. These tracts and others like them made the struggle in Nova Lima a national issue.[64]

While nationalism divided the British and Brazilian communities, communism divided the Brazilians. Labor organizers from the Communist party of Brazil (PCB) began their work in Nova Lima in 1932, planting three "seeds" in the company and the community. With the formation of the miners' union in 1934, party members working in both the Raposos and Morro Velho mines began to assume key positions in the union movement. With the exception of a brief interlude in which the PCB operated legally, party members in Nova Lima worked either clandestinely or as members of legal political parties. In the latter case the ideology of the party members was well known to all in the community. In 1935 a failed coup led by Communists and the PCB under the leadership of Luís Carlos Prestes triggered a decade of repression by the Vargas regime.[65] Despite the persecution of the PCB after the Intentona Comunista in 1935, the PCB in Nova Lima maintained a low profile and fairly good relations with the government until the postwar period. With the rise of the cold war, and the renewed repression of the PCB after 1947, the struggle between Communists and anti-Communists in the union and in Nova Lima produced a deep division within the community. Political violence and labor conflict became commonplace in Nova Lima for two decades after the war.[66]

The struggle in Nova Lima between Briton and Brazilian, Communist and anti-Communist, took place on three fronts: in the workplace, in the union hall, and in local politics. In the workplace management, Communists, and anti-Communists, all vied for the loyalty of workers. British management tried to weaken the labor movement by pitting the two opposing forces against each other. Despite their bitter disagreements, the union movement grew stronger and more powerful in the late forties and early fifties. Both sides agreed on the need for wage increases, more benefits, and better working conditions in the mine. While Communists and anti-Communists struggled for control of the union and local politics, they continued to confront the company in a series of bitter strikes and negotiations.

As table 20 indicates, workers went out on strike repeatedly between 1943 and 1955. Eight strikes in twelve years, two lasting for more than three weeks, earned the workers significant wage and benefit increases and brought the company to its knees financially. By 1954 the superintendent was telling the board of directors that it was "difficult to see where the money is coming from to meet our cash commitments." By 1956 the company had opened its books to bureaucrats and the union to convince them of the difficulty of further concessions—and to hold off additional strikes. Workers and government officials agreed to less confrontational tactics, realizing that they could not afford to "kill the goose that lay the golden

Table 20 Strikes Against the St. John d'el Rey Mining Company, Limited, 1943–1955

Dates	Major Issues
5 November–6 November 1943	Wage increase for travel time to work (strike limited to Raposos Mine)
26 December–28 December 1944	General strike for wage hike
26 November–2 December 1947	Sitdown strike/work slowdown for wage hike
12 October–14 October 1948	Wage hike
4 May–12 May 1953	Wage hike and health benefits
14 October–15 November 1953	Wage hike and better working conditions
12 May–31 May 1955	Insalubrity pay
15 December–16 December 1955	Late payday

Sources: Grossi, *Mina de Morro Velho*, p. 224; Correspondence, SJNL.

eggs."[67] In the late 1950s the company, the union, and the government became partners in negotiations to keep the mine open. The specter of a closed mine in this company town compelled the Brazilian government and workers to end two decades of labor strife. After the mine passed to Brazilian ownership in 1960, strikes and labor strife returned until the military government "intervened" the union in 1964. The miners of Morro Velho went on strike on 1 April 1964 to protest the military coup that deposed President João Goulart, and the regime immediately sent troops into the so-called "red city" to shut down all protest. Under the military regime the union movement was repressed, and many activists paid dearly for the work of the previous twenty years.[68]

Although the union normally formed a unified front when challenging the company, the rank and file were not a homogenous group. Workers identified themselves by the type of work they did for the company. The value placed on different jobs is apparent when they are placed in rank order by pay. Underground, for example, the highest-paid employees were the supervisors (*feitores*) and those who worked at the rock face. Rock drill men made the highest salaries (after the supervisors), with the pinchers (who pulled down the loose rock after blasting) and timbermen also making good wages. Carmen and trammers were next on the scale, followed by machinists such as winding enginemen and pumpsmen. The lowest-paid jobs were those requiring the least skill and with less hazardous conditions: cleanup, sanitary work, and handling mules. Aboveground, the same general pattern followed with the more skilled labor, especially those working with machinery, making the highest wages. In general, skilled labor made twice as much per hour as unskilled labor. Interestingly, a very high number of machinists and highly skilled workers were Communists.[69] Despite a clear hierarchy and differentiation within the working class, the approach of the union was to win wage increases across the board for all workers.

Most of the strikes and collective bargaining between union and company focused on wage increases and the extension of benefits. Chronic inflation and a rapidly rising cost of living in the post-1930 period constantly eroded real wages and produced demands for higher wages. Between 1938 and 1954 the average daily wage of borers rose more than 600 percent, roughly at the same rate as the cost of living.[70] The company acknowledged in private that inflation was consuming wage increases and impoverishing the working class in the community. The management had witnessed a similar pattern in the 1920s and, prompted by a strike, had raised wages.[71] Nevertheless, management also recognized the high price of new labor costs. After 1945 the stable price of gold established at Bretton Woods, as well as rising labor costs in Brazil, squeezed the St. John. Each new strike, each new wage and benefit concession, brought the company closer to insolvency.

In addition to higher wages, workers demanded and received a wide range of benefits: production bonuses, paid holidays, pay for travel time to the workplace, and increased pension and health benefits. Company management bitterly resented "this d— social legislation" as creeping socialism promoted by the Brazilian government.[72] The benefits of the new social legislation came through constant bargaining and bitter strikes and, almost always, with the mediation of the state government and the ministry of labor. The revolution in social and labor legislation begun by Vargas in the 1930s provided the union with the legal foundations it needed to pressure the company and to extract concessions.[73] The Brazilian government periodically readjusted minimum wages for the mining industry, established the right to paid holidays, regulated safety and health conditions in the workplace, and created a pension and unemployment compensation system. The government became the third party arbiter in labor-management relations, continually pressuring the St. John to make concessions and implement the new social legislation.[74] Although the company maintained powerful friendships in government and politics, the tide had turned against this British enterprise by the 1930s. The state and national governments wanted the company to stay and invest, but on terms more favorable to Brazil, terms that would keep more of the profits in Brazil.

The struggle for health or "salubrity" pay is a good example of the influence of the new labor legislation on the St. John and its labor costs.[75] In the 1930s legislation called for bonus pay to those working in especially unhealthy or hazardous conditions. At Morro Velho the workers called for salubrity pay for those exposed to the fine silica dust in drilling areas. Initially, the company fought the demand, claiming that no evidence existed that the borers and their teams were exposed to especially hazardous work. The union countered with charges that the silica dust incapacitated workers, causing high rates of tuberculosis and silicosis (white lung). The disease had been recognized (and compensation awarded to the afflicted) in South Africa since the early 1930s.[76] A team of physicians from the Ministry of Labor and an independent study by a Canadian physician provided the workers with powerful proof of their claims, and the company conceded the pay to those in areas of maximum exposure.[77] As a result of the strikes and negotiations after 1940, the union gradually extended the pay to an increasingly larger segment of the work force. The resulting cost of this special pay was enormous, contributing to the company's financial woes.[78]

In addition to working conditions, the escalating cost of living spurred worker militancy. Much of the discontent of the workers over the cost of living was directed at the dominant retail outlet, the Casa Aristides. Operating in the same location since the 1860s, the Casa had made special arrangements with the St. John to extend credit to workers. Although not a company store in the classic form, at the Casa an employee received credit by showing his company time card and hours accumulated on it. He was then given a passbook that was continually updated with credit purchases. On monthly paydays the company cashier subtracted the debt owed the store and handed over the remainder of the wages to the worker. For this service the St. John charged the Casa Aristides a small commission. The practice, along with cheap housing, served to tie the worker to the community and make his departure less likely. In the 1940s the Brazilian government, after union petitions, informed the company that the practice was illegal and could not continue. Workers continued to complain of the prices at the Casa, and in the 1940s and 1950s they forced the St. John to help establish food cooperatives to make basic foodstuffs available at wholesale prices.[79]

The struggles for salubrity pay and for access to cheap foodstuffs are but two examples of the impact of the new politics in Brazil after 1930. The corporatist tendencies of the Vargas regime provided labor with the means to organize and, with government support, to extract previously unthinkable concessions from the English. The populist political environment in Brazil after 1945, with its emphasis on economic nationalism and social welfare programs, brought the St. John under increasing public and private pressure. The ever-present fear of nationalization hung over the enterprise beginning in the 1930s and became a very real possibility in the 1950s. In public, politicians scored points by attacking this foreign company's control of a vital national resource and its treatment of Brazilian workers. In government offices, increasingly nationalistic bureaucrats pressured the St. John with fiscal and tariff regulations while implementing increasingly costly social and labor legislation. An activist state contributed to rising labor costs and threatened profit remittances.

The Party, the Union, and the Community

Although economic nationalism came between the Brazilian government and the St. John d'el Rey, the Communist movement in Brazil brought them together in a common alliance. After the Intentona by the PCB in 1935, the Vargas regime cracked down on Communists, and in Nova Lima the Ministry of Labor intervened in the union during 1936–37. The company seized the opportunity to dismiss eighteen employees, among them the seventeen founders of the union. The group had just successfully established the new pension fund (Caixa de Aposentadoria e Pensões) electing a governing board antagonistic to the company. Although most had more than ten years' seniority, providing them with job "stability" protecting them from dismissal, the Ministry of Labor allowed the firings to stand.[80] Party members remained active in the union but maintained a low profile until the early 1940s.

For a brief period (1945–47) the PCB reemerged from clandestinity to operate legally, but renewed repression by the Dutra government drove the party underground once again. As it had in 1936, the St. John took advantage of the government's anti-Communist drive to rid itself of "troublemakers." In a dramatic case that became a cause célèbre for the Brazilian Left, the company dismissed fifty-one Communists (thirty-six with stability) claiming that party members were sabotaging production.[81] In fact, production levels were declining due to labor problems in the mine, including a serious breakdown in discipline. The government quietly reclassified the mine as a vital national industry, and a government commission agreed with the company position.[82] The "fifty-one" fought their dismissal in labor courts for four years, ultimately losing in the supreme labor court in Rio de Janeiro.[83] Without the close cooperation of government officials and security forces the action would never have been possible. The government had carefully compiled police dossiers detailing the Communist activities of all the dismissed miners, and the files were key evidence in the hearings.[84]

The company management made a clear distinction between "agitators" and "sympathizers." The action against the "fifty-one" was designed to eradicate the so-called troublemakers. As for the large following of the PCB in the union, and their understanding of communism, management took a condescending and paternalistic view. Superintendent Davies neatly summed up the attitude in 1945 in a letter to Managing Director L. E. Langley in London: "I do not think the great majority of our Morro Velho and Raposos Communists have any conception of the real meaning of Communism, their ideas being mostly limited to the theory that when they finally win, one of them (how chosen is not clear) will come up and run things in my office, while I will have to go underground and fill cars."[85]

While not academic experts on Marxism, Morro Velho's miners were much better informed about politics and economics than British managers could imagine. Party activists had well-organized discussion groups to educate miners on ideology as well as politics and economics. The testimony of major figures in the labor movement attests to their firm grounding in theory and the reality of their economic and social situation. Orlando de Sá Bandeira, one of the key PCB activists, was well read in Brazilian and foreign literature, as well as Marxist texts, works he was encouraged to read after becoming involved in the miners' movement as a young man.[86] He was not alone in his pursuit of knowledge.

The conflict between Communists and anti-Communists divided

community as well as union, as each group attempted to gain control of local politics. Up until the 1930s the St. John could count on friendly and cooperative local politicians. The clan networks and local elite families of the nineteenth century continued to control municipal government up to the fall of the First Republic in 1930, and they maintained close ties with the company. Many worked for the company. Two of the key political officials were Anglo-Brazilians, Jorge Morgan and Carlos Henrique Roscoe. The parents and grandparents of both had come to Brazil to work for English mining companies in the mid-nineteenth century, and they had married into the local Brazilian elite. (Despite management's efforts to isolate the British, some did establish close ties to the Brazilian community. See chapter 7.) Morgan, at one time the company slave manager, was head of the local elections board during the 1880s and 1890s, and Roscoe was president of the local political machine from 1910 through the 1920s. The posts in the town council in the late nineteenth and early twentieth centuries were filled with Ribeiros, Limas, Barbosas, Rochas, and other sons of the local elite family networks.[87]

Local politics in the Vargas years did not shift dramatically. The appointed *prefeito* was normally an individual from the traditional elite with close company ties. For a number of years Carlos Galery ran local government. Son of a French mining company officer at nearby Faria, and one of the Ribeiro Wanderley family, Galery was a longtime, loyal company employee in the Casa Grande offices. His brother-in-law, Braulio Carsalade, was the St. John's public relations man in Belo Horizonte and Rio de Janeiro. Although listed on the payroll as a clerk and translator, Galery essentially handled public relations in Nova Lima and Belo Horizonte. He was, as A. G. N. Chalmers put it, "of very great use to the Company, politically."[88] The dramatic shift in local politics did not take place until the fall of Vargas in 1945 and the emergence of mass politics in Brazil.

During the next two decades local politics became a battleground for the two contending forces, with the Communists exerting powerful influence in local affairs. The party reached the height of its power in the late 1940s. In the open national elections at the end of the Vargas dictatorship in 1945 the PCB took 16 percent of the vote in Nova Lima, placing second behind the Social Democratic party (PSD) of Eurico Dutra.[89] Although the PCB was officially banned after 1947, party members ran on the ticket of the PSD. In 1947 *novalimenses* elected four Communist *vereadores* (councilmen) and a Communist *vice-prefeito*. Led by William Dias Gomes and Anélio Marques Guimarães, both councilmen and company employees, the Communists made council meetings a forum to denounce the St. John d'el Rey. Minutes of the meeting reveal contentious and bitter debates in the late forties and early fifties.[90] To honor Luís Carlos Prestes, the head of the PCB, the councilmen called themselves the *vereadores de Prestes*. With the election of Waldomiro Lobo as state congressman, militant workers found an ally in state politics who regularly denounced the company, calling for nationalization of the mine. For the first time in over a century of operations, the St. John d'el Rey faced a hostile and nationalistic local government.[91]

The anti-Communist movement in Nova Lima took shape around the União Novalimense de Assistência Social (UNAS), founded with the stimulus of the local Catholic church in 1949.[92] Ideologically the UNAS was part of the rising Christian Democratic movement in Latin America in the postwar years. In Nova Lima the UNAS became the focal point of opposition to the rising power of the Communists in the union and in local government. Each side denounced the other in vitriolic speeches in council meetings, in mass rallies, and in countless pamphlets in the 1940s and 1950s. The conflict between Communists and anti-Communists reached a crescendo very quickly in 1947–48 with the intervention of the union by the government and bloody confrontations in the streets of Nova Lima.

As a part of the nationwide crackdown on the PCB in 1947, the Ministry of Labor took over control of the union and supported company efforts to dismiss Communist workers.[93] The intervention lasted until 1950, but Communists continued to play key roles in the union. In the 1950s three union presidents were party members. Government control of the union did not mean labor peace, as table 20 indicates. Most of the strikes were instigated without official union sanction. (In fact, in several strikes the union leadership dissociated itself from the strikers.) Union leadership often found itself following the rank and file when strikes erupted.

The divisions in the community produced rising levels of violence culminating in the killing of three Communists during a mass rally in the town plaza in November 1948. Violence generated by political and labor conflict had been growing in the community since the 1890s, reaching new levels after 1930. The violence prior to the 1930s had been largely restricted to confrontations between strikers and police. Homicides (rarely more than one a year) were normally the result of personal disputes among workers.[94] Beginning in the midthirties, violence directed at the British, and between Communist and anti-Communist, became a major characteristic of local life. In 1935 a disgruntled miner shot a British foreman, and in 1942 and 1944 British supervisors were shot down and killed. In the latter two cases the Englishmen were killed by employees they had disciplined for insubordination. In 1955 a disgruntled employee ambushed the company labor lawyer, leaving him paralyzed from the waist down with a bullet near the spine.[95]

The most spectacular violent confrontation, however, was between the contending forces within local politics and the union. In late 1948 under the militant leadership of councilman William Dias Gomes, the Communists tried to foment a strike. Despite warnings by local police, the Communists held a mass rally in the plaza on the evening of 7 November 1948 celebrating the thirty-first anniversary of the Bolshevik Revolution.[96] A group of armed anti-Communist agitators were at the rally and attacked Gomes and the other Communist speakers. A gun battle broke out, apparently initiated by the attackers, and Gomes and two others were gunned down while attempting to flee the union hall. At least two dozen more were wounded seriously enough to be hospitalized. Nearly all those involved were company employees. No one was ever arrested for the shootings—hardly surprising given the government's anti-Communist stance at the time. Six months later another prominent Communist was killed in front of the Bonfim Chapel near the center of town. The killer claimed self-defense and was never tried.[97] By 1949 Nova Lima was a community severely split by political and labor violence.

The emergence of a Catholic Action movement and pragmatism by local PCB members in the early 1950s began to heal wounds and mediate conflict. Under a new parish priest, the Catholic church in Nova Lima turned to the Ação Católica Operária (ACO) as a means of supporting the working class while diminishing the confrontational tactics of UNAS. Under the leadership of a highly respected miner, José Gomes Pimenta (Dazinho), the ACO sought conciliation with the local branch of the PCB. In turn, the Communists in Nova Lima, under the intense government repression, began to pursue less confrontational and more conciliatory tactics. Although ordered by the national leadership to pursue efforts at creating an alternative union movement, local leaders refused, knowing well the consequences that this divisive move would bring. In the early fifties the ACO and the Communists cooperated to elect mutually acceptable leaders in the union and in the town council. The result was diminishing conflict among *novalimenses* as well as a united working-class movement confronting the St. John d'el Rey.[98]

From its founding in 1934 until intervention by the military regime in 1964, the working-class movement in Nova Lima benefited from developments outside of the community, yet remained fiercely independent. The union was organized by workers and only later sanctioned by the Ministry of Labor. The government repeatedly sought to control the union, which repeatedly ignored government restrictions on strikes and organizing. The growth of the Communist influence in the union directly challenged the corporatist nature of labor-government relations, and despite severe repression and harassment the PCB maintained a powerful influence in the union until 1964. At the same time the local PCB membership remained fiercely independent of outside control. Although the local organization participated fully in national campaigns, sent members for training, and supported party policies, the local cell refused to follow the most important order from above: to create an alternative union and divisions in the community. Instead, local Communists chose to cooperate with the ACO to achieve a stronger union and peace in the community. The miners of Morro Velho were first and foremost concerned about their own community.

Conclusion

By the 1950s Nova Lima had become an industrial, working-class city having gradually lost its rural, agrarian past. Although the rise of the technological system at Morro Velho had created an industrial complex by the 1860s, it was a complex built on slave labor. As the composition of the community gradually shifted in the late nineteenth century with the demise of slavery, the emergence of a free labor economy was not accompanied by the rise of an industrial working class. The surrounding peasantry balked at working in the mine, and when they did enter the work force it was on a seasonal basis as they moved back and forth between field and factory. Between the 1870s and 1920s the St. John attempted to combat this resistance with the importation of foreign labor, an effort that ultimately failed. Despite the construction of a sophisticated industrial complex beginning in the 1890s, the company did not succeed in its efforts to promote the formation of a working class and an industrial order out of the surrounding agricultural population.

The rise of the working class and the transformation of Nova Lima into an industrial city came in the 1930s. A depressed agricultural economy suffering from the Depression, new social and labor legislation, a favorable international gold market, and the existence of a complex technological system at Morro Velho all combined to produce an industrial working class in Nova Lima. The government-sanctioned union movement provided the industrial working class with an instrument to confront management in an era of rising nationalism. The union gave the workers a powerful means to influence events and attempt to forge their own future.

Beginning in the 1930s, workers and management entered into a "dance of death" marked by confrontations, conflict, and bitter strikes. The workers succeeded in extracting important wage and benefit concessions from management. Unfortunately, inflation in Brazil continued to erode these gains and forced workers to confront the company again and again. The stagnation of the world gold market trapped workers and management, limiting the company's ability to meet new demands and the workers' ability to extract new concessions without destroying the company—and with it their livelihood. By the 1950s an activist Brazilian state had become the mediator in the fate of both company and community. It was the Brazilian government that presided over the end of the British era at Morro Velho. The demise of British control, however, did not signify victory for the Brazilian workers. The striking contrast between the poverty of this industrial working-class community and the enormous wealth it produced had not—and has not—changed.

7

British Society in the Tropics

[Morro Velho] is a delightful place, a proper English colony, and without a doubt as finely a managed place as there is in the world.[1]

The growth and expansion of the Morro Velho gold mine made Nova Lima a thriving multiracial and multicultural community despite its geographical isolation in the Brazilian interior. Just as the development of the mine spurred the formation of a diverse working-class community, it also created and perpetuated a small but thriving British community in the mountains of Minas Gerais. The expansion of company operations at Morro Velho shaped the growth of a dual community of a small, British managerial elite and a large, predominantly Brazilian, working-class population. The British community's impact far outweighed its small numbers, and through its managerial and supervisory roles guided the technological system at Morro Velho, and thereby played a key, if not *the* key, role in local life. For nearly a century and a quarter the British at Morro Velho played the central role in shaping the rise of the mine and the community around it. This chapter analyzes this resilient cultural and social enclave of Britons in the Brazilian interior.[2]

The British at Morro Velho formed an elite sector in the local community. With few exceptions, the British filled supervisory positions and dominated the upper echelons of company management. Even the working-class British employees enjoyed a living standard that placed them above the majority of the local population. This community of managers, supervisors, and workers, as well as their families, by no means formed a homogeneous group. They were, however, bound together by a common bond: their common cultural heritage reinforced by life in a foreign land. The Brazilians clearly perceived the British community as separate and self-contained, and they referred to the British as *ingléses*, although not all were English. Some of the community came from Ireland, Scotland, or Wales, and a number were not British at all. A few North Americans, South Africans, and a smattering of Europeans through the decades formed a small part of the British community. Yet the community was overwhelmingly British, and the majority consciously set themselves apart from Brazilian society as they maintained their common linguistic, cultural, and social heritage.

From the perspective of the St. John d'el Rey management and the employees, the dividing line in the community roughly followed the dividing line in the payroll account books. The St. John maintained two sets of payroll sheets until the late 1940s. The larger one carried the names of the "natives" and included the non-British working class—Brazilian and foreign. The smaller, and more exclusive, account book listed "European" employees on signed contracts. The company paid the "natives" their wages in local currency, with the "European" salaries paid in sterling—part in "home pay" deposited in banks in Britain and part in Brazilian currency at the current rate of exchange. This payroll division reflected the cultural and social separation in the community throughout the history of British presence in Nova Lima and Morro Velho.[3]

Growth of the Community

Although the St. John created this strong foreign enclave in Nova Lima, British presence in the community predated the arrival of the company in the 1830s. A small number of British families had taken up residence in Congonhas de Sabará in the 1820s with the opening of the interior after independence. Local notarial records show British citizens purchasing property in the community in the mid-1820s. John and Mary Alexander, for example, came to the area in 1827, began to buy property, and established a dry-goods business. A number of British merchants bought mining properties, although most did not reside in Congonhas.[4] The former superintendent of the Gongo Soco mine settled in Congonhas and purchased a portion of the Morro Velho estate, along with some London merchants. When

Table 21 British Employees at Morro Velho, 1835–1950 (selected years)

Year	Employees	Total Labor Force	Percentage of Total Labor Force
1835	18	64	28.0
1840	44	660	6.7
1845	65	733	8.9
1867	165	2,521	6.5
1880	108	1,327	8.1
1892	46	545	8.4
1910	148	2,524	5.9
1932	126	5,000	2.5
1950	50	5,172	1.0

Sources: AR and SJNL.

the St. John began operations in Congonhas, the British community probably already numbered at least a dozen.

Superintendent Charles Herring, Jr., brought with him around twenty miners and craftsmen to Morro Velho in 1833.[5] Apparently, none brought families with them. With the expansion of operations in the late 1830s and early 1840s the company began to encourage miners to take their families to Morro Velho.[6] Imbued with the Victorian morality of the era, the board of directors firmly believed in promoting social and moral responsibility in their workers. They saw family life as a stabilizing force that would keep miners away from the temptations of liquor, gaming, and women. They encouraged miners to take their families out to Brazil, hoping to build up a stable and hardworking community as well as a productive enterprise. Good family men would stay out of fights, would not show up drunk for work, and would ensure a steady, dependable work schedule.[7]

After 1840 the ups and downs of mining operations became the determining factor in the rise and decline in the size of the British community. By 1850 the number of British employees at Morro Velho had risen to around 100, and the size of the community reached 200 (see tables 21 and 22). This upward trend continued until the disaster of 1867. At the time of Richard Burton's visit on the eve of the disaster the community numbered close to 350, about half of those employees. In the wake of the collapse of the mine the company laid off its free Brazilian force and sent home many of the British. At the

Table 22 British Community at Morro Velho, 1835–1950 (selected years)

Year	Number
1835	20
1851	200
1867	343
1880	256
1901	202
1915	300
1925	146
1950	161

Sources: AR 1852, p. 10; Burton, *Explorations,* I; *AR 1880,* p. 79; John Spear to Consul General, Rio de Janeiro, Papers of British Vice-Consul, 3 April 1901, SJNL; C. F. W. Kup to George Chalmers, 7 January 1915; A. G. N. Chalmers to Board, 14 March 1925; and Loose Papers, 17 October 1950, SJNL.

time of Chalmers's arrival in the mid-1880s the community probably numbered around 250 with a little less than half of those on the
payroll. The crush of 1886 once again cut into the size of the community as miners returned to Britain or hired on with other British
mining companies in Minas Gerais.

By the First World War the phenomenal expansion under Chalmers's direction pushed the community back over the 300-mark, and
the payroll now included around 150 British employees. With the
outbreak of the war in Europe in 1914 began a long and gradual process of decline, which continues in its final stages today. Although
the company expanded at a record pace in the 1930s, the number of British employees and dependents slowly diminished. Company management in London pursued a policy of replacing British
labor with Brazilians whenever possible for one fundamental reason:
British labor cost more than Brazilian labor. Rather than pay high
sterling wages to an employee on contract and incur the expenses of
training him and then possibly losing him after one contract period,
the company felt it could be better served by cheaper, local labor.[8]
Consequently, the number of lower-level employees diminished and
the disparity between British technicians and managers presiding
over a Brazilian labor force became more pronounced.

The financial crisis of the 1940s and 1950s accentuated the decline of the British community. The expansion of the company under
Chalmers had left the St. John with a large number of employees who

had settled and stayed with the company for decades. Some families had even predated the Chalmers era by several decades. The arrival of the Canadian superintendent, G. P. Wigle, in the 1950s brought a belt-tightening, managerial reorganization. Wigle proceeded to lay off and retire a large contingent of the British force, many of whom had been with the company for more than twenty years. The departure of this large contingent of Britons left a deep impression on both the British and Brazilian communities. The former still look back on the cutback by a non-British superintendent with considerable bitterness. The Brazilians who witnessed the exodus continue to marvel at the organizational ax wielded by Wigle.[9] By 1950 the St. John employed around fifty British citizens at Morro Velho, and the community numbered just over 150.

The final dismantling of this community followed the sale of the mine to North Americans and then Brazilians in the late 1950s and early 1960s. With the end of British control the vast majority of the community chose to return to the British Isles. A small number stayed on to work for the Brazilians. Retirement and personal decisions further diminished the size of the community through the 1960s and 1970s. A few families continued to reside in Nova Lima, mainly those with deep roots in the area. The once-impressive British community today numbers some two dozen, but the complete assimilation of the last surviving members of that community into Brazilian society seems inevitable.

Composition and Hierarchy

The British who came to Morro Velho were from all parts of the British Isles, with the majority coming from the mining regions of Cornwall and Durham. This was especially true in the nineteenth century when the company brought over large groups of miners. In the mid-nineteenth century mining in Cornwall had begun a long period of decline, but it continued to supply the rest of the mining world with its surplus miners.[10] The Cornish played prominent roles in the mining booms all over Latin America in the 1820s and 1830s. In the 1850s they streamed to the western United States and then Australia. With the collapse of Cornish mining in the 1870s even more migrated to these areas and other parts of the globe. The Cornish miner took part in every significant mining boom in the nineteenth century.[11]

Both company records and parish registers indicate that the majority of the working-class British came from Cornwall. By the 1920s the number of Cornishmen at Morro Velho had diminished in both absolute and relative terms, probably due to the decline of mining in Cornwall itself. Fewer Cornish were being trained in mining. Also the St. John brought over fewer and fewer miners in the early twentieth century preferring to place Englishmen in supervisory positions and leave the manual labor to the Brazilians. Local management increased as members of the British working class were elevated to supervisory positions. The rest of the community came from a wide variety of locations in Britain. A few of the superintendents were Irish (Keogh and Gordon, for example), and a high proportion of the company physicians were Scots (no doubt a reflection of the quality of Scottish medical schools). Occasionally, a South African or Welshman appeared on the payroll, but the remainder of the community generally came from England.

In the 1920s a survey of some sixty employees on the European payroll provides us with a composite picture of the geographical origins of the British community.[12] By the twenties over one-quarter of the employees had been born in Brazil of English-speaking parents. Nearly all of these Anglo-Brazilians had been born at Morro Velho. With the exception of one Irishman, the rest of the British came from areas in England. Of these forty-two people about one-third (fourteen) came from the North country. Fully one-fifth (nine) came from Durham alone. About 24 percent (ten) came from the Midlands. The South contributed the single largest contingent, accounting for nearly 43 percent (eighteen) of the British community. The largest counties represented were Cornwall with 17 percent (seven) and London with 12 percent (five). The British community at Morro Velho in the first quarter of the twentieth century then was mainly English, from the South, and heavily represented by native *morrovelhenses*.

Within the British community the position of a person depended, for the main part, on his or her position in the company hierarchy. Embedded in this small, foreign colony was a pecking order derived from the company payroll sheets. At the top stood the "officers" of the company. This group traditionally included the superintendent and the department heads. (When the parson was in residence he was

Table 23 Salaries of Department Heads, 1867–1955 (selected years in pounds sterling)

Year	Mine	Reduction	Shops	Store	Estate	Cashier	Hospital
1867	240	350	300	250	—	350	350
1871	350	300	250	200	—	200	350
1881	250	250	450	300	—	300	500
1891	250	—	450	350	250	350	350
1901	700	700	700	700	200	350	700
1911	700	700	600	700	400	400	700
1924	—	—	—	700	—	—	700
1939	—	—	800	800	750	—	—
1950	900	1,200	1,000	1,100	1,100	1,020	1,320
1955	1,600	1,700	1,600	960	1,600	1,600	1,280

Sources: European Payroll and Loose Papers, SJNL.
Note: (—) means figures not available. The estate department did not come into existence until the 1890s.

also counted among the top echelon but did not participate in business operations.) The superintendent reigned over the small British community. Throughout the history of the St. John d'el Rey the superintendent was handpicked by the board, and he usually came from a fairly well-to-do socioeconomic background. The company kept the superintendent's salary high, much higher than any other employee. The first few superintendents received £1,000 per annum. James Newell Gordon's long tenure and achievements pushed his salary up to £1,800 after twenty years' service. George Chalmers started at the traditional £1,000 plus perquisites.[13] His extraordinary business and engineering performance pushed his salary up to £4,000 by 1910 and to £5,000 by the 1920s.[14] This was nearly six times the salary of the highest-paid department head. When A. H. Millett took charge in 1930 he started at £2,500, and his successors followed suit at similar salary levels.

Below the superintendent, the department heads and their families manned the highest social and economic positions in the British community. The heads of the major departments reigned over their personal domains and were privy to all but the most confidential information from London. In a sense they were the local board of directors discussing and making decisions with the approval of the superintendent. Heads of departments made annual salaries ranging from £240 to £350 in the mid-nineteenth century (see table 23). These salary levels remained relatively constant until the reopening of the

Table 24 Typical Yearly Wages of British Working Class, 1865–1915
(in pounds sterling)

Year	Miner	Carpenter	Smith/Fitter	Reduction
1865	120–216	96	120	108
1870	120–180	96	120	120
1875	120–840	120	132	120
1880	84–408	120	120	120
1885	84–144	132	96	96
1890	96–168	108	156	—
1895	204–228	144	156	144
1900	120–300	240	156	216
1905	120–396	—	192	168
1910	132–300	—	204	192
1915	144–300	—	204	216

Source: European Payroll, SJNL.
Note: The category of fitter appears in the payroll around 1900, and carpenters disappear from the payroll at roughly the same time.

mine in the early twentieth century brought renewed prosperity. By the turn of the century the most important department heads made around £700 per annum. This rose slowly but surely with inflation, the erosion of the pound sterling, and market demands until by 1950 department heads earned salaries in the £1,000-to-£1,700 range, with the average closer to the higher end of the scale.

The officers of the St. John d'el Rey, nevertheless, made up a small percentage of the British community. They normally numbered no more than a dozen or so and accounted for less than 10 percent of the European payroll. The vast majority of the British employees worked on a much lower monthly salary basis. The standard contract called for four (sometimes six) years of service with a home leave paid by the company halfway through the term of the contract. As can be seen from the figures in table 24, these employees made significantly less than the department heads. The gap between officers and regular monthly employees was substantial.

The vast majority of these employees were blue-collar workers, with a smattering of clerical employees. In the nineteenth century the miners, carpenters, smiths, and fitters apparently handled more direct labor than their twentieth-century successors. As time went by the English increasingly became supervisory personnel and left manual labor to the Brazilians. The European payroll in the twentieth century became increasingly loaded with managers, supervisors, and foremen, as manual laborers decreased. Miners became shift bosses and captains. Smiths became shop supervisors. Carpenters became crew supervisors, and fitters gave way to metallurgical engineers. To some extent this also reflects the increasingly scientific and technical nature of mining. This trend accentuates the growing separation of the vast majority of the company payroll—the Brazilian laborers—from the small, supervisory staff of foreign technicians. By the 1930s the company employed eight Brazilians for every European.[15]

The Europeans received their salaries in pounds sterling, while the "natives" were paid in local currency. (This system was designed to protect the British against any sudden fluctuation in the exchange rate and maintained them on a British standard of living.) The Europeans had the option of receiving their pay in the equivalent of local currency at the current exchange, or receiving part of it in local currency and the rest in a bank account in Britain. This "home pay" enabled the employee to accumulate pounds back home as savings or expenses for family and friends left in Britain. Currency laws in the 1930s made this practice increasingly difficult.[16] Although the dual-pay system had to be done away with in the 1940s, a number of British employees continued to receive their salaries partly in cruzeiros and partly in pounds.[17]

Unlike the high salaries of the officers, the rest of the Europeans received less than £200 per annum. In the mid-1860s a miner made somewhere between £10 and £18 a month, a carpenter about £8, a smith around £10, and a reduction worker around £9. By the 1880s these figures had risen very little with all of these workers receiving around £10 per month with some of the older, more experienced miners making between £15 to £20. (The average monthly wage for a Brazilian borer was around £5 in 1890.) By the First World War a miner made as much as £25 a month, with the average being closer to £20 (compared with the average Brazilian borer at around £6 in 1910). Carpenters had disappeared from the payroll by then, as had smiths. The latter were replaced by pipe fitters making around £17 per month. Reduction workers made about the same. By the 1950s an assistant mine captain made about £85 a month, an assistant in reduction about £70, and an assistant in the mechanical department about £80 a month. These salary levels were negatively affected by an unfavorable exchange rate after World War I.

Looking at the salary history of individual employees provides another perspective on movement within company ranks. At the highest level one can see the rewarding of valuable service in the career of George Chalmers as he moved from the beginning salary of £1,000 to £5,000 per annum at the time of his retirement forty years later. As the minutes of stockholders' meetings indicate, the board and stockholders felt that he was certainly worth every shilling of his salary.[18] A. H. Millett started with the company in 1912 at £27 a month working as an assistant cashier. He worked his way up to business manager in the 1920s, and in 1930 he became superintendent at £2,500 per annum. The careers of his successors followed a similar pattern. Both Eric Davies and W. R. Russell had started in low clerical positions in the second decade of the century. Both rose through the ranks, the former on the technical side of operations, and the latter on the business side. Both eventually became superintendent.[19]

In the middle ranks of the company the case of H. W. Cocking shows another type of career pattern. Cocking's father, H. D., had arrived at Morro Velho in the 1850s as a smith and eventually became foreman of the smiths before retiring in the 1880s. H. W. began work as a reduction assistant in the 1890s at £20 per month. He gradually rose to head of the reduction department in the early 1920s making over £700 per annum (nearly £60 per month). The career of R. J. Clemence followed a similar pattern. His father, Samuel, was also a smith and also rose to the position of foreman before retiring after four decades of service in 1892. R. J. started with the company as a clerk in the company store at £11 a month in the late 1870s. By 1883 he had become cashier at £17, and by 1888 he headed the store and cashier departments at £25 per month. In the mid-1890s he became storekeeper and estate agent at £50 per month, and at the turn of the century he served exclusively as estate agent at £58 per month. In the nineteenth century miners who rose through the ranks were not rewarded as handsomely as clerical workers. John Jackson, a Cornishman, joined the company in the mid-1860s as a miner at £10 per month. In just a few years he had become an assistant mine captain at £14. In the mid-1870s he became mine captain, the most important position underground, and head of the mine department. His salary for this position came to a mere £15 per month, rising to £17 before his retirement in 1876.

Housing

Housing and housing patterns in the British community also reflected the dual nature of local society. The St. John d'el Rey owned most of the real estate in the vicinity of Nova Lima and either bought or built most of the physical structures. Housing for the European employees had been put up by the company since the beginning of operations at Morro Velho. The housing for the British community generally clustered on the hill around the Casa Grande, and to the southwest of the hill in the area known as the Retiro (see map 3). A few of the English lived on the Mingu hill where the "C" and "D" shafts were later built. A few did live in the village. This placed the British close to the mine and the superintendent's house and office. It also separated most of the British from the majority of the townspeople in Nova Lima, which lay in the Cristais basin just over the ridge to the east. The size and location of the British community varied through the years as did the British population. The growth of the mine under Chalmers and then Millett increased the size of the community. By the end of World War II the British had covered most of the Casa Grande hill and the Retiro. British housing also covered the hillside to the south between the Retiro and the town, an area that came to be known as the Bairro das Quintas. The Quintas neighborhood faced the Casa Grande hill and the homes of the management; it eventually housed the British club.

Although the British and Brazilian communities knew no absolute physical boundaries, both were more or less separate entities. The Brazilians referred to the British neighborhoods as the *colônia inglêsa*, and the British spoke of "the village" when referring to Nova Lima.[20] As the Brazilian community expanded outward along with the British neighborhoods, the two communities began to merge physically in the first decades of this century. By the Second World War the physical separation of the two communities had become less clearly defined. By then a few Brazilians on the European payroll had access to privileged housing and no well-defined physical boundary separated the "village" from the *"colônia inglêsa."* With the departure of the British staff in 1960, Brazilian staff members replaced them in the company's best housing. Today the housing is known as "staff" instead of "European."

Staff housing varied, of course, depending on the importance of the occupant. The highest echelons of the British community lived in the largest and most spacious homes on the Casa Grande hill. The superintendent, beginning with Herring in the 1830s, occupied the Casa Grande. Under Chalmers in the early twentieth century the Casa Grande became more of a guest house and offices; the superintendent lived at Jaguara on holidays and in a large home on an isolated hill west of the Casa Grande at Morro Velho. A. G. N. Chalmers initially resided in the Casa Grande, later deciding to move into the isolated home his father had built, thereby avoiding the constant interruptions from social life in the Casa Grande.[21] All subsequent British superintendents lived in the Retiro house as the Casa Grande became a guest residence and museum.

The home of the average British employee by the late 1920s normally contained four rooms, a kitchen, and a lavatory.[22] Built by the company with local materials, the homes resembled local architecture, but with a definite British touch. As far back as the 1860s, travelers had noted the quaint English-style gardens and cottage appearance of the homes.[23] The houses contained four twelve-by-twelve-foot rooms, with wood floors raised off the ground on a light, concrete foundation. Built with sun-dried company bricks and wood, they had a tile roof. One of these houses cost the company about £1,000 to construct. At the turn of the century the company owned about seventy houses occupied by Europeans.[24] In 1911 Chalmers estimated that European housing contained about 522 rooms occupied by 357 people (161 being employees), or about .75 persons per room.[25] This compares with a ratio of about 1.3 persons per room in the company-owned Brazilian housing. Most of the British homes used woodburning stoves until the mid-twentieth century when they were replaced with electric stoves and appliances.[26] In 1896 the company built a boarding house/club for the single men in the Retiro. This hotel provided the men with a room, meals, and leisure facilities in the form of billiards, a library, and occasional dances.[27]

Life in the Bairro Inglês

The St. John d'el Rey also built and operated a company school for the children of British employees. As a small part of company efforts to provide British employees with all the services they might receive in England, the company had long sought to offer schooling at the primary level. With the consolidation of the community in the 1840s and 1850s formal efforts began to educate the growing number of British children. The chairman of the board clearly outlined to the superintendent at Morro Velho the board's views on education: "I think it the duty of the upper classes and especially of large employers of labour to assent, and as much in their power, insist on the education of the young people committed to their care as it were."[28] After 1850 the arrival of an Anglican clergyman-and-wife team set a pattern that would be followed in general terms for the next century. The husband-and-wife team handled the religious needs of the community as well as the education of the British children in the company school. During the periods when no clergyman resided at Morro Velho the usual practice was for the wife of an employee, or a young, single woman from one of the British families, to take over the teaching duties. For a brief period in the 1870s a Confederate expatriate couple from Tennessee ran the school.[29]

The population of the company school never reached great numbers; in the 1870s around thirty children attended classes regularly. This number rose to forty by the 1880s. The collapse of operations and the subsequent rebuilding years eliminated the school for some time, but by the 1930s the chaplain again had about thirty students in the classroom. The number remained in the upper thirties into the 1950s.[30] Only those children between the ages of approximately five and fifteen could be given basic instruction. As children finished their primary education, their parents had several options, generally dictated by family income. The less affluent simply put their children to work—normally for the company—when they were teenagers. For those who could afford to send their children on to a secondary education, Nova Lima had a high school after 1909. However, few chose to send their children there.[31] Older children normally went to high school in Belo Horizonte, and the Izabel Hendricks School run by North American Methodist missionaries was a popular choice for teenage girls. Another option open to parents was the British school in Rio de Janeiro.[32] The most affluent members of the staff could afford the luxury of sending their children off to boarding school in England, as George Chalmers had at the beginning of the century.[33]

The existence of an English-language school for the children of British employees provided one more symbol of the cultural separation between foreigners and nationals. At the same time the company school mirrored the class distinctions within the British community. Close to half of the children of the community between the ages of five and fifteen did not even attend school. Instead, their parents arranged private tutoring at home, at their own expense. These parents chose to tutor their children privately for a number of reasons: some wished their children to receive a more intense and rigorous education; others felt that the mixture of levels and ages in the school worked to the disadvantage of the students; perhaps a more important factor was the desire to keep children from being exposed to the speech and social habits of lower-class British children. Simply stated, some parents did not want their children going to school with the children of lower-class employees.[34]

Another social and cultural dilemma faced by the teachers was presented by children who bridged both cultural communities. The composition of the student body ranged from children born and raised in England, to children born and raised in English-language homes in Brazil, to those raised in bilingual homes in Brazil. Finally, some students came from British homes where Portuguese dominated. These linguistic and cultural traditions reflected the marriage and settlement patterns of the British staff. Consequently, a number of children entering the school often encountered English instruction for the first time, although they had at least one English parent. Teachers had to handle the English-language transition from Portuguese much as teachers of English as a second language do today.[35]

In the 1930s the cultural nationalism of the Vargas period extended into the educational system, and the St. John was compelled to provide instruction in Portuguese for at least one-half of the school day. The company hired local teachers to handle Portuguese instruction in the morning hours and British teachers to teach the British curriculum in the afternoon. In effect, the school became truly bilingual and bicultural.[36] Along with the other services set up for the British community, the company school disappeared with the sale of the St. John in the late 1950s. The departure of the majority of the British staff removed the school's very raison d'être. The Brazilianization of the St. John d'el Rey after 1960 brought an end to this unique institution.

The social and cultural life of the British community at Morro Velho further set it apart from the surrounding Brazilian milieu. Perhaps the most prominent feature of this distinct social and cultural life was the religion of the British. With the possible exception of the Irish, the community contained few Roman Catholics. The Protestant heritage of the British set them apart from the single most important cultural influence in Brazilian society. In Catholic Brazil one was born, baptized, confirmed, married, and buried within the realm of the Catholic church. The calendar of the nation weighed heavy with saints' days, feast days, and other religious celebrations. In short, the lives of the Brazilians were inextricably entwined in the fabric of Roman Catholicism. Whether one was devout or not, the influence of Catholicism permeated all aspects of Brazilian culture.

The religious division between Briton and Brazilian served to further divide both communities. The British applied for and received permission to set aside their own cemetery as Protestant dead could not be buried in the local parish burial grounds.[37] To this day the existence of a separate burial ground leads to misunderstanding and a strong sense of division between the two communities.[38] The British also built their own church on the store hill. Beginning in the 1840s with the expansion of the community, the board constantly urged the superintendent to press employees to observe the Sabbath and attend worship services in the Casa Grande.[39] The company built a small chapel in the 1840s and an even larger one in the early 1850s. The building of the second chapel coincided with the arrival of the first Anglican parson.

Not surprisingly, church services did not attract the entire community. The company tried to present the services in a manner that would attract those not of Anglican faith. Those who chose not to attend most probably reflected the sentiments of nonconformity, hostility to institutional religion, or merely apathy. Attendance also reflected the popularity (or lack of popularity) of the pastor.[40] The parson held services on Sunday, ran the English school with his wife, and sought to improve the morality of the British community. (The parsons also kept the parish registers, for which at least one historian is eternally grateful!) The board in London kept a close eye on local morality, tolerating little sexual or social deviance. In the nineteenth century the heavy drinking of the miners constantly perplexed and annoyed management. Company correspondence contains countless schemes to produce sobriety, including fines and dismissals for drinking. Alcohol seems to have been less a problem in later years than concern for sexual mores. Company records occasionally register fines or dismissals for a sexual dalliance with a slave or for cohabitation without marriage.[41]

In the twentieth century the company management acted quickly to send home those found having illicit relationships. Quick action was taken to prevent discord within the community or between communities.[42] In one notable case an Anglican Englishman married a Catholic Brazilian in the local Catholic church, but not in the Anglican church to the dismay of George Chalmers. In a letter to the board Chalmers warned menacingly, "According to the religion this man professed he is not married, and is therefore living with this woman in an unlawful way; and for the sake of the morality of this Establishment, I feel bound to dispense with the services of this man. It is evident to me that if the matter were passed unnoticed by me it might lead to others *weak in such matters to follow his example.*"[43]

Aside from religion the most important social and cultural institution in the community was the sports club. The company sponsored sporting events from the beginnings of British settlement in the nineteenth century. On company holidays miners often competed in wrestling, running, and tests of strength.[44] With the consolidation of the enterprise under Chalmers and the growth of the community, the St. John built a sports club overlooking the Quintas neighborhood and the mine. Complete with soccer, cricket, and pool facilities, the club became the central social institution among the British. The company formed a cricket team that from time to time competed with the British team from Rio de Janeiro.[45] Tennis and sport shooting were also popular. The company, as well as some individual employees, also participated in the formation of a local soccer club (Vila Nova) that continues to compete in the first division of Brazilian national soccer leagues. The club also divided the two communities. Open only to members of the British community, it became an exclusive enclave rarely visited by Brazilians—only those with the highest confidence of the management. In effect, the club became the playground of a foreign elite and a source of bitterness for Brazilians who looked upon it as a reminder of foreign domination of the local economy.[46]

In addition to the sports activities at the club, the St. John constantly sponsored films, dances, and parties for the British. These events generally took place in the upper level of the old company store on the hill above the Casa Grande. In the nineteenth century the company provided the superintendent with a crude image-projecting device called a "magic lantern." Local management regularly entertained slaves and free persons alike with showings of slides.[47] Another popular nineteenth-century social event was a weekly gathering of the officers and families in the Casa Grande. These social gatherings often featured readings from English literature and music performed by members of the staff. During one of these gatherings in 1867 Sir Richard Burton dazzled the community with slides and lectures on his African travels.[48] In this century the company regularly provided films attended by large crowds. Dances and parties on holidays brought together the entire community, and prominent members of the local and regional elites often attended.[49] These festivities created the greatest amount of interaction between all sectors of the British community. Those who lived at Morro Velho in the early twentieth century were left with indelible memories of these occasions, and today they recall the old social life with fond nostalgia.[50]

Throughout the history of the community, clubs took shape around the changing interests of the local families. For decades (beginning in the nineteenth century) the Horticultural Society met annually to award prizes for the gardening successes of its members. A Boy Scout troop was formed, and women banded together in sewing clubs to support servicemen in both world wars.[51] The biggest festivities in the community, however, were reserved for St. John's Day at midsummer each June. From the earliest days of the company's existence employees were given a holiday of three days to celebrate the day of the company's patron saint.[52] The following is the superintendent's description of these festivities in 1867.[53]

The proceedings of the day commenced at 9:30 A.M., when the English Brass Band of Morro Velho waited on the Superintendent at the Casa Grande and accompanied the party from thence to the Store Hill where a Play Ground had been previously prepared, and enclosed with poles & chains, within which space the greater part of the sports and games were carried on.

The Blacks attended at 1 P.M. and took part in the proceedings, giving some of the National Dances in dress costume. A number of Brazilians (Borers) were tastefully dressed and danced the Ribbon Dance with loops and half circles, dressed very neatly. The May Pole dance was also performed by them. The sports of the day terminated at 5 P.M.

The evening entertainment in the large Store well decorated for the purpose commenced at 6:15 P.M. and continued until Midnight when a splendid series of Fire Works prepared by the R[oman]. C[atholic]. Chaplain, illuminated the whole neighbourhood and formed a striking contrast; being very superior to any previously exhibited in this part of Brazil.

The visits of important political figures also became occasions for grand festivities. In 1881 the Emperor Dom Pedro II visited the mine on his tour of Minas Gerais and the company put on a huge banquet for his entourage and for local notables.[54] In 1904 President Rodrigues Alves visited the mine, and Chalmers entertained the presidential entourage in splendid style.[55] Royalty again toured the mine in 1920 as King Albert of Belgium inspected investment opportunities of the region. The most memorable visit in this century for the British was a whirlwind tour of the mine by the Prince of Wales (later Duke of Windsor) and his younger brother in 1931.[56] On all these festive occasions prominent local Brazilians attended, but the contact between working-class Brazilians and British seems to have diminished over the years as the latter constructed their own clubs and facilities. Relations between the local Brazilian elite and the British were also not the smoothest as company correspondence often suggests. The social and linguistic isolation of the British was perceived as cultural condescension by some Brazilians.[57] With the increasing nationalism of the 1940s and 1950s the community seems to have become more and more isolated with the exception of those families with the longest and closest ties to the Brazilian community.

Morrovelhenses: Family Histories

The history of the families in the British community at Morro Velho reveals a great deal about the internal dynamics of local society. Although the majority of the company employees viewed their residence in Brazil as temporary, a small core of families provided the community with a sense of stability and continuity. A number of these families stretch across the entire history of the British presence at Morro Velho, and their individual family histories provide us with a glimpse of a number of important aspects of community life: marriage patterns, linguistic habits, acculturation processes, and class boundaries.

Interviews with descendants of this community, parish registers from both Catholic and Anglican parishes, vice-consular archives, and company records have contributed to the reconstruction of a number of these family histories. These histories tell us a great deal about the British community, but one must always keep in mind that the sample has its inherent biases. First, the selection represents the most stable members of the community, and those more transient families and individuals escape the sample. Second, the parish registers reflect an imprecise record. They cover only the events in Nova Lima and do not throw light on those families that moved to or have ties with other communities, particularly those at Passagem or other British mines. Also, we cannot be sure that all marriages, births, and deaths were registered. Less religious individuals and those less concerned with formalities often disappear from the historical record through lack of registration. Furthermore, the movement of families within Brazil and across the Atlantic often leads to registration in locations outside of Morro Velho.

One of the most remarkable aspects of the history of the British community is the long-term stability of certain families. Beginning with the arrival of considerable numbers of British families in the 1840s and 1850s, a small group of families settled into Morro Velho and their descendants continue to form a portion of the local community up to the present. Through intermarriage and migration, family names sometimes disappear, but the nucleus of these families remain. Perhaps the best manner in which to illustrate this is through the example of the Clemence family.

Samuel Clemence, a blacksmith, probably arrived in Morro Velho in the late 1840s or early 1850s. His father was an English blacksmith. In November 1852 Samuel married Julia Stephens, the daughter of one of the British miners at Morro Velho. Samuel and Julia had several children. One daughter, Julia Ann, married a Morro Velho miner; her brother, Thomas Syne, worked for the St. John. Samuel and Julia's first-born, Richard John (b. 1853), joined the company as a store clerk in the late 1870s. In 1880 he married Caroline Julia Cocking. Her father, H. D. Cocking, was also a blacksmith and had come to Morro Velho in the mid-1850s. H. D. had married Louisa Ellen

Rouse in 1861. She was one of the many daughters of John Rouse, a mechanic who joined the company in 1836.[58]

Caroline Julia Clemence (née Cocking) had a sister, Florence Ellen, who married J. W. P. Heslop in the 1890s. Heslop had come over with the crew of sinkers to drive the new shafts for George Chalmers in 1888. Richard John and Caroline Julia Clemence, along with Florence Ellen Heslop, represent the children of working-class immigrants who settled at Morro Velho and whose children were born in Brazil. Richard and Caroline Clemence also had a large family born and raised in Brazil at Morro Velho. Some married into the British community to company employees. Mabel, born in 1885, married George William Mayo, another Briton who came to Morro Velho to build the Chalmers mine at the turn of the century. Their children were also born and raised at Morro Velho and some worked for the company. These children represented the third generation born at the mine; some were still alive in 1988 and were in their sixties.

For our purposes the most important of R. J. Clemence's children was Leslie Melville, born at the turn of the century. As a young man Leslie Clemence went to England for schooling. When he returned to Morro Velho he began to work for the company as a surveyor and married a daughter of C. H. Raborg, the head of the electrical department. The son of a Baltimore physician, Raborg had shipped out to South America in the 1890s as a teenager in search of adventure. He jumped ship in Rio de Janeiro and, after a short stay, ended up in Morro Velho. Beginning as an apprentice in the electrical department in 1898, Raborg worked his way to the top of the department by the 1920s. He married Georgina Morgan Birchal, the daughter of Frederick Birchal and Catherine Morgan. Frederick was the company storekeeper for many years in the Gordon era, and his wife was the daughter of George Morgan, the supervisor of the company slaves. Frederick and Catherine's daughter, Georgina, was born at Morro Velho.

C. H. and Georgina Raborg had six daughters and a son. The son has spent his life moving back and forth between the United States and Brazil. Two daughters, Diva Georgina and Emily, both married *morrovelhenses*. Diva married Leslie Clemence, who gradually rose through the company hierarchy to head the estate department in the 1950s. He continued to work for the Brazilian owners of the mine into the 1960s before retiring to Belo Horizonte with his wife. Diva's sister, Emily, married a son of J. W. P. and Florence Ellen Heslop. In other words, the two Raborg sisters married cousins. H. D. Heslop, Emily's husband, had also been born at Morro Velho and gradually worked his way up through the company to head the shops department. His son, John Christopher, today heads the accounting department for the company.

The Clemences, both directly and through intermarriage with the Cockings and the Heslops, span five generations, four of those born and raised in Morro Velho. These generations span the history of the company from the 1830s to the 1980s. The life of Mary Henrietta Cocking alone (a daughter of H. D. Cocking) spanned nearly a century of the British presence at Morro Velho. Born in 1865, she worked at various times for the St. John d'el Rey, and she helped her family raise four generations, although she never married. Dying in 1959 at the age of ninety-three, her lifetime touches the present generation of *morrovelhenses* who reminisce about the stories she told them when they were children.

The longevity of these families at Morro Velho also demonstrates the heavily concentrated intermarriage within the British community. Never more than three hundred persons at its height, this community contained few men and women of marriageable age. Those few, however, grew up together and often chose one another as mates. Witness the complex interconnections between families created by this endogamy. The Clemences were married into the Cocking, Mayo, and Goddard families. Indirectly, they were related to the Heslops, Gills, and Goddards. Among the old families of the community nearly everyone is related through marriage somewhere along the line.

In between those families who came and settled and those who stayed for a short time and moved on were those who settled for some time before disappearing from the scene. Good examples are the Morgan and Woods families. George Morgan came to Brazil in the mid-nineteenth century and managed the company's blacks, the store, and other operations. His daughter married Frederick Birchal, the company storekeeper. His son, George Morgan, Jr., bought into the old Gongo Soco property. He had dealings with the St. John from time to time, and he eventually died in the rundown Casa Grande at Gongo Soco still dreaming of rediscovering its lost wealth.[59] Numerous Morgans took Brazilian spouses, assimilated into *mineiro* society, and spread out in the major cities and towns of the region.[60] William Woods came to Brazil from England as a wandering young man; he hired on in the store, working as an agent procuring goods in the surrounding countryside where he made many valuable business contacts and perfected his Portuguese. He too left the company, settling near the old Cata Branca mine in what is today the city of Itabirito in 1872. He married the daughter of a prominent local figure, and the couple had seven daughters. The daughters married into some of the most prominent families in Minas Gerais (Carvalho, Souza, Soares, Barcellos, and Lacerda), and their descendants are scattered throughout Brazil today.[61]

As is evident from the preceding examples, the British community at Morro Velho did not form a cohesive and monolithic block of families and individuals all acting in the same fashion. Although the vast majority of the community did not settle, did not acculturate, and did not assimilate into Brazilian life, some members of the community did. As a rule, the British chose to form their own separate society. This was reinforced by the transience of the group, their lack of fluency in Portuguese, and the strong sense of being a foreigner in a land with (what seemed to them) strange and exotic customs. Those who did assimilate were members of families who settled, had children at Morro Velho, and raised them in both cultures and languages.

Company employees who migrated to Brazil and remained did not always learn Portuguese. George Chalmers spoke the language poorly to the end of his life.[62] These people also had the normal disadvantages of anyone learning a language as an adult. As anyone who has tried knows, the acquisition of a second language as an adult is difficult and rarely does one achieve the fluency of a native speaker. Also, the English (especially those in higher positions) could—and did—operate daily in an English-language environment, thereby losing the constant and necessary contact with Portuguese. Language served as an important and vital indicator of social distance and cultural division. Inability to speak Portuguese forced the English speakers to fall back on their own "kind" and to separate themselves from the Brazilian community. From the standpoint of the Brazilians this represented an affront by foreigners unwilling to meet them on local terms. At its worst, the English attitude reeked of paternalism and cultural condescension.

Those English children born in Brazil had the advantage of growing up in a bilingual atmosphere with tremendous linguistic flexibility. This enabled them to achieve bilingualism, at least in speech. Those unschooled in Portuguese grammar often learned to speak by their association with maids and cooks. In the process they often acquired lower-class speech patterns, causing them to be mocked by educated Brazilians in later years.[63] In the 1930s the English school began instruction in both languages, producing truly bilingual children. These bilingual Anglo-Brazilians became a valuable resource for the St. John d'el Rey. They served as effective cultural and commercial brokers between Brazilians and Englishmen. Men like Leslie Clemence, at home in both languages, were ideal for handling the legal and linguistic duties of departments such as estate and personnel. They could deal with the subtleties of both languages and nationalities. By the 1930s this group numbered well over two dozen.[64]

The tendency to follow English culture and the English language, to some extent, was determined by marriage patterns. When both parents were native English speakers, the language at home was usually English. Assimilation into the Brazilian community and into local culture normally occurred only when an Englishman married a Brazilian. A prominent example is the Jones family.[65] Arriving in Brazil at the turn of the century from Manchester, Harold Jones hired on with the St. John d'el Rey in 1904. He eventually became the head of the reduction department, retiring at the beginning of the Second World War. Jones married one of the daughters of an old and prominent *novalimense* family. His wife, Alcinda, was the daughter of Belisário Ribeiro. The latter had begun working for the company as a store clerk in the 1870s. His father was the head of the local militia, justice of the peace, and a supplier of goods to the company. His daughters were well schooled, and Alcinda even spoke English. At home, however, the children of Harold and Alcinda Jones grew up speaking only Portuguese, and despite trips to England the family was essentially Brazilianized. Harold's son, Cecil, was a monolingual Portuguese speaker who worked for the St. John and its successor. In the 1950s and 1970s he was *prefeito* of Nova Lima and the president of the company. In this particular case the family was completely acculturated into the Brazilian community.

The Roscoe family presents a similar case. James Roscoe migrated from Cornwall to Minas Gerais in the early nineteenth century to manage the Cata Branca mine near Santa Barbara. He brought with him his son, Edward William, who married a Brazilian. His wife gave birth to several sons, among them João Roscoe, who ran a hotel in Sabará, and Carlos Henrique, born in 1866. The latter grew up fluent in English and Portuguese, became an important company employee (cashier) and a prominent leader in Nova Lima. He also married a Brazilian who bore him ten children. One son, Mário, took a medical degree and worked for the company for a brief period in the 1930s and 1940s. Edward's grandchildren had completely acculturated, and today their descendants are among the prominent business leaders of Belo Horizonte.[66]

Settlement and gradual assimilation offered a longer and different path to assimilation. This can best be seen in the Clemence and Heslop families. Over the generations the children maintained both cultures and languages, though in habits and customs they would be picked out by the foreigner as more British than Brazilian. By choice they associated with the British community. These Anglo-Brazilians, however, despite intermarriage with "Britons" gradually became *morrovelhenses*, marrying *morrovelhenses*. They rarely returned to England except for short vacations or schooling. Consequently, their entire lives were spent in Brazil. England was probably more foreign to them than many of them suspected. With the departure of the British owners and most of the community in the late 1950s, only these "old-timers" remained. Without the benefit of an English school and English social institutions, the children of the young people have gradually lost contact with the English language and culture. It will be extremely difficult for these *morrovelhenses* to raise bilingual, bicultural children now that the supporting community has departed. As a result, the last of the British community cling to their memories and attempt to pass on the remnants of British culture to their children. The memory and the language will dim as local culture becomes more influential.

Birth, Death, and Marriage

Although the marriage registers at Morro Velho do not present a complete picture of the marital patterns of the British community, they do seem to indicate that marriage, not surprisingly, followed class lines. Working-class men took the daughters of working-class employees as their wives, and management employees married the daughters of management-level employees. This seems to be true throughout the century for which relatively good records exist. James Newell Gordon, the superintendent in the mid-nineteenth century, married off two of his daughters while at Morro Velho. In 1862 Gordon's nineteen-year-old daughter, Jane, married the company physician, Henry F. Meadows. In 1874 his daughter Mary married James Crichton Bushman, one of the owners of the Morro Santa Anna mine near Mariana. A third daughter appears to have wed James Pennycook Brown, the manager at Cocais.[67] Some of the highest employees in the company returned to England to marry. In a small community where the majority of eligible females normally came from the working class, few options were open to upper- and middle-class bachelors. George Chalmers, for example, married twice in England, and his two sons also found wives in England. A. H. Millett returned to England after a decade at Morro Velho to take a wife.[68]

Almost without fail the daughters of miners married miners or other working-class men such as smiths. The Hodge family provides us with the best example of marriage among the working class. Both Thomas and Richard Hodge were miners and married the daughters of another Morro Velho miner, Joseph Walker. All were born in Cornwall or were the children of Cornishmen. Richard William Hodge, also a miner like his father Richard, married the daughter of another miner. Both were born at Passagem where their fathers toiled underground for British mining companies. Richard William and Emily Jane Hodge's daughter, Livia Eugenia, also married a miner, E. J. Sanders, who came from Cornwall in the early twentieth century to work at Morro Velho.

Although marriage tended to take place along class lines, some degree of social mobility over generations did take place in the established families. Although Richard Hodge was a miner—and his son as well—his granddaughter, Alda, married a white-collar Brazilian; their son Pedro today works in a white-collar job in the accounting department at the mine. A much better example of mobility over several generations can be seen in the Clemence/Heslop/Cocking families. Samuel Clemence was a smith and married a miner's daughter. He eventually rose to the position of foreman of the smithy. His son, Richard, married the daughter of H. D. Cocking, also a foreman of the smithy at one time. Richard John began working for the company as a clerk and over more than three decades rose through the ranks to head the store and then the estate department. His son, Leslie, married the daughter of another department head, C. H. Raborg, of the electrical department. Leslie eventually followed his father's footsteps to head the estate department.

The demography of the British community at Morro Velho presents special problems making any type of generalization difficult. The community never numbered more than a few hundred at any one time, and since it was a small, foreign enclave built around a business enterprise, inhabitants came and left frequently. This high mobility complicates demographic analysis. Furthermore, the basic source for the vital statistics of the population is flawed. No census other than very broad inquiries by the London office ever took place at Morro Velho. Consequently, we lack good figures on age distribution, male-female ratios, and other such vital indicators. The best records extant are the baptismal, marriage, and burial registers of the Anglican parish.[69] These records do provide a glimpse of local demography, but these too are severely limited. First, they record only the baptisms of the faithful, leaving out the less devout and the nonconformists. Second, they may contain gaps in years during which a vice-consul, clergyman, or proper official were not in residence to record events.[70] Finally, the movement of the Anglo-Brazilians between the various British communities means that for some families we have the records only for those born, married, or buried at Morro Velho. (The Hodge family is a good example.) The following analysis, therefore, remains necessarily limited in scope. It does provide an interesting, though imperfect, glimpse at the demography of the British community at Morro Velho.

Some five to ten baptisms took place each year at Morro Velho. All that can be said about the crude birthrate is that it probably ranged somewhere between twelve and thirty-five per thousand.[71] From the few family histories that can be reconstructed it is apparent that families in the late nineteenth century were generally large. The H. D. Cockings had six children, the Samuel Clemences four, the R. J. Clemences eight, the Richard Hodges seven, the Thomas Hodges seven, and the James Hodges eight. In all these cases the wives married before the age of twenty and normally gave birth for the last time in their mid-to-late thirties. Childbearing often took place over a fifteen- to twenty-year period. Children were spaced as close as a year apart, and sometimes as much as ten years apart.

Generally, Morro Velho rarely witnessed more than one marriage per year, although in some years as many as five couples took their vows. (The bunching of a large number of marriages in some years reflects the arrival of a clergyman after several years of absence.) From the limited records of the Anglican parish it is possible to make a crude calculation of age at marriage for males and females for certain periods. In the 1850s and 1860s the registers merely state whether the bride and groom are of "full age" or not, and if not, the age under twenty-one. Of twenty-nine marriages between 1851 and 1867 all the males were over twenty-one, while only fifteen of the females had reached the age of majority. Of the remaining fourteen females (nearly half the group), the average age at marriage was 18.2 years. (This was lower than European females who normally married in their twenties.)[72] After 1881 the age of both parties appears in the registers. For purposes of comparison I have split the marriages into two periods: 1881–1919 and 1920–39. During the first period twenty-three couples took vows, with the average age of the man being 25.7 and the woman 22.6, a difference of 2.1 years. In the later period the average age rose to 29.6 for males and 25.1 for females, with a difference of 4.5 years. It seems that as time went by the young people of the community waited longer to marry. Once again, one must keep in mind the small statistical base.[73]

Along with the marriage registers the burial registers at Morro Velho are probably the most complete and accurate. Every non-Catholic member of the community was buried in the English cemetery, burial in the parish cemetery in Nova Lima being denied to Protestants. Although the lack of a large statistical sample and age-distribution pyramids prohibits the construction of life-expectancy tables, the burial registers do allow for some limited statements about local demography. The number of deaths each year varied widely, from as low as zero to as high as eleven. In a "normal" year the British community buried three or four of its members. (Once again, the numbers are deceptive, principally due to the high mobility of the community. Older people in many cases retired and died in Great Britain, and many who were sick returned to England for treatment and died away from Morro Velho.)

One thing that clearly stands out is the large number of deaths before the age of one and in the first five years of life. In both centuries infant mortality seems to have been very high. In the twentieth century the number of child deaths seemed to decrease. By far the largest number of deaths occurred in the adult years from twenty-one to sixty-five. This no doubt reflects the working adult population and spouses in the community. A distinct trend is the difference between the two centuries in the number of deaths over age sixty-five. This century's register records a much larger number of deaths over age sixty-five. This could be due to several factors. First, in the nineteenth century the community was not as established, and more of the older group probably returned to the British Isles in the later years. Finally, and most importantly, this trend no doubt reflects the settling of a number of families in Morro Velho and the deaths of the elders of these families. Instead of returning to Great Britain, the older people chose to live out their lives in their "native" land. A perusal of the names of those people dying after age sixty-five seems to confirm this assumption.

Among the British, the most prominent causes of death were accidents, pulmonary disease, and natural causes. Accidents both in the mine and around the plant (drowning, falls) were the main cause of death among adults in their working years. Pulmonary diseases, especially influenza and bronchitis, killed a large number of people in the nineteenth century and during the Spanish Influenza in the First World War. Infants died in significant numbers mainly from intestinal and bronchial problems, although not at the rate of their Brazilian counterparts.

The management of the St. John d'el Rey worked constantly to improve the health of the British employees and their families. The climate and local diseases presented the company with special challenges that management confronted with special steps. As Sir Richard Burton pointed out in the 1860s, the community lay in a depression surrounded by mountains. Lack of ventilating winds, the cool, damp mornings and hot afternoons, and heavy rains made the locale a tough one for the two communities.[74] Management often advised employees to boil water before using it and provided all its European quarters with water closets and running water. The company physician paid special attention to British employees, and the latter had the comfort of being able to deal with a physician of the same language and culture. Severely ill employees were at times sent home to England to recuperate.

Throughout its history the company store took pains to keep employees on both payrolls supplied with basic foodstuffs. British employees had easier access to these and imported goods. On a number of occasions the company ran its own farms, and when unable to produce sufficient crops, purchased supplies in the surrounding region. The most important foodstuffs, especially in the nineteenth century when the community was more isolated than today, were beans, flour, rice, and pork. The flour consisted of wheat, corn, or manioc, or of a mixture known as *fubá*. Under Chalmers an experimental farm began to produce milk, butter, beef, and grains. The St. John also set up its own bakery and soft-drink factory, butcher shop, and dairy. In town the major store, Casa Aristides, did a good deal of special ordering of British goods for employees' individual needs. The St. John, in any case, pursued a definite policy of providing British employees with as healthy a diet and environment as it possibly could. Healthy employees, after all, would be productive employees.

Community and Control

Throughout the preceding pages the image that has taken shape is that of a dual society revolving around the operations of the Morro Velho gold mine. Despite the wide variety of cultures and races present at various times in the last two centuries, only two cultures and societies have survived for any length of time in Nova Lima. Italians, Germans, Japanese, Chinese, Africans, and others have slowly but surely been absorbed into Brazilian life. For nearly 125 years the British, however, survived and persisted alongside Brazilian society in Nova Lima. The picture I have painted is one of a society and culture that maintained and protected its integrity despite its small numbers. The strength and persistence of British culture created two coexisting societies—local Brazilian society in Nova Lima, and within, British society at Morro Velho. Despite ties between the two communities, despite bilingualism, biculturalism, and intermarriage, British society persisted with its own language, religion, school, neighborhoods, and social institutions. This tiny enclave in the interior became a solitary outpost of British life in the tropics—surrounded by Brazilian society.

British society persisted at Morro Velho because the British there maintained their way of life in the face of all types of obstacles. The British constructed the social and cultural institutions necessary for the maintenance and transmission of their way of life to the next generation. The ability to construct these institutions, however, hinged on one incontrovertible reality: the existence of the St. John d'el Rey Mining Company, Limited. The British would never have come to Morro Velho, and they would never have stayed and flourished, had it not been for the existence of the mine that gave life to British society in the Brazilian interior. The creation, expansion, and tenacity of British society at Morro Velho hinged on the company. The fortunes of the community rose and fell with the financial fortunes of the St. John d'el Rey.

The British became the technical and managerial guiding force of the technological system at Morro Velho. They sat at the controls. The positions of leadership and power also set them apart from the masses of Brazilians whose lives the St. John dominated. For good or bad, British control of the technological system that dominated life in Nova Lima created a situation where a small colony of foreigners became the dominant force in the lives of the Brazilian community. The British, nevertheless, did not have total control over Nova Lima or of their own destinies. They too often fell victim to larger forces beyond their control. As nationalism waxed hot in the mid-twentieth century, as the world gold market weakened, and as the Brazilian working class organized, the fate of the British community was sealed. The last half-century of operations became a steady process of erosion, wearing away at British control of the St. John and of the resilience of British society at Morro Velho. The financial decline of the St. John and its sale in the late 1950s pulled the rug from under the British community. With the end of British control came the end of the raison d'être of the community. One hundred and twenty-five years of social and cultural institutions crumbled as control of the company slipped from British hands.

The history of the British community at Morro Velho has not ended. Those few families that put down roots in Brazil have remained. Their numbers dwindle and the last traces of British culture slowly but surely fade away. Traces of the British era confront the observer everywhere in Nova Lima today. The British left their mark and they left it deep in the very heart and soul of the community. Life in Nova Lima goes on without the British, but the mine they built and ran continues to dominate the lives of the novalimenses. In a sense, the British created and controlled Nova Lima. For better or worse, they made Nova Lima what it is today. They built the technological system that continues to dominate local life. Ultimately, it was the control of this technological system that gave the British their power and their hand in creating Nova Lima's past. The heirs of the British now take into their hands this same power and the ability to shape Nova Lima's future.

Conclusion

8

British Enterprise in Brazil

So, if one were to strike a balance sheet for British actions in Brazil,
one would find them more often connected to disruptive and, therefore,
transforming influences than to preserving ones. But they appear as
well on the other side of the ledger, an ambiguity which is not
surprising to any observer of the human past.[1]

As the late afternoon sun begins to drop behind the mountains surrounding Nova Lima, long shadows fall across the English cemetery.
The visitor surveys the broken gravestones amid the tall grass, reflecting on how the desolate graveyard symbolizes the rise and decline of British influence in the community. Thirty years ago this
was a neat and tidy cemetery with carefully kept shrubs and flowers.
Today weeds and vandals have taken over. Just below the English, on
the eastern slope of the hill, the old slave cemetery has disappeared.
A smooth field, without a single marker or sign, is all that remains
of the slaves' burial ground. The British picked a wonderful location
to bury their dead. High atop a hill, the Afro-Brazilian and the British
dead look northward into the original Morro Velho excavations on
the slopes of the "Old Hill" itself. To the east, George Chalmers's
mine and mill cover the Cardoso basin, and to the southwest they
survey the ancient Casa Grande and old British cottages. Off in the
distance to the southeast rise the towers of the Rosário Church on
the ridge separating the center of Nova Lima from the mine. Buried
in a country far from where most of them were born, the slaves and
their British masters look out across the fruits of their labor—and
their Brazilian inheritors.

The British and Africans buried at Morro Velho came to Brazil as
one small part of the rise of British power around the globe in the
nineteenth century. The neglected and desecrated graves reflect the
decline of that power in this century. The extent of British influence,
and its impact, have been bitterly debated since the early nineteenth

century. The goal of this modest study has been to examine a key example of British power through the history of the St. John d'el Rey Mining Company, Limited, its operations, politics, and impact. Although the focus in the preceding chapters has been on the local or regional level, I have made a consistent effort to place local history within the larger context of national and international affairs. Indeed, a central premise of this study has been the need to understand the connections between local developments and national and international events.

Without a doubt, the St. John d'el Rey was an immensely successful enterprise. One hundred and thirty years of continuous operation, millions of pounds of profit and dividends, and enormous assets testify to the company's success. That success was determined by a complex mixture of forces—some controlled by the company, others beyond its control. Most certainly, this powerful foreign business did not act as an autonomous force within Brazil, Minas Gerais, or even Nova Lima. The St. John d'el Rey marshaled powerful means to shape its own destiny, but at the same time its history was shaped by powerful market forces, national and state politics, and even by the people of Nova Lima. In short, the company was powerful, but its power had limits.

Although influential and well connected, the company did not wield very much power in national affairs, and surprisingly little in Minas Gerais. As a minor industry in a coffee economy, isolated in the interior for most of its history, the St. John could not mobilize a powerful political lobby, despite the Anglophilia of the Brazilian elites. The company identified and cultivated receptive Brazilians to promote the goals of the St. John in the political arena, but it was rarely able to translate this influence into more than minor victories that were often short-lived. Furthermore, the company could not always count on support from its own Foreign Office during the height of British influence in nineteenth-century Brazil. At least in this case, British business and diplomatic interests did not always coincide.

In addition to the generally weak political influence of the St. John d'el Rey, company power was often limited by shifting forces in Brazil and the international economy. The company could not control the price of gold, inflation in Brazil, or financial crises in the world economy. Furthermore, the political weakness of the St. John became even more apparent with its inability to influence the response of the

Brazilian government to these economic dislocations. The rise of an activist and nationalistic state in the twentieth century, spurred on by two world wars and the Depression, brought intense pressure on the company in the form of greater government regulation and social legislation. Ultimately, the convergence of these unfavorable market forces, economic crises, and an activist state drove the company to insolvency.

The true power of the St. John d'el Rey was not its influence in national or state affairs, but rather its ability to transform the community around the Morro Velho mine. The St. John d'el Rey introduced and promoted the creation of an industrial order in the rural, agrarian interior of Brazil. The coming of this industrial order was a process that took shape over decades and was largely restricted to the surrounding community. Despite the industrialization of Nova Lima, and to a lesser extent Raposos, the St. John operated as an enclave, with little transfer of technology or industrial spin-off. As economists would say, company operations had few spread effects.

This case highlights the need to examine the role of technology in development and underdevelopment. Industrial operations like that of the St. John are the concrete points of encounter between so-called external forces and local society. In places like Nova Lima foreign capital brings together foreigners, local elites, and workers around the point of encounter I have called the technological system. At the local level this system draws together the key forces in the process of development and underdevelopment. More microlevel studies will help clarify the long and heated debates over the role of foreign capital in Latin America. Capitalism's critics and supporters alike would do well to turn their attention to microlevel studies and to place greater emphasis on the role of technology in social change.

Technological innovation was at the heart of the process of industrialization and the transformation of Nova Lima. Yet this innovation depended on a complex set of factors involving the interrelationships of geology, labor, and machines at the local level and intimately linked into political and economic affairs of Brazil and the international economy. The British attempted to guide the process of technological innovation, and thereby, industrialization, but they encountered powerful limits to their ability to direct change. The British response to these limits demonstrates the tremendous adaptability of capitalism and capitalist enterprise. Rather than acting as a transforming agent, in some cases the company simply adapted to local conditions. The British management of the St. John, for example, desperately wanted to employ free Brazilian labor and could not. They turned reluctantly (but profitably) to slave labor for their industrial complex. With the slow death of slavery and the continuing resistance of the surrounding peasantry to work in the mine, the company turned to imported labor. Ultimately, the St. John had to wait (for nearly a century) for sweeping changes in Brazilian politics and a world economic crisis before it finally acquired an adequate free Brazilian labor force. The company responded to the constraints of the social and political systems just as it had responded to the constraints of geology and politics. In each case management adapted as best it could to maintain a profitable enterprise.

For a century the company responded to social, economic and political challenges, and the company grew and profited. The convergence of changes in the international economy, Brazilian politics, and local society in the 1930s made the decade a turning point in the history of both company and community. The politics of economic and cultural nationalism, inflation in the Brazilian economy, a stagnant world gold market, and militant labor halted technological innovation and brought an end to this British enterprise. These changes also converged to complete the transformation of Nova Lima from a small, rural village to a large, industrial city. The process took shape over decades, culminating in the 1930s as all the pieces fell into place.

In the quarter-century after 1930 Nova Lima acquired the characteristics of a modern, industrial city: housing for workers, running water, electricity, transportation systems, declining death rates, improvements in health care, schools, high levels of literacy, and a large working-class population. The stark contrast, however, between the immense wealth the *novalimenses* produced and the general poverty of this working-class community remained. The St. John d'el Rey had initiated and guided the creation and development of this industrial community, but it did not control it. The company was the most powerful force in the community, but the influences of external economic and political forces, as well as the response of the local peasantry (and later, the working class), had shaped the community's growth.

The intertwined histories of the St. John d'el Rey and Nova Lima highlight the need for more sophisticated theories of the role of foreign business in Latin America. Clearly, evolutionary and diffusionist theories have been too uncritical of the negative impact of foreign capital and the weak position of Latin American nations in the world economy. These theories generally fail to appreciate the difficulties of this subordinate position and Latin America's late entry into the world economy. Theories of imperialism and dependency have generally erred in the other direction, overemphasizing the power of foreign capital and the negative effects of capitalism. These theories too often overestimate the power and autonomy of foreign businesses. The time has come for Marxists and radicals to recognize that foreign capital also acts under certain constraints. For those who understand the need to place Latin American history within the larger context of the developing world system, Cardoso and Faletto seem to offer the most promising approach. While they stress the subordinate position of Latin America in the international economy, and the power of external forces, they also argue for the primacy of internal forces in their model. Better than anyone else, Cardoso and Faletto offer an approach that recognizes the interplay of external and internal forces and the diversity of historical experiences in Latin American nations.

Theories of dependency and imperialism have correctly stressed the immense power of external forces in shaping the history of the region, and those theories have demonstrated the role of foreign business as one of the key mechanisms through which these forces operate. Clearly, the St. John d'el Rey was a powerful agent of change, a potent external force. Yet this study also stresses the need to recognize the complex relationship between this potent force, its own place within the international economy, and the power of forces internal to Brazil and Nova Lima. The St. John d'el Rey was not a mere tool of British foreign policy; it even found itself in conflict with the Foreign Office. The company did achieve political influence through collaboration with local elites, but that influence was limited. An increasingly activist state and a recalcitrant peasantry further mediated the power of this external force. In short, this case emphasizes the need to recognize the power and influence of the external sector in Latin American history and the equally pressing need to seek a better understanding of internal forces and how they link up with the external sector. British capitalism does not simply sweep away all before it in Brazil. The social structure, political divisions, and economic patterns within Brazil (and its various regions) prior to the full-scale entry of the British in the nineteenth century also shape the expansion of capitalism within its borders.

Finally, this study points out the need to focus attention on the concrete linkages between external and internal sectors at the local and regional levels, for it is at this level that the abstract theorizing becomes flesh and blood. As Ian Roxborough has pointed out, "*The central defect of a great deal of writing on the Third World is that of overgeneralisation.*"[2] The time has come to combine the best features of grand theories with careful empirical analysis and, in the process, to produce sophisticated theories grounded in the concrete realities of Latin America. Only then will we be able to understand the complex interaction of internal and external forces that produces development and underdevelopment in Latin America.

Appendixes

Appendix 1

Original Directors, St. John d'el Rey Mining Company

Robert Addison, of Somerset Coffee House, Strand, in the county of Middlesex

Joseph Constantine Carpue, of Dean Street, Soho, in the said county of Middlesex

Stuart Donaldson, Merchant of Old Broad Street, in the city of London

James Mackenzie, Merchant of Leadenhall Street, in the said city of London

John Diston Powles, Merchant of Freeman's Court, Cornhill, in the said city of London

John Routh, Merchant of Austin Friars, in the said city of London

James Vetch, of Leicester Square, in the county of Middlesex

Source: "Wharrier Notes," Pasta Histórica, sjnl/p, quoting power of attorney given to Charles Herring, Jr., 28 June 1830.
Note: The original name of the association formed by these men was the Sociedade para minerar as Minas de São João de El Rey em a Província de Minas Geraes Império do Brazil.

Appendix 2

Chairmen of the Board, St. John d'el Rey Mining Company, Limited, 1830–1960

John Diston Powles	1830–1867
John Hockin	1867–1890
Frederick J. Tendron	1890–1910
Sir Henry P. Harris, K.B.E.	1910–1941
The Rt. Hon. Lord Rathcavan, P.C.	1941–1956
The Rt. Hon. Lord Remnant, M.B.E.	1956–1957
Isidore Kerman	1957–1958
Leo Model	1958–1960

Source: AR.

Appendix 3

Description of the Morro Velho Estate, 1834

A fazenda named Morro Velho consisting of residence, houses and other buildings, stone-breaking machinery, mill, arable and mineral lands, watersources, mines, regos and water rights, pastures on the slopes of the Serra do Curral d'el Rey; the site (property) called Aguas Claras, the site called Cardozo which belonged to Rodrigo Carvalho da Costa, the farm for rearing cattle which consists of houses and enclosures on the land which belonged to José Pinto Saco, named Marmeleiro, arable and mineral lands, water rights, pastures, fields and mining explorations on the slopes to Raposos and Gambá or the Espirito Santo hill, Morro Novo and the slopes of the Morro Velho stream, mines and mineral lands in Garcez, water rights, woods, and mineral lands in the Campo do Pires and Batatal, finally all that constitutes and is actually known as belonging to Fazenda Morro Velho.

Source: Doc. No. 1/2A, SJNL/P, a certified copy of the original notarial registration of the purchase of the estate.

Appendix 4

Superintendents, St. John d'el Rey Mining Company, Limited, 1830–1960

Charles Herring, Jr.	1830–1846
George D. Keogh	1846–1853
Thomas Walker	1853–1857
James Newell Gordon	1857–1876
Pearson Morrison	1876–1882
Alexander Buchanan	1882[a]
George H. Oldham	1882–1884
George Chalmers	1884–1924
A. G. N. Chalmers	1924–1930
A. H. Millett	1930–1940
Eric Davies	1940–1948
W. R. Russell	1948–1953
G. P. Wigle	1953–1954
A. L. Yarnell	1954–1956
H. C. Watson	1956–1960

Source: AR.
a. Acting superintendent (March to August 1882).

Appendix 5

Lima Family

ca 1800

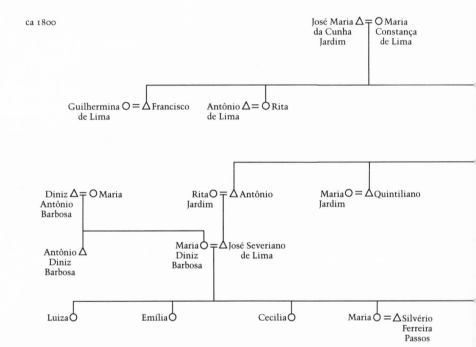

ca 1950

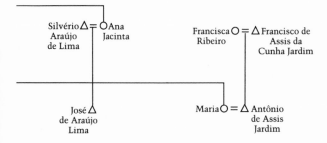

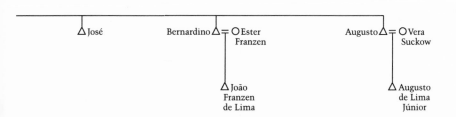

Appendix 6

Ribeiro Family

ca 1780

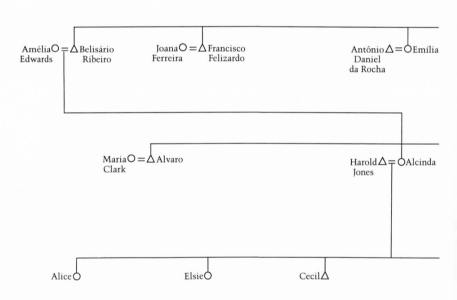

ca 1980

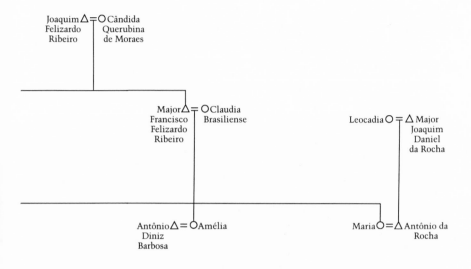

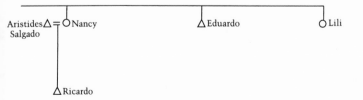

Abbreviations

ACM	Atas da Câmara Municipal, Nova Lima
AEB	*Anuário estatístico do Brasil*
AEMG	*Anuario estatistico de Minas Gerais*
APM	Arquivo Público Mineiro
AR	*Annual Report of the St. John d'el Rey Mining Company, Limited*
B-CLB	Brazil. *Coleção das leis do Império do Brasil*
CMS	Câmara Municipal de Sabará
CPRC	Cartório de Paz e Registro Civil, Nova Lima
CRH	Companies Registration House, London
FO	Foreign Office, Great Britain, Public Records Office
HAHR	*Hispanic American Historical Review*
HYR	*Half-Yearly Report of the St. John d'el Rey Mining Company, Limited*
IBGE	Instituto Brasileiro de Geografia e Estatística
JLAS	*Journal of Latin American Studies*
MJ	*Mining Journal*
MWER	*Mining World and Engineering Record*
PR	Parish Registers, Anglican Church, Nova Lima
PRO	Public Records Office, London, England
RAPM	*Revista do Arquivo Público Mineiro*
RE	*Recenseamento do Brasil*
RP	Registros Paroquiais, Congonhas de Sabará
SAG	Secretaria de Agricultura. Minas Gerais
SIP	Secretaria do Interior. Chefe de Polícia
SJNL	St. John d'el Rey Archive, Nova Lima
SJNL/P	St. John d'el Rey Archive, Patrimônio Department, Nova Lima
SJUT	St. John d'el Rey Archive, University of Texas

Notes

Preface

1. Of the few recent book-length scholarly studies of foreign firms in Latin America the most notable are Robert W. Randall, *Real del Monte: A British Mining Venture in Mexico* (Austin: University of Texas Press, 1972); Thomas L. Karnes, *Tropical Enterprise: The Standard Fruit and Steamship Company in Latin America* (Baton Rouge: Louisiana State University Press, 1978); Allen Wells, *Yucatán's Gilded Age: Haciendas, Henequen, and International Harvester, 1860–1915* (Albuquerque: University of New Mexico Press, 1985). Two outstanding "community" or "*município*" studies that have influenced this work are Stanley J. Stein, *Vassouras: A Brazilian Coffee County, 1850–1900* (Cambridge: Harvard University Press, 1957), and Warren Dean, *Rio Claro: A Brazilian Plantation System, 1820–1920* (Stanford: Stanford University Press, 1976). Both focus on communities in the coffee zone of the southeast.

2. Several recent works have emphasized the adaptability of foreign capitalist enterprise to local and regional conditions. See, for example, Florencia Mallon, *The Defense of Community in Peru's Central Highlands: Peasant Struggle and Capitalist Transition, 1860–1940* (Princeton: Princeton University Press, 1983), and Barbara Weinstein, *The Amazon Rubber Boom, 1850–1920* (Stanford: Stanford University Press, 1983).

3. Francisco Iglésias, *Política econômica do govêrno provincial mineiro (1835–1889)* (Rio de Janeiro: Ministério da Educação e Cultura, 1958); and John D. Wirth, *Minas Gerais in the Brazilian Federation, 1889–1937* (Stanford: Stanford University Press, 1977).

4. Iraci del Nero da Costa, *Vila Rica: população (1719–1826)* (São Paulo: Instituto de Pesquisas Econômicas, 1979); Francisco Vidal Luna, *Minas Gerais: escravos e senhores: análise da estrutura populacional e econô-*

mica de alguns centros mineratórios (1718–1804) (São Paulo: Instituto de Pesquisas Econômicas, 1981); Francisco Vidal Luna and Iraci del Nero da Costa, Minas colonial: economia e sociedade (São Paulo: Instituto de Pesquisas Econômicas, 1982); Laura de Mello e Souza, Desclassificados do ouro: a pobreza mineira no século XVIII (Rio de Janeiro: Graal, 1982); Amilcar Vianna Martins Filho, A economia política do café com leite (1900–1930) (Belo Horizonte: UFMG/PROED, 1981); Donald Ramos, "A Social History of Ouro Preto: Stresses of Dynamic Urbanization in Colonial Brazil, 1695–1726," Ph.D. Diss., University of Florida, 1972; Jeffry Adelman, "Urban Planning and Reality in Republican Brazil: Belo Horizonte, 1890–1930," Ph.D. Diss., Indiana University, 1974; Lawrence James Nielsen, "Of Gentry, Peasants, and Slaves: Rural Society in Sabará and Its Hinterland, 1780–1930," Ph.D. Diss., University of California–Davis, 1975; Roberto Borges Martins, "Growing in Silence: The Slave Economy of Nineteenth-Century Minas Gerais, Brazil," Ph.D. Diss., Vanderbilt University, 1980; William Stuart Callaghan, "Obstacles to Industrialization: The Iron and Steel Industry in Brazil During the Old Republic," Ph.D. Diss., University of Texas, 1981; Peter Louis Blasenheim, "A Regional History of the Zona da Mata in Minas Gerais, Brazil, 1870–1906," Ph.D. Diss., Stanford University, 1982.

5. Douglas Cole Libby, Trabalho escravo e capital estrangeiro no Brasil: o caso de Morro Velho (Belo Horizonte: Itatiaia, 1984); Yonne de Souza Grossi, Mina de Morro Velho: a extração do homem: uma história de experiência operária (Rio de Janeiro: Paz e Terra, 1981).

6. Bernard Hollowood wrote a brief, anecdotal history of the company and mine for the St. John's 125th anniversary in 1955. The handsomely bound volume, The Story of Morro Velho (London: Samson Clark & Co. Ltd., 1955), was distributed to stockholders, employees, and (in Portuguese translation) to Brazilian friends.

7. Alan K. Manchester, British Preeminence in Brazil: Its Rise and Decline (Chapel Hill: University of North Carolina Press, 1933), and Richard Graham, Britain and the Onset of Modernization in Brazil, 1850–1914 (Cambridge: Cambridge University Press, 1968).

8. See, for example: D. C. M. Platt, ed., Business Imperialism 1840–1930 (Oxford: Clarendon Press, 1977).

9. Stanley J. Stein, The Brazilian Cotton Manufacture: Textile Enterprise in an Underdeveloped Area, 1850–1950 (Cambridge: Harvard University Press, 1957), and Graham, Britain and the Onset of Modernization in Brazil.

Gold Mining in Minas Gerais

1. Euclides da Cunha, Rebellion in the Backlands, trans. Samuel Putnam (Chicago: University of Chicago Press, 1944), p. 5.

2. Geological information in this section comes from Jacob E. Gair, Geology and Ore Deposits of the Nova Lima and Rio Acima Quadrangles, Minas Gerais, Brazil, Geological Survey Professional Paper 341-C, United

States Geological Survey (Washington, D.C.: U.S. Government Printing Office, 1962), especially pp. 1 and 55–57; and John Van N. Dorr, II, *Physiographic, Stratigraphic and Structural Development of the Quadrilátero Ferrífero, Minas Gerais, Brazil*, Geological Survey Professional Paper 641-A, U.S. Geological Survey (Washington, D.C.: U.S. Government Printing Office, 1969).

3. Pierre Monbeig, *O Brasil*, 2d ed., trans. Dirceu Lino de Mattos (São Paulo: Difusão Européia do Livro, 1958), p. 18. Rainfall and temperature figures have been taken from Joel B. Pomerene, *Geology and Ore Deposits of the Belo Horizonte, Ibirité, and Macacos Quadrangles, Minas Gerais, Brazil*, Geological Survey Professional Paper 341-D, United States Geological Survey (Washington, D.C.: U.S. Government Printing Office, 1964), p. 4.

4. C. R. Boxer, *The Golden Age of Brazil, 1695–1750: Growing Pains of a Colonial Society* (Berkeley: University of California Press, 1962), p. 31. Richard M. Morse, ed., *The Bandeirantes: The Historical Role of the Brazilian Pathfinders* (New York: Knopf, 1965).

5. Morse, *The Bandeirantes*, p. 25; and Boxer, *Golden Age*, p. 35.

6. Boxer, *Golden Age*, p. 29. One of the few comparative studies of world gold rushes is W. P. Morrell, *The Gold Rushes* (New York: Macmillan, 1941).

7. For an excellent overview of silver mining in Mexico and Peru see D. A. Brading and Harry E. Cross, "Colonial Silver Mining: Mexico and Peru," *HAHR*, 52:4 (November 1972), pp. 545–79.

8. See, for example, Ramos, "A Social History of Ouro Preto."

9. Vila Rica d'Albuquerque was later renamed Vila Rica de Ouro Preto, known as Vila Rica in the colonial period and as Ouro Preto since independence. Sabará was originally called Nossa Senhora da Conceição do Sabará, and Mariana was known as Ribeirão do Carmo. Boxer, *Golden Age*, p. 82, and Waldemar de Almeida Barbosa, *Dicionário histórico-geográfico de Minas Gerais* (Belo Horizonte: Promoção-da-Família Editora, 1971), p. 290.

10. This back-breaking and tedious procedure dates back to ancient times in Europe and the Middle East, and it may have been known to many of the slaves brought to Minas Gerais from the gold-bearing regions of Africa. Paulo Aníbal Marques de Almeida Rolff, "Síntese Histórica da Batéia," *Mineração e Metalurgia*, 40:378 (September 1976), pp. 48–58.

11. The best descriptions of these mining techniques come from John Mawe, *Travels in the Interior of Brazil* (London: Longman, Hurst, Rees, Orme, and Brown, 1815), pp. 78–79; and W. L. von Eschwege, *Pluto brasiliensis*, trans. Domício de Figueiredo Murta, 2 v. (Belo Horizonte: Itatiaia, 1979), I, pp. 167–80. For the role of slaves in eighteenth-century Minas Gerais, see A. J. R. Russell-Wood, *The Black Man in Slavery and Freedom in Colonial Brazil* (New York: St. Martin's Press, 1982).

12. João Pandiá Calogeras, *As minas do Brasil e sua legislação*, 3 v. (Rio de Janeiro: Imprensa Nacional, 1904–1905). Virgílio Noya Pinto, *O ouro brasileiro e o comércio anglo-português (uma contribuição aos estudos da economia atlântica no século XVIII)* (São Paulo: Companhia Editora Nacional, 1979), p. 112, presents a more recent evaluation and arrives at figures close to those of Calogeras.

13. Pierre Vilar, *A History of Gold and Money, 1450–1920*, trans. Judith White (London: NLB, 1976), pp. 222–31.

14. Caio Prado, Jr., *The Colonial Background of Modern Brazil*, trans. Suzette Macedo (Berkeley: University of California Press, 1971), p. 31; Vilar, *History of Gold*, pp. 225–27. The legendary *Inconfidência Mineira* in 1789 has long been viewed as the first great expression of the new commercial group. See Kenneth R. Maxwell, *Conflicts and Conspiracies: Brazil and Portugal, 1750–1808* (Cambridge: Cambridge University Press, 1973).

15. Augusto de Lima, "Um municipio de ouro," *RAPM*, 6 (1901), p. 326; and Nielsen, "Of Gentry, Peasants, and Slaves," chap. 1.

16. Barbosa, *Dicionário*, pp. 320–21.

17. The original will of Anna Corrêa da Silva, listing the complete inventory of slaves and goods of the Morro Velho estate, is on file in the SJNL/P, along with thousands of other notarial records pertaining to the Morro Velho mine. Lima discusses some of the *datas* and principal families in "Um municipio de ouro."

18. The Crown hired Eschwege to revive the iron-mining industry in Portugal. After the royal family fled to Brazil in 1808, he began to work on iron and gold mining in São Paulo and Minas Gerais. His *Pluto brasiliensis* remains one of the most important historical documents on the mining region.

19. Eschwege, *Pluto brasiliensis*, I, pp. 46–47.

20. Augusto de Saint-Hilaire, *Viagens pelo distrito dos diamantes e litoral do Brasil*, trans. Leonam de Azeredo Pena (São Paulo: Companhia Editora Nacional, 1941), p. 139.

21. Eschwege, *Pluto brasiliensis*, II, pp. 20–49.

22. Mawe, *Travels in the Interior of Brazil*.

23. "St. John d'el Rey Mining Company, Limited: Historical Notes," Pasta Histórica, SJNL/P. The exchange rate comes from José do Nascimento Brito, *Economia e finanças do Brasil* (Rio de Janeiro: Freitas Bastos, 1945), p. 65.

24. J. Fred Rippy, "Early British Investments in the Latin American Republics," *Inter-American Economic Affairs*, 6:1 (Summer 1952), p. 40; D. C. M. Platt, *Latin America and British Trade 1806–1914* (New York: Barnes & Noble, 1973), pp. 36–37; and Irving Stone, "British Direct and Portfolio Investment in Latin America Before 1914," *Journal of Economic History*, 37:3 (1977), pp. 690–722.

25. Stone, "British Direct and Portfolio Investment," p. 694.

26. Rippy, "Early British Investments," p. 41; J. Fred Rippy, "The Most Profitable British Mining Investments in the Hispanic World," *Inter-American Economic Affairs*, 8:2 (Autumn 1954), p. 43; and J. Fred Rippy, *British Investments in Latin America, 1822–1949: A Case Study in the Operations of Private Enterprise in Retarded Regions* (Minneapolis: University of Minnesota Press, 1959), pp. 24 and 50.

27. Randall, *Real del Monte*, pp. 32–42; Leland Hamilton Jenks, *The Migration of British Capital to 1875* (New York: Knopf, 1927), pp. 52–64; Benjamin Disraeli, *An Inquiry into the Plans, Progress, and Policy of Ameri-*

can Mining Companies (London: John Murray, 1825); and Stone, "British Direct and Portfolio Investment," p. 692.

28. Rippy, *British Investments*, p. 32; and J. Fred Rippy, "The British Investment 'Boom' of the 1880's in Latin-American Mines," *Inter-American Economic Affairs*, 1:4 (March 1948), p. 72. Alfred Tischendorf estimated that of 210 British mining companies registered in Mexico between 1885 and 1910 some fifty-seven actually began mining. Fifteen returned a dividend, and just three paid dividends for longer than five years. Alfred Tischendorf, *Great Britain and Mexico in the Era of Porfirio Diaz* (Durham, North Carolina: Duke University Press, 1961), pp. 78–86.

29. For the economic history of Minas Gerais, see Iglésias, *Política econômica do govêrno provincial mineiro*; Wirth, *Minas Gerais in the Brazilian Federation*; and Amilcar Martins Filho and Roberto B. Martins, "Slavery in a Nonexport Economy: Nineteenth-Century Minas Gerais Revisited," *HAHR*, 63:3 (August 1983), pp. 537 and 544–47.

30. Blasenheim, "A Regional History of the Zona da Mata."

31. APM/SAG, *Relatório, 1906*, Table 6, "Exportações comparativas de 1853–54, 1873–74 e 1904."

32. The best sources on British mining company operations are Othon Henry Leonardos, *Geociências no Brasil: a contribuição britânica* (Rio de Janeiro: Forum, 1970); Paul Ferrand, *L'Or à Minas Geraes, Brésil* (Belo Horizonte: n.p., 1913); Pasta Histórica, SJNL/P; and Marshall C. Eakin, "The Role of British Capital in the Development of Brazilian Gold Mining," in Thomas Greaves and William W. Culver, eds., *Miners and Mining in the Americas* (Manchester, England: Manchester University Press, 1985), pp. 10–28.

33. Ferrand, *L'Or à Minas Geraes*, pp. 104–19; and Eschwege, *Pluto brasiliensis*, II, pp. 51–82. George Gardner, *Travels in the Interior of Brazil* (London: Reeve, 1846) gives a firsthand account of the Gongo Soco mine at the height of its prosperity.

34. Gongo Soco Account Book, SJNL.

The St. John d'el Rey Mining Company, Limited

1. Carlos Drummond de Andrade, *Poesia completa e prosa* (Rio de Janeiro: Companhia José Aguilar Editora, 1973), p. 262.

2. Decree of 5 November 1828, *B-CLB, 1828*, pp. 158–61; "Contract for the Mines of San João d'el Rey and San José . . . ," SJUT; and "Wharrier Notes on Company History," Pasta Histórica, SJNL/P. *AR 1831* describes the formation of the company. Appendix 1 lists the original directors of the St. John d'el Rey.

3. Susan Berglund, "Mercantile Credit and Financing in Venezuela, 1830–1870," *JLAS*, 17:2 (November 1985), pp. 377–79; Vicente Lecuna, ed., *Cartas del Libertador*, 12 v. (New York: Colonial Press, 1948) XI, pp. 318–19, 335–37, and 356–57; Benjamin Disraeli, *An Inquiry into the Plans*, pp. 7, 25, and

54; Robert Blake, *Disraeli* (New York: St. Martin's Press, 1967), pp. 24–26; John Diston Powles, *New Granada: Its Internal Resources* (London: A. H. Baily and Co., 1863). See appendix 2 for a complete list of the company chairmen.

4. "Charles Herring's Papers Relating to the British Legion," English Family Papers, HA 157, sections 2 and 6, County Record Office, Ipswich, England. James Vetch's exploits in Mexico are discussed in Randall, *Real del Monte*, pp. 40–76.

5. Nathan Rosenberg and L. E. Birdzell, Jr., *How the West Grew Rich: The Economic Transformation of the Industrial World* (New York: Basic Books, 1986), pp. 196–98; Board Minutes, v. 3, 26 March 1858, SJUT. The records of the companies registered under this act, and all changes in registrations, are located in CRH.

6. Extracts of Advices from Morro Velho, SJUT, contains the early correspondence from Herring to the board of directors. Fortnightly reports to the London office continued up to the 1870s when the superintendent began to send weekly reports. A transatlantic telegraph link became available in the 1870s, with a message taking a week for the transit in each direction. Messages were sent in code. Airmail became available after the Second World War and improved the flow of communications, making the company less dependent on the sailing of mail packets. In the mid-nineteenth century a letter took about four to six weeks to move between Morro Velho and London, making the round-trip two to three months, excluding the time required to ponder and draw up a reply.

7. Herring's disillusionment with the mines fills his letters in the Extracts, SJUT, during 1832. These letters also recount the wandering from mine to mine in search of a new base of operations. Pasta Histórica, SJNL/P, and Board Minutes, 8 February 1833, and 23 July 1833, SJUT, contain the legal notices of the St. John's abandonment of the mines leased from Süch and his partners.

8. For a favorable view of Padre Freitas see Alexander Cladcleugh, *Travels in South America During the Years 1819–20–21*, 2 vols. (London: John Murray, 1825), I, pp. 270–75.

9. Ledger 1, SJNL; and Document 1/A, SJNL/P. George Francis Lyon, R.N., Luiz Morethsohn, John Tom, and Frederick Warre purchased the sixteen portions of the estate from the heirs.

10. *AR 1835*, p. 23. The contract to purchase the Morro Velho from its English owners was signed on 13 February 1834. Board Minutes, 3 March 1834, SJUT. The original imperial concession that Süch had transferred to the St. John in 1830 allowed the company to operate anywhere in the province of Minas Gerais. Document 1/2C, SJNL/P, contains the original bill of sale as registered with the local notary. Appendix 3 contains a copy of the estate contents.

11. The Casa Grande (literally the "Big House" on a Brazilian estate) has undergone numerous modifications during the past two centuries and remains at the center of the Morro Velho enterprise. Until 1924 the house

served as the home and office of the superintendent. Today it serves as a museum and guesthouse.

12. "Wharrier Notes," SJNL/P; and Slave Register, SJNL.

13. The lengthy committee report appears in *AR 1837*.

14. See, for example, *London Times*, 2 July 1849, 9 July 1851, and 2 July 1853.

15. Notices from Superintendent to Employees, SJNL.

16. *AR 1844*, p. 34, and *AR 1852*, pp. 10–11. "An Act to Legalise Certain Marriages Solemnized at Morro Velho, in Brazil, 1867," *British Parliamentary Papers. General Index, 1852–1869*, 8 vols. (Shannon: Irish Universities Press, 1968) IV, p. 447.

17. William Harrison and Company were the original agents. P. S. Nicolson and Company handled the firm's business from the 1860s to the 1920s when Wilson Sons and Company took over for the next forty years. John Hockin to J. N. Gordon, 8 November 1859; A. G. N. Chalmers to Board, 11 March 1926, SJNL.

18. In 1905 the St. John built a spacious building with modern surgical equipment on the Boa Vista hill to the west of the old hospital and Casa Grande. This facility continues to serve the company. Until the first decade of this century it was the only hospital in the community. See map 5. M. A. M'Call to George Chalmers, 14 February 1906, SJNL.

19. The company dismantled the dual pay system and home pay in the 1940s in response to currency restrictions and rising nationalism. Salaries and Wages (European Employees), 1865–1918, 3 vols.; and L. E. Langley to Superintendent, 7 March 1952, SJNL.

20. According to Burton, Bahú in mines is "the hollow where the drainage gathers and forms a well; thus it is opposed to a 'Cachoeira,' ground where the water falls over and does not sink. Hence many great mines have a Bahú and a Cachoeira." Richard F. Burton, *Explorations of the Highlands of the Brazil*, 2 vols. (London: Tinsley Brothers, 1869), I, p. 231.

21. A stope is any underground excavation, other than development workings, for the purposes of removing ore. Underhand stoping involves the cutting of steplike portions out of the rock face and shoveling ore down the steps. Overhand stoping involves cutting the reverse of these steps into the rock above the miner instead of below him. George J. Young, *Elements of Mining* (New York: McGraw-Hill, 1923), chap. 15, "Underground Methods," pp. 495–549.

22. Superintendent's Diary, 28 January 1881, SJNL.

23. *AR 1851*, p. 63.

24. *AR 1849*, p. 29; Libby, *Trabalho escravo*, p. 92.

25. Slave Tax Receipts File, SJNL; Livro de Escripturas, No. 2, CPRC; Libby, *Trabalho escravo*, p. 93. According to Emilia Viotti da Costa, slave prices in Rio rose from 1,000 milreis in the 1850s to 2,500/3,000 in the 1870s, figures that would seem to be higher than those at Morro Velho. Emilia Viotti da Costa, *The Brazilian Empire: Myths and Histories* (Chicago: Dorsey Press, 1988), p. 144. The figures of Katia M. de Queirós Mattoso for Bahia, 595

milreis in 1840 and 1,230 in 1870, are somewhat closer to the Morro Velho numbers. Katia M. de Queirós Mattoso, *To Be a Slave in Brazil, 1550–1888*, trans. Arthur Goldhammer (New Brunswick, N.J.: Rutgers University Press, 1986), p. 80.

26. Superintendent's Diary, 1861, SJNL.

27. Martins, "Growing in Silence," p. 65; Martins and Martins, "Slavery in a Nonexport Economy," pp. 537–68; Libby, *Trabalho escravo*.

28. Libby, *Trabalho escravo*, pp. 96–97.

29. Libby, *Trabalho escravo*, p. 108.

30. David Brion Davies, *The Problem of Slavery in the Age of Revolution, 1770–1823* (Ithaca: Cornell University Press, 1975), p. 419; Board Minutes, v. 2, 16 June 1843, and Letter Book 4, 17 June 1843, SJUT.

31. Superintendent's Diary, 18 September 1861, and 17 June 1877; John Hockin to Thomas Walker, 8 May 1857 and 7 August 1857, SJNL.

32. Superintendent's Diary, 31 August 1861, SJNL.

33. Burton describes a Sunday service in the slaves' church. *Explorations*, I, p. 229.

34. Superintendent's Diary, 1 May 1859, SJNL. Nova Lima, Registros Paroquiais, 1843–1891.

35. Burton, *Explorations*, I, pp. 236–37.

36. Examples of some letters of freedom are APM/CMS, Codices 205, 206, 209, 225, and 226.

37. The manumission procedure is discussed in John Hockin to James Buchanan, 22 July 1882, SJNL.

38. Ibid. and John Hockin to Pearson Morrison, 22 March 1879, SJNL.

39. Leslie Bethell, *The Abolition of the Brazilian Slave Trade* (Cambridge: Cambridge University Press, 1970); Robert Brent Toplin, *The Abolition of Slavery in Brazil* (New York: Atheneum, 1975), p. 51. Company officials grew concerned about rising slave prices as early as the 1850s. *AR 1856*, p. 59.

40. "Papers Relating to Catta Branca Slaves," FO 131, Embassy and Consular Archives, [Miscellanea], Brazil, 1879–1881, vol. 18; "Sessão em 26 de agosto de 1879," *Annaes do parlamento brazileiro, camara dos srs. deputados* (Rio de Janeiro, 1897), pp. 182–87; "Illegal Slavery," *The Rio News*, 5 September 1879.

41. Superintendent's Diary, 23 October 1877, 3 November 1879, and 11 June 1882; John Hockin to James Buchanan, 22 July 1882, SJNL; CPRC, Livro de escripturas No. 3, pp. 1v–7 (4 August 1882), and 13v–15 (13 October 1882).

42. Mine Report Book, June 1886 and December 1887, SJNL.

43. Burton had been appointed British Consul in São Paulo in 1865, and in 1867 he made his way through Minas Gerais and up the São Francisco river to the coast. His travel account in two volumes, *Explorations of the Highlands of the Brazil*, was published in 1869. Burton is perhaps best known for his translation of the *Thousand and One Nights* and for his travels in the Middle East. Byron Farwell, *Burton: A Biography of Sir Richard Francis Burton* (New York: Holt, Rinehart and Winston, 1963), pp. 248–65.

44. *AR 1868* gives a full account of the disaster. Accounts of the fire also appeared in the *Diário de Minas* (Ouro Preto), 5 December 1867, p. 1; and, *O Constitucional* (Ouro Preto), 7 December 1867, p. 2.

45. The Passagem mine has been worked on and off during the last two centuries by a variety of companies. In the 1860s and 1870s the Anglo Brazilian Gold Mining Company Limited ran the mine. In 1884 the Ouro Preto Gold Mines of Brazil Limited took over control of the mine and worked it until 1927 when the Guimarães banking family of Minas Gerais took control. Next to the Morro Velho the Passagem mine has been the most successful deep-shaft gold mine in Brazilian history. The mine no longer operates except for tours for visitors. Leonardos, *Geociências no Brasil*, pp. 74–76.

46. *AR 1874.*

47. *AR 1890.*

48. Board Minutes, 7 July 1862, SJUT; and *AR 1868.*

49. John Hockin to Pearson Morrison and Frederick J. Tendron, 21 April 1877, SJNL. Morrison had been the manager of the Anglo Brazilian Company at Passagem. An accountant and shareholder, Tendron became the company auditor in 1873, later director, and then chairman of the board (1890–1910). *MJ*, 5 July 1873.

50. John Hockin to G. H. Oldham, 23 April 1883, SJNL.

51. Treloar had apparently come to Brazil in the 1830s and during the next forty years worked for at least a half-dozen mining companies in Brazil. He hired on with the Morro Velho in 1845 after the collapse of the Cata Branca mine. In the 1860s and 1870s Treloar worked as superintendent at Passagem and other mines. Letter Book 4, 5 February 1845, and 3 December 1845; Board Minutes, 15 January 1862, SJUT; and "Captain Thomas Treloar," (mss.), SJNL.

52. He also claimed that many miners never received cash but remained in debt to the store, which Gordon partially controlled. Board Minutes, 1 November 1876, SJUT.

53. John Hockin to Pearson Morrison and Frederick J. Tendron, 8 June 1877, SJNL. Gordon and his family remained large stockholders in the company even after its reorganization in the 1880s. Gordon later dabbled in other Brazilian mines and at times appeared at company meetings, much to the discomfort of Tendron. John Hockin to George Chalmers, 8 November 1887, SJNL; and Stock Register, B-1, SJUT.

54. John Hockin to S. E. Illingworth, 4 November 1884, SJNL. S. E. Illingworth (1842–1910) was on the board from the early 1880s until his death in 1910. His father, Richard S. Illingworth, was a member of the board from 1848 until his death in the 1880s. S. E. visited Morro Velho as a young man in 1871–72. Stonehewer Edward Illingworth, "Journal and Letter Book," Duke University Library.

55. John Hockin to S. E. Illingworth, 4 November 1884, SJNL; and, Board Minutes, 15 and 30 October 1884, SJUT.

56. "Foreign Establishment," v. 1, SJUT; John Hockin to George Chalmers,

23 September 1884; John Hockin to S. E. Illingworth, 4 November 1884; and Superintendent's Diary, 3 December 1884, SJNL.

57. George Chalmers to Board, 12 November 1886, SJNL, contains a full account of the mine disaster. Captain Rogers's account has been preserved in a partially decomposed letter copybook, Mine Department Correspondence, SJNL.

58. George Chalmers to Board, 23 November 1886, SJNL.

59. George Chalmers to Board, 18 December 1886, SJNL. Chalmers first mentions his plan to reopen the mine in George Chalmers to Board, 28 February 1887, SJNL. The liquidation process is described in *MWER*, 22 January 1887.

60. George Chalmers to Board, 19 January and 28 February 1887, SJNL.

61. *Memorandum and Articles of Association of the St. John d'el Rey Mining Company, Limited*, printed by the company, contains the St. John's new structure. The reorganized company registered in London on 24 July 1888, CRH. *MWER*, 24 December 1887; and *MJ*, 16 June 1888.

62. *MJ*, 16 June 1888, contains a detailed description of the plans.

63. John Hockin to George Chalmers, 2 January 1889; Superintendent's Diary, 8 May 1890, SJNL; A. G. N. Chalmers, "Mining Methods Past and Present in the Morro Velho Mine of the St. John del Rey Mining Company, Ltd., and Lode-Changes which have Necessitated an Alteration of System," *Proceedings of the Institution of Civil Engineers*, 226 (1929), esp. pp. 189–240; and *AR 1893*, pp. 5–7.

64. J. Arthur Phillips, *Elements of Metallurgy*, 3d ed. rev. (London: Charles Griffin and Company, 1891), pp. 849–53, contains an excellent description of the Morro Velho reduction process.

65. John Temple, *Mining: An International History* (New York: Praeger, 1972), pp. 108–9.

66. *AR 1893*, pp. 34–35.

67. *MWER*, 24 June 1893, p. 879; "Minutes of Annual Meeting," 28 June 1894, pp. 14–15, SJNL.

68. Frederick J. Tendron to George Chalmers, 4 February 1896; M. A. M'Call to George Chalmers, 17 December 1895, 14 May and 12 November 1896, SJNL.

69. Chalmers had begun to push the idea of hydroelectric power at least as early as 1887. George Chalmers to Board, 4 October 1887, SJNL.

70. *AR 1892*, p. 8; C. F. W. Kup to George Chalmers, 26 August 1910, SJNL.

71. A.M.I.C.E. stands for Associate Member of the Institution of Civil Engineers, the British professional organization.

72. John Hockin to J. N. Gordon, 8 July 1859, and John Hockin to Pearson Morrison, 22 February 1879, SJNL, are but two examples of the endless complaints of company management about the shortage.

73. *HYR 1893*, p. 10. George Chalmers to Board, 14 November 1924, SJNL, discusses the seasonal fluctuations in the labor force.

74. J. Routh to G. D. Keogh, 8 July 1852; John Hockin to J. N. Gordon, 7 January 1860, SJNL. The company pursued the defection of the "lads" in

the courts of Cornwall for breach of contract. Several were fined in court. John Hockin to G. H. Oldham, 23 May 1883, SJNL.

75. The government of Minas Gerais paid labor agents to recruit and pay the passage for immigrants from Italy. In the 1890s the state attracted only around ten thousand new immigrants a year, while the figure for São Paulo was closer to sixty to seventy thousand annually. *Minas Geraes*, 17 July 1897, p. 6; Thomas H. Holloway, *Immigrants on the Land: Coffee and Society in São Paulo, 1886–1934* (Chapel Hill: University of North Carolina Press, 1980), p. 40.

76. John Hockin to G. H. Oldham, 23 June 1883, SJNL. George Chalmers to Board, 20 April 1887, SJNL, reported that some twenty-two "old and infirm Chinamen" remained at Morro Velho, with many "literally starving." For the Brazilian political debate over Chinese immigration in the late nineteenth century, see Emília Viotti da Costa, *Da senzala à colônia*, 2d ed. (São Paulo: Livraria Editora Ciências Humanas Ltda, 1982), pp. 124–28.

77. The Japanese minister plenipotentiary to Brazil visited Belo Horizonte and Morro Velho in 1905, hosted by Teófilo Ribeiro. *Minas Geraes*, 30 July 1905, p. 7. *AR 1914*, p. 27; M. A. M'Call to George Chalmers, 4 September 1913, and C. F. W. Kup to George Chalmers, 5 March 1914, SJNL. For more on the efforts to recruit Japanese workers for Brazilian jobs, see Arlinda Rocha Nogueira, *A imigração japonesa para a lavoura cafeeira paulista (1908–1922)* (São Paulo: Instituto de Estudos Brasileiros, Universidade de São Paulo, 1973), and Alan Takeo Moriyama, *Imingaisha: Japanese Immigration Companies and Hawaii, 1894–1908* (Honolulu: University of Hawaii Press, 1985), pp. 154–56.

78. George Chalmers to Board, 24 November 1925, SJNL.

79. Strikes primarily instigated by Spanish laborers broke out in 1897, 1898, 1900, 1903, 1904, and 1925. Board Minutes, 10 June 1897, SJUT; APM/SIP, *Relatório 1898*, p. 95; *Minas Geraes*, 15 and 16 July 1900, p. 2; *O Operário* (Belo Horizonte), 29 July 1900, p. 3; APM/SIP, *Relatório 1903*, p. 112; M. A. M'Call to George Chalmers, 30 March 1904; and George Chalmers to Board, 24 November 1925, SJNL. One of Chalmers's undercover agents in the labor movement reports back to him in R. Robson to George Chalmers, 24 November 1919, SJNL.

80. A. G. N. Chalmers to L. E. Langley, 10 December 1924, SJNL.

81. T. A. Rickard, "The Deepest Mine," *Mining and Scientific Press*, 2 October 1920, pp. 477–78. The development in depth reached 2,453 meters (8,051 feet) below the surface in 1934 when further work in depth was halted. A. H. Millett to Board, 17 September 1937, SJNL.

82. Eric Davies describes the plant in "The Air-Cooling Plant at the Morro Velho Mine of the St. John Del Rey Mining Company, Limited, Brazil," *Transactions of the Institution of Mining Engineers*, 43 (August 1922), pp. 326–41.

83. "Labor Force," SJNL, and *Annuario demographico de Minas Geraes* (Belo Horizonte: Imprensa Official, 1928–1935), p. 96.

84. *AR 1920*, pp. 46–47.

85. In the 1880s the company purchased the Jaguara estate north of Sabará

near Pedro Leopoldo to insure an adequate lumber supply. John Hockin to G. H. Oldham, 23 December 1882, SJNL. Later the company sold the estate to Chalmers, and it became his personal retreat.

86. "List of Documents by which the Company Acquired Its Several Properties," SJNL.

87. Board Minutes, 28 August 1902 and 28 February 1907, SJUT.

88. George Chalmers to E. C. Harder, 6 January 1920; M. A. M'Call to George Chalmers, 14 May 1908, SJNL; Callaghan, "Obstacles to Industrialization," chapter four, pp. 208–80.

89. In the 1910s and 1920s the government offered subsidies and rebates for planting eucalyptus trees to encourage reforestation. *AR 1917*, p. 57.

90. W. O. Rooper, Report upon the Manufacture of Steel by Electricity, October 1907; and Report upon Smelting and Refining of Iron from the Iron Lands of the St. John Del Rey Mining Co., Ltd., November 1909, SJNL.

91. This experiment is summarized in "Brief Report on Wood Distillation Plant," Superintendent's Files, SJNL.

92. *AR 1899*, p. 27.

93. The railway was dismantled in the early 1960s, and a modern, asphalt highway now covers much of the old railway bed. *AR 1915*, pp. 62–63; *AR 1919*, pp. 52–54; and Decree No. 3,516 of March 1912 published in APM/SAG, *Relatório 1912*, pp. 170–72.

94. Callaghan, "Obstacles to Industrialization," chapter four; M. A. M'Call to George Chalmers, 30 March 1899, and 11 August 1904; A. H. Millett to H. P. Harris, 14 May 1926; A. G. N. Chalmers to Board, 24 December 1927, SJNL; *Minas Geraes*, 6–8 August 1904.

95. Callaghan, "Obstacles to Industrialization," chapter six; John Wirth, *The Politics of Brazilian Development* (Stanford: Stanford University Press, 1970), chapter 4.

96. Martins, *A economia política*; Steven Topik, *The Political Economy of the Brazilian State, 1889–1930* (Austin: University of Texas Press, 1987); and Annibal Villanova Villela and Wilson Suzigan, *Política do governo e crescimento da economia brasileira 1889–1945* (Rio de Janeiro: IPEA/INPES, 1973).

97. J. S. Paris to H. P. Harris, 9 September 1931; A. H. Millett to L. E. Langley, 6 June 1934; and Eric Davies to Board, 16 October 1942, SJNL.

98. *AR 1918*, p. 35; and *AR 1919*, p. 34; Villela and Suzigan, *Política do governo*, pp. 207–8 and 323–28.

99. British Vice-Consulate Files, SJNL.

100. H. P. Harris to George Chalmers, 21 March and 12 June 1918, SJNL. At the outbreak of both world wars the company fired its few German employees. *AR 1917*, pp. 34–35.

101. Chalmers's first wife had died of tuberculosis soon after arriving in Brazil. He soon returned to England and married his deceased wife's sister who gave birth to his two sons in 1887 and in 1889. She died of tuberculosis in 1900. Superintendent's Diary, 7 August 1885, SJNL; Register of Burials in Morro Velho, p. 8, SJNL; Foreign Establishment, v. 1, SJUT; John Hockin to George Chalmers, 9 October 1889; George Chalmers to M. A. M'Call,

15 September 1911, M. A. M'Call to George Chalmers, 24 July 1912; C. F. W. Kup to George Chalmers, 19 November 1914, 22 April 1915, and 7 November 1919, SJNL.

102. H. P. Harris to George Chalmers, 7 October 1920, SJNL.

103. *AR 1925* and *AR 1927*.

104. "Chalmers Folder," SJNL, contains hundreds of telegrams and newspaper obituaries from all over Brazil that were sent to Morro Velho shortly after Chalmers died.

105. Foreign Establishment, v. 1, SJUT; A. G. N. Chalmers to A. H. Millett, January 1931, SJNL. Chalmers remained in Brazil, with the exception of brief vacations in England, for the rest of his life. His two sons also remained in Brazil. The oldest, John, died in 1980 and was buried beside his grandmother at Morro Velho. The younger son, William, lives a few kilometers south of Nova Lima. Interview, William Frederick Chalmers, Nova Lima, 25 July 1985.

106. Interview, Mrs. A. H. Millett and Eileen Millett Nixson, Belo Horizonte, 22 March 1980.

107. A. M. Mackilligin to A. H. Millett, 25 September 1930, SJNL.

108. The St. John coined a large number of centennial medallions, designed by the chairman's wife and struck in the Brazilian mint. The company planned to have a special ceremony with all the country's major leaders, but the October revolt forced management to distribute the medals to major figures in separate, private ceremonies. A. H. Millett to H. P. Harris, undated, SJNL.

109. Hobart A. Spalding, Jr., *Organized Labor in Latin America: Historical Case Studies of Urban Workers in Dependent Societies* (New York: Harper Torchbooks, 1977), pp. 151–206; and Kenneth Paul Erickson, *The Brazilian Corporative State and Working Class Politics* (Berkeley: University of California Press, 1977).

110. A. H. Millett to Board, 24 May 1934, SJNL.

111. *AR 1940*.

112. Eric Davies to Board, 12 December 1941; and W. R. Russell to Board, 7 May 1952, SJNL.

113. *AR 1920*, pp. 72–73; Villela and Suzigan, *Política do governo*, pp. 207–8 and 323–28.

114. A. H. Millett to Board, 10 November 1932, SJNL.

115. The $20.67 standard (£3.17s.10.5d) had stood since 1717 when set by the master of the mint, Isaac Newton. Roy Jastram, *The Golden Constant: The English and American Experience 1560–1976* (New York: John Wiley & Sons, 1977), pp. 50–53.

116. Some of the problems the company faced when dealing with the bureaucracy and its shifting policies are detailed in Eric Davies to Board, 4 November 1946, SJNL.

117. A. H. Millett to L. E. Langley, 9 March 1933; D. W. J. Grey to A. H. Millett, 9 November 1937, SJNL; *AR 1935*, p. 26; *AR 1948*, p. 22.

118. "25 anos de política cambial," *Conjuntura Econômica*, 26:11 (November 1972), pp. 77–81; Villela and Suzigan, *Política do governo*, p. 424;

Sir Albert Feavearyear, *The Pound Sterling: A History of English Money*, 2d ed. (Oxford: Clarendon Press, 1963), p. 417.

119. Grossi, *Mina de Morro Velho*, esp. chaps. 3–5.

120. Private and Confidential Correspondence, 1956, SJNL.

121. "Average Daily Wage," SJNL.

122. *AR*, 1940–1954.

123. *AR 1918, AR 1944*, and *AR 1945*.

124. Jastram, *Golden Constant*, p. 53; Temple, *Mining*, pp. 115–17.

125. See, for example, Committee of Inquiry into the Economics of the Gold Mining Industry, *Gold Mining in Ontario* (Toronto: Baptist Johnston, 1955). In 1949 Canada had ninety-seven lode mines. In 1968 the figure had dropped to twenty. Eric Cousineau and Peter R. Richardson, *Gold: The World Industry and Canadian Corporate Strategy* (Kingston, Ontario: Centre for Resource Studies, 1979), p. xi.

126. Leonardos, *Geociências no Brasil*, pp. 93–94; Superintendent to Board, 28 January 1953; and Lord Rathcavan to G. P. Wigle, 29 April 1954, SJNL.

127. *The Financial Times* (London), 26 January 1957.

128. A. L. Yarnell to H. C. Watson, 22 January 1958, SJNL.

129. Raymond F. Mikesell, "Hanna in Brazil: The Story of an Iron-Mining Venture," in Raymond F. Mikesell, ed., *Foreign Investment in Mining Projects* (Cambridge: Oelgeschlager, Gunn & Hain, 1983), pp. 471–96.

130. The Canadian government also attempted to aid the national gold-mining industry through the Emergency Gold Mining Assistance Act of 1949. Cousineau and Richardson, *Gold*, p. xi.

131. João Pinheiro Filho, Conselho Nacional de Economia, to Lord Rathcavan, Chairman of the Board, 3 June 1955; and Superintendent to A. L. Yarnell, 9 May 1956, SJNL.

132. *AR 1960*.

133. Leonardos, *Geociências no Brasil*, pp. 95–96; *Jornal do Brasil*, 8 February 1980, p. 3; Lionel F. Gray, ed., *Jane's Major Companies of Europe, 1971 Edition* (London: Sampson, Low, Marston & Co., 1970), pp. F191–92; Francis Wilson, *Labour in the South African Gold Mines, 1911–1969* (Cambridge: Cambridge University Press, 1972), pp. 24–27.

134. *Brasil Mineral*, 1:7 (June 1984), pp. 14–15.

135. After the takeover, the new board raised the capital stock to £1,300,000. *AR 1957*.

136. American Bureau of Metal Statistics, *Yearbook for 1960* (New York: Maple Press Company, 1961), pp. 106–7.

137. During the First World War the company also purchased British government war bonds (1915–19).

138. Rippy, "Most Profitable British Mining Investments."

139. Graham, *Britain and the Onset of Modernization in Brazil*, p. 147; Robert Howard Mattoon, Jr., "The Companhia Paulista de Estradas de Ferro, 1868–1900: A Local Railway Enterprise in São Paulo, Brazil," Ph.D. Diss., Yale University, 1971, p. 227; Colin M. Lewis, *British Railways in Argentina 1857–1914: A Case Study of Foreign Investment* (London: Athlone, 1983),

pp. 199 and 218–19; Platt, *Business Imperialism*, p. 12; Michael Edelstein, *Overseas Investment in the Age of High Imperialism: The United Kingdom, 1850–1914* (New York: Columbia University Press, 1982), p. 335.

140. The rate of return on capital equals net profits divided by capital stock. Following the standard definition, capital stock is equal to the value of a firm's physical and cash assets. I have subtracted the value of investments in other companies' stocks from total assets to arrive at the figures for capital stock. Rates have been calculated from the *AR*.

141. The California rush, for example, produced 83,600,000 grams per year from 1848–56, with Australia roughly the same from 1851–56. The large mines of the Transvaal produce three to five times the output of the Morro Velho mine. Vilar, *History of Gold*, pp. 326–27.

142. Gold production at Morro Velho in 1983 stood at 4,200,000 grams. Paulo Sarmento, "Cento e cinqüenta anos de mineração em Morro Velho," *Mineração e Metalurgia*, 48:453 (May 1984), pp. 18–32.

143. *AR 1861, 1884, 1906, 1937, 1951*.

144. *AR 1860* and *AR 1935*; and AEMG (1929), p. 1147.

145. This compares with the 4 to 9 percent paid on the value of sales by the North American Cerro de Pasco Corporation in Peru. Adrian W. DeWind, Jr., "Peasants Become Miners: The Evolution of Industrial Mining Systems in Peru," Ph.D. Diss., Columbia University, 1977, p. 67.

146. *AR 1930, AR 1937,* and *AR 1939*.

147. A. H. Millett to L. E. Langley, 25 May 1940, SJNL. Company accounting procedures make the precise tax figures difficult to ascertain from the *AR*.

148. *AR 1861, 1906, 1924, 1937, 1951*.

149. Graham, *Britain and the Onset of Modernization in Brazil*, pp. 152–53.

The Politics of a Foreign Enterprise

1. Chairman of the Board to Superintendent Wigle, 19 June 1953, SJNL.

2. Ronald H. Chilcote, *Theories of Comparative Politics* (Boulder: Westview Press, 1981), esp. chap. 7, "Theories of Development and Underdevelopment." For the classic example of evolutionary diffusionist theory, see W. W. Rostow, *The Stages of Economic Growth: A Non-Communist Manifesto* (Cambridge: Cambridge University Press, 1960). For a devastating critique of conventional liberal theories of development, see André Gunder Frank, "Sociology of Development and Underdevelopment of Sociology," *Catalyst*, III (Summer 1967), pp. 20–73.

3. Chilcote, *Theories of Comparative Politics*, chapter 7; Christopher Abel and Colin M. Lewis, "General Introduction," in Christopher Abel and Colin M. Lewis, eds., *Latin America, Economic Imperialism and the State: The Political Economy of the External Connection from Independence to the Present* (London: Athlone, 1985), pp. 1–25.

4. Wolfgang J. Mommsen, *Theories of Imperialism*, trans. P. S. Falla (New York: Random House, 1980), esp. chaps. 1 and 2.

5. John Gallagher and Ronald Robinson, "The Imperialism of Free Trade," *Economic History Review*, 2d series, 6:1 (August 1953), pp. 1–15.

6. Gallagher and Robinson, p. 13.

7. For the most sophisticated effort to explain the emergence of industrialization in dependent societies, see Peter B. Evans, *Dependent Development: The Alliance of Multinational, State, and Local Capital in Brazil* (Princeton: Princeton University Press, 1979).

8. See, for example, Samir Amin, *Imperialism and Unequal Development*, trans. Alfred Ehrenfeld and Joan Pinkham (New York: Monthly Review Press, 1977); Arghiri Emmanuel, *Unequal Exchange: A Study of the Imperialism of Trade*, trans. Brian Pearce (New York: Monthly Review Press, 1972); Ernest Mandel, *Late Capitalism*, trans. Joris De Bres (London: NLB, 1975).

9. Philip J. O'Brien, "Dependency Revisited," pp. 40–69, in Abel and Lewis's *Latin America*, provides a useful review of the various "theories" and the literature.

10. For an early and influential example of this analysis, see André Gunder Frank, *Capitalism and Underdevelopment in Latin America* (New York: Monthly Review Press, 1967).

11. Fernando Henrique Cardoso and Enzo Faletto, *Dependency and Development in Latin America*, trans. Marjory Mattingly Urquidi (Berkeley: University of California Press, 1979).

12. For an excellent survey of different theoretical approaches and a perceptive analysis of Cardoso and Faletto, see Ian Roxborough, "Unity and Diversity in Latin American History," *JLAS*, 16 (1984), pp. 1–26.

13. See, for example, D. C. M. Platt, *Latin America and British Trade 1806–1914* (New York: Barnes & Noble, 1973), and "Dependency and Nineteenth-Century Latin America: An Historian Objects," *Latin American Research Review*, 15:1 (1980), pp. 113–30. Stanley and Barbara Stein comment on Platt's article, and he replies to their comment in the same issue, pp. 131–49.

14. Platt, *Business Imperialism*.

15. See, for example, Thomas McCann, *An American Company: The Tragedy of United Fruit* (New York: Crown, 1976); Oscar Zanetti, "The United Fruit Company: Politics in Cuba," in Warren Dean, ed., *Diplomatic Claims: Latin American Historians View the United States* (Lanham, Md.: University Press of America, 1985), pp. 157–91; Gilbert M. Joseph and Allen Wells, "Corporate Control of a Monocrop Economy: International Harvester and Yucatán's Henequen Industry during the Porfiriato," *Latin American Research Review*, 17:1 (1982), pp. 69–99; and Wells, *Yucatán's Gilded Age*.

16. Iglésias, *Política econômica*; Wirth, *Minas Gerais*; Blasenheim, "A Regional History of the Zona da Mata."

17. Graham, *Britain and the Onset of Modernization in Brazil*.

18. Imperial decree of 16 September 1824 conceding mining rights to

Edward Oxenford, and decree of 5 November 1828 conceding mining rights to George Süch. *RAPM*, 20 (1924), pp. 146–47.

19. Imperial decree of 28 October 1848; *AR 1857*, p. 12; and *AR 1860*, p. 10.

20. Neill Macaulay, *Dom Pedro: The Struggle for Liberty in Brazil and Portugal, 1798–1834* (Durham: Duke University Press, 1986), pp. 216–17.

21. *O Universal* (Ouro Preto), no. 88 (1 September 1837), pp. 2–3.

22. Leonardos, *Geociências no Brasil*, pp. 60–63.

23. Superintendent's Diary, 9 January 1861; and John Hockin to Pearson Morrison, 3 August 1877, SJNL.

24. John Hockin to Pearson Morrison, 2 August 1878, SJNL.

25. Superintendent's Diary, 8 November 1866, SJNL.

26. Imperial decree of 26 September 1867. For a summary of mining tax laws in the nineteenth century, see *Minas Geraes*, 18 August 1904, pp. 8–9.

27. Provincial decree of 25 November 1875; Lord Salisbury to Mr. St. John, 17 January 1879, FO 13/549, no. 1, PRO.

28. Graham, *Britain and the Onset of Modernization in Brazil*, p. 101.

29. John Hockin to Pearson Morrison, 23 September 1878 and 8 January 1879; John Hockin to Baron of Penedo, 20 October 1881, SJNL.

30. Lord Salisbury to Mr. St. John, 17 January 1879, FO 13/549, no. 1, PRO.

31. John Hockin to George Chalmers, 8 November 1884, SJNL.

32. Letter Book 1, 20 January 1831, SJUT.

33. Hélio Viana, ed., "Viagem à Província de Minas Gerais em 1881," *Anuário do Museu Imperial*, XVIII (1957), pp. 80–83; *AR 1881*, p. 83.

34. Superintendent's Diary, 9 April 1867 and 23 July 1873, SJNL.

35. Topik, *Political Economy*.

36. Imperial decree of 5 November 1828, B-CLB, 1828, pp. 159–61.

37. Aristides A. Milton, *A constituição do Brazil: noticia historica, texto e comentario*, 2d ed. (Rio de Janeiro: Imprensa Nacional, 1898), title VI, section II, article 17. See also Calogeras, *As minas do Brasil*, III, pp. 3–46 and 57–110.

38. *AR 1905*, pp. 48–49.

39. Nícia Vilela Luz, *A luta pela industrialização do Brasil (1808–1930)* (São Paulo: Difusão Europeia do Livro, 1961), pp. 186–90.

40. Callaghan, "Obstacles to Industrialization," pp. 226–28; *Minas Geraes*, 28 July 1899, p. 11; 29 July 1899, p. 7.

41. "Parecer apresentado a commissão organizadora do Congresso Industrial de Bello Horizonte, pelo Dr. George Chalmers, em 1903," in Calogeras, *As minas do Brasil*, III, pp. 227–38; *Minas Geraes*, 4–5 May 1904, p. 2; 19 June 1904, p. 8. Chalmers was one of the six organizers of the Congress —the other five were Brazilians. *Minas Geraes*, 7–8 January 1903, p. 3.

42. Nascimento Brito, *Economia e finanças do Brasil*, p. 93; *AR 1900*, p. 27; *HYR 1907*, p. 36.

43. *HYR 1899*, p. 9; *AR 1900*, p. 27; *Minas Geraes*, 28 March 1899, p. 3; and George Chalmers to Rui Barbosa, 3 January 1899, Fundação Casa Rui Barbosa, Rio de Janeiro.

44. Some examples of exemptions granted to mining companies are *Minas Geraes*, 14 March 1900, p. 5; 4 February 1901, p. 3; 26–27 October 1903, p. 3; and 18 September 1904, p. 3.

45. *AR 1907*, pp. 46–48; *AR 1921*, p. 39; and A. G. N. Chalmers to Board, 3 January 1927, SJNL.

46. *AR 1913*, p. 71.

47. *AR 1899*, p. 27.

48. *AR 1905*, p. 45.

49. Decree 3,516 of 25 March 1912 in *Colleção das leis e decretos do Estado de Minas Gerais, 1912* (Belo Horizonte: Imprensa Official, 1912), p. 301; and decree 3,914 of 17 May 1913 in *Colleção 1913*, p. 161; APM/SAG, *Relatório 1912*, pp. 170–72; and *AR 1914*, p. 46; *AR 1915*, pp. 62–63.

50. *AR 1916*, p. 62; and *AR 1919*, p. 53.

51. A. G. N. Chalmers to Board, 11 June and 27 October 1925, SJNL.

52. A. H. Millett to Board, 11 May 1926, SJNL.

53. A. G. N. Chalmers to H. P. Harris, 25 September 1926, SJNL. Ribeiro was the first president (1901–11) of the Associação Comercial de Minas, and director of the state secretariat of finance. *Mensagem Econômica*, (December 1980), p. 6; *Minas Geraes*, 1 January 1901, p. 3.

54. Villela and Suzigan, *Política do governo*, pp. 135–50.

55. C. F. W. Kup to George Chalmers, 12 October 1917, SJNL.

56. *AR 1918*, p. 35; *AR 1920*, pp. 72–73; *AR 1925*, pp. 20–21; decrees 3,446 (31 December 1917); 3,533 (3 September 1918); and 3,644 (31 December 1918); C. F. W. Kup to Board, 17 January 1931, SJUT.

57. *AR 1920*, pp. 72–73.

58. Vilela Luz, *A luta pela industrialização do Brasil*.

59. George Chalmers to Augusto de Lima, 2 August 1917, SJNL.

60. For one laudatory portrayal of Chalmers, see: Daniel D. Carvalho, "A Mina de Morro Velho e um Grande Superintendente," and "George Chalmers e os Brasileiros," in *Novos estudos e depoimentos* (Rio de Janeiro: José Olympio, 1959), pp. 133–43.

61. Antônio Luiz de Bessa, *História financeira de Minas Gerais em 70 anos de república*, 2 v. (Belo Horizonte: APM, 1981), II, p. 442; M. A. M'Call to George Chalmers, 13 October 1904, SJNL; *Minas Geraes*, 3 December 1901, pp. 2–3.

62. Unsigned letter to A. H. Millett, 27 July 1934, SJNL.

63. A. H. Millett to H. P. Harris, 9 September 1931, SJNL.

64. Paris's work was well known to management and workers alike. When he died in June 1934 an anonymous flier distributed in Nova Lima exulted in the passing of "that wicked and vile individual, who used to enslave and plunder the workpeople" and whom God had now sent "to the bottom of Hell." A. H. Millett to Board, 28 June 1934, SJNL.

65. Decree No. 575, 10 January 1894, cited in *Minas Geraes*, 2 August 1897, p. 6.

66. "Decrees and Statutes of the Company," Pasta Histórica, SJNL/P; and *Memorandum and Articles of Association*.

67. Jacques Paris to H. P. Harris, 9 September 1931, SJNL. The company reregistered once again in 1933.

68. Jacques Paris to A. H. Millett, 11 June 1932, SJNL.

69. CPRC, Casamentos, 6 January and 11 August 1894; *Minas Gerais*, 8 May 1945, p. 10; and Eric Davies to Board, 16 October 1942, SJNL.

70. A. H. Millett to L. E. Langley, 11 June 1934, SJNL.

71. Obituary in *Minas Gerais*, 16 February 1939, p. 21.

72. Obituary in *Minas Gerais*, 1 June 1966, p. 13; Wirth, *Minas Gerais*, pp. 93–94, 251, and 256; and A. H. Millett to Board, 15 August 1930, SJNL.

73. José Augusto de Lima, *Augusto de Lima, seu tempo, seus ideais* (Rio de Janeiro: Ministério da Educaçâo e Cultura, 1959).

74. Superintendent's Diary, 12 February 1859; A. G. N. Chalmers to Board, 11 June 1925; S. S. Tegner to A. H. Millett, 24 August 1937, SJNL; and Callaghan, "Obstacles to Industrialization," p. 224.

75. See, for example: A. H. Millett to Board, 13 January 1933, SJNL.

76. A. H. Millett to H. P. Harris, 1930, SJNL.

77. Thomas E. Skidmore, *Politics in Brazil, 1930–1964: An Experiment in Democracy* (New York: Oxford University Press, 1967), pp. 3–21.

78. A. H. Millett to H. P. Harris, 10 October, 17 October, 24 October, and 4 November 1930, SJNL.

79. A. G. N. Chalmers to Board, 24 December 1927; A. H. Millett to C. F. W. Kup, 23 February 1931; A. H. Millett to Board, 22 October 1935; Eric Davies to A. H. Millett, 19 July 1938, SJNL.

80. A. H. Millett to Board, 17 January and 18 June 1938, SJNL.

81. C. F. W. Kup to Board, 17 January 1931, SJNL.

82. A. H. Millett to Board, 10 November 1932, SJNL.

83. C. F. W. Kup to Eric Davies, 3 April 1941, SJNL.

84. *AR 1930* and *AR 1938*.

85. A. G. N. Chalmers to Board, 1 March 1930, SJNL.

86. See, for example: A. H. Millett to Board, 17 April 1934, SJNL.

87. Confidential Memo to Getúlio Vargas, 1 June 1935, Arquivo Nacional, SPR, Banco do Brasil, lata 1.

88. Decrees 24,023 (21 March 1934); 24,195 (May 1934); 24,491 (June 1934); A. H. Millett to Board 17 January 1931 and 1 July 1932, SJNL.

89. A. H. Millett to Board, 1 February 1938, SJNL, and Decree Law No. 67 of 20 January 1938.

90. *AR 1930, AR 1937,* and *AR 1939*.

91. Constitution of 1934, Article 118; Constitution of 1937, Article 143. The Constitution of 1946 maintained the same system. The mining code came into effect under decree 1,985 of 29 January 1940.

92. Wirth, *The Politics of Brazilian Development*, p. 94.

93. *AR 1935*, p. 11; General Manager to Board, 10 September 1958, SJNL; and *Estatutos (Reformados) da Companhia de Mineraçāo Novalimense* (Rio de Janeiro: Jornal do Commercio, 1942).

94. Constitution of 1937, Article 153.

95. A. H. Millett to L. E. Langley, 14 August 1934, SJNL.

96. Decree Law No. 1,545 of 25 August 1939.

97. Spalding, *Organized Labor in Latin America*, pp. 94–206; Erickson, *The Brazilian Corporative State*.

98. Grossi, *Mina de Morro Velho*, p. 96.

99. Grossi, *Mina de Morro Velho*, p. 224, lists thirteen major labor conflicts in the company's last decade of operation.

100. A. H. Millett to Board, 15 August 1939, SJNL; and Carlos Martins Teixeira, et al., *Higiene das minas de ouro. silicose. Morro Velho—Minas Gerais* (Rio de Janeiro: Departamento Nacional da Produção Mineral, Boletim No. 44, 1940).

101. A. H. Millett to Board, 1 December 1932 and 7 January 1936, SJNL.

102. *AR 1946* and *AR 1951*.

103. Grossi, *Mina de Morro Velho*, p. 98.

104. For a history of the Communist party in Brazil during these years, see John W. F. Dulles, *Brazilian Communism, 1935–1945* (Austin: University of Texas Press, 1983).

105. Grossi, *Mina de Morro Velho*, pp. 122–42.

106. Skidmore, *Politics in Brazil*, pp. 65–67.

107. Grossi, *Mina de Morro Velho*, pp. 181–85.

108. The St. John began publishing yearly accounts in the *Diário Oficial* and *Minas Gerais* in December 1941. Eric Davies to Board, 16 January 1942, SJNL.

109. Roberto C. Costa, *A cortina de ouro (Morro Velho)* (Belo Horizonte: E. G. Santa Maria, 1955), is one notable example of bad press for the St. John. Costa, a former union leader, wrote a scathing denunciation of the company, emphasizing the dangerous working conditions in the mine, the poverty of the town, and high company profits.

110. A. L. Yarnell to Board, 6 April 1955; Anthony Vereker to H. C. Watson, 25 September 1956; and Anthony Vereker to J. K. Gustafson, 13 June 1959, SJNL.

111. Lord Rathcavan to General Nelson de Melo, March 1954; and H. C. Watson to Board, 19 January 1956, SJNL.

112. Letter to stockholders, 5 March 1958, SJNL.

113. *Financial Times*, 26 January 1957; and *AR 1957*, p. 13.

114. E. M. Irving, "Alternative Solutions Re Gold Mine," 7 July 1959, SJNL.

Technology and Labor in the Workplace

1. Karl Marx, *Capital*, 3 vols. (New York: International Publishers, 1967), III, p. 791.

2. The system encompasses what Marxists would call the social relations of production: human labor, the tools laborers employ, the materials that the laborers transform, and the interaction between these three and those in control of the labor process. See, for example, Marta Harnecker, *Los conceptos*

elementales del materialismo histórico, 18th ed. (México: Siglo Veintiuno, 1973), pp. 33–56.

3. See, for example, Daniel R. Headrick, *The Tools of Empire: Technology and European Imperialism in the Nineteenth Century* (New York: Oxford University Press, 1981).

4. *Technology and Culture,* 8:3 (July 1967), contains a series of articles on causal factors in the relationship between technology and society. For a strong statement of technological determinism, see Robert Heilbroner, "Do Machines Make History?" pp. 335–45, in the same issue. See also Nathan Rosenberg, *Inside the Black Box: Technology and Economics* (Cambridge: Cambridge University Press, 1982).

5. Otis E Young, Jr., *Black Powder and Hand Steel: Miners and Machines on the Old Western Frontier* (Norman: University of Oklahoma Press, 1976), p. 91; Alan Probert, "Bartolome de Medina: The Patio Process and the Sixteenth Century Silver Crisis," *Journal of the West,* 8 (January 1969), pp. 90–124; and Temple, *Mining.*

6. The rise of the mining engineer in the United States is traced by Clark C. Spence, *Mining Engineering & the American West: The Lace-Boot Brigade, 1849–1933* (New Haven: Yale University Press, 1970).

7. Timothy Green, *The World of Gold Today* (New York: Walker and Company, 1973), pp. 54–55.

8. Green, *World of Gold,* pp. 72–81. Wilson's *Labour in the South African Gold Mines, 1911–1969* is an exhaustive survey of the labor situation in the South African mines.

9. Otis E Young, *Western Mining: An Informal Account of Precious-Metals Prospecting, Placering, Lode Mining, and Milling on the American Frontier from Spanish Times to 1893* (Norman: University of Oklahoma Press, 1978), pp. 285–86; Temple, *Mining,* pp. 108–9.

10. W. H. Dennis, *A Hundred Years of Metallurgy* (London: Gerald Duckworth, 1963), pp. 271–72.

11. Young, *Western Mining,* pp. 285–88.

12. This description has been synthesized from L. C. Graton and Guy N. Bjorge, *Report on the Geology and Prospects of the Morro Velho and the Espirito Santo, Raposos and Morro das Bicas Prospects as of April 1929* (Minas Geraes, Brasil: St. John del Rey Mining Company, Ltd., July 10, 1929); and Gair, *Geology and Ore Deposits.*

13. Throughout the nineteenth century, and up until the 1930s, the assay value at Morro Velho hovered around twenty to twenty-five grams per ton. This dropped to around ten to twenty per ton in the 1940s and 1950s. Today high gold prices allow the Anglo American Corporation to run operations with an assay as low as three to five grams per ton.

14. Rickard, in "The Deepest Mine," criticized Chalmers's stairstep method. Chalmers stridently rebutted Rickard's arguments in *AR 1921,* pp. 51–52.

15. Although the standard for the workday was eight hours, the labor shortage forced the company to employ about 15 percent of the underground

force on twelve-hour shifts. The company paid four hours of overtime to this group. *AR 1913*, p. 25; *AR 1918*, pp. 26–27. The company began using eight-hour shifts in 1851, roughly at the same time as mining companies in Great Britain. Raphael Samuel, "Mineral Workers," in Raphael Samuel, ed., *Miners, Quarrymen and Saltworkers* (London: Routledge & Kegan Paul, 1977), pp. 52–53; *AR 1851*, p. 29.

16. "Managing Director's Report on Visit to Morro Velho," July–October 1911, John W. F. Dulles Files, SJUT; A. H. Millett to L. E. Langley, 11 February 1935, SJNL.

17. John Hockin to George Chalmers, 20 December 1888, SJNL.

18. John Hockin to G. H. Oldham, 8 March 1884, SJNL.

19. Black Books (1934–56), SJNL, contain statistics on all aspects of production. This appears to be slightly higher than in mines in Britain. Samuel, "Mineral Workers," pp. 52–53.

20. Described in Young, *Western Mining*, pp. 183–84.

21. *AR 1878*, p. 62, and *AR 1894*, p. 19. The two-to-ten ratio comes from *AR 1899*, p. 21, as does the information on wet and dry seasons.

22. The Morro Velho mine has been converting entirely to wet drilling in the past few years. This has been made possible with the installation of a new cooling plant in the lower levels of the mine. Interview, Juvenil T. Félix, Diretor-Presidente, Mineração Morro Velho S.A., Nova Lima, November 1979.

23. In the nineteenth century the St. John annually consumed several thousand barrels of castor (*mamona*) oil for lighting in the mine. *AR 1830–1888*; Burton, *Explorations*, I, p. 245.

24. Interview, Janis Karklin, Nova Lima, 3 April 1980.

25. The St. John made its own blasting caps and fuses throughout the nineteenth century. Blasting materials were kept in isolated locations above and below ground. For a detailed description of the blasting process used in the North American West, see Young, *Western Mining*, pp. 187–91.

26. The St. John imported its dynamite from Europe prior to World War I. The war, and growing import restrictions, eventually forced the company to purchase materials made in Brazil. *AR 1911*, p. 53.

27. I rely heavily on the Karklin interview for my description of the blasting process.

28. Fatality figures come from *AR 1919*, p. 27. Eric Davies to Board, 18 July 1947, SJNL. Mark Wyman argues that the industrial revolution in mining in the western United States made mining more hazardous than it had been for miners prior to the 1860s, in *Hard Rock Epic: Western Miners and the Industrial Revolution, 1860–1910* (Berkeley: University of California Press, 1979), chapter 4, "Betrayed by the New Technology."

29. Larry D. Lankton and Jack K. Martin, "Technological Advance, Organizational Structure, and Underground Fatalities in the Upper Michigan Copper Mines, 1860–1929," *Technology and Culture*, 28:1 (January 1987), pp. 56–57; Wyman, *Hard Rock Epic*, p. 115; Wilson, *Labour*, p. 21; William H. Worger, *South Africa's City of Diamonds: Mine Workers and*

Monopoly Capitalism in Kimberly, 1867–1895 (New Haven: Yale University Press, 1987), p. 264.

30. Two good descriptions of the labor systems in England are D. B. Barton, "The Cornish Miner in Fact and Fancy," in *Essays in Cornish Mining History, Volume One* (Truro, Cornwall: D. Bradford Barton Ltd., 1968), pp. 13–66, and Roger Burt, ed., *Cornish Mining: Essays on the Organisation of Cornish Mines and the Cornish Mining Economy* (Newton Abbot, Devon: David & Charles, 1969), pp. 133–35. The St. John wanted very much to employ the contract system and tried it without success in the 1860s. Superintendent's Diary, January to March 1861, SJNL. Janis Karklin worked on a contract basis in the 1920s, but the system was limited to development works and not normal stoping.

31. *AR 1904*, pp. 19–20.

32. Assistant Superintendent to Board, 25 August 1955, SJNL.

33. Eric Davies to A. G. N. Chalmers, 24 July 1925, SJNL.

34. Ibid.

35. Karklin interview; *AR 1922*, p. 45; *AR 1950*, p. 17. Dermeval José Pimenta, *Estradas de ferro eletrificadas do Brasil* (n.p.: Oficinas Gráficas do R.M.V., 1957), p. 12.

36. *AR 1925*, p. 22; *AR 1926*, p. 25; *AR 1939*, p. 23.

37. *AR 1849*, p. 29.

38. At Morro Velho wire rope replaced the dangerous chainlink hauling by the 1860s at about the same time as other mines around the world. John Hockin to J. N. Gordon, 8 March 1860, SJNL; and Young, *Black Powder and Hand Steel*, pp. 97–98.

39. "The cages are mainly constructed of steel; they are double decked, carrying two cars each deck, and weigh with chains about 26.5 cwts [2,968 lbs.]." *AR 1881*, pp. 57–58.

40. My understanding of the role of machine operators has benefited from an interview with Modesto Sérgio da Silva, Nova Lima, 26 March 1980, who worked as a machinist in the mine for over fifty years.

41. A. G. N. Chalmers to Board, 22 February 1929, SJNL.

42. When Chalmers opened the new mine he had to bore into the old workings to pump out the water that had accumulated there. The draining began in 1896 and continued for more than a decade. A. C. R. Medrado, "The Morro Velho Gold Mine, Brazil," *The Engineering and Mining Journal*, 72 (19 October 1901), pp. 486–87.

43. To keep foreign laborers content, the company experimented using experienced Spanish, German, and Italian *feitores* with their own newly arrived countrymen. M. A. M'Call to George Chalmers, 14 February 1901; A. G. N. Chalmers to Board, 9 September 1925, SJNL; and *AR 1927*, p. 21.

44. "Staff List, December 1951," SJNL.

45. José Murilo de Carvalho, *A Escola de Minas de Ouro Preto: o peso da glória* (São Paulo: Companhia Editora Nacional, 1978), p. 84; Eric Davies to Board, 23 December 1940, SJNL.

46. A. H. Millett to L. E. Langley, 10 May 1934, SJNL.

47. Burton, *Explorations*, I, pp. 274–75.

48. Karklin interview.

49. "Contrary to past experience, the Reduction is now the principal factor determining tonnage . . ." A. H. Millett to C. F. W. Kup, 5 July 1930, SJNL.

50. Gold purity is measured on a scale of one thousand. A "good delivery" bar accepted on the world market today normally requires a purity of 995 parts of gold per thousand. Most South African gold is 996 pure. Gold bars minted at Morro Velho are 999.9 pure. Green, *World of Gold*, p. 95; and Abel Gower, "Morro Velho: A Gold Mine Old But Not Over the Hill," *Optima*, 28:1 (12 January 1979), pp. 22–35.

51. Sulphides are composed of a metal and a sulphur. The major sulphides at Morro Velho are pyrrhotite, pyrite, chalcopyrite, and arsenopyrite. Pyrites are a combination of iron and sulphur. Arsenopyrites contain arsenic, iron, and sulphur. Graton and Bjorge, *Report*, pp. 70–71.

52. Jack H. French and Harold Jones, "Reduction Works Practice at Morro Velho, Brazil," *Transactions of the Institution of Mining and Metallurgy*, 42 (1933), p. 232.

53. SJUT contains a fabulous collection of photographs taken circa 1903 depicting each step of the reduction process. The following discussion relies heavily on the excellent French and Jones article cited above.

54. French and Jones, "Reduction Works," p. 199.

55. *AR 1867*, p. 51.

56. *AR 1878* and *AR 1924*.

57. A. H. Millett to Board, 16 February 1940, and W. R. Russell to Board, 12 April 1949, SJNL.

58. Interview, Dennis Kemp, former reduction employee and second-generation *morrovelhense*, Belo Horizonte, October 1979; and French and Jones, "Reduction Works," p. 200.

59. French and Jones, "Reduction Works," pp. 201 and 232.

60. J. Arthur Phillips, *The Mining and Metallurgy of Gold and Silver* (London: E. and F. Spon, 1867), p. 215.

61. French and Jones, "Reduction Works," p. 207.

62. For a good description of this process, see L. DeLaunay, *The World's Gold*, trans. Orlando Cyprian Williams (New York: Putnam's, 1908), pp. 146–49.

63. *AR 1840*, p. 16.

64. Burton, *Explorations*, I, pp. 253–61; and Phillips, *Mining and Metallurgy*, pp. 210–20, provide excellent descriptions of the Morro Velho reduction practices in the 1860s and 1880s, respectively.

65. Burton, *Explorations*, I, p. 257.

66. Flux is a generic term for substances that lower the melting point of metals when added to the melting process.

67. Burton, *Explorations*, I, pp. 258–59.

68. *AR 1837*, p. 33.

69. C. F. W. Kup to George Chalmers, 10 November 1910; A. H. Millett to Board, 8 February 1932; A. G. N. Chalmers to Harold Jones, 19 May

1932; A. H. Millett to Board, 19 July 1934; A. H. Millett to L. E. Langley, 23 November 1937, 23 May and 29 June 1939, SJNL.

70. *AR 1956*, p. 22.

71. DeLaunay, *The World's Gold*, pp. 127–53.

72. French and Jones, "Reduction Works," p. 208.

73. Ibid., p. 213.

74. Ibid., pp. 224–26.

75. Burton, *Explorations*, I, pp. 260–61; photograph collection, SJUT.

76. Prior to the 1920s the London firm of Mocatta and Goldsmid (founded 1684) remelted the cast bars and refined them for the company. Unrefined Morro Velho gold contained about 20 percent silver. Consequently, the gold produce figures at the mine in the nineteenth century are inflated.

77. Personal communication, E. P. Dempster, Mineração Morro Velho S.A. and Anglo American Corporation.

78. This is roughly comparable to the wage costs for British coal mining companies. Roy Church, *The History of the British Coal Industry. Volume 3. 1830–1913: Victorian Pre-eminence* (Oxford: Clarendon Press, 1986), pp. 501–2.

79. John Hockin to J. N. Gordon, 8 May 1860, SJNL.

80. *AR 1916*, p. 27.

81. For a parallel example in early nineteenth-century North America, see Judith A. McGaw's excellent *Most Wonderful Machine: Mechanization and Social Change in Berkshire Paper Making, 1801–1885* (Princeton: Princeton University Press, 1987), esp. p. 304.

82. A. G. N. Chalmers to H. P. Harris, 30 January 1926, SJNL.

83. *AR 1907*.

84. The same process took place in British mining. Samuel, "Mineral Workers," p. 4.

85. Eric Davies to A. G. N. Chalmers, 24 July 1926, SJNL.

86. The company hired A. M. MacKilligin, a graduate of the Camborne School of Mines in Cornwall, to handle underground operations. MacKilligin had experience in the gold fields of the Sudan, Rhodesia, and West Africa. Loose Papers, SJNL. L. C. Graton, a Harvard geologist, and his consultant colleague, Guy N. Bjorge of San Francisco, prepared the comprehensive *Report on the Geology and Prospects of the Morro Velho and the Espirito Santo, Raposos and Morro das Bicas Prospects as of April 1929*. Bjorge was later superintendent of the Homestake Mine in South Dakota. Joseph H. Cash, *Working the Homestake* (Ames: Iowa State University Press, 1973), pp. 20–21.

87. During the 1930s the St. John d'el Rey built its last major hydroelectric projects on the Rio do Peixe. The company built three large dams and raised power generation significantly. Power production rose from around 4,000 HP at the turn of the century to around 12,000 HP by 1950. Electrical and Mechanical Engineer to A. L. Yarnell, 9 July 1954, SJNL.

88. Mine Engineer to A. H. Millett, 14 May 1938, SJNL. Assay value dropped from around fifteen grams per ton in 1934–35 to an average of ten to twelve grams per ton in the 1940s and 1950s. Black Books (1934–56), SJNL.

89. "List of Documents by which the Company Acquired its Several Properties," SJNL. The Raposos and Morro Velho lodes may be part of the same mineral formation. During the 1930s the company contemplated connecting the two lodes via an underground tunnel. A. G. N. Chalmers to H. P. Harris, 24 March 1927, SJNL.

90. *AR 1932*, p. 27, and *AR 1935*, p. 26.

91. *AR 1935*, pp. 24 and 34.

92. Black Books, SJNL.

From Rural Village to Industrial City

1. Burton, *Explorations*, I, p. 194.

2. Saint-Hilaire, *Viagens*, p. 139.

3. "Datas e aguas minerais de Rio Acima, Congonhas, Raposos (Guarda-moria), 1726–1730," APM/CMS, Codice 5. Congonhas do Sabará became Congonhas de Sabará in the nineteenth century. A *guarda-mor* (chief officer) was in charge of distributing and inspecting the *datas* of an area (*guardamoria*) to insure compliance with royal mining law. Prado, Jr., *Colonial Background of Modern Brazil*, pp. 202–3.

4. Lima, "Um municipio de ouro," pp. 321–64; Barbosa, *Dicionário*, p. 320.

5. Raimundo José da Cunha Matos, *Corografia histórica da provincia de Minas Gerais (1837)*, 2 vols. (Belo Horizonte: APM, 1979), I, p. 136.

6. *AEMG* (1921), II, p. 849; Lima, "Um municipio de ouro," p. 362.

7. Ibid., pp. 339–40 and 362.

8. Ibid., p. 362; ACM, 1922–1926. Votes for the "official" candidate were nearly unanimous. See, for example, *Minas Geraes*, 5 March 1898, p. 5; 12 July 1902, p. 6; 30–31 July 1906, p. 3.

9. "Governo de Minas Geraes," *RAPM*, 1 (1896), p. 19.

10. APM, Letter from 3a. Commissão da Estatistica do Estado de Minas Geraes em Ouro Preto, 19 April 1890, to Governor of Minas Geraes, in "Relações de comarcas e divisões," Secretaria do Governo, 1a. Diretoria, Section 10, vol. 74.

11. Superintendent's Diary, 15 March 1891, SJNL.

12. Lima, "Um municipio de ouro," pp. 321–26; Barbosa, *Dicionário*, p. 320; Instituto Brasileiro de Geografia e Estatística, *Enciclopédia dos municípios brasileiros*, 36 vols. (Rio de Janeiro: IBGE, 1959), v. 26, pp. 189–91.

13. Superintendent's Diary, 1 June 1890, SJNL.

14. APM/SAG, *Relatório, 1892*, p. 47.

15. *Atlas chorographico municipal*, 2 vols. (Belo Horizonte: Imprensa Official, 1926), I, p. 347. The state had around 7,500 motor vehicles in 1923. APM/SAG, *Relatório, 1922–26*, p. 366.

16. ACM, 14 December 1923, 27 April and 31 October 1926, 16 December 1927.

17. Pamphlet dated 7 September 1943, IBGE branch office, Nova Lima.

18. See, for example, Robert A. Huttenback, *Racism and Empire: White Settlers and Colored Immigrants in the British Self-Governing Colonies 1830–1910* (Ithaca, N.Y.: Cornell University Press, 1976), esp. pp. 13–25; David Avery, *Not on Queen Victoria's Birthday: The Story of the Rio Tinto Mines* (London: Collins, 1974), esp. pp. 210–38; sign (ca. 1900) preserved in Casa Grande museum, Nova Lima.

19. *AR 1913*, p. 61.

20. *Atlas chorographico*, I, p. 345; RE 1960, vol. I, tomo IX, p. 84.

21. Raposos, a satellite community, ranked sixth overall with 109 inhabitants per square kilometer. Nova Lima ranked eighty-seventh in population (in the top 18 percent of all *municípios*). *AEB 1961*, pp. 35–38.

22. "Report on Blacks Department," (undated), Loose Papers, SJNL.

23. "Extracts of Advices," vol. 2, 18 August 1849, SJUT.

24. *AR 1853*, p. 40; George Chalmers to Board, 19 May 1887, SJNL.

25. *AR 1915*, pp. 54–55.

26. RE 1920, vol. IV, part 6, p. 310.

27. *AR 1930–1944*; and RE 1950, vol. 21, part 1, p. 264.

28. "Notes from Snr. Carlos Galery re Housing for Employees, 12 September 1938," SJNL; and Armin K. Ludwig, *Brazil: A Handbook of Historical Statistics* (Boston: G. K. Hall, 1985), p. 171.

29. RE 1920, v. 4, pt. 6, pp. 256–57, 274–75, and 310–11. According to June Hahner, the mean number of people in an average household in Rio de Janeiro in 1906 was 9.6. *Poverty and Politics: The Urban Poor in Brazil, 1870–1920* (Albuquerque: University of New Mexico Press, 1986), p. 169.

30. W. Pollard to A. G. N. Chalmers, 18 January 1923, SJNL. Workers in Rio at identical wages faced rents from 20$000 to 120$000 per month. Hahner, *Poverty and Politics*, p. 169.

31. A. G. N. Chalmers to C. F. W. Kup, 14 February 1925, SJNL; ACM, 15 March 1927 and 27 April 1926; RE 1960, vol. I, tomo IX, p. 168.

32. M. A. M'Call to George Chalmers, 4 June 1909 and 30 January 1913, SJNL.

33. A. H. Millett to H. P. Harris, 3 September 1931, SJNL.

34. RE 1920, vol. 5, part 3, pp. 130–39 and 154–61; *AEMG 1921*, vol. 4, part 1, pp. 15 and 25.

35. ACM, 14 September 1923 and 15 September 1924; *AR 1923*; and Victor Silveira, *Minas Geraes em 1925* (Belo Horizonte: Imprensa Official, 1926), p. 25.

36. *Minas Geraes*, 20 January 1897, p. 1; 28 January 1903, p. 8; 23 December 1903, pp. 7–8; 1 July 1905, p. 5; George Chalmers to C. H. Roscoe, 22 September 1923, SJNL.

37. ACM, 6 December 1922.

38. Martins and Martins, "Slavery in a Nonexport Economy," p. 538.

39. Wirth, *Minas Gerais*, p. 32.

40. Clélio Campolina Diniz, *Estado e capital estrangeiro na industrialização mineira* (Belo Horizonte: UFMG/PROED, 1981), especially part 1.

41. RE 1920, vol. 3, part 2, pp. 58–59 and 228–29.

42. *AEMG*, vol. I, pp. 406–7 and 493; vol. II, pp. 398–414.

43. RE 1940, vol. 13, part 3, p. 362.

44. *Atlas chorographico*, p. 347; *Almanak . . . de Minas Gerais* (Ouro Preto, 1865), pp. 218–19.

45. RE 1872, reel 4, part 9, p. 228. The slave population of Rio Claro, São Paulo, was almost identical in size to that of Congonhas, yet 76.4 percent were engaged in agricultural labor with 17.4 percent in domestic service and day labor. The slaves in Congonhas were almost evenly divided between agriculture (40.9 percent) and domestic service/day labor (45.8 percent). The difference reflects the slave-labor structure of a coffee county versus that of a mining county and the flaws of the 1872 census in Congonhas. Dean, *Rio Claro*, p. 52.

46. RE 1920, vol. 5, part 1, pp. 274–95, 422–23, and 441.

47. *AEB* 1947, pp. 134–35.

48. RE 1872, reel 4, part 9.

49. Ricardo Pinheiro Penna, "Development and Population Distribution in Minas Gerais, Brazil," Ph.D. Diss., Cornell University, 1983, pp. 150–56.

50. RE 1980, *Sinópse preliminar do censo demográfico, Minas Gerais*, p. 215; and Wirth, *Minas Gerais*, p. 76.

51. As Martins and Martins cogently point out, the numbers for the 1872 census are seriously flawed. For example, many of the aggregate figures do not correspond with the tabulations from the individual parish statistics! Martins and Martins, "Slavery in a Nonexport Economy," p. 550.

52. Stuart Schwartz, "Patterns of Slaveholding in the Americas: New Evidence from Brazil," *American Historical Review*, 87:1 (February 1982), pp. 55–86. According to Vidal Luna and da Costa, *Minas colonial*, pp. 38–39, 70 percent of the slave owners in Congonhas had five or fewer slaves in the late eighteenth century (1771 and 1790).

53. Vidal Luna and da Costa, *Minas colonial*, p. 50, show identical figures for Congonhas de Sabará in 1771.

54. See, for example, Philip D. Curtin, *The Atlantic Slave Trade: A Census* (Madison: University of Wisconsin Press, 1969), p. 239.

55. In 1900, for example, 24.1 percent of the city of Rio de Janeiro was foreign born, 21 percent of the state of São Paulo. Thomas W. Merrick and Douglas H. Graham, *Population and Economic Development in Brazil: 1800 to the Present* (Baltimore: Johns Hopkins University Press, 1979), p. 94, table V-3.

56. The city comprised 64.2 percent of the *município* population. Assuming roughly the same proportions in the age groups would mean that there were 3,479 males between the ages of fifteen and sixty-nine in the city. The work force of the company would be 91.2 percent of this figure.

57. Brazilian census officials in Rio de Janeiro in the 1870s estimated that the registers probably undercounted actual births by around 15 percent. Robert Wayne Slenes, "The Demography and Economics of Brazilian Slavery: 1850–1888," Ph.D. Diss., Stanford University, 1976, p. 281.

58. RP, Baptisms. The unusually high number of slave marriages may have reversed (or at least attenuated) the common Latin American pattern of higher levels of bastardy among slaves than free persons. Stuart B. Schwartz,

Sugar Plantations in the Formation of Brazilian Society: Bahia, 1550–1835 (Cambridge: Cambridge University Press, 1985), p. 389.

59. Slenes, "Brazilian Slavery," p. 298; *AEB—1954*, p. 55. For the purpose of comparison, the rate in the United States in the twentieth century has never risen above 127 per thousand. Donald J. Bogue, *The Population of the United States: Historical Trends and Future Projections* (New York: Free Press, 1985), p. 255.

60. Nicolás Sánchez Albornoz, *The Population of Latin America: A History*, trans. W. A. R. Richardson (Berkeley: University of California Press, 1974), pp. 171 and 189.

61. See, for example, *AR 1848*, p. 41; and *AR 1919*, pp. 24–25.

62. *AR 1902*, p. 21; *AR 1904*, p. 37; *AR 1907*, p. 37–39.

63. The major causes of death in Belo Horizonte in the 1940s appear to have been similar to those in Nova Lima. F. M. Salzano and N. Freire-Maia, *Populações brasileiras: aspectos demográficos, genéticos e antropológicos* (São Paulo: Companhia Editora Nacional, 1967), p. 59.

64. Ludwig, *Brazil*, p. 84; *AEB 1967*, p. 40; CPRC.

65. N. Irving Sax, ed., *Industrial Pollution* (New York: Van Nostrand Reinhold Company, 1974), pp. 584, 606, and 637–39.

66. Mary Karasch, *Slave Life in Rio de Janeiro, 1808–1850* (Princeton: Princeton University Press, 1987), p. 92; Slenes, "Brazilian Slavery," p. 281.

67. Stein, *Vassouras*, p. 76; Dean, *Rio Claro*, p. 59.

68. *AR 1851*, pp. 69–70.

69. On a few occasions slaves married *libertos*. RP, Casamentos, 1843–91.

70. RE 1872, reel 4, part 9, p. 226. In 1888 17 percent of the slaves in Minas were married; 22 percent in São Paulo; and less than 1 percent in the city of Rio de Janeiro. Emilia Viotti da Costa, *The Brazilian Empire: Myths and Histories* (Chicago: Dorsey Press, 1988), p. 135.

71. Dean, *Rio Claro*, p. 78.

72. Ludwig, *Brazil*, p. 68.

73. Widows outnumbered widowers 857 to 180 in 1920; and 1,142 to 254 in 1940. Life expectancy of Brazilian males and females does not differ enough to explain the imbalance. Ibid., p. 85.

74. Silvia Marina Arrom, *The Women of Mexico City, 1790–1857* (Stanford: Stanford University Press, 1985), p. 149. Donald Ramos found a much higher age differential for marriages in early nineteenth-century Minas Gerais (5.7 to 9.7 years) than the figures for Congonhas. Donald Ramos, "City and Country: The Family in Minas Gerais, 1804–1838," *Journal of Family History*, 3:4 (Winter 1978), p. 368. Robert McCaa calculated the mean age at marriage at 25.9 years for females and 28.5 for males in the Petorca Valley, Chile (1863–95). For the years 1930–69 the mean age for females at marriage was 24.0 years and for males, 28.4 years. Robert McCaa, *Marriage and Fertility in Chile: Demographic Turning Points in the Petorca Valley, 1840–1976* (Boulder: Westview Press, 1983), pp. 66 and 68.

75. In a study of early nineteenth-century Minas Gerais, Donald Ramos could not find a single example of black/white marriage in a sample of over three hundred marriages. Ramos, "City and Country," p. 369.

76. See, for example, DeWind, Jr., "Peasants Become Miners"; Donald Reid, *The Miners of Decazeville: A Genealogy of Deindustrialization* (Cambridge: Harvard University Press, 1985), pp. 26–27; and Roland Trempé, *Les mineurs de Carmaux, 1848–1914*, 2 vols. (Paris, Les Editions Ouvrières, 1971), vol. 1, pp. 147–53 and 169–200.

77. For a Chilean example of the demographic transition, see McCaa, *Marriage and Fertility in Chile.*

78. Michael Haines, *Fertility and Occupation: Population Patterns in Industrialization* (New York: Academic Press, 1979).

From Slave Society to Working-Class Society

1. Anonymous miner quoted in Grossi, *Mina de Morro Velho*, p. 135.

2. The 1872 national census actually took place in Minas Gerais in 1873. Martins and Martins, "Slavery in a Nonexport Economy," p. 541.

3. Slave purchases by the St. John d'el Rey have been calculated from the original sales tax receipts collected in a folder in SJNL.

4. For a description of the "middle passage" of one Morro Velho slave, Agostinho, see Robert Edgar Conrad, *Children of God's Fire: A Documentary History of Black Slavery in Brazil* (Princeton: Princeton University Press, 1983), pp. 37–39.

5. A detailed breakdown of the occupations of Cata Branca slaves is presented in the pamphlet, *O supremo tribunal pela verdade, e a justiça: victoria dos pobres ex-escravos da extincta companhia Catta-Branca contra a prepotente Companhia S. João d'El-Rei Limited (Morro Velho)* (Rio de Janeiro: Typographia Perseverança, 1881), in FO 131/18, pp. 271–98.

6. Extracts of Advices, August 1837, SJUT; and *AR 1838*, p. 25.

7. *AR 1851*, p. 57; John Hockin to Pearson Morrison, 8 January 1878, SJNL; and *AR 1884*, p. 74.

8. Burton, *Explorations*, I, p. 236.

9. *AR 1851*, pp. 58–59.

10. *AR 1851*, p. 60.

11. The Morro Velho slave diet does not seem to be significantly different from that of slaves in Rio de Janeiro except that they did not regularly eat seafood. Karasch, *Slave Life*, pp. 138–45.

12. Superintendent's Diary, 31 July 1862, SJNL.

13. Walker was also the brother-in-law of chairman of the board John Diston Powles. Christopher Richardson, *Mr. John Diston Powles* (London: printed privately, 1855), p. 37.

14. Walker's report was printed privately as a *Circular*. Soon after, Walker became the third superintendent at Morro Velho.

15. Superintendent's Diary, 7 May 1859, 1 October 1871, 2 May 1875, and 2 July 1876, SJNL.

16. John Hockin to J. N. Gordon, 8 August 1867, SJNL.

17. RP, 1830–91; Schwartz, *Sugar Plantations*, pp. 406–7.

18. *Circular*, p. 39.

19. Superintendent's Diary, 8 February 1859, SJNL.

20. Burton, *Explorations*, I, pp. 237–38.

21. In contrast to Herbert S. Klein's work on the "middle passage," Karasch argues that many of the slaves arriving in Rio de Janeiro in the early nineteenth century were children. Herbert S. Klein, *African Slavery in Latin America and the Caribbean* (New York: Oxford University Press, 1986), p. 148; and Karasch, *Slave Life*, pp. 31–35.

22. John Hockin to J. N. Gordon, 8 August 1860, SJNL. Emphasis added.

23. Burton, *Explorations*, I, pp. 228–29, describes a Sunday service in the slave church.

24. Superintendent's Diary, 6 August 1861 and 31 July 1877, SJNL.

25. *Circular*, p. 32. According to Burton, a prominent slave vice was the use of marijuana (*ariri*), which slaves purchased at very low prices. Burton, *Explorations*, I, p. 276.

26. Board Minutes, v. 2, 13 April 1852, SJUT.

27. Ibid., v. 3, 6 March 1855.

28. John Hockin to Thomas Walker, 8 May 1857, SJNL.

29. Board Minutes, v. 3, 12 July 1859, SJNL.

30. John Hockin to Pearson Morrison, 17 August 1877, SJNL.

31. Superintendent's Diary, 3 February and 3 March 1867, SJNL. The *revista* ceremony dates from the beginning of operations in Brazil. Warre Report (1834), SJUT.

32. John Hockin to Pearson Morrison, 22 September 1877, SJNL.

33. John Hockin to Pearson Morrison, 8 January 1878, SJNL.

34. *Circular* (London: R. Clay, 1850), pp. 52–53. Emphasis added.

35. A. G. N. Chalmers to C. F. W. Kup, 10 December 1924, SJNL; Hahner, *Poverty and Politics*, pp. 196–99.

36. The 1872 and 1920 censuses indicate that the majority of the economically active population in the surrounding parishes and *municípios* was involved in agriculture. The major nonagricultural employer was the textile industry. RE 1872, reel 4, part 9, pp. 216–43; RE 1920, vol. IV, part 5, tome II, pp. 32–33, 52–53, 100–103, and 136.

37. *AR 1913*, pp. 27 and 60; *AR 1940*; Business Manager to Superintendent, 26 February 1930; Superintendent to Board, 1 March 1930, SJNL.

38. See, for example, Wells, *Yucatán's Gilded Age*; DeWind, "Peasants Become Miners," esp. pp. 155–77. For a provocative discussion of debt peonage see Arnold J. Bauer, "Rural Workers in Spanish America: Problems of Peonage and Oppression," *HAHR*, 59:1 (February 1979), pp. 34–63.

39. For a sophisticated treatment of these networks elsewhere in Brazil, see Linda Lewin, *Politics and Parentela in Paraiba: A Case Study of Family-Based Oligarchy in Brazil* (Princeton: Princeton University Press, 1987). For a view of a comparable local elite, see Alida C. Metcalf, "Fathers and Sons: The Politics of Inheritance in a Colonial Brazilian Township," *HAHR*, 66:3 (August 1986), pp. 455–84, esp. pp. 461–62.

40. The collective biography of the Lima family has been compiled from the following sources: Lima, *Augusto de Lima*; Mercês Maria Moreira Lopes,

Augusto de Lima (Belo Horizonte: Imprensa Oficial, 1959), pp. 26–70; Silveira, *Minas Geraes em 1925*, p. 411; *Almanak . . . de Minas Gerais* (Ouro Preto, 1873), p. 144; *Minas Geraes*, 19–20 May 1924, p. 4; APM/CMS, Codice 227, 4 April 1867 and 9 November 1868; CPRC, Births, book 1, 20 July 1880; CPRC, Livro de Escripturas No. 1, 25 April 1877; SJNL/P, Doc. 12/1; RP, Casamentos, 11 November 1854; and personal interview with João Franzen de Lima, Belo Horizonte, July 1988.

41. Raimundo Trindade, *Velho troncos mineiros*, 3 v. (São Paulo: Revista dos Tribunais, 1955), vol. 1, pp. 335–37; APM/CMS, Codice 202, 28 June 1837; APM/Seção Governo 33, v. 737, p. 10; CPRC, Marriages, book B-01, 3 August 1879; SJNL/P, Docs. 12/1 and 32/1; *Almanak . . . de Minas Gerais* (Ouro Preto, 1864), p. 164.

42. Ibid., p. 163; *Folha Sabarense*, 4 April 1886, p. 1.

43. *Almanak . . . de Minas Gerais* (Ouro Preto, 1864), p. 163; *Minas Gerais*, 2 November 1944, p. 5; APM/CMS, Codice 226, 11 August 1862; APM/ Seção Governo 25, p. 104, 11 May 1875; CPRC, Marriages, book B-09, 3 July 1920, book B-14, 9 November 1940; Births, book 1, 21 August 1879 and 12 April 1885; Deaths, book C-03, entry No. 1440; Livro de Escripturas No. 4, pp. 32v–34v; SJNL/P, Docs. 7/2, 10/2, 18/1–4, 34/6; and Register 1, p. 91; A. G. N. Chalmers to Board, 11 May 1927; Establishment Book, 1 April 1903, SJNL.

44. Superintendent's Diary, 26 August 1878, SJNL; CPRC, Marriages, book 2, 10 July 1892, 16 July 1894; book 14, 23 October 1940; Livro de Escripturas No. 1, 5 May 1877 and 9 July 1879.

45. Periodically during the past half-century brief (four-page) "newspapers" have appeared, the most prominent examples being the *Terra do Ouro* and the *Minerador* in the 1940s and 1950s. None of the papers contained much more than announcements and advertisements.

46. Grossi, *Mina de Morro Velho*, pp. 80–81.

47. *AEMG*, IV, part 1, pp. 423 and 436; *Terra do Ouro*, 6 July 1957; "A caminho dos 80 anos, o Vila mostra seu passado de glória," *Estado de Minas*, 21 February 1988, p. 38.

48. A. H. Millett to Board, 6 December 1934; Eric Davies to Board, 17 December 1943, SJNL; *AEMG*, IV, part 1, pp. 134–35.

49. According to the 1920 census literacy in Juiz de Fora was 29.8 percent; 25 percent in Barbacena; 24.7 percent in Carangola; and 18.1 percent in Caratinga.

50. John Hockin to Thomas Walker, 8 January 1857, SJNL.

51. John Hockin to Pearson Morrison, 3 September 1879, SJNL.

52. Superintendent's Diary, 12 November 1880, SJNL.

53. *Minas Geraes*, 26 November 1903, pp. 2–3.

54. Board Minutes, 10 June 1897, SJUT; *Minas Geraes*, 6 May 1897, p. 5 and 8 May 1897; APM/SIP *Relatório—1898*, p. 95; *Minas Geraes*, 15–16 July 1900, p. 2; *O Operário*, 29 July 1900, p. 3; APM/SIP, *Relatório—1903*, p. 112; M. A. M'Call to George Chalmers, 30 March 1904, SJNL; and John W. F. Dulles, *Anarchists and Communists in Brazil, 1900–1935* (Austin: University of Texas Press, 1973).

55. Notices to Employees, 14 January 1891 and 29 October 1906; Ledger, Club dos Broqueiros, SJNL. The Superintendent's Diary, 29 August 1861, SJNL, contains a passing reference to a "borers' club."

56. *Minas Geraes*, 20 November 1901, p. 3.

57. *Estatutos da junta auxiliar dos operarios, fundada a 2 novembro de 1902* (Villa Nova de Lima: Typ. Clark, 1904); *Minas Geraes*, 7 July 1906, pp. 5–7.

58. *Carta constitutiva club internacional de Congonhas de Sabará* (Rio de Janeiro: Typographia de Thiago Dias & C., 1891); George Chalmers to C. F. W. Kup, 12 August 1914, SJNL.

59. George Chalmers to Eleodoro Vazques, 9 December 1919, SJNL.

60. *AR 1913*, pp. 58–59; Letter to Jorge Charmens (*sic*), 8 April 1912, SJNL; *Correio da Manhã*, 27 April 1912.

61. Teófilo Ribeiro, "Morro Velho Workmen on Strike," SJNL. This manuscript is a translation of Ribeiro's article from the *Diário de Minas*, 11 December 1925.

62. *Sindicato dos Trabalhadores na Indústria da Extração do Ouro e Metais Preciosas de Nova Lima*; Grossi, *Mina de Morro Velho*, p. 121.

63. A. H. Millett to L. E. Langley, 24 May, 7 June, and 28 June 1934, SJNL. Quote is from A. H. Millett to L. E. Langley, 6 June 1934, SJNL. The best description of the rise of the union movement and its development is Grossi, *Mina de Morro Velho*, esp. 94–98.

64. A. Tenório d'Albuquerque, *Escándolo no Morro Velho* (Rio de Janeiro: Gráfica Labor, 1940) and Costa, *A cortina de ouro*. D'Albuquerque published numerous works promoting fascism, including *A Grã-Bretanha a serviço dos judeus*.

65. Two key works on the PCB in the 1930s and 1940s are Dulles, *Brazilian Communism, 1935–1945*, and Manuel Caballero, *The Comintern and Latin America, 1919–1943* (Cambridge: Cambridge University Press, 1986), esp. pp. 109–20.

66. Grossi's *Mina de Morro Velho* is a fine analysis of the labor movement in Nova Lima and the role of the PCB based on extensive interviews.

67. Superintendent to Board, 5 May 1954 and 18 April 1956, SJNL.

68. The intervention of the union is carefully analyzed in Grossi, *Mina de Morro Velho*, esp. pp. 229–30.

69. "Loose Papers on Wages" and "Police Files on Communists," SJNL.

70. "Average Daily Wage Charts," SJNL.

71. "It is obvious that the Company's interests cannot be served by workmen who are insufficiently fed [due to the rising cost of living]. They cannot do good work and naturally seize any opportunity they can get of seeking better conditions." H. P. Harris to George Chalmers, 10 July 1924, SJNL.

72. A. H. Millett to L. E. Langley, 5 January 1933, SJNL.

73. Erickson, *The Brazilian Corporative State*, esp. pp. 27–46.

74. A. H. Millett to Board, 8 December 1932; 24 January, 31 January, and 31 December 1934; 25 May 1935; 11 February 1936, SJNL.

75. Grossi, *Mina de Morro Velho*, p. 137, provides a list of worker complaints about health and sanitary conditions in the mine.

76. Often misdiagnosed as pneumonia or tuberculosis in the nineteenth century, the disease was also called phthisis or pneumoconiosis. Wilson, *Labour in the South African Gold Mines*, pp. 50–51.

77. Teixeira et al., *Higiene das minas de ouro*; Superintendent to Board, 29 August 1941, SJNL. The company diagnosed an average of thirty-four new cases of silicosis per year from 1945–54. Folder on Company Closing, 24 May 1955, SJNL.

78. Social legislation costs accounted for 6 percent of all expenses in 1945 or nearly £75,000. Superintendent to Board, 12 July 1947, SJNL.

79. Grossi, *Mina de Morro Velho*, pp. 72–76; George Chalmers to C. F. W. Kup, 1 March 1920; Eric Davies to L. E. Langley, 27 January 1941, SJNL.

80. Apparently the St. John made considerable payments to government officials to guarantee their cooperation in the dismissal of the workers. A. H. Millett to L. E. Langley, 14 May 1936 and 16 May 1939; and A. H. Millett to Board, 7 January 1936, SJNL.

81. The "fifty-one" were actually "forty-one." One had been assassinated, one pensioned, two left the company on their own, one had been previously dismissed, and five had accepted an indemnity from the company. W. R. Russell to L. E. Langley, 9 July 1949, SJNL.

82. Superintendent to Board, 11 December 1948, SJNL.

83. Superintendent to Board, 15 September 1952, SJNL.

84. "Police Files on Communists," SJNL. The government also helped the company compile a list of all Communists and Communist "sympathizers" on the company payroll.

85. Eric Davies to L. E. Langley, 24 December 1945, SJNL.

86. Grossi, *Mina de Morro Velho*, pp. 237–47.

87. CPRC, Livros de Escripturas, No. 3, 23–29; No. 4, 23–26v; No. 7, 11–15, 17v–21, 44v–49v, 73v–75v, 82–83v, 89–90; No. 13, 70–72v; *Herma ao Marquez de Sapucahy em Villa Nova de Lima* (Rio de Janeiro: Lyceo de Artes e Officios, 1919), p. 33; ACM, 1922–26.

88. A. G. N. Chalmers to C. F. W. Kup, 25 May 1925, SJNL; "Carlos Galery," Foreign Establishment, SJUT.

89. Eric Davies to L. E. Langley, 13 June 1947, SJNL; Grossi, *Mina de Morro Velho*, p. 235.

90. ACM, 1947–59.

91. Superintendent to Board, 20 May 1953, SJNL.

92. Grossi, *Mina de Morro Velho*, pp. 176–79.

93. Eric Davies to L. E. Langley, 13 June 1947, SJNL; Grossi, *Mina de Morro Velho*, p. 235.

94. Summaries of crimes in Nova Lima (and other municipios) are in APM/SIP, *Relatórios—1897–1917*.

95. Superintendent to Board, 6 November 1935, 31 October 1942, 14 November 1944, and 10 October 1955, SJNL.

96. Superintendent to Board, 12 November 1948, SJNL; Grossi, *Mina de Morro Velho*, p. 177.

97. Superintendent to Board, 19 June 1949, and Communist flier dated 25 June 1949, SJNL.

98. Grossi, *Mina de Morro Velho*, pp. 192–202; Superintendent to Board, 22 October 1958, SJNL.

British Society in the Tropics

1. Illingworth, "Journal and Letter Book," 10 December 1871.

2. Some interesting works on other overseas British communities are Avery, *Not on Queen Victoria's Birthday* on the Rio Tinto zinc mines in southern Spain; Deborah Lynn Jakubs, "A Community of Interests: A Social History of the British in Buenos Aires, 1860–1914," Ph.D. Diss., Stanford University, 1986; and Vera Blinn Reber, *British Mercantile Houses in Buenos Aires, 1810–1880* (Cambridge: Harvard University Press, 1979).

3. Payroll Books, SJNL.

4. Pasta Histórica, SJNL/P; *Almanak . . . de Minas Gerais* (Ouro Preto, 1864), p. 163; PR, Burials; *Registro de estrangeiros, 1822–1830* (Rio de Janeiro: Publicações do Arquivo Nacional, vol. 49, 1961), p. 3.

5. Cash Book 1, 1833, SJNL.

6. Letter Book 4, SJUT.

7. John Hockin to Thomas Walker, c. 1855, SJNL.

8. Eric Davies to L. E. Langley, 25 February 1946, SJNL.

9. Silva, Karklin, and Heslop interviews.

10. The standard work on mining life in Cornwall is A. K. Hamilton Jenkin, *The Cornish Miner* (London: George Allen & Unwin, 1962); see esp. pp. 321–43.

11. Some works dealing with Cornish miners overseas are Randall, *Real del Monte*; A. L. Rowse, *The Cousin Jacks: The Cornish in America* (New York: Scribner's, 1969); John Rowe, *The Hard-Rock Men: Cornish Immigrants and the North American Mining Frontier* (Liverpool: Liverpool University Press, 1974); and Philip Payton, *Pictorial History of Australia's Little Cornwall* (Melbourne: Rigby, 1978).

12. In the 1920s the Brazilian government ordered the registration and issuing of identity cards (*carteiras*) to foreign nationals. The company list made up for this purpose in 1926 undoubtedly leaves out some British citizens born in Brazil and must, therefore, be viewed with caution.

13. These perquisites included a furnished home (the Casa Grande), four servants, a cleaning woman one day per week, and £200 per year to cover the costs of entertaining. John Hockin to Frederick Tendron and Pearson Morrison, 23 June 1877; and John Hockin to George Chalmers, 8 November 1884, SJNL.

14. This compares with the £2,500 per year that the superintendent of the British-owned Rio Tinto zinc mines in Spain was receiving in 1879. The assistant superintendent at Rio Tinto, in the same period, received £1,500. Rio Tinto was the largest mining operation in Europe at the end of the nineteenth century. Avery, *Not on Queen Victoria's Birthday*, pp. 145–46. The Morro Velho superintendent's salary appears to be comparable to, or even

slightly higher than, those of his peers in the British coal industry. Church, *History of the British Coal Industry*, pp. 463–64.

15. European Payroll, SJNL. In 1950 the company had 5,203 employees, of whom 5,177 (99.5 percent) were Brazilian nationals. (This included one naturalized Brazilian and fifty-two foreigners born in Brazil.) "Labour," SJNL.

16. A. H. Millett to H. P. Harris, 17 January 1934, and Eric Davies to Board, 4 November 1946, SJNL.

17. W. R. Russell to L. E. Langley, 20 May 1952, SJNL.

18. For a typical example of stockholder opinion of Chalmers, see the *Report of the Ordinary General Meeting on 28 June 1906*, printed in pamphlet form by R. Clay and Sons, Ltd., SJNL.

19. European Payroll, SJNL. All the following examples come from this source.

20. Millett, Clemence, and Heslop interviews.

21. Chalmers interview.

22. The best description of European housing comes from H. Foster Bain and Thomas Thornton Read, *Ores and Industry in South America* (New York: Harper & Brothers, 1934), p. 118. Another detailed description is given in *AR 1915*, p. 55.

23. Burton, *Explorations*, I, p. 198.

24. *AR 1903*, p. 39, and *AR 1915*, p. 25.

25. *AR 1911*, p. 66.

26. W. R. Russell to Board, n.d., SJNL.

27. *AR 1896*, p. 53.

28. John Hockin to Thomas Walker, 7 March 1857, SJNL. The company offered evening classes for those children who worked in the mine during the day. *AR 1851*, p. 10.

29. Mr. and Mrs. Joseph Malone had teaching degrees from the Nashville Educational Institute and had farmed near Congonhas for several years. Superintendent's Diary, 2 April 1874, SJNL.

30. Superintendent's Diary, 2 April 1874; John Hockin to Pearson Morrison, 23 October 1878; Superintendent to C. F. W. Kup, 4 April 1930; A. H. Millett to Board, 5 December 1936; and W. R. Russell to Board, 30 August 1949, SJNL.

31. *AR 1911*, p. 66.

32. Raborg, Clemence, and Heslop interviews.

33. Board Minutes, 11 October 1906, SJUT.

34. Superintendent to C. F. W. Kup, 4 April 1930, SJNL.

35. Ibid.

36. Brazilian social studies became a required subject as a part of the government guidelines. General Manager to Board, 27 August 1957, SJNL.

37. *AR 1844*, pp. 25 and 34.

38. See, for example, Grossi, *Mina de Morro Velho*.

39. J. D. Powles to Charles Herring, Jr., 25 July 1842, SJNL.

40. Superintendent to C. F. W. Kup, 4 April 1930, SJNL.

41. "Notices to Employees," SJNL.

42. A. G. N. Chalmers to C. F. W. Kup, 25 January and 27 March 1927; and A. G. N. Chalmers to Board, 7 September 1928, SJNL.

43. Superintendent's Diary, 31 August 1893, SJNL. Emphasis in original.

44. Superintendent's Diary, 24 June 1867, SJNL.

45. M. A. M'Call to George Chalmers, 11 January 1900; and A. G. N. Chalmers to L. E. Langley, 19 October 1928, SJNL.

46. Relations between the British and Brazilians and tension between the two communities is dealt with in George Chalmers to C. H. Roscoe, 13 January 1919, SJNL.

47. Board Minutes, v. 3, 5 November 1862, SJUT.

48. Superintendent's Diary, 14 February and 12 March 1861; August 1867, SJNL.

49. Daniel de Carvalho reminisces about some of these parties in *Novos estudos e depoimentos*, pp. 133–68.

50. Interviews, Millett, Clemence, Heslop, and Raborg.

51. *AR 1917*, pp. 62–63; A. H. Millett to Board, 3 January 1938, SJNL; *AR 1944*; and interview, Alda Hodge Vasconcelos, 8 April 1980, Nova Lima.

52. The Midsummer Day celebration was a tradition in the Cornish mining industry transplanted to Morro Velho. D. B. Barton, *Essays in Cornish Mining History*, I (Truro, Cornwall: D. Bradford Barton, 1968), p. 43.

53. Superintendent's Diary, 24 June 1867, SJNL.

54. Viana, "Viagem à Província de Minas Gerais," pp. 80–83; and *AR 1881*, p. 83.

55. M. A. M'Call to George Chalmers, 11 August 1904, SJNL.

56. Millett, Clemence, and Heslop interviews.

57. George Chalmers to C. H. Roscoe, 13 January 1919, SJNL.

58. Board Minutes, v. 1, 16 September 1836, SJUT; PR; Superintendent's Diary, 21 April 1882, SJNL; *Registro de estrangeiros, 1831–1839* (Rio de Janeiro: Publicações do Arquivo Nacional, v. 50, 1962), p. 439.

59. A. H. Millett to Board, 16 October 1931, SJNL.

60. Obituary of Margarida Branca Morgan, *Minas Gerais*, 17 September 1947, p. 8.

61. British Vice-Consul at Morro Velho to A. Chapman, 17 February 1906, and John Spear to Nicholson & Cook, 12 January 1906, SJNL. Interview with Woods Lacerda family, 1980, Belo Horizonte.

62. George Chalmers to Augusto de Lima, 2 August 1917, SJNL.

63. Interview with Eileen Millett Nixson, 22 March 1980, Belo Horizonte.

64. A. H. Millett to L. E. Langley, 14 August 1934, SJNL.

65. The following information is based largely on an interview with Cecil Jones, 17 April 1980, Belo Horizonte.

66. A. H. Millett to Board, 20 July and 15 November 1935, 25 May 1936; Eric Davies to Board, 23 September 1940 and 12 September 1941, SJNL.

67. PR, Marriages.

68. C. F. W. Kup to George Chalmers, 19 November 1914 and 24 June 1915, SJNL; Mrs. A. H. Millett interview.

69. The late Reverend Ariel Alvin of Nova Lima and the Reverend Roger

Blankley of Christ Church, Rio de Janeiro, kindly allowed me to photocopy the extant registers.

70. During a number of years no clergyman resided at Morro Velho and the registers during these years are either blank or filled in by company employees. At the end of the nineteenth century a vice-consulate was set up at Morro Velho, and for the next sixty years a company official always served as vice-consul. This consular official had the power to marry couples and also registered births and deaths. British consul-general M. Irvin kindly allowed me to examine these records in Rio de Janeiro in April 1980.

71. The birthrate in England and Wales in the last half of the nineteenth century hovered around thirty to thirty-five per thousand. B. R. Mitchell, ed., *European Historical Statistics 1750–1970*, abridged ed. (New York: Columbia University Press, 1978), p. 16.

72. PR, Marriages; John Hajnal, "European Marriage Patterns in Perspective," in D. V. Glass and D. E. C. Eversley, eds., *Population in History: Essays in Historical Demography* (Chicago: Aldine, 1965), pp. 101–43.

73. The figures at Morro Velho are nearly identical to those in a "special study carried out by the Registrar General in 1884–5 [that] revealed that miners and their wives had the lowest age of first marriage of nine occupational groups (24.06 for men and 22.46 for women)." Church, *History of the British Coal Industry*, p. 616.

74. Burton, *Explorations*, I, pp. 220–25.

British Enterprise in Brazil

1. Graham, *Britain and the Onset of Modernization in Brazil*, p. 320.

2. Ian Roxborough, *Theories of Underdevelopment* (London: Macmillan, 1979), p. ix.

Bibliographical Essay

This study relies heavily on the use of unpublished archival materials, as well as a broad range of published primary and secondary sources. Rather than list the hundreds of items consulted, the following essay describes the archival materials and the most useful of the published sources. Discussion of the latter does not pretend to be exhaustive but rather indicates the most important materials consulted.

Archives and Interviews

The *St. John d'el Rey Archive (Nova Lima)* may be one of the richest business-history archives in all of Latin America. When the English management left Morro Velho in 1960 many of the company records were stored in two basement rooms in the office annex to the Casa Grande. The materials were in almost complete disarray when I located them in 1979. The present management of the company, Mineração Morro Velho S. A., gave me complete access to all the available records, which I proceeded to organize in a very rough fashion. The most valuable of the materials is a very complete set of the correspondence between Morro Velho and the London office between the 1830s and 1960 in more than one hundred binders. An additional forty-two binders or copybooks contain correspondence between various superintendents, managing directors, and other company officials. In this century management divided correspondence between regular, special, and confidential series.

The archive also contains more than fifty binders of department reports (going into great detail) from widely varying periods in this century. Some records have survived from the British vice-consulate, but little of any importance. In addition to a wide variety of files and notebooks on different aspects of operations, some of the original ledger books have been preserved, most prominently: accounts from the Gongo Soco mine; Cash Book 1; Cost Book (1830–45); purchasing accounts from the nineteenth century; notices to employees; salaries and wages for European employees; and a slave hire register (1867–79). Unfortunately, the only cumulative records on slavery are the latter ledger and a file of tax receipts from the purchase of slaves (1830–43).

The archive also contains thousands of photographs of the mine and Nova Lima, dating back to the nineteenth century, and an almost complete set of *Annual Reports*. Finally, the Departamento do Patrimônio (on the hill above the Casa Grande) has collected and filed thousands of documents over decades to help establish claims to land ownership. These files contain wills, contracts, datas, and numerous other sources systematically collected and copied from around the region. R. H. Wharrier, the company estate agent in the 1940s, began the collection; he wrote up a series of notes on the history of the company in the 1950s based on his documentary search. His notes are collected in a file in the department labeled "Pasta Histórica."

St. John d'el Rey Archive (Austin, Texas). When the company offices moved to Cleveland, Ohio, in 1960 many of the London office records were burned. Others had been destroyed in the blitz during the Second World War (although the company office had moved out of London for the war). In the early 1970s William Callaghan, a graduate student from the University of Texas, located the remaining records in a very damp warehouse in London. These records were then donated to the Latin America Collection at the University of Texas in 1974. Callaghan describes these materials in "Gold Mining on the Brazilian Frontier: The Archives of the St. John d'el Rey Mining Company," *The Library Chronicle of the University of Texas* 11 (1979), pp. 27–32.

In addition to a complete run of the *Annual Reports*, the collection in Austin contains a disparate group of materials including the minutes of board meetings, copybooks with the earliest correspondence from Brazil, some share registers from the 1880s, some accounting ledgers, and various paintings and maps. The most valuable part of the collection is a marvelous series of photographs taken circa 1903 to give shareholders a systematic and comprehensive view of all operations at the mine. Other albums document life at the mine back to the 1860s.

The *Arquivo Público Mineiro (Belo Horizonte)* has documents relating to Nova Lima dating back to the early eighteenth century. The most useful materials are located under the headings *Seção Colonial* and *Câmara Municipal de Sabará*. The *RAPM*, 28 (1977) contains a complete listing of the materials, which include *livros de guardamoria* and some notarial registers from the early nineteenth century. The APM also has a large collection of *mineiro* newspapers and magazines, reference materials, and provincial and state government reports and documents up to 1930.

Parish Registers for Nova Lima and Morro Velho are widely scattered. The local Catholic parish has preserved some of the original baptismal, marriage, and burial registers for the nineteenth century. Twentieth-century registers are located in Belo Horizonte. The Anglican church has maintained registers since the 1850s, and they are still in Nova Lima. Christ Church in Rio de Janeiro also has copies of the Morro Velho registers as well as early registers for the British settlements at Gongo Soco, Cata Branca, and other mines. The British Consulate General in Rio de Janeiro has the vital statistics registers that were kept by the vice-consul at Morro Velho beginning in the 1890s.

The *Cartório de Paz e Registro Civil (Nova Lima)* was critical in the collection of demographic material. A tiny, one-room office, the *cartório* has birth, death, and marriage registers dating back to the late nineteenth century for the entire *município*. In addition, a series of *livros de escrituras* contain contracts of sales, letters of freedom, and important business transactions. The *cartório* also has some electoral registers for the late nineteenth and early twentieth centuries.

Other *cartórios* with records for Nova Lima are located in the courthouse on the main plaza, but they did not begin to function until Nova Lima received its own judicial *comarca* in 1938. Records for property and judicial matters prior to 1938 were handled in Sabará. In 1985 these records were transferred to the Museu de Ouro in Sabará and had barely begun to be unpacked and sorted.

The *Câmara Municipal (Nova Lima)* has a small archive that contains bound volumes of the minutes of the meetings of the *câmara*. The archive has eleven volumes covering the years 1947–59. Unfortunately, only one volume (1922–26) has survived for the period before 1947. The *prefeitura municipal* has no materials on the period covered in this study.

Additional Archives that were helpful included the Centro de Estudos do Ciclo de Ouro, Casa dos Contos, in Ouro Preto. This collection has a number of the early eighteenth-century land records for the area around Nova Lima. The Arquivo Edgard Leuenroth at the Universidade Estadual de Campinas has a fine collection of working-class newspapers from the early nineteenth century, although very few were published in Minas Gerais, and coverage of the state by São Paulo and Rio papers was minimal. The Arquivo Nacional in Rio de Janeiro has a few collections with materials on Nova Lima and Morro Velho, in particular the papers of Afonso Pena. Movietonews, Inc., a division of Twentieth Century Fox Film Corporation in New York City, has a newsreel—and outtakes—of mining operations at Morro Velho in the 1930s.

Interviews with Brazilians and Anglo-Brazilians were invaluable in the reconstruction of life in Morro Velho and Nova Lima. Mrs. A. H. Millett and her daughter Eileen Millett Nixson (22 March 1980, Belo Horizonte); Diva Clemence and Emily Heslop (27 March 1980, Belo Horizonte); John and Vivien Heslop (7 April 1980, Nova Lima); Alda Hodge Vasconcelos (8 April 1980, Nova Lima); and Fred Raborg (30 June 1981, Carlsbad, California) helped me understand life in the British community. Dr. Ricardo Salgado Guimarães (11 March 1980, Nova Lima) and Cecil Jones (17 April 1980, Belo Horizonte) helped me understand Nova Lima. Modesto Sérgio da Silva (26 March 1980, Nova Lima) and Janis Karklin (3 April 1980, Nova Lima), both of whom worked in the mine for more than fifty years, gave me insights into life underground and in the Brazilian community. Earl M. Irving (17 February 1981, Los Angeles) talked to me about his work for the Hanna Mining Company at Morro Velho in the final years of the British era. Frederick William Chalmers (25 July 1985, Nova Lima) spoke to me about his father and grandfather. João Franzen de Lima (4 July 1988, Belo Horizonte) kindly talked to me about his family and his role in regional politics. Finally, I had countless conversations with company officials and workers on all aspects of operations at the mine and life in the community.

Printed Sources

Great Britain and Latin America

The standard accounts of British influence in Brazil are Alan K. Manchester, *British Preeminence in Brazil: Its Rise and Decline* (Chapel Hill: University of North Carolina Press, 1933), and Richard Graham, *Britain and the Onset of Modernization in Brazil, 1850–1914* (Cambridge: Cambridge University Press, 1968). J. Fred Rippy's *British Investments in Latin America, 1822–1949: A Case Study in the Operations of Private Enterprise in Retarded Regions* (Minneapolis: University of Minnesota Press, 1959) is a good overview of British investment in Latin America. A more recent accounting is Irving Stone, "British Direct and Portfolio Investment in Latin America Before 1914," *Journal of Economic History*, 37:3 (1977), pp. 690–722.

The classic statement on British informal empire is John Gallagher and Ronald Robinson, "The Imperialism of Free Trade," *Economic History Review*, 2d series, 6:1 (August 1953), pp. 1–15. Peter Winn applies this theoretical approach to Latin America in "British Informal Empire in Uruguay in the Nineteenth Century," *Past and Present*, 73 (November 1976), pp. 100–26. D. C. M. Platt is the most prominent critic of this perspective. *Business Imperialism 1840–1930: An Inquiry Based on British Experience in Latin America* (Oxford: Clarendon Press, 1977), edited by Platt, brings together a series of detailed studies challenging the "informal empire" thesis. Vera Blinn Reber, *British Mercantile Houses in Buenos Aires, 1810–1880* (Cambridge: Harvard University Press, 1979), and Colin M. Lewis, *British Railways in Argentina 1857–1914: A Case Study of Foreign Investment* (London: Athlone, 1983), helped place the British experience at Morro Velho in comparative perspective.

Brazil

I have found a number of works on Brazilian history helpful in my research. Nathaniel H. Leff, *Underdevelopment and Development in Brazil*, 2 vols.

(London: Allen & Unwin, 1982), and Annibal Villanova Villela and Wilson Suzigan, *Política do governo e crescimento da economia brasileira 1889–1945* (Rio de Janeiro: IPEA/INPES, 1973), are indispensable for understanding Brazilian economic history. June Hahner's *Poverty and Politics: The Urban Poor in Brazil, 1870–1920* (Albuquerque: University of New Mexico Press, 1986) was useful in comparing working-class conditions in Nova Lima with other Brazilian cities. Steven Topik's *The Political Economy of the Brazilian State, 1889–1930* (Austin: University of Texas Press, 1987) is a valuable guide to the economic history of the First Republic. Two classic "município studies" that influenced my thinking are Stanley J. Stein, *Vassouras: A Brazilian Coffee County, 1850–1900* (Cambridge: Harvard University Press, 1957), and Warren Dean, *Rio Claro: A Brazilian Plantation System, 1820–1920* (Stanford: Stanford University Press, 1976). Robert Howard Mattoon, Jr.'s "The Companhia Paulista de Estradas de Ferro, 1868–1900: A Local Railway Enterprise in São Paulo, Brazil," Ph.D. Diss., Yale University, 1971, is one of the very rare studies of a business in Brazil. Barbara Weinstein's *The Amazon Rubber Boom, 1850–1920* (Stanford: Stanford University Press, 1983) is an outstanding blending of theory and careful empirical analysis to explain the interaction of foreign business and local society.

Minas Gerais

The most useful general works on Minas Gerais are Francisco Iglésias, *Política econômica do govêrno provincial mineiro (1835–1889)* (Rio de Janeiro: Ministério da Educação e Cultura, 1958); John D. Wirth, *Minas Gerais and the Brazilian Federation 1889–1937* (Stanford: Stanford University Press, 1977); and Amilcar Vianna Martins Filho, *A economia política do café com leite (1900–1930)* (Belo Horizonte: UFMG/PROED, 1981). Three unpublished theses were helpful in understanding the nature of *mineiro* politics: Maria Efigênia Lage de Resende, "Formação da estrutura de dominação em Minas Gerais: o novo PRM (1889–1906)," Tese de Livre-Docência, Universidade Federal de Minas Gerais, 1976; Peter Louis Blasenheim, "A Regional History of the Zona da Mata in Minas Gerais, Brazil, 1870–1906," Ph.D. Diss., Stanford University, 1982; and David Verge Fleischer, "Political Recruitment in the State of Minas Gerais, Brazil (1890–1970)," Ph.D. Diss., University of Florida, 1972.

Accounts of foreign travelers in the nineteenth century provide firsthand descriptions of the region and Morro Velho. Hélio Gravatá has compiled a complete list of travelers in Minas Gerais in "Viajantes estrangeiros em Minas Gerais, 1809 a 1955: contribuição bibliográfica," *Minas Gerais (Suplemento Literário)*, 10 October 1970, pp. 11–12. The best, and most complete, account of Morro Velho is in Richard F. Burton, *Explorations of the Highlands of the Brazil*, 2 vols. (London: Tinsley Brothers, 1869). George Gardner, *Travels in the Interior of Brazil* (London: Reeve, 1846), and John Mawe,

Travels in the Interior of Brazil (London: Longman, Hurst, Rees, Orme, and Brown, 1815), also provide excellent descriptions of the mining region in the early nineteenth century.

The best overview of the geology of Minas Gerais comes from a series of papers by the U.S. Geological Survey, especially, John Van N. Dorr II, *Physiographic, Stratigraphic and Structural Development of the Quadrilá-tero Ferrífero, Minas Gerais, Brazil*, Geological Survey Professional Paper 341-C (Washington, D.C.: U.S. Government Printing Office, 1969); and Jacob E. Gair, *Geology and Ore Deposits of the Nova Lima and Rio Acima Quadrangles, Minas Gerais, Brazil* (Washington, D.C.: U.S. Government Printing Office, 1962).

Mining

C. R. Boxer's *The Golden Age of Brazil, 1695–1750: Growing Pains of a Colonial Society* (Berkeley: University of California Press, 1962) remains the standard source on the Brazilian gold-rush period. Virgílio Noya Pinto, *O ouro brasileiro e o comércio anglo-português (uma contribuição aos estudos da economia atlântica no século XVIII)* (São Paulo: Companhia Editora Nacional, 1979), provides a more recent assessment of gold production and its impact. João Pandiá Calogeras, *As minas do Brasil e sua legislação*, 3 vols. (Rio de Janeiro: Imprensa Nacional, 1904–1905), remains an invaluable catalog of laws, mineral deposits, and all types of mining and mining companies in Brazil. W. L. von Eschwege, *Pluto brasiliensis*, trans. Domício de Figueiredo Murta, 2 vols. (Belo Horizonte: Itatiaia, 1979), offers a comprehensive survey of mining in early nineteenth-century Brazil, while Othon Henry Leonardos, *Geociências no Brasil: a contribuição britânica* (Rio de Janeiro: Forum, 1970), gives the most comprehensive treatment of British mining companies in Brazil.

Rodolphe Jacob, *Minas Geraes no XX século* (Rio de Janeiro: Gomes e Simões, 1911), Paul Ferrand, *L'or à Minas Geraes, Brésil* (Bello Horizonte: n.p., 1913), and M. A. de Bovet, *L'industrie minérale dans la province de Minas-Geraes* (Paris: Dunod, 1883), are the best overviews of mining in Minas Gerais in the nineteenth century. All three were French professors at the Escola de Minas in Ouro Preto. Albert F. Calvert, *Mineral Resources of Minas Geraes (Brazil)* (London: E. & F. N. Spon, 1915), gives the best survey in English.

My views on Brazilian gold mining have been shaped by a wide comparative reading of the literature on mining history around the globe. The best bibliography for Latin America can be found in Thomas Greaves and William W. Culver, eds., *Miners and Mining in the Americas* (Manchester, England: Manchester University Press, 1985), pp. 277–347. Carlos Prieto, *Mining in the New World* (New York: McGraw-Hill, 1973), is a general history. Some important case studies which I found helpful are David G. Becker, *The New Bourgeoisie and the Limits of Dependency: Mining, Class and Power in "Revolutionary" Peru* (Princeton: Princeton University Press, 1983); Marvin D. Bernstein, *The Mexican Mining Industry 1890–1950: A Study of the Interaction of Politics, Economics, and Technology* (Albany: State University of New York, 1964); D. A. Brading and Harry E. Cross, "Colonial Silver Mining: Mexico and Peru," *HAHR*, 52:4 (November 1972), pp. 545–79; Robert W. Randall, *Real del Monte: A British Mining Venture in Mexico* (Austin: University of Texas Press, 1972); and Kenneth Vergne Finney, "Precious Metal Mining and the Modernization of Honduras: In Quest of El Dorado," Ph.D. Diss., Tulane University, 1973.

For the United States experience I relied heavily on Joseph H. Cash, *Working the Homestake* (Ames: Iowa State University Press, 1973); Richard E. Lingenfelter, *The Hardrock Miners: A History of the Mining Labor Movement in the American West, 1863–1893* (Berkeley: University of California Press, 1974); Mark Wyman, *Hard Rock Epic: Western Miners and the Industrial Revolution, 1860–1910* (Berkeley: University of California Press, 1979); and two works by Clark C. Spence, *British Investments and the American Mining Frontier, 1860–1901* (Ithaca, N.Y.: Cornell University Press, 1958), and *Mining Engineering and the American West: The Lace-Boot Brigade, 1849–1933* (New Haven: Yale University Press, 1970).

Roy Church, *The History of the British Coal Industry. Volume 3. 1830–1913: Victorian Pre-eminence* (Oxford: Clarendon Press, 1986), provides excellent comparative material on British mining. David Avery's lavishly illustrated *Not on Queen Victoria's Birthday: The Story of the Rio Tinto Mines* (London: Collins, 1974) recounts the history of the British Rio Tinto zinc mines—Spain's version of Morro Velho. The most important works on the Cornish role in world mining are D. B. Barton, *Essays in Cornish Mining History*, 2 vols. (Truro, Cornwall: D. Bradford Barton Ltd., 1968 and 1971); Roger Burt, ed., *Cornish Mining: Essays on the Organisation of Cornish Mines and the Cornish Mining Economy* (Newton Abbot, Devon: David & Charles, 1969); A. K. Hamilton Jenkin, *The Cornish Miner* (London: George Allen & Unwin, 1962); and John Rowe, *The Hard-Rock Men: Cornish Immigrants and the North American Mining Frontier* (Liverpool: Liverpool University Press, 1974).

Robert V. Kubicek, *Economic Imperialism in Theory and Practice: The Case of South African Gold Mining Finance 1886–1914* (Durham: Duke University Press, 1979), and Francis Wilson, *Labour in the South African Gold Mines, 1911–1969* (Cambridge: Cambridge University Press, 1972), taught me a great deal about mining in South Africa. Finally, Pierre Vilar's *A History of Gold and Money 1450–1920*, trans. Judith White (London: NLB, 1976), is an invaluable comparative work.

Two old handbooks guided me in my understanding of the mining of gold: C. Le Neve Foster, *A Text-Book of Ore and Stone Mining*, 4th ed. (London: Charles Griffin and Company, 1901), and J. Arthur Phillips, *Elements of Metallurgy*, 3d ed. rev. (London: Charles Griffin and Company, 1891). Otis E Young, Jr. has written two excellent technical histories of mining in the American West, *Black Powder and Hard Steel: Miners and Machines on the Old Western Frontier* (Norman: University of Oklahoma Press, 1976) and *Western Mining: An Informal Account of Precious-Metals Prospecting, Placering, Lode Mining, and Milling on the American Frontier from Spanish Times to 1893* (Norman: University of Oklahoma Press, 1978).

Slavery

The comparative works on slavery which have shaped my views are too numerous to list and are often incorporated into the best work on Brazilian slavery. I have relied heavily on Herbert S. Klein, *African Slavery in Latin America and the Caribbean* (New York: Oxford University Press, 1986); Katia M. de Queirós Mattoso, *To Be a Slave in Brazil, 1550–1888*, trans. Arthur Goldhammer (New Brunswick, N.J.: Rutgers University Press, 1986); Stuart B. Schwartz, *Sugar Plantations in the Formation of Brazilian Society: Bahia, 1550–1835* (Cambridge: Cambridge University Press, 1985); and Mary Karasch, *Slave Life in Rio de Janeiro, 1808–1850* (Princeton: Princeton University Press, 1987). Other fine works on Brazilian slavery and the slave trade are Leslie Bethell, *The Abolition of the Brazilian Slave Trade* (Cambridge: Cambridge University Press, 1970); Robert Wayne Slenes, "The Demography and Economics of Brazilian Slavery," Ph.D. Diss., Stanford University, 1976; A. J. R. Russell-Wood, *The Black Man in Slavery and Freedom in Colonial Brazil* (New York: St. Martin's Press, 1982); and Robert Brent Toplin, *The Abolition of Slavery in Brazil* (New York: Atheneum, 1975).

Roberto Borges Martins, "Growing in Silence: The Slave Economy of Nineteenth-Century Minas Gerais, Brazil," Ph.D. Diss., Vanderbilt University, 1980; and Amilcar Martins Filho and Roberto B. Martins, "Slavery in a Nonexport Economy: Nineteenth-Century Minas Gerais Revisited," *HAHR*, 63:3 (August 1983), pp. 537–68, are the finest works on slavery in Minas Gerais. Douglas Cole Libby, *Trabalho escravo e capital estrangeiro no Brasil: o caso de Morro Velho* (Belo Horizonte: Itatiaia, 1984), uses secondary sources, government documents, and the company's *Annual Reports* to produce the most complete account of slavery at Morro Velho.

Labor

Yonne de Souza Grossi has produced an exceptional study of the labor movement at Morro Velho (1934–64) based on dozens of interviews with former militants: *Mina de Morro Velho: a extração do homem: uma história de experiência operária* (Rio de Janeiro: Paz e Terra, 1981). Eliana Regina de Freitas Dutra, *Caminhos operários nas Minas Gerais* (São Paulo: Hucitec/UFMG, 1988), discusses the regional context of workers' movements in early twentieth-century Minas. Terezinha Gascho Volpato, *A pirita humana: os mineiros de Criciúma* (Florianópolis: UFSC, 1984), looks at coal miners in contemporary southern Brazil. The best overviews of labor in Brazil are

Hobart A. Spalding, Jr., *Organized Labor in Latin America: Historical Case Studies of Urban Workers in Dependent Societies* (New York: Harper Torchbooks, 1977), and Kenneth Paul Erickson, *The Brazilian Corporative State and Working Class Politics* (Berkeley: University of California Press, 1977). Thomas H. Holloway's *Immigrants on the Land: Coffee and Society in São Paulo, 1886–1934* (Chapel Hill: University of North Carolina Press, 1980) offers a useful contrast to the working class in Nova Lima. Several works were useful in understanding the role of the Communist party in Nova Lima: Manuel Caballero's excellent *The Comintern and Latin America, 1919–1943* (Cambridge: Cambridge University Press, 1986); Ronald H. Chilcote, *The Brazilian Communist Party: Conflict and Integration, 1922–1972* (New York: Oxford University Press, 1974); and two volumes by John W. F. Dulles, *Anarchists and Communists in Brazil, 1900–1935* and *Brazilian Communism, 1935–1945* (Austin: University of Texas Press, 1973 and 1983). John Benson, *British Coalminers in the Nineteenth Century: A Social History* (New York: Holmes & Meier, 1980), was useful for comparative purposes. For a highly theoretical sociological approach to the rise of the working class in another foreign mining enclave, see Dirk Kruijt and Menno Vellinga, *Labor Relations and Multinational Corporations: The Cerro de Pasco Corporation in Peru (1902–1974)* (Assen, The Netherlands: Van Gorcum, 1979).

Demography

Armin K. Ludwig, *Brazil: A Handbook of Historical Statistics* (Boston: G. K. Hall, 1985); Thomas W. Merrick and Douglas H. Graham, *Population and Economic Development in Brazil: 1800 to the Present* (Baltimore: Johns Hopkins University Press, 1979); and the Brazilian national censuses were the most important sources for Brazilian demographic statistics. A number of important demographic studies of Minas Gerais have appeared during the past decade. These include Iraci del Nero da Costa, *Populações mineiras: estudo sobre a estrutura populacional de alguns núcleos mineiros no alvorecer do século XIX* (São Paulo: Instituto de Pesquisas Econômicas, 1981); Francisco Vidal Luna, *Minas Gerais: escravos e senhores: análise da estrutura populacional e econômica de alguns centros mineratórios (1718–1804)* (São Paulo: Instituto de Pesquisas Econômicas, 1981); Ricardo Pinheiro Penna, "Development and Population Distribution in Minas Gerais, Brazil," Ph.D. Diss., Cornell University, 1983; Donald Ramos, "A Social History of Ouro Preto: Stresses of Dynamic Urbanization in Colonial Brazil, 1695–1726," Ph.D. Diss., University of Florida, 1972; and Lawrence James Nielsen, "Of Gentry, Peasants, and Slaves: Rural Society in Sabará and Its Hinterland, 1780–1930," Ph.D. Diss., University of California-Davis, 1975.

Morro Velho

Until the 1980s the only monograph on the Morro Velho mine in any language was Bernard Hollowood's anecdotal *The Story of Morro Velho* (London: Samson Clark & Co. Ltd., 1955), commissioned by the company for its 125th anniversary. Two masters theses on Morro Velho, both done at the Universidade Federal de Minas Gerais, were published in the 1980s. Douglas Libby's *Trabalho escravo e capital estrangeiro* and Yonne de Souza Grossi's *Mina de Morro Velho* both focus on labor at the mine. Neither author had access to company records. Two scathing attacks on the St. John d'el Rey were published in the 1940s and 1950s, A. Tenório d'Albuquerque's *Escándolo no Morro Velho* (Rio de Janeiro: Gráfica Labor, 1940), and Roberto C. Costa's *A cortina de ouro (Morro Velho)* (Belo Horizonte: E. G. Santa Maria, 1955).

Three technical articles provide the best general overview of mining operations in this century: A. G. N. Chalmers, "Mining Methods Past and Present in the Morro Velho Mine of the St. John del Rey Mining Company, Ltd., and Lode-Changes which have Necessitated an Alteration of System," *Proceedings of the Institution of Civil Engineers*, 226 (1929), pp. 189–240; Eric Davies, "The Air-Cooling Plant at the Morro Velho Mine of the St. John Del Rey Mining Company, Limited, Brazil," *Transactions of the Institution of Mining Engineers*, 43 (August 1922), pp. 326–41; and Jack H. French and Harold Jones, "Reduction Works Practice at Morro Velho, Brazil," *Transactions of the Institution of Mining and Metallurgy*, 42 (1933), pp. 189–265. The most complete description of Morro Velho in the nineteenth century is Richard Burton's *Explorations*. Nearly a quarter of volume I is devoted to a detailed description of his lengthy stay at the mine in 1867. For a nostalgic view of Morro Velho during the Chalmers era, see Daniel de Carvalho's *Novos estudos e depoimentos* (Rio de Janeiro: José Olympio, 1959), pp. 133–68.

Comparative Works

Several theoretical works helped shape my thinking on the role of British enterprise in Brazil. These included Ian Roxborough, *Theories of Underdevelopment* (London: Macmillan, 1979); Peter B. Evans, *Dependent Development: The Alliance of Multinational, State, and Local Capital in Brazil* (Princeton: Princeton University Press, 1979); and Peter B. Evans, Dietrich Rueschemeyer, and Theda Skocpol, eds., *Bringing the State Back In* (Cambridge: Cambridge University Press, 1985); Wolfgang J. Mommsen, *Theories of Imperialism*, trans. P. S. Falla (New York: Random House, 1980); Fernando Henrique Cardoso and Enzo Faletto, *Dependency and Development in Latin America*, trans. Marjory Mattingly Urquidi (Berkeley: University of California Press, 1979); Daniel R. Headrick, *The Tools of Empire: Tech-*

nology and European Imperialism in the Nineteenth Century (New York: Oxford University Press, 1981); Lance E. Davis and Robert A. Huttenback, *Mammon and the Pursuit of Empire: The Political Economy of British Imperialism, 1860–1912* (Cambridge: Cambridge University Press, 1986); and Christopher Abel and Colin M. Lewis, eds., *Latin America, Economic Imperialism and the State: The Political Economy of the External Connection from Independence to the Present* (London: Athlone, 1985).

Two works on industrialization in North America gave me a broader perspective on the process in Nova Lima: Michael B. Katz, Michael J. Doucet, and Mark J. Stern, *The Social Organization of Early Industrial Capitalism* (Cambridge: Harvard University Press, 1982) and Steven Hahn and Jonathan Prude, eds., *The Countryside in the Age of Capitalist Transformation: Essays in the Social History of Rural America* (Chapel Hill: University of North Carolina Press, 1985). Allen Wells, *Yucatán's Gilded Age: Haciendas, Henequen, and International Harvester, 1860–1915* (Albuquerque: University of New Mexico Press, 1985), and Adrian W. DeWind, Jr., "Peasants Become Miners: The Evolution of Industrial Mining Systems in Peru," Ph.D. Diss., Columbia University, 1977, are two fine studies of the impact of foreign business on other Latin American locales. The finest study of the impact of capitalist development on local society is Florencia Mallon's *The Defense of Community in Peru's Central Highlands: Peasant Struggle and Capitalist Transition, 1860–1940* (Princeton: Princeton University Press, 1983).

Index

Marshall C. Eakin is Associate Professor of History
at Vanderbilt University.

The first five photographs following page 164 are from A. Riedel, *Viagem de S.S. A.A. Duque de Saxe Augusto Irmão D. Luís Philippe ao interior do Brazil no anno 1868*, courtesy of the archive of Robert Bosch GmbH, Stuttgart. The others are from the archives of Mineração Morro Velho, S.A.

Library of Congress Cataloging-in-Publication Data
Eakin, Marshall C. (Marshall Craig), 1952–
British enterprise in Brazil : the St. John d'el Rey Mining
Company and the Morro Velho Gold Mine, 1830–1960 / Marshall C.
Eakin.
p. cm.
Bibliography: p.
Includes index.
ISBN 0-8223-0914-9
1. Saint John d'el Rey Mining Company—History. 2. Gold industry—
Brazil—Nova Lima—History. 3. Investments, British—Brazil—Nova
Lima—History. 4. Corporations, British—Brazil—Nova Lima—
History. 5. Nova Lima (Brazil)—Industries—History. I. Title.
HD9536.B83N684 1989
338.7'6223422'098151—dc20 89-33441